# The Moral Foundations of Social Institutions
*A Philosophical Study*

In this book, Seumas Miller examines the moral foundations of contemporary social institutions. Offering an original general theory of social institutions, he posits that all social institutions exist to realize various collective ends, indeed, to produce collective goods. He analyzes key concepts such as collective responsibility and institutional corruption. Miller also provides distinctive special theories of particular institutions, including governments, welfare agencies, universities, police organizations, business corporations, and communications and information technology entities. These theories are philosophical and, thus, foundational and synoptic in character. They are normative accounts of a sampling of contemporary social institutions, not descriptive accounts of all social institutions, both past and present. Miller also addresses various ethical challenges confronting contemporary institutional designers and policy makers, including the renovation of the international financial system, the "dumbing down" of the media, the challenge of world poverty, and human rights infringements by security agencies combating global terrorism.

Seumas Miller is Foundation Director of the Centre for Applied Philosophy and Public Ethics and Professor of Philosophy at Charles Sturt University and the Australian National University. He is also a senior research Fellow at the Centre for Ethics and Technology at Delft University of Technology. He is the author of a number of books, including *Social Action: A Teleological Account*, *Corruption and Anti-Corruption* (with P. Roberts and E. Spence), *Ethical Issues in Policing* (with J. Blackler), and *Terrorism and Counter-Terrorism: Ethics and Liberal Democracy*.

# The Moral Foundations
# of Social Institutions

## A Philosophical Study

SEUMAS MILLER

*Australian National University, Charles Sturt University,
and Delft University of Technology*

CAMBRIDGE
UNIVERSITY PRESS

CAMBRIDGE UNIVERSITY PRESS
Cambridge, New York, Melbourne, Madrid, Cape Town,
Singapore, São Paulo, Delhi, Mexico City

Cambridge University Press
32 Avenue of the Americas, New York, NY 10013-2473, USA

www.cambridge.org
Information on this title: www.cambridge.org/9780521744393

First published 2010
Reprinted 2012

*A catalog record for this publication is available from the British Library.*

*Library of Congress Cataloging in Publication Data*

Miller, Seumas.
The moral foundations of social institutions : a philosophical study / Seumas Miller.
   p.   cm.
Includes bibliographical references and index.
ISBN 978-0-521-76794-1 (hardback) – ISBN 978-0-521-74439-3 (pbk.)
1. Social institutions.   2. Social ethics.   I. Title.
HM826.M55   2010
306.01–dc22      2009000780

ISBN 978-0-521-76794-1 Hardback
ISBN 978-0-521-74439-3 Paperback

*For my parents, Crawford Miller (1913–2001) and Kathleen Miller*

# Contents

# Acknowledgements

Thanks to the following for comments on parts of this book at some stage of its genesis: Andrew Alexandra, Christian Barry, John Blackler, Michael Boylan, Thom Brooks, Tom Campbell, Tony Coady, Dean Cocking, Michael Collingridge, John Kleinig, Pekka Makela, Larry May, Justin O'Brien, Thomas Pogge, Peter Roberts, Frederick Schmitt, Edward Spence, T. S. Tsohatzidis, Raimo Tuomela, Jeroen van den Hoven, and John Weckert.

Thanks also to the various publishers and editors in relation to the use of elements of the following earlier publications of mine: *Terrorism and Counter-terrorism: Ethics and Liberal Democracy* (Oxford: Blackwell Publishing, 2008); "Collective Responsibility and Information and Communication Technology" in (ed.) J. van den Hoven and J. Weckert, *Moral Philosophy and Information Technology* (New York: Cambridge University Press, 2008); "Institutions, Integrity Systems and Market Actors" in (ed.) J. O'Brien, *Private Equity, Corporate Governance and the Dynamics of Capital Market Regulation* (Imperial College of London Press, 2007); "Joint Action: The Individual Strikes Back" in (ed.) S. L. Tsohatzidis, *Intentional Acts and Institutional Facts: Essays on John Searle's Social Ontology* (Dordrecht: Springer Press, 2007); "Against the Moral Autonomy Thesis," *Journal of Social Philosophy* 38, no. 3, 2007; "Social Institutions" in (ed.) Edward N. Zalta, *Stanford Encyclopedia of Philosophy*, Winter 2007 edition; "Torture" in (ed.) Edward N. Zalta, *Stanford Encyclopedia of Philosophy*, Spring 2006 edition; *Professionalisation, Ethics and Integrity* (co-authors Andrew Alexandra et al.), Report for the Professional Standards Council, 2006; "Collective Moral Responsibility: An Individualist Account" in (ed.) Peter A. French, *Midwest Studies in Philosophy*, vol. XXX, 2006; *Corruption and Anti-Corruption: A Study in Applied Philosophy* (co-authors Peter Roberts and Edward Spence) (Saddle River, N.J.: Prentice Hall, 2005); *Ethical Issues in Policing* (co-author John Blackler) (Aldershot: Ashgate, 2005); "Corruption" in (ed.) Edward N. Zalta, *Stanford Encyclopedia of Philosophy*, Fall 2005 edition; "Human Rights and the Institution of the Police" in (eds.) Tom Campbell and Seumas Miller, *Human Rights and the Moral Responsibilities of Corporate and Public Sector Organisations* (Dordrecht: Kluwer, 2004); "Individual Autonomy and Sociality" in (ed.) Frederick Schmitt, *Socialising Metaphysics: Nature of Social Reality* (Lanham: Rowman & Littlefield, 2003); "Institutions, Collective Goods and Individual Rights," *ProtoSociology: An International Journal of Interdisciplinary Research* 18–19, 2003; "Academic Autonomy" in (ed.) Tony Coady, *Why Universities Matter* (Sydney: Allen and Unwin, 2000); *Social Action: A Teleological Account* (New York: Cambridge University Press, 2001); "Corruption and Anti-Corruption in the Profession of Policing," *Professional Ethics* 6, nos. 3 & 4, 1998; "Filial Responsibility and the Care of the Aged," *Journal of Applied Philosophy* (co-author M. Collingridge) 14, no. 2, 1997; "Needs, Moral Self-consciousness and Professional Roles," *Professional Ethics* (co-author Andrew Alexandra) 5, nos. 1 & 2, 1996; "Freedom of the Press," *Politikon* 22, no. 1, June 1995; "Joint Action," *Philosophical Papers* XXI, no. 3, 1992.

Thanks finally to various anonymous Cambridge University Press reviewers, and to Ewen Miller for preparing the index.

# Introduction

## 1. OVERVIEW

This book is concerned with contemporary social institutions that are also complex organizations or systems of organizations. Thus its field of concern includes governments, police services, business corporations, universities, welfare institutions, and the like; it also includes criminal justice systems (comprised of a police organization, courts, correctional facilities, etc.), legal systems (comprised of a legislature, the law, courts, legal firms, etc.), financial systems (comprised of retail and investment banks, a stock exchange, regulators, auditing firms, etc.), and so on. On the one hand, it offers a *general* theory of social institutions – a teleological account, according to which all social institutions exist to realize various collective ends, indeed, to produce collective goods. On the other hand, it provides *special* theories of particular institutions, for instance, a theory of government.

Lest this field of concern appear too broad, and hence the ambitions of this book overblown, let me immediately add that the theories on offer are philosophical and, as a consequence, foundational and synoptic in character. Moreover, these theories are *normative* accounts of *some contemporary* social institutions, not accounts of all social institutions, both past and present. Much less are these theories descriptive or normative accounts of *all* organizations and associations; private clubs with restricted entry, for example, lie outside the scope of the normative theory of contemporary social institutions.

Roughly speaking, a descriptive theory is concerned with *what is* (the state of the institution as it happens to be), whereas a normative theory is concerned with *what ought to be* (the institutional processes that ought to be taking place, and the purposes that the institution ought to be

1

serving). Thus – to foreshadow part of the discussion in Chapters 1, 2, and 9 – an institution, such as a police organization, might have as its institutional purpose the protection of human and other moral rights, *normatively speaking;* nevertheless, as a matter of fact the police officers in question and, therefore, the police organization per se, might not pursue this collective end but rather engage in purely repressive action on behalf of the government of the day.

A normative theory is not a fanciful story about some utopian state; rather, it provides an account of what an institution realistically could be, and ought to be. Normative theory thereby gives direction to institutional actors, policy makers, citizens, and other stakeholders in the actual world.

My assumption in writing this book is that contemporary social institutions, including international institutions, are extraordinarily important for the well-being of humankind, but that in many cases the responses of institutions to the various challenges that they confront are manifestly inadequate, and the institutions in question in need of ethical renovation, if not redesign and rebuilding. Consider in this connection global poverty in Africa and elsewhere (Chapter 7) or the current crisis in the international financial sector (the greatest financial crisis since the 1929 stock market crash). The latter has thrown the global economy into recession and has involved the collapse and government bailout of a whole range of leading U.S. and European financial institutions: Lehman Brothers (United States), Northern Rock (United Kingdom), Fortis (Belgium), Hypo Real Estate (Germany), Fanny Mae and Freddie Mac (the United States' two largest home mortgage lenders), and AIG (the world's largest insurer) (Chapter 10). Consider also abuse of power and other forms of corruption in leading liberal democratic governments, such as by the Bush administration in the United States (Chapter 12), officially sanctioned use of torture in security agencies (Chapter 9), and the deleterious effect of the "dumbing-down" of the mainstream media on its role as the Fourth Estate (Chapter 10).

In Part A of this book I address a range of theoretical issues that arise in the context of the philosophy of social institutions. Part B applies the fruits of this theoretical work to specific institutions and challenges.

The material in Part A is somewhat conceptually complex, at least by the standards of some of those who are not academic philosophers. However, the book is written in such a way that readers who are interested only in the applications of this theoretical work can go straight to Part B without first having absorbed the content of Part A; indeed, even within

Part B it is possible to focus only on chapters dealing with institutions of specific interest.

In Chapter 1 I elaborate my normative, teleological account of social institutions. In my earlier book, *Social Action: A Teleological Account* (Miller 2001b), I provided a detailed analytical account of this theory and applied it to a variety of social forms, including joint action, conventions, and social norms. In this book I take over this account, extend it somewhat, and apply it to social institutions. On my teleological account, social institutions exist to serve various collective ends that are also collective goods, such as security (police services) or the acquisition, transmission, and dissemination of knowledge (universities). The extent to which actual institutions fail to serve these collective ends is the extent to which they are in need of redesign or renovation.

In Chapter 2 I elaborate an account of the general normative character of social institutions based on my individualist, teleological model, and according to which social institutions have a multifaceted normative dimension with multiple sources. These sources include ones that are logically prior to institutions, such as basic human needs and (institutionally prior) human rights, such as the rights to life, to freedom, and not to be tortured.

The normative character of social institutions includes the collective goods that they produce, the moral constraints on their activities, and a variety of *institutional* moral rights and duties (as opposed to moral rights and duties that are logically prior to institutions, that is, natural rights and duties). Such institutional moral rights and duties include ones that are derived from institutionally produced collective goods and, indeed, that are constitutive of specific institutional roles, such as the rights and duties of a fireman or a banker. They also include more broad-based institutional (moral) rights and duties that are dependent on community-wide institutional arrangements, such as the duty to obey the law in the jurisdiction in which one resides, the duty to assist the national defense effort of one's country in time of war, the right of access to paid employment in an economy in which one participates, the right to own land in some territory, and the right to freely buy and sell goods in an economy in which one participates.

These moral rights and duties are institutionally relative in the following sense. Even if they are in part based on an institutionally prior human right (e.g., a basic human need, the right to freedom), their precise content, stringency, context of application (e.g., jurisdiction, national territory, particular economy), and so on can be determined only by reference to the institutional arrangements in which they exist and, specifically, in the light of their contribution to the collective good(s) provided by those institutional arrangements.

On my account, collective ends are collective goods by virtue of their possession of the following three properties: (1) they are produced, maintained, or renewed by means of the *joint activity* of members of organizations, for example, schools, hospitals, welfare organizations, agribusinesses, electricity providers, police services – that is, by institutional role occupants; (2) they are *available to the whole community*, for example, clean drinking water, clean environment, basic foodstuffs, electricity, banking services, education, health, safety, and security; and (3) they *ought* to be produced (or maintained or renewed) and made available to the whole community because they are desirable (as opposed to merely desired) and such that the members of the community have an *(institutional) joint moral right* to them.

Note that my notion of a collective good, as defined, is different from standard notions of so-called public goods deployed by economists[1] and others, for example, in respect of a good's being jointly produced and having an explicitly normative character as the object of a joint moral right. Moreover, I do not make any sustained attempt to quantify these collective goods in the manner of, say, classical utilitarianism ("util" or mental states of pleasure). However, this is not to say that collective goods in my sense cannot be quantified, at least in some limited ways: for example, the quantification of police organizations' provision of security by recourse to rates of reported crime, clearing-up rates, and so on.

An important underlying assumption here is that *contra* much economic theory, human beings are not always and everywhere motivated by self-interest, albeit self-interest is a powerful and pervasive driver; moral beliefs and, specifically, doing one's moral duty for its own sake – as the German philosopher Immanuel Kant stressed – are an important additional motivation for action and one not reducible to self-interest – no matter how self-interest is conceived; for example, self-centeredness or pursuit of one's own goals (whatever they might be) at the expense of the goals of others (Sen 2002, 28–36). So, institutional design needs

---

[1] Economists typically define public goods as being nonrival and nonexcludable. If a good is nonrival, then my enjoyment of it does not prevent or diminish the possibility of your enjoyment of it; for example, a street sign is nonrival because my using it to find my way has no effect on your likewise using it. Again, a good is nonexcludable if it is such that if anyone is enjoying the good, then no one can be prevented from enjoying it, for instance, national defense.

to proceed on the assumption that both self-interest and morality are important motivations for human action, neither of which necessarily dominates the other when they come into conflict, as they often do.

In Chapter 3 I discuss the relationship between institutional structures and individual autonomy; to a degree, therefore, my concern is with the threat to the moral rights of institutional actors posed by some of the institutions in which they are housed. I argue, among other things, that well-functioning, well-designed, morally responsive social institutions enable individual autonomy, rather than necessarily diminish it. I also argue against the view that the reproduction of institutions is simply the unintended result of the actions of institutional actors.

By contrast, I emphasize the importance of the members of institutions strongly identifying with the institutional ends, constitutive activities, and social norms that are in part definitive of those institutions. Indeed, particular institutional actors have *special* moral rights and duties and, as such, are to a degree subject to a partialist ethic. Hence the limitations of so-called impartialist ethical theories, such as utilitarianism (Hoff Sommers 1986). Thus a journalist (but not an ordinary citizen) may be required to publish the truth, or protect her source, notwithstanding the predictable harmful consequences of her doing so (Bradley 1927). Here the partialism is with respect to an objectively specified category of persons, such as journalists' sources, and not simply individual persons as individuals, as in the case of partialism toward one's friends (Chapter 6). Unlike partialism in respect of one's friends, the partialism exhibited by journalists in relation to their sources, by lawyers in relation to their clients, and by various other institutional actors with special duties to specific categories of persons is impersonal.

Moreover, members of a given institution typically share a common structure of motivating moral beliefs in relation to their institutional roles and do so notwithstanding a diversity of prior and continuing, motivating, preference structures, for instance, with respect to why they joined the institution in the first place or why they do not leave it, and in relation to the lives that they lead outside the institution in question. Indeed, from the perspective of this book such preferences are extraneous to the analysis of institutions per se. Naturally, some extraneous preferences – specifically, some aggregated, widely shared, extraneous preferences – play an important role in the explanation of institutional change and performance (Hirschman 1970; North 1990). For example, those imbued with a strong desire to succeed in life may well enhance the performance of the government department of finance that they join, whereas those principally looking for job security do not. Nevertheless, these motivational differences are not constitutive of the organization in question *qua* institution, that is, *qua* government department of finance. On the other hand, the motivation to act in the public interest is constitutive of government departments *qua* institutions.

Needless to say, there are multiple, important, unintended consequences of the actions of institutional actors, both on themselves and on their institutions (Graham 2002, introduction). Of particular relevance to our concerns in this book are those unintended institutional outcomes, such as institutional corrosion, consequent on the failure of institutional actors to discharge adequately their institutional responsibilities (Hirschman 1970).

In Chapter 4 I provide a detailed analysis of the moral notion of collective moral responsibility, a notion that underpins institutions and, often indirectly, the duties of institutional actors. My account of collective moral responsibility is in part based on my teleological theory of joint action (the Collective End Theory [CET] elaborated in Chapter 1) and is individualist in character. I argue against corporatist accounts of collective moral responsibility, that is, accounts that ascribe moral responsibility to entities other than individual human beings.

In Chapter 5 my focus is on the dark side of institutions. Specifically, I provide a detailed analysis of the concept of institutional corruption. I proffer five hypotheses in relation to institutional corruption: (1) the personal character of corruption, (2) the causal character of corruption, (3) the moral responsibility of corruptors, (4) the asymmetry between corruptors and those corrupted, and (5) the involvement in institutional corruption of institutional actors who corrupt or are corrupted. An important assumption here is that social institutions, including economic institutions, are subject to processes of decline (Hirschman 1970) – notably corruption and, relatedly, loss of rationality. As Hirschman argues, these processes of decline typically activate counterforces, such as (in the case of economic institutions) exit (Hirschman 1970, chap. 2), for instance, loss of customers, and (in the case of political institutions) voice (Hirschman 1970, chap. 3), for instance, political protest. However, I suggest that an important motivational component of these counterforces is moral belief, for example, the belief that bribery, nepotism, and abuse of authority are morally wrong. It is not simply a matter of activating self-interest by increasing levels of competition or threatening sanctions.

Chapters 6–12 of this book are concerned with various applications of the theoretical work undertaken in Chapters 1–5. Thus in addition to the *general* normative theory of social institutions outlined in Chapters 1 and 2, I provide *special* and derived (from the general theory) normative theories of a number of importantly different contemporary institutions, namely, the so-called traditional (and emerging) professions (Chapter 6), welfare institutions (Chapter 7), the university (Chapter 8), police organizations (Chapter 9), the business corporation (Chapter 10), institutions in part constituted by information and communication technology (Chapter 11), and government (Chapter 12).

In a book of this size I need to be selective, and some central institutions are omitted or only treated in a cursory manner, for instance, correctional and military institutions. However, I content myself with the thought that my task here is not to provide a detailed treatment of each of these social institutions, but rather to apply my teleological theory to a selection of the main contemporary social institutions.

I have also selected social institutions that are in large part grounded in one or another of the following basic human needs (Wiggins 1991, 6), rights, and/or desirable (as opposed to merely desired) goods: food, water, and shelter (economic institutions that produce basic foodstuffs, medicines, houses, etc., and welfare institutions), the right to personal physical security (police organizations), the acquisition/transmission/dissemination of knowledge/understanding (universities), the storage/retrieval/communication of knowledge (institutions in part constituted by information and communication technology), and the organization, maintenance, and direction of other institutions (government).

On my teleological, normative account (roughly speaking) the university has as its fundamental collective end the acquisition, transmission, and dissemination of knowledge, whereas police organizations have as their fundamental collective end the protection of the human and other moral rights (including institutional moral rights) of members of the community. Again, the traditional professions have a range of specific collective ends, for example, the administration of justice (lawyers). The collective end of each of these institutions is a collective good: a jointly produced good that is, and ought to be, produced and made available to the whole community because it is a desirable good and one to which the members of the community have a joint moral right.

By contrast with these social institutions, business corporations and markets in general do not have ethico-normative purposes (collective goods, in the above sense) that are *internal* to them. Rather they should be understood in instrumentalist terms, for example, as an institutional means for the production of desired (but not necessarily desirable) goods. Accordingly, a business organization in a competitive market is not deficient *qua* institution merely because it produces candy rather than basic foodstuffs; obviously, many business organizations operating in competitive markets produce material goods and services that are desired but not needed, or otherwise desirable – and they should continue to do so. Nevertheless, there are moral and other value-driven purposes that should give direction to the design and operation of at least some markets and business organizations. Specifically, there are collective goods, for instance, aggregated needs-based rights to basic foodstuffs, clean water, clean air, clothing, housing, medicines, that markets and business organizations ought to produce as a matter of priority.[2]

In addition, business organizations operating in competitive markets – including organizations that produce only desired (as opposed to desirable) goods – provide jobs; in doing so they fulfill a moral right, namely, the right to paid work. In contemporary societies there is a (derived) moral right (and corresponding moral obligation) to work for a wage, that is, a right to a job (some job or other), because (other things being equal) without a job one cannot provide for one's basic needs and one cannot contribute to the production, maintenance, and renewal of collective goods, such as via taxes. In short, although business organizations in competitive markets per se do not serve inherently valuable collective ends that are internal to them, they do have enormous instrumental value. Accordingly, they are available to serve value-driven, including moral, purposes and should be made to do so by way of regulation, incentive structures, and the like, as required.

Note that I argue in Chapter 2 against market fundamentalism (Soros 2008) and, in particular, against the view that the moral right to property is such that it overrides aggregated needs-based rights and other collective goods. Indeed, *contra* market fundamentalism, property rights are in fact based in part on needs-based rights; to this extent needs-based rights are available to override property rights and, specifically, the transfer rights of property owners whose own needs are well catered for. Moreover, transfer rights – the right that the owner of property has to transfer the right to use, exclude, and in turn transfer the good in

---

[2] My use of the term *aggregated* is not meant to imply that rights fulfillment is subject to some simple process of addition such that the fulfillment of, say, the respective rights to life of two individuals is worth twice that of one person. See Miller (2008b, chap. 5) for further discussion.

question to others – are a very weak link in market fundamentalism's argumentative chain. From the fact that I might have certain use and exclusion rights to something because I produced it – or otherwise "mixed my labor with it" (to use John Locke's famous phrase) – it simply does not follow that I have the right to transfer all those rights to someone else or that, if I do, the transferred rights have the same stringency as they had when they attached to me as the producer of the good in question.

Morality, and ethical values more generally, is implicated in business organizations operating in competitive markets in a variety of ways, aside from in terms of any collective goods that they might produce or property right that they might embody. Thus business organizations are constrained by human rights, they facilitate the exercise of the institutional moral right to buy and sell property (itself a joint right; see Chapter 2, Section 2), their constitutive activities often reflect a strong work ethic, and so on.

It is also important to stress that business organizations operating in competitive markets cannot necessarily be expected to achieve adequately the larger (indirect) purpose that justifies their existence, that is, the production of a collective good, by simply being left alone; there is a need for incentivization, regulation, accountability, and, where appropriate, institutional redesign to ensure that Adam Smith's famous invisible hand actually delivers on its promises. If the current global financial crisis has demonstrated nothing else about free markets, it has surely demonstrated this.

In the course of discussing specific social institutions I examine some of the moral problems, including forms of institutional corruption, that these institutions face in the contemporary setting, for example, in the case of police and military organizations the practice of torture. I also attempt to offer practical solutions to some of these ethical problems, for instance, an outline of the key elements of an integrity system for the professions. I seek to frame these various practical ethical issues in terms of my individualist, teleological (normative) theories, both general and special, and to apply the various other theoretical understandings developed in Chapters 1–5.

I deliberately do not offer a philosophical theory of the institution of language for a somewhat different reason than my reasons (mentioned above) for excluding some other social institutions. Human languages are, as is often noted, a more fundamental kind of institution than the others and, indeed, are a logical presupposition of other institutions and have general properties not possessed by other institutions[3] – so much so that, arguably, they are not really a species of *social* institution at all.

Accordingly, I restrict my focus in this book to nonlinguistic institutions and, in particular, to contemporary social institutions that are also large complex organizations (Etzioni 1975) or systems of organizations. However, at various points I invoke the program of agent-semantics (Grice 1989) – itself a species of teleological individualism, as I see it – and make use of accounts of assertion, truth telling, and the like that I have elaborated in detail elsewhere, and that are congruent with the conception of social institutions that I am putting forward in this book (Miller 1985, 2003a). In Chapter 11 in particular, I offer accounts of certain contemporary institutions that are in part constituted by information and communication technology; these institutions are dependent on, and closely related to, the institution of language (on an agent-semanticist account of language).

An important reason for philosophical interest in social institutions – a reason additional to ontological interest – stems from the specifically normative concerns of philosophers. Philosophers, such as John Rawls (1972), have developed elaborate normative theories concerning the principles of justice that ought to govern social institutions. Yet they have done so in the absence of a developed theory of the nature and point of the very entities (social institutions) to which the principles of justice in question are supposed to apply. Surely the adequacy of one's normative account of the justice or otherwise of any given social institution, or system of social institutions, will depend at least in part on the nature and point of that social institution or system. For example, the principles of justice governing the distribution of benefits and burdens in relation to prisons differ in substance and application from those operative in relation to universities. This is presumably in large part because prisons have as a fundamental purpose to prevent ordinary people being harmed by dangerous persons, whereas universities have as a fundamental purpose to ensure the acquisition, transmission, and dissemination of knowledge.

In this book I elaborate a conception of social institutions according to which key elements of human morality, notably the human rights to life, to freedom, and not to be tortured, are logically prior to, albeit

---

[3]  The institution of the family and kinship systems are arguably another kind of social institution that is more fundamental than other social institutions (with the exception of human languages).

profoundly shaped by, social institutions.[4] However, this is not to make the implausible claim that human morality is logically prior to *inter-personal* interaction: the interpersonal is not to be confused with the institutional. The human right to life, for example, is a right with respect to some other persons that they not take one's life, but rather, at least in some circumstances, preserve and protect it. (Nor is the interpersonal to be confused with the social, in the sense of the societal. To reiterate, this time with respect to the societal: human rights, such as the right to life, are logically prior to the societal; see Miller 2001b, introduction).

Accordingly, I reject constructivist views such as that of John Searle (1995) and that of Raimo Tuomela (2002); Searle in particular tries – unsuccessfully, in my view – in effect to derive morality, specifically certain moral rights and duties, from social institutions (Chapter 2). But surely the right not to be killed and the right not to be tortured, for example, are logically prior to any social institution. Indeed, these human rights provide the raison d'être for some institutions, such as police organizations (Chapter 9), and give direction to others, such as governments (Chapter 12). Nevertheless, social institutions provide the medium and setting in which human moral activity typically takes place. As such, they strongly condition the nature and shape of many moral rights, values, and principles. For example, and as argued in Chapter 8, the prior human rights to freedom of thought and communication

---

[4] There are, of course, complications with some moral principles, such as theft and breaking promises; these seem institution-bound in ways not true of others, such as the moral principle not to take innocent life. Self-evidently, theft presupposes the institution of property. As far as promises are concerned, I regard these as a species of speech act and, therefore, not part of my concerns in this book. Nevertheless, it might be held that promises support a (institutional) constructivist conception of moral obligations; after all, promise making enables a given promise maker to *create* a moral obligation he or she did not already have. However, my unavoidable acceptance of the existence of this interesting phenomenon is not a concession to constructivism as a general theory of moral obligation, because the concept of a moral obligation is, in my view, already in play before the institution of making and keeping promises. On the other hand, the grain of truth in constructivism is that we do have institutions that have at their core a performative convention such that performing a certain act counts as putting one's self under an obligation; for example, my utterance of the sentence "I promise to meet you at 7 p.m." counts as putting myself under a moral obligation to meet you at 7 p.m. (or at least does so under certain conditions) (see Miller 1984, 2001b, introduction). Such an entrenched and widespread convention realizes a morally significant collective end, namely, *assurance* that future actions that might not be in the promisor's interest will, nevertheless, be performed. Moreover, the fact that participation is on any occasion mutually consensual (on pain of there being no promise) affords a further moral underpinning to the "obligation" created being an actual moral obligation.

underpins in part the institution of the university; nevertheless, these prior freedoms are transformed and further specified in various ways in the institutional setting of the university before finally emerging as academic freedom. A similar point can be made about freedom of speech in relation to the freedom of the press and the media as an institution (Chapter 10).

Moreover, once an institution, or set of institutions, based on prior human rights has been established, then this first-order (so to speak) layer of institutions may in turn give rise to a further set of second-order institutions. Thus the institutionally prior need for food, shelter, and so on might give rise to economic institutions that produce and distribute food. These are first-order institutions. However, these first-order economic institutions might in turn need a further set of institutions to facilitate their endeavors, for example, financial institutions such as banks. These financial institutions are second-order institutions.

## 2. THEORIZING ABOUT INSTITUTIONS

The term *social institution* is somewhat unclear both in ordinary language and in the philosophical literature (see below). However, contemporary sociology is rather more consistent in its use of the term. Typically, contemporary sociologists use the term to refer to complex social forms that reproduce themselves, such as governments, the family, human languages, universities, hospitals, business corporations, and legal systems. A typical definition is that proffered by Jonathan Turner: "a complex of positions, roles, norms and values lodged in particular types of social structures and organizing relatively stable patterns of human activity with respect to fundamental problems in producing life-sustaining viable societal structures within a given environment" (Turner 1997, 6). Again, Anthony Giddens says: "Institutions by definition are the more enduring features of social life." He goes on to list as institutional orders modes of discourse, political institutions, economic institutions, and legal institutions (1984, 31). The contemporary philosopher of social science Rom Harre follows the theoretical sociologists in offering this kind of definition: "An institution was defined as an interlocking double-structure of persons-as-role-holders or office-bearers and the like, and of social practices involving both expressive and practical aims and outcomes" (1979, 98). He gives as examples schools, shops, post offices, police forces, asylums, and the British monarchy (97).

In this book the above-noted contemporary sociological usage will be followed. Doing so has the virtue of grounding philosophical theory in the most salient empirical discipline, namely, sociology.

At this point it might be asked why a theory of social institutions has, or ought to have, any philosophical interest; why not simply leave such theorizing to the sociologists? Here we need to separate at least three different, albeit related, theoretical concerns, namely, descriptive, explanatory, and normative concerns. Roughly speaking, a descriptive theory of a social institution provides an account of the nature, structure, and other features of that institution as it *is*. An explanatory theory provides an explanation, for example, a causal explanation, of how the institution came to be the way it is (an explanation of its establishment and development) and, possibly, a set of predictions in relation to its future shape and direction based (presumably) on the underlying causal laws that in part enabled the explanatory developmental account. By contrast with description, and explanation and prediction, a normative theory provides an account of what a social institution *ought to be* like and what directions it *ought to* take.

Social institutions are constituted and animated by human beings, and human beings are intrinsically moral agents.[5] Since human beings are intrinsically moral agents, there is no adequate description of a human being that does not involve the ascription of moral properties, such as moral virtues and vices, moral responsibility, and the like.

Here it might be worth reminding ourselves of some of the obvious defining properties of human beings. Human beings have desires, beliefs, and intentions; they have visual, tactile, and other perceptions; experience pleasure and pain; have a range of emotions, such as love, hate, sympathy; plan and realize projects, both individually and jointly with others; have interpersonal relations with others; have interests, needs, and human rights; and so on and so forth. So human beings have properties above and beyond the physical properties studied in the so-called natural sciences – physics, chemistry, biology, and the like. Importantly, they have moral properties, such as interests, needs, and human rights. Nevertheless, these properties, including moral properties, are *natural* properties: that is, they are properties that human beings have *qua* human beings (Griffin 1996, chap. 3; Griffin 2008, 35–6).

---

[5] It does not follow from this that all human beings are moral agents; some may not be, but, if so, then they would be defective *qua* human beings.

The contrast I wish to make at this point is between the natural and the institutional (Miller 2001b, introduction). A human being *qua* human being is not an institutional role occupant; so a human being is not necessarily a politician, police officer, teacher, or even citizen. Moreover, moral properties, or at least some moral properties, such as basic needs, are logically prior to institutions, or, at least, are logically prior to those institutions that are also organizations (the type of institutions that are under discussion in this book). Hence, as already mentioned, I am excluding from consideration the institution of language. Although language is a necessary condition for reasoning, and hence moral reflection, a human language is not necessarily an organization (even if it is an institution).[6] Moreover, again as mentioned above, I am distinguishing between interpersonal relations and institutional relations. Interpersonal relations are not logically prior to morality; rather, they are in large part constitutive of it. Accordingly, I must hold, and do hold, that the interpersonal realm is logically prior to the institutional (insofar as the institutions in questions are organizations).

Notwithstanding the logical priority of basic elements of the moral over the institutional, there is no adequate description of a social institution that does not involve the ascription of moral properties. Crucially, however, these moral properties are (properly speaking) properties only of the individual human beings that constitute the social institution in question, or so I will argue.

There is an important connection between a normative theory of a social institution and a descriptive theory of that institution; specifically, if the ideal institution outlined in the normative theory bears no relationship to the actual institution detailed in the descriptive theory, then the normative theory is defective *qua* theory. Nevertheless, the descriptive does not collapse into the normative or vice versa; there remains a *conceptual* distinction between the institution as it is and the institution as it ought to be, even for those extremely rare (nonexistent?) institutions that are exactly as they ought to be.

There are radically different types of explanatory theories. Some focus on causal explanation and deploy the much vaunted covering-law model according to which causal explanations of particular events are to

---

[6] Speech acts such as assertions and promises are not institutions in the required sense of being organizations. Rather they are convention- and social-norm-governed communicative practices. Moreover, they are often institutionalized, such as in legal contexts. See also Chapter 11, Section 3.

be understood as logically dependent on, and therefore derivable from, universal causal laws of which the particular causal explanations are instances (Hempel 1965). Others seek to provide causal explanations, but insist that causes are powerful particulars in their own right rather than merely instances of lawlike generalizations (Harre and Madden 1975). Accordingly, *contra* the Scottish philosopher David Hume and other regularity theorists of causation, the notion of a cause should be decoupled from the notion of a regular co-occurrence of events. Indeed, on this view de facto *generalizable* causal explanations might be few and far between, especially in the social sciences. Thus it is unlikely, for example, that there would ever be a specific causal explanation applicable to all, or even most, wars. Still other explanatory theories eschew causal explanation in favor of interpretative, including rational, explanations. These latter theories might, or might not, leave room for causal explanations in addition to interpretative ones.

In this book the working assumption is that explanation in the social sciences is, at least in the first instance, reason based, albeit not in the restrictive sense deployed by rational choice theory and the like. (Amartya Sen, among others, has provided a sustained critique of rational choice theory; see Sen 2002.) Thus conformity to the convention (in some countries) to drive on the left-hand side of the road, for example, can be explained by recourse to reasons in the heads of the relevant actors, namely, road users strongly desire to avoid fatal car collisions. On the other hand, many reasons, such as many desires, are also causes of behavior; so a given reason-based explanation can cohere with a causal explanation. Moreover, action-guiding reasons are not necessarily rational in the sense that they provide *good* and/or decisive reasons for the actions they guide. Indeed, many reason-based explanations explain irrational behavior. Thus a husband serving a life sentence for murdering in a fit of jealous rage the wife he loved evidently acted irrationally but, nevertheless, acted for a reason.

As far as predictive theories of social institutions are concerned, these are typically causal explanatory theories framed in terms of the covering-law model; however, predictive theories are likely to be only partial and of limited application. This is surely because social institutions are constituted and animated by individual human beings, and the lives of the latter – including their institutional lives – tend to resist de facto generalizable causal explanation and certainly prediction.

There are, of course, well-confirmed, causal explanatory theories of some of the physical aspects of human beings in particular, such as human perception. Although such theories undoubtedly contribute to our understanding, and capacity for manipulation, of the physical world by describing the workings of the underlying causal mechanisms, they do not necessarily enable us to predict reliably particular physical events (other than the relatively small number of such events that take place under conditions of controlled experimentation).

As Peter Manicas points out (Manicas 2006, chap. 2) even in the physical sciences, outside closed experimental settings and more or less closed systems such as the solar system, reliable predictions of particular events are not nearly as common as the covering-law model in particular should lead us to expect. This is in large part because there are manifold causal contributors to most outcomes, and these contributors typically interact in a dynamic, nonlinear manner (Manicas 2006, 40). Consider the science of meteorology: predictions are often unreliable, almost always imprecise, and in constant need of updating as multiple variables (e.g., air temperature, wind velocity, and direction) in dynamic interaction give rise to new and emerging weather patterns.

Whatever the situation in the natural sciences, when one considers more generally the actions, projects, and lives of individual human beings, the prospects for generalizable causal explanatory/predictive theories seem slim indeed. Certainly, to date there are no well-confirmed, moderately comprehensive, causal explanatory/predictive accounts of the life narrative of a single, individual, rational, adult human person, let alone ones that are generalizable to other human persons.

We do, of course, "predict" on a daily basis the future actions of individual human persons including role occupants; however, we do so in large part on the basis of their stated intentions/ends/policies and so on and the rules/conventions/laws/social norms and so on that regulate their actions. Since intentions – including the standing intentions manifest in rule-governed behavior – are causes, these everyday predictions are to this extent based on so-called folk knowledge (as opposed to expert scientific knowledge) of causes. However, such banal "predictions" of future actions based on explicitly stated intentions and/or on past conformity to rules are hardly the stuff of a social theory with pretensions of becoming a mature generalizable, causal explanatory/predictive science constituted by laws of the kind governing, say, the movements of the planets in the solar system.

In addition to such everyday prediction of future actions, there are backward-looking, historical accounts, for example, biographies or criminal investigators' reports, that provide an explanation in a somewhat different sense from that standardly (but not universally; see Manicas 2006, chap. 2) assumed to be on offer in the natural sciences; but they are particularist and essentially nonpredictive in character. They do not have the ambitions of generalization to other human beings, and of prediction of future life events, that counterpart explanatory/predictive causal theories in operation in the natural sciences would have if applied to the lives of human beings.

In sum, then, although social institutions are susceptible to a degree of explanatory theorizing, including some causal – even predictive – theorizing, the fact that they are constituted and animated by individual human beings gives them a particularist character and lends them more to particularist-historical explanation than to generalizable causal explanation/prediction, or so I contend.

Social institutions are like individual human beings in another very important respect: they are malleable, and they make plans and pursue projects – or, at least, the individuals who constitute them collectively do so. Herein lies the opportunity for, and potential importance of, normative institutional theory. Just as ethics and ethical reasoning can, and should, give direction to the life of an individual human being, so normative institutional theory can, and should, give direction to the establishment, and the trajectory of development, of social institutions. In short, ethics can be *designed in* to social institutions (Van den Hoven 1997; Miller 2008b).

In the light of the above, we can see that one important reason for philosophical interest in social institutions stems from – or ought to stem from – the, so to speak, ontological concerns of philosophers. Doubtless, social institutions are in part constituted and animated by individual human persons; but in what respects, if any, might individual human persons be constituted by social institutions, such as by institutional roles? Moreover, do social institutions have mental or moral properties, or properties of rationality, above and beyond those possessed by the individual human beings who at least in part constitute the institutions in question? As already mentioned, I think not. However, historically these issues have been at the heart of the social thought of philosophers such as Hegel (and, in a contrasting, assumptive, and atomistic mode, David Hume). Recently the issues have again come to the fore, albeit in a somewhat different form, in the work of philosophers of social action, such as John Searle (1995) and Raimo Tuomela (2002).

### 3. A TELEOLOGICAL ACCOUNT: RELATIONAL
### INDIVIDUALISM

In Chapter 1 I put forward and defend an individualist and teleological (normative) account of social institutions (Miller 2001b, chap. 6). The individualism in question is *relational individualism,* as opposed to atomistic individualism. Relational individualism does not adhere to the implausible doctrine that social entities can be reduced to the individual human beings who constitute them; Australia, for example, is more than the sum of Australians.

Moreover, relational individualism posits sui generis interpersonal attitudes and relations, but eschews social entities possessed of mental properties or rationality. By sui generis interpersonal attitudes and relations I mean attitudes and relations that are not, and logically cannot be, possessed by single individuals considered as such. Consider the mutual, simultaneous recognition by two people of who the other is, or two people "looking into one another's eyes" (Miller 2001b, 3–8).

No doubt the notion of mutuality in play here serves in part to rule out the possibility that one agent, A, is conscious of the other agent, B, without B being likewise conscious of A (or of A being conscious of B being conscious of A, without B being likewise conscious of B being conscious of A, etc.; see Lewis 1969, 52). However, mutual consciousness is not simply a construction out of ordinary one-way directed consciousness, where by ordinary one-way consciousness I mean the one-way consciousness that a person has of something other than him or herself, like a person's consciousness of a table, a horse, or another person. In particular, mutual consciousness in the sense that I have in mind does not refer to a phenomenon comprised of two sets of iterated attitudes of ordinary one-way consciousness that mirror one another: first set – A is conscious of B, A is conscious that B is conscious of A, and so on; second set – B is conscious of A, B is conscious that A is conscious of B, and so on. Rather, mutual consciousness is a ground-level, two-way relation between conscious beings, A and B, that is not reducible to such sets of iterated attitudes of ordinary one-way consciousness, or so I contend (but cannot argue here for reasons of space; see Eitan et al. 2005, 2).

So there are sui generis interpersonal attitudes and relations, and they are manifested in mind to other mind interactions (e.g., extraspection; see Broad, 1928, 328), as opposed to mind to own-mind interactions (e.g., introspection) or mind-to-material world interactions (e.g., perception). However, these sui generis extraspective attitudes are all cognitive attitudes; they do not include conative attitudes, such as willings, intentions, ends, and the like. So I have no objection to – indeed, I endorse – the project of reducing putative group or joint willings, intentions, ends, and the like to sets of (possibly iterated) individual willings, intentions, ends, and so on.

I also hold, and need to hold on pain of inconsistency, that from the fact that there are such sui generis extraspective *cognitive* attitudes it does not follow that there are sui generis extraspective *conative* attitudes, such as sui generis joint intentions (Searle 1995, 24). As will become evident, I resist the notion of sui generis joint intentions in particular. What does follow is that at least some interpersonal interactions are not reducible to combinations of mind to own-mind and mind-to-material world interactions (Eitan et al. 2005, chap. 14). Such cases include, but are not restricted to, interpersonal interactions in which there is mutual consciousness.

A paradigm of interpersonal interaction is joint action. Joint action can, but does not necessarily, involve sui generis interpersonal attitudes. So sui generis interpersonal attitudes do not necessarily present a barrier to the reduction of joint actions to individual actions, albeit other relational elements in joint actions do present such a barrier (e.g., the relational bodily configuration of two dancing partners). On the other hand, as I will argue in Chapter 1, joint action does necessarily involve beliefs and intentions.

The notion of joint action provides the core of my individualist, teleological theory. As such, the theory is based on cooperative, as opposed to conflictual, action. Therefore, my account fits the following (admittedly cumbersome) description: it is an individualist, teleological, cooperation (normative) theory of social institutions. For the sake of brevity, I will continue to refer to my account simply as an individualist, teleological account.

Individualism of the kind I defend rejects the ascription of moral obligations or of moral responsibility to social entities per se, as opposed to the individual human beings who constitute and animate them. Ultimately, morality pertains to individual human beings and their interpersonal relations, and only derivatively to social entities. This is not to deny that social entities, like natural entities such as the HIV virus, can be evil in the sense that they can cause great harm to humans who come in contact with them, or that they are morally deficient in the *derived* sense that the individual human beings who constitute them are, say, corrupt.

Although teleological and consequentialist normative theories are often conflated, they ought not to be. According to consequentialism the rightness or wrongness of actions, procedures, or policies is logically dependent only on their outcomes and, therefore, is not logically dependent on whether or not they were intended or otherwise aimed at. Indeed, consequentialism is committed to the implausible view that an action is morally right or morally wrong by virtue of its consequences, even though those consequences might be unknown and unknowable. This collapses the distinction between harmful actions and morally wrong actions (and also the parallel distinction between beneficial actions and morally right actions) and puts moral rightness and wrongness implausibly beyond the epistemic reach of moral agents. For the harmful or beneficial consequences of human actions over the long term are quite often unknowable by the agents who perform the actions, either at the time of their performance or at any future time; consider, for instance, past members of an immigrant group who settled on a fertile coastal strip rather than on the less fertile and less accessible high ground. Suppose that the second generation of the immigrant group is largely wiped out by a freak, once-in-a-million-years tsunami, a fate that they would have avoided if the first generation had opted to establish the community on the high ground. The actions of the first generation ultimately causally contributed to the near destruction of the community, but they could not possibly have known that their apparently reasonable actions would have these untoward effects. Although it is true that what these people did was ultimately harmful, the claim that it was also morally wrong is implausible; yet consequentialism seems committed to just this claim.

By contrast, according to teleological theories, the intentions and, in particular, the outcomes aimed at, that is, *ends*, are in part *definitive* of the rightness or wrongness of actions, procedures, and policies – and, indeed, of social institutions themselves. On this kind of view the outcome of an action cannot be morally significant – as opposed to good or evil in some more general sense – unless it was in fact intended, or could have been intended (or was or could have been otherwise aimed at).

As will become apparent, my own favored account of normative ethical theory is a species of *moral pluralism*. I see little prospect of the nontrivial accommodation of, for example, moral rights within virtue theory (or vice versa). In my view the distinctions between, say, intrinsically right action, virtues, and morally significant consequences are just that: conceptual and morally relevant distinctions that need to be respected as basic, rather than set against one another in the service of a monistic ethical theory that seeks to privilege one of these conceptual moral categories at the expense of the others.

Moreover, the moral pluralism that I have in mind is substantive, as opposed to formalist, in character. By this I simply mean that purely formal or otherwise highly abstract principles, such as the principle of universalizabilty and the principle of utility maximization, have a relatively minor role to play in theoretical and practical ethics, and, certainly, in individual and collective moral or ethical decision making (Miller 2009a).

Is there, for example, a viable criminal justice system anywhere in which the principle of utility is taken to override the principle of convicting the guilty and ensuring the innocent go free, utilitarian philosophers notwithstanding? And in relation to the media as an institution, ought the principle of utility override the principle of objective and balanced reporting, if and when they conflict? Arguably a commitment to a principle of utility is a very large part of the problem with contemporary media organizations (Chapter 10). In maximizing consumer satisfaction the media has "dumbed down" its communicative content to the point that it is abnegating its institutional responsibilities as the Fourth Estate. What of the principle of universalizability: does it provide much-needed guidance in the kinds of institutional contexts in question? No doubt the principle of universalizability has a contribution to make, but evidently it is a limited one. It appears to be little more than a consistency test, and, as such, it offers only very limited guidance to moral agents, including institutional actors, seeking to know what they ought to do or not do. Moral decision making relies heavily on substantive principles; purely formal ones are largely impotent.

Nor is it self-evident that a "system" of social institutions, such as the contemporary nation-state, can be adequately normatively framed in terms of even a relatively sophisticated set of abstract principles such as that provided by John Rawls (Rawls 1972). The set of institutions that allegedly comprises the contemporary nation-state is far from being an organic or otherwise unitary whole. Accordingly, it is doubtful that there is a single, bounded, system of institutions to which these principles can be applied (albeit they might well be able to be applied to the nation-state's population conceived as a set of individual citizens). Some of the institutions in question straddle different nation-states, for instance, the global financial system (Chapter 10); their nature and purposes transcend national boundaries, and, indeed, their organization and maintenance requires multiple governments. Others, such as universities, have a normative institutional reach that goes well beyond the nation-state in which they are located: for example, research into HIV/AIDS at an Australian university has, or ought to have, practical implications for sufferers in Africa.

The particularity of social institutions and their trajectories of development are partially analogous to the lives of individual human persons. Indeed, in one respect the degree of particularity of social institutions is much greater than that of individual human lives; for example, police organizations and universities are different in kind in a way in which two human beings are not. At any rate, to make good on my claim regarding the impotence of formal principles in normative theorizing about social institutions, and in relation to the practical ethical problems of institutional actors – as well as in relation to unifying normative frameworks for all institutions in a given society – I am relying on the various normative analyses of specific social institutions and associated ethical problems provided in Part B of this book.

## 4. GENERIC PROPERTIES OF SOCIAL INSTITUTIONS

Any account of social institutions must begin by informally marking off social institutions from other social forms.[7] Unfortunately, as noted above, the terms *institutions* and *social institutions* are used to refer to a miscellany of social forms, including conventions, rituals, organizations, and systems of organizations. Moreover, there are a variety of theoretical accounts of institutions, including sociological as well as philosophical ones. Indeed, many of these accounts of what are referred to as institutions are not accounts of the same phenomena; they are at best accounts of overlapping fields of social phenomena. Nevertheless, it is possible, first, to mark off a range of related social forms that would be regarded by most theorists as being properly describable as social institutions, and, second, to compare and contrast some of the competing theoretical accounts of the "social institutions" in question.

Social institutions need to be distinguished from less complex social forms such as conventions, social norms, roles, and rituals. The latter are among the constitutive elements of institutions.

Social institutions also need to be distinguished from more complex and more complete social entities, such as societies or cultures, of which any given institution is typically a constitutive element. A society,

---

[7] Much of the material in the following sections is taken from Miller (2007a).

for example, is more complete than an institution, because a society – at least as traditionally understood – is more or less self-sufficient in terms of human resources, whereas an institution is not. Thus, arguably, for an entity to be a society it must sexually reproduce its membership, have its own language and educational system, provide for itself economically, and – at least in principle – be politically independent.[8]

Social institutions are often organizations (Scott 2001). (For a contrary view see Douglass North's work, e.g., North 1990, 4.) Moreover, many institutions are *systems* of organizations. For example, capitalism is a particular kind of economic institution, and in modern times capitalism consists in large part of specific organizational forms – including multinational corporations – organized into a system. Further, some institutions are *meta-institutions:* they are institutions (organizations) that organize other institutions (including systems of organizations). For example, governments are meta-institutions. The institutional end or function of a government consists in large part of directing, regulating, assisting, maintaining, or otherwise organizing other institutions (both individually and collectively); thus governments regulate and coordinate economic systems, educational institutions, police and military organizations, and so on. Moreover, governments are hierarchical organizations and regulate largely by way of enforceable legislation; as such, they not only have internal relations of power and authority, they also stand in relations of authority and power to the institutions and institutional actors thus regulated.

Nevertheless, some institutions are not organizations, or systems of organizations, and do not require organizations. For example, the English language is arguably an institution, but it is not an organization. Moreover, it would be possible for a language to exist independently of any organizations specifically concerned with language. Again, consider an economic system that does not involve organizations, such as a barter system involving only individual traders. An institution that is not an organization or system of organizations comprises a relatively specific

---

[8]  The fact that a society might engage in trade with other societies and, as a consequence, rely on other societies for certain purely physical resources does not affect this point. However, if it came to rely on cultural or educational resources, then matters would be different. Moreover, increased economic interdependence and integration with other societies certainly puts pressure on the concept of a society. As far as political independence is concerned, perhaps a society that is temporarily politically subsumed by another society, as in an empire, might nevertheless remain a society if it maintained a degree of integrity and distinctiveness in relation to its governance structures.

type of agent-to-agent interactive activity, for instance, communication or economic exchange, that involves (1) differentiated actions – communication involves speaking and hearing/understanding, economic exchange involves buying and selling – that are (2) performed repeatedly and by multiple agents, (3) in compliance with a structured unitary system of conventions, such as linguistic conventions, monetary conventions, and social norms, such as truth telling and property rights.

As already mentioned, in this book the concern is with social institutions (including meta-institutions) that are also organizations or systems of organizations. However – again, as mentioned above – the institutions of language, such as the English language, are often regarded as more fundamental than most other institutions. The reason for this is that these institutions of language are presupposed by, or in part constitutive of, other kinds of social institution. Members of legal, economic, and political institutions, for example, reflect, communicate, and act on the basis of reasons; to do this they must have a language. A case might also be made that the family is a more fundamental institution than most others for related reasons; for example, it is the site of sexual reproduction and initial moralization/socialization.

Note also that uses of the term *institution* in such expressions as "the institution of government" are often ambiguous. Sometimes what is meant is a particular token, such as the current government in Australia, sometimes a type, such as the set of properties instantiated in any actual government, and sometimes a set of tokens, such as all governments. Restricting the notion of an institution to organizations is helpful in this regard; the term *organization* almost always refers to a particular token. On the other hand, the term *institution* connotes a certain gravity not connoted by the term *organization;* so arguably those institutions that are organizations are organizations that have a central and important role to play in or for a society. Being central and important to a society, such roles are usually long-lasting ones; hence institutions are typically transgenerational.

Having informally marked off social institutions from other social forms, let us turn to a consideration of some general properties of social institutions. At a fundamental level, different types of institutions are differentiated from one another by the different generic kinds of joint action and activity that principally constitute them: for example, communicative, economic, sexual, and religious activity. However, in addition to their constitutive activity, institutions have four salient properties, namely, structure, function, culture, and sanctions.

Roughly speaking, an institution that is an organization or system of organizations consists of an embodied (occupied by human persons) structure of differentiated roles. These roles are defined in terms of tasks, an agent who performs those tasks (the role occupant), and rules regulating the performance of those tasks. Moreover, there is a degree of interdependence between these roles, such that the performance of the constitutive tasks of one role cannot be undertaken, or cannot be undertaken except with great difficulty, unless the tasks constitutive of some other role or roles in the structure have been undertaken or are being undertaken. Further, these roles are often related to one another hierarchically and hence involve different levels of status, degrees of authority, and relationships of power. Finally, on teleological and functional accounts, these roles are related to one another in part in virtue of their contribution to (respectively) the *end(s)* or *function(s)* of the institution; and the realization of these ends or functions normally involves interaction between the institutional actors in question and external noninstitutional actors. (The assumption here is that the concept of an end and of a function are distinct concepts.)[9] The constitutive roles of an institution and their relations to one another can be referred to as the *structure* of the institution, albeit strictly speaking structure is simply an abstraction – it is an abstraction from the reality that consists of those individual human beings who perform the tasks that define the roles in question (Chapter 3). In the case of hierarchical structures, the role occupants will stand to one another in relationships of authority and power.

Note that on this conception of institutions as *embodied* structures of roles and associated rules, the nature of any institution at a given time will to some extent reflect the personal character of different role occupants, especially influential role occupants; for example, the British government during the Second World War reflected to some extent Winston Churchill's character. Moreover, institutions in this sense are dynamic, evolving entities; as such, they have a history, the diachronic structure of a narrative, and (usually) a partially open-ended future.

---

[9] One way of drawing the distinction is as follows. Having an end is some form of mental state; but mentality is not necessarily an element of a function or possessed by the things that have functions; for example, the function of the heart is to ensure that blood is circulated throughout the body. Naturally, the explanations for the possession of an end are multifarious; perhaps, for example, some collective ends are "wired in." Consider the desired end for sexual union. And if "wired in" they might, nevertheless, exist in a relatively inchoate form; hence the need for social forms to refine and articulate prior collective ends.

Aside from the formal and usually explicitly stated, or defined, tasks and rules, there is an important implicit and informal dimension of an institution roughly describable as institutional *culture*. This notion comprises the informal attitudes, values, norms, and ethos or "spirit" that pervades an institution; importantly, it includes the extent and degree of institutional loyalty. Culture in this sense determines much of the activity of the members of that institution, or at least the manner in which that activity is undertaken. So although the explicitly determined rules and tasks might say nothing about being secretive or "sticking by one's mates come what may" or having a hostile or negative attitude to particular social groups, these attitudes and practices might in fact be pervasive; they might be part of the culture. Here it is worth noting that the sources of this culture might be predominantly internal or external. The reckless, break-the-rules, greed-is-good culture of Enron, for example, appears to have been predominantly intraorganizationally spawned (Fusaro and Miller 2002; Jackall 1988). On the other hand, the racist culture within a particular business organization in apartheid South Africa might have been predominantly driven by racist attitudes and institutions in the wider external society. Naturally, there can be competing cultures within a single organization; the culture comprised of attitudes and norms that is aligned to the formal and official complex of tasks and rules might compete with an informal and "unofficial" culture that is adhered to by a substantial subelement of the organization's membership.

In one sense culture is a contingent feature of social institutions; hence multiple cultures can inhabit a single institution, and institutions of the same kind can have widely divergent cultures. Moreover, the contingency of culture is reflective of its pronounced expressive character; culture is less instrumentalist in character than is, for instance, structure.[10] Nevertheless, it is necessarily the case that an institution has some culture(s) or other. Moreover, normatively speaking, some aspects of culture are definitive of institutions, for example, a collective commitment to institutional purposes (the relevant collective goods).

It might be claimed that in addition to structure, function, and culture, social institutions necessarily involve sanctions. It is uncontroversial that social institutions involve *informal* sanctions, such as moral disapproval following nonconformity to institutional norms, or acts of disloyalty to the institution. However, some theorists argue that formal

---

[10] Although the expressive aspect of social forms, including institutions, is important, limitations of space prevent detailed treatment of it in this book.

sanctions, such as punishment, are a necessary feature of institutions (Elster 1989, chap. 15). Here formal sanctions are being contrasted with informal sanctions, such as social disapproval.

Formal sanctions are certainly a feature of most contemporary institutions, especially institutions that are hierarchical organizations; hierarchical organizations have structures of authority and power, and formal sanctions are required for purposes of enforcement. However, sanctions do not seem to be a feature of all institutions; specifically, they do not seem to be a feature of all *nonhierarchical* institutions. Consider, for example, an elaborate and long-standing system of economic exchange between members of different societies that have no common system of laws or enforced rules.

Although I have argued that formal sanctions are not a *defining* feature of social institutions, they are a characteristic of those contemporary social institutions that are also hierarchical organizations: that is, most contemporary institutions. Since the latter are my principal concern in this book, I will for the most part treat formal sanctions as if they were on all fours with the other general properties of social institutions identified, namely, constitutive activity, structure, function, and culture.

Thus far we have informally marked off social institutions from other social forms, and we have identified a number of general properties of social institutions. It is now time to outline some of the main general theoretical accounts of social institutions.

## 5. ATOMISTIC, HOLISTIC, AND MOLECULARIST ACCOUNTS OF INSTITUTIONS

Notwithstanding our understanding of social institutions as complex social forms, some accounts of institutions identify institutions with relatively simple social forms – especially conventions, social norms, or rules. At one level this is merely a verbal dispute; *contra* our procedure here, such simpler forms could simply be termed *institutions*. However, at another level the dispute is not merely verbal, because what we are calling institutions would on such a view consist simply of sets of conventions, social norms, or rules. Let us refer to such accounts as *atomistic* theories of institutions (Schotter 1981; North 1990).

Here the "atom" itself typically consists of the actions of individual human persons, for example, conventions as regularities in action that solve coordination problems (Lewis 1969). The individual agents are not themselves defined in terms of institutional forms, such as institutional roles. Hence atomistic theories of institutions tend to go hand in hand with atomistic theories of all collective entities: for instance, a society consists of an aggregate of individual human persons. Moreover, atomistic theories tend to identify the individual agent as the locus of moral value. On this kind of view, social forms, including social institutions, have moral value only derivatively, that is, only insofar as they contribute to the prior needs or other requirements of individual agents.

The regularities in action or rules made use of in such atomistic accounts of institutions cannot simply be individual regularities in action or individual rules for action; rather there must be interdependence of action such that, for example, agent A performs only action X if other agents, B and C, do likewise. Moreover, some account of the interdependence of action in question is called for, for example, that it is not the sort of interdependence of action involved in conflict situations.

Assume that the conventions, norms, or rules in question are social in the sense that they involve the required interdependence of action: for example, the parties to any given convention, or the adherent to any such norm or rule, conform to (respectively) the convention, norm, or rule on condition the others do. Nevertheless, such interdependence of action is not sufficient for a convention, norm, or rule, or even a set of conventions, norms, or rules, to be an institution. Governments, universities, corporations, and the like are structured, unitary entities. Accordingly, a mere *set* of conventions (or norms or rules) does not constitute an institution. For example, the set of conventions comprising the convention to drive on the left, the convention to utter "Australia" to refer to Australia, and the convention to use chopsticks does not constitute an institution. Accordingly, a problem for atomistic accounts of social institutions is the need to provide an account of the structure and unity of social institutions, and an account that is faithful to atomism, for instance, that the structure is essentially aggregative in nature.

Some theorists have sought to identify institutions with a particular species of rule, namely, so-called constitutive rules. Constitutive rules have the form "Doing X counts as Y in circumstances C" (Searle 1995). (They are often also held to be self-referential and/or self-validating; see Bloor 1997, chap. 3.) No doubt many such constitutive rules are an integral element of larger structures of rule-governed activity that are in fact institutions. (Constitutive rules also raise the issue of constructivist, e.g., collective acceptance, accounts of institutional properties – an issue taken up in Chapter 3.) However, the mere fact that some regularity in action has the form of a constitutive rule does not make it an institution per se. Consider a child who collects pebbles on the beach, and counts or treats them as money by getting his mother to give him a lollipop for each pebble. He has not thereby established an institution, even an institution that is only derivative from, or a pale reflection of, a monetary institution. Nor would it make any difference if a number of children engaged in this practice, and if each did so only on condition the others did.

By contrast with atomistic accounts of social institutions, *holistic* – including *structuralist-functionalist* – accounts stress the interrelationships of institutions (structure) and their contribution to larger and more complete social complexes, especially societies (function). Thus according to Barry Barnes:

> Functionalist theories in the social sciences seek to describe, to understand and in most cases to explain the orderliness and stability of entire social systems. In so far as they treat of individuals, the treatment comes after and emerges from analysis of the system as a whole. Functionalist theories move from an understanding of the whole to an understanding of the parts of that whole, whereas individualism proceeds in the opposite direction. (1995, 37)

Moreover, "such accounts list the 'functions' of the various institutions. They describe the function of the economy as the production of goods and services essential to the operation of the other institutions and hence the system as a whole" (Barnes 1995, 41). Theorists in this tradition include Durkheim, Radcliffe-Brown, and Talcott Parsons (Radcliffe-Brown 1958; Durkheim 1964; Parsons 1968, 1982).

Of particular concern to many of these holistic theorists has been the moral decay consequent (in their view) on the demise of strong, mutually supportive social institutions. Durkheim, for example, advocated powerful professional associations:

> A system of morals is always the affair of a group and can operate only if the group protects them by its authority. It is made up of rules which govern individuals, which compel them to act in such and such a way, and which impose limits to their inclinations and forbid them to go beyond. Now there is only one moral power – moral, and hence common to all – which stands above the individual and which can legitimately make laws for him, and that is collective power. To the extent the individual is left to his own devices and freed from all social constraint, he is unfettered by all moral constraint. It is not possible for professional ethics to escape this fundamental condition of any system of morals. Since, the society as a whole feels no concern in professional ethics, it is imperative that there be special groups in the society, within which these morals may be evolved, and whose business it is to see that they are observed.(Durkheim 1957, 61)

The meta-institution of government obviously has a pivotal directive, maintenance, and integrative role in relation to other institutions and their interrelationships, albeit government is itself simply one institution within the larger society. Moreover, government stands in a relation of formal authority and of power (backed by formal sanctions) in relation to other institutions, as well as to the citizenry per se. Further, holistic accounts of institutions lay great stress on institutional roles defined in large part by social norms; institutional roles are supposedly largely, or even wholly, constitutive of the identity of the individual human agents who occupy these roles. (Individuals participate in a number of institutions and hence occupy a number of institutional roles – hence the alleged possibility of their identity being constituted by a number of different institutional roles.)

Many such holistic accounts deploy and depend on the model, or at least analogy, of an organism. A salient historical figure here is Herbert Spencer (Spencer 1971, part 3, B – *A Society Is an Organism*). On this holistic, organicist model, social institutions are analogous to the organs or limbs of a human body. Each organ or limb has a function, the realization of which contributes to the well-being of the body as a whole, and none can exist independently of the others. Thus the human body relies on the stomach to digest food to continue living, but the stomach cannot exist independently of the body or of other organs, such as the heart. Likewise, it is suggested, any given institution, such as law courts, contributes to the well-being of the society as a whole, and yet is dependent on other institutions, such as government.

Here the "well-being" of the society as a whole is sometimes identified with the stability and continuation of the society as it is – hence the familiar charge that holistic, organicist accounts are inherently politically conservative. This political conservatism transmutes into political authoritarianism when society is identified with the system of institutions that constitute the nation-state, and the meta-institution of the nation-state – the government – is assigned *absolute* authority in relation to all other institutions: hence the contrasting emphasis in political liberalism on the separation of powers between, for example, the executive, the legislature, and the judiciary.

Holistic accounts of social institutions often invoke the terminology of internal and external relations. An internal relation is one that is definitive of, or in some way essential to, the entity it is a relation of; by contrast, external relations are not in this way essential. Thus being married to someone is an internal relation of husbands; if a man is a husband, then necessarily he stands in the relation of being married to someone else. Likewise, if someone is a judge in a court of law, then necessarily he stands in an adjudicative relationship to defendants. Evidently, many institutional roles are possessed of, and therefore in part defined by, their internal relations to other institutional roles.

However, the existence of institutional roles with internal relations to other institutional roles does not entail an holistic account of social institutions. For the internal relations in question might not be relations between institutional roles in different institutions; rather, they might simply be internal relations between different institutional roles in the same institution, such as the institutional relation between a Ph.D. supervisor and her Ph.D. student.

On the other hand, the existence of institutional roles with internal relations does undermine the attempts of certain forms of atomistic individualism to reduce institutions to the individual human persons who happen in part to constitute them. By the lights of atomistic individualism, the individual human persons who happen to constitute an institution at a particular time are not *qua* individual human persons even in part defined in terms of their relations to institutional roles; they would be the individual human persons that they are even if they did not occupy the institutional roles in question. Therefore, *qua* individual human persons, these agents are not, and cannot be, fully constitutive of the institutional roles that they might come to occupy; for *qua* role occupant (but not *qua* individual human person) these agents have institutional relations to other institutional role occupants, and (crucially) these (internal) relations are definitive of them as role occupants.

Here it is important to distinguish the plausible view that institutions are not reducible to the individual human persons who constitute them from the highly implausible view that institutions are themselves agents possessed of minds and a capacity to reason (French 1984). Elsewhere I have provided a detailed rebuttal of this implausible view (Miller 2001b, chap. 4). Here I offer only one kind of rather obvious objection to it.

If we ascribe intentions to organizations, for example, ascribe to Gulf Oil the intention to maximize profits, then we are apparently committed to ascribing to Gulf Oil a whole network of sophisticated propositional attitudes concerning economic production, the workings of markets, and so on. Moreover, a being with such a network of propositional attitudes would be capable of high-level thought and therefore be possessed of a language in which to do this thinking. Further, this agent's thought processes would include planning for its future and doing so on the basis of its past mistakes and the likely responses of other corporations. Such a corporate agent is self-reflective; it not only distinguishes its present from both its past and its future, and itself from other corporations, but it also reflects on itself for the purpose of transforming itself. Such a being has higher-order propositional attitudes, including beliefs about its own beliefs and intentions, and conceives of itself as a unitary whole existing over time. In short, it looks as though we now have a fully conscious, indeed, self-conscious, being on our hands. Nor do matters rest here. For if we are prepared to grant Gulf Oil a mind, then why not all its subsidiaries, as well as all other companies and subsidiaries worldwide? Indeed, how can we stop at corporations? Surely governments, universities, schools, supermarkets, armies, banks, political parties, trade unions, English soccer teams' supporters' clubs (at least) now all have minds, albeit in some cases smaller minds (so to speak). Not only do we have a self-conscious mind, but we have an ever expanding community of self-conscious minds!

If we reject the notion that corporations and other collectivities are agents possessed of minds, as it seems we must, then it follows that these collective entities cannot be *moral* agents; moral agency presupposes mentality, indeed, rational agency. The denial of moral agency to collective entities, such as corporations and nation-states, has important practical implications. It reveals the incoherence, for example, in the claim that the ascription of legal rights, such as intellectual property rights, to corporations is grounded in some prior moral right that those entities possess. From the fact that some new medicine was developed by the employees of a pharmaceutical company, for example, it simply does not follow, indeed, it cannot be the case, that the company has a moral (as opposed to legal) right to patent the medicine; collectivities, such as companies, are not conceptually appropriate bearers of moral rights. There are, of course, a variety of justifications for the ascription of legal rights to collective entities, and these legal rights include intellectual property rights; my point is simply that no such justification is acceptable if it relies on the ascription of moral properties to collectivities as such (Chapter 7).

Thus far we have discussed atomistic and holistic accounts of social institutions. However, there is a third possibility, namely – what might be termed – *molecularist* accounts. Roughly speaking, a molecularist account of an institution would not seek to reduce the institution to simpler atomic forms, such as conventions; nor would it seek to define an institution in terms of its relationships with other institutions and its contribution to the larger societal whole. Rather, each institution would be analogous to a molecule; it would have constitutive elements ("atoms") but also have its own structure and unity. Moreover, on this conception each social institution would have a degree of independence vis-à-vis other institutions and the society at large; on the other hand, the set of institutions might itself under certain conditions form a unitary system of sorts, for example, a contemporary liberal democratic nation-state comprised of a number of semiautonomous public and private institutions functioning in the context of the meta-institution of government.

A general problem for holistic organicist accounts of social institutions – as opposed to molecularist accounts – is that social institutions can be responses to *trans-societal* requirements or needs. Accordingly, an institution is not necessarily a constitutive element of some given society in the sense that it is both in part constitutive of that society and wholly contained within that society. Examples of such trans-societal institutions are global institutional arrangements such as the World Trade Organization (Chapter 7), the international financial system (Chapter 10), the Internet (Chapter 11), the international legal system, the United Nations, and some multinational corporations. Indeed, arguably, any given element of such a trans-societal institution stands in some *internal* relations to elements of other societies.

This raises the question as to whether or not the category of social institution might be *conceptually* independent of the category of society in the sense that it might be conceptually possible for there to be an institution without there being a society. This is consistent with the impossibility of there being a society without institutions: that is, perhaps societies presuppose social institutions, but not vice versa.

Here we need to distinguish conceptual (or logical) impossibility from *practical* impossibility. For example, it might well be that no society and no system of institutions can exist, practically speaking, without the meta-institution of government; absent government, societies and social institutions tend to disintegrate. However, it would not follow from this that the institution of government is logically necessary for the existence of societies and (nongovernment) institutions.

The claim that institutions are conceptually independent of societies goes hand in glove with the proposition that human social life is dependent on institutions, but not necessarily on societies as such. The picture here is of human beings who are members of many different social groups, such as academic philosophers, EU citizens, and speakers of the Spanish language, each group sustained by one or more social institutions; however, there are no societies as such. For those who lived, or are living, in traditional tribes or clans, this picture might be incomprehensible. However, it does have some resonance for those living in contemporary cosmopolitan settings.

In response to this claim of the independence, and perhaps priority, of institutions vis-à-vis societies it can be pointed out that trans-*societal* institutions presuppose societies. This is true enough. However, this would not rescue the holistic organicist conception, for such trans-societal institutions are not generally – and certainly not necessarily – constitutive "organs" of some larger society. Moreover, international institutions presuppose only nation-states, and the latter might be conceived of in narrowly political terms. Contemporary nation-states are not, it might be insisted, complete and self-sufficient societies, such as traditional tribes or clans might have been. At any rate, it is an assumption of this book that social institutions are necessary for human social life, and that the notion of a social institution is logically independent of the notion of a society per se.

In this introductory chapter a preliminary account of social institutions has been provided. In the next chapter I turn to my own account of social institutions – a teleological account. This account is consistent with institutional molecularism, broadly conceived.

# PART A

# THEORY

# A Teleological Account of Institutions

Teleological accounts of social action in general, and of social institutions in particular, fall within the individualist philosophy of action tradition that has its intellectual roots in Aristotle, Hume, and Kant and is associated with contemporary analytic philosophers of social action such as Michael Bratman (1987), John Searle (1995), and Raimo Tuomela (2002).[1] However, this way of proceeding also has a place outside philosophy in sociological theory. Broadly speaking, it is the starting point for the voluntaristic theory of social action associated with the likes of Max Weber (1949) and (the early) Talcott Parsons (1968). Consider, for example, the following idea in relation to social action expressed by Parsons (1968, 229): "actions do not take place each with a separate, discrete end in relation to the situation, but in long complicated chains ... [and] the total complex of means-end relationships is not to be thought of as similar to a large number of parallel threads, but as a complicated web (if not a tangle)."

## 1. JOINT ACTION

The central concept in the teleological account of social institutions is that of *joint action*.[2] Joint actions are actions involving a number of agents performing interdependent actions to realize some common goal. Examples of joint action are two people dancing together, a number of tradesmen building a house, and a group of robbers burgling a house. Joint action is to be distinguished from individual action, on the one hand, and from the "actions" of corporate bodies, on the other. Thus an

---

[1] Much of the material in this chapter is taken from Miller (2007c).
[2] Earlier versions of the material in this section appeared in Miller (2001b, chap. 2).

individual walking down the road or shooting at a target is an instance of individual action. A nation declaring war or a government taking legal action against a public company is an instance of *corporate* action.

Over the last decade or two a number of analyses of joint action have emerged.[3] These analyses can be located on a spectrum at one end of which there is so-called (by Frederick Schmitt [2003]) strict individualism, and at the other end of which there is so-called (again by Schmitt) supra-individualism.

A number of these theorists have developed and applied their favored basic accounts of joint action to account for a range of social phenomena, including conventions, social norms, and social institutions. Elsewhere I have elaborated and defended a relatively strong form of individualism, namely, the Collective End Theory (CET)[4] against arguments emanating from the supra-individualists and from their fellow traveler antireductionists, such as Searle, who try to occupy middle ground. I cannot rehearse all these arguments and counterarguments here. However, I do need to set forth CET and briefly locate it within the overall spectrum of intellectual options.

Individualism, as I see it, is committed to an analysis of joint action such that ultimately a joint action consists of (1) a number of singular actions and (2) relations between these singular actions. Moreover, the constitutive attitudes involved in joint actions are individual attitudes; there are no sui generis we-attitudes. Here it is important to stress that individualism can be, and in the case of CET certainly is, a form of relationalism. It is relational in two senses. First, as mentioned above, singular actions often stand in relations to one another, for example, two partners dancing, and the joint action in part consisting of the singular actions also in part consists of the relations between the singular actions. Second, the agents who perform joint actions can have intersubjective attitudes to one another – for example, they mutually recognize who one another is – and, mentioned in the Introduction, some (but not all) of these attitudes are sui generis. Specifically, some *cognitive* (but no conative) intersubjective attitudes are sui generis, such as mutual consciousness of one another's consciousness (Eitan et al. 2005, chap. 14). In virtue of

[3]  See Tuomela and Miller (1988), Tuomela (1995, 2002), Gilbert (1989, esp. sect. 4), Searle (1990, 1995, esp. chaps. 1 and 2), Cohen and Levesque (1991), Bratman (1992, 1993), and Miller (1992a, 1995a, 2001b, chap. 2).
[4]  For a detailed elaboration of CET see Miller (2001b, chap. 2; see also Miller 1992a). For earlier applications of this account in relation to conventions, speech acts, and social contracts, see Miller (1986a, 1986b, 1987, 1992b).

such intersubjective attitudes they will also typically have interpersonal relations to one another. Intersubjectivity and interpersonal relations in this sense are not necessarily, or at least are not by definition, social or institutional. To suggest otherwise would be to beg the question against individualism (specifically, relational individualism) in any interesting sense of the term.

By contrast, according to supra-individualists, when a plurality of individual agents perform a joint action the agents necessarily have the relevant propositional attitudes (beliefs, intentions, etc.) in an irreducible "we-form" that is sui generis, and as such not analyzable in terms of individual or I-attitudes. Moreover, the individual agents constitute a new entity, a supra-individual entity not reducible to the individual agents and the relations between them.

Individualism can be, and has been, targeted by supra-individualist- or, at least, antireductionist-, style arguments of a number of kinds. Some of these arguments miss their mark by virtue of the fact that they ascribe claims or positions to individualism that it does not make or need not occupy.

For example, it is sometimes argued that individualism must hold that the attitudes involved in joint actions must not make any reference to irreducibly collective entities. However, this kind of argument confuses irreducibly collective *entities* with irreducibly collective *attitudes.* An individualist account of joint action does not need to hold the implausible view that there are no irreducibly collective entities, for example, Australia, the United States, Finland, and the European Union. Clearly there are irreducibly collective entities, and such entities can and do figure in the content of individual attitudes; for example, Raimo Tuomela believes that Finland but not Australia or the United States is a member of the European Union. However, the existence of collective entities does not entail the existence of collective *agents,* and specifically, it does not entail the existence of supra-individual attitudes.

A related error among those who attack individualist accounts of joint action is to confuse *atomistic* individualism with *relational* individualism. The former is open to well-known difficulties, but CET is a species of the latter. Margaret Gilbert is guilty of this confusion, so let us consider one of her examples and accompanying argument against individualist accounts of joint action. Gilbert correctly claims that from the fact that agents A and B (successfully) perform a joint action properly describable as Xing, it does not follow that A performed some individual action properly describable as Xing. Thus A and B might be dancing together, but it does not follow that if A were doing the same movements alone A would be dancing (Gilbert 1989, 165). But this is not required of *relational* individualist accounts, and certainly not of CET. CET in helping itself to the notion of a collective end enables a joint action description that outruns the description of any of the individual actions considered without reference to the end. Thus Fred can dial a number and Bill can pick up a receiver, and there is the joint action of communication. But this is the case only if each had as a (collective) end that there be communication. In the dancing example each has as an end that they dance. Here it is the bodily movement of each coupled with the *relations* between those individual bodily movements that is the end that each has. So this end is not adequately described by a description of the bodily movements of one of the partners.

A second kind of argument pertains to normativity. It is argued that joint actions are an inherently normative phenomenon and that individualists deny this. Here there is often a confusion between types of normativity. On any account, individualist or otherwise, joint actions involve beliefs, intentions, ends, and the like, that is, attitudes that are normative in the weak sense that they are subject to some form of evaluation, such as truth and falsity, success and failure. So much individualists can and do acknowledge. Moreover, on any account, individualist or otherwise, many joint actions are as *a matter of contingent fact* going to be normative in some stronger sense, for instance, possess institutional properties. However, the critical question is whether or not joint actions are *necessarily* normative in some stronger sense that would be antithetical to individualism, for example, *necessarily* have *institutional* properties. Individualists deny that joint actions necessarily have institutional properties and have offered counterexamples by way of support. For example, two strangers from different cultures traveling in opposite directions whose common pathway is blocked by a large fallen tree might spontaneously jointly act to remove the tree; but this might be a one-off joint action not governed by any institutional rule or regularity. I conclude that the charge against individualism that it has a normative deficit is at best not sustained.

Other arguments against individualist accounts of joint action get it more or less right about individualism per se, but get it wrong about the power and flexibility of individualism to accommodate a variety of features of social forms. Here the work of John Searle is salient. According to Searle, "In addition to individual intentionality there is collective intentionality. Obvious examples are cases where I am doing something only as part of *our* doing something. ... In my view all these efforts to reduce collective intentionality to individual intentionality fail" (Searle 1995, 23–6). An important claim here is that individualism cannot deal with the fact that an individual agent sometimes acts *qua* member of a group and, more specifically, *qua* occupant of an institutional role. One of my aims in this chapter is to show that, *contra* Searle and others, CET can accommodate the concept of acting *qua* member of a group and *qua* occupant of a role.

## 2. THE COLLECTIVE END THEORY OF JOINT ACTION

Basically CET is the theory that joint actions are actions directed to the realization of a collective end.[5] However, this notion of a collective end is a construction out of the prior notion of an individual end. As a first shot, let us say that a collective end is an individual end that more than one agent has, and that is such that, if it is realized, it is realized by all, or most, of the actions of the agents involved; the individual action of any given agent is only part of the means by which the end is realized. Thus when one person dials the phone number of another person, and the second person picks up the receiver, then each has performed an action in the service of a collective end: a collective end that each has, namely, that they communicate with each other. (See below for more detail on collective ends.)

So a joint action simply consists of at least two individual actions directed to the realization of a collective end. Accordingly, individual actions, X and Y, performed by agents A and B (respectively) in situation S, constitute a joint action if and only if

(1)  A intentionally performs X in S and B intentionally performs Y in S;

(2)  A X's in S if and only if (he believes)[6] B has Y'd, is Y'ing, or will Y in S, and B Y's in S if and only if (he believes) A has X'd, is X'ing, or will X in S;

---

[5]  The notion of a collective end was introduced in Miller (1982, 6). See Miller (1986a, sect. 6; 1986b, 133–7). See also Searle (1990) and Gilbert (1989, sect. 4).

[6]  Something weaker than belief is probably sufficient here – perhaps thinks it is likely, or even thinks it is quite possible. Ditto for the other beliefs – including the mutual true beliefs – involved in the definition. However, absence of any degree of belief would not be sufficient. For if the first agent did not think there was any chance the other agent would do his part, then how could the first agent be thought to have the end in question? After all, the end can be achieved only if both agents do their parts.

(3)   A has end E, and A X's in S to realize E, and B has E, and B Y's in S
      in order to realize E;

(4)   A and B each mutually truly believes that A has performed, is
      performing, or will perform X in S, and that B has performed, is
      performing, or will perform Y in S;

(5)   Each agent mutually truly believes that (2) and (3).

In respect of this account the following points need to be noted.

First, with respect to clause (2), the conditionality of the action is
internal to the agent in the sense that if the agent has performed a
conditional action, then the agent has performed the action in the
*belief* that the condition obtains. Moreover, the conditionality of the
agent's action is relative to the collective end. A X's *only if* B Y's *relative
to the collective end E*. So B's Y'ing is not a necessary condition for A's
X'ing, tout court. Thus, it might be that A has some other individual
end E1, and that A's X'ing realizes E1 (in addition to E). If so, A will
X, even if B does not Y. For example, A might dial B's phone number
having as a collective end that A and B communicate with one another
but, in addition, having as an individual end that he give his annoying
colleague the impression that he is on the phone and is, therefore, not
to be disturbed. Accordingly, A might well have dialed B's phone number even if he knew that B was unable to communicate at that time
and, indeed, had his phone switched off. Nevertheless, it remains true
that A X's only if B Y's *relative to the collective end E*. Again, A X's *if* B Y's
*relative to the collective end, E*. So B's Y'ing is not a sufficient condition
for A's X'ing, tout court. Other things being equal, if for some reason
A abandons the end E, then even if B Y's, A will not X. Naturally, other
things might not be equal; for example, A might pick up the phone to
give the impression to his annoying colleague that he is busy on the
phone, and do so even though he does not have as a collective end to
communicate with B.

Second, the notion of a collective end is an individualist notion. The
realization of the collective end is the bringing into existence of a state
of affairs. Each agent has this state of affairs as an individual end. (It is
also a state of affairs aimed at more or less the same description by each
agent.) So a collective end is a species of individual end. Thus CET is to
be distinguished from the accounts of theorists such as Searle who favor
irreducibly collectivist notions of collective intentions.[7]

---

[7]   See note 5.

A collective end is the same as an ordinary individual end in that *qua* end it exists only in the heads of individual agents. But it is different from an ordinary individual end in a number of respects. For one thing, it is a *shared* end. By shared end I do *not* mean a set of individual ends that would be realized by qualitatively identical, but *numerically different*, multiple states of affairs (one state of affairs for each individual end). Rather I mean a set of individual ends that would be realized by *one single* state of affairs; so the coming into existence of the one single state of affairs in question constitutes the realization of *all* of the individual ends that exist in the heads of each of the agents. For another thing, although collective ends are shared (individual) ends, they are ends that are *necessarily* shared by virtue of being interdependent; they are not ends that are shared only as a matter of *contingent* fact. Suppose you and I are soldiers being shot at by a single sniper. Suppose further that we both happen to see the sniper at the same time and both fire at the sniper to kill him. I have an individual end, and you have an individual end. Moreover, my individual end is one that I share with you; for not only will the death of this one sniper realize my individual end, it will also simultaneously realize your individual end.[8] However, this is not yet a collective end; for the fact that I have as an end the death of sniper is not dependent on your having as an end the death of that very same sniper, and vice versa for you.

A further point about collective ends is that they are "open" to those that have them; collective ends are objects of mutual true belief. So if end E is a collective end, then the agents who possess E mutually truly believe that they each have E.

Third, a collective end is not an intention. On CET ends are distinguished from intentions. The notion of an end is coordinate with that of a means, but this is not so for intentions. To say that an action was intended is not in itself to say that the action is a means or that it is an end. Indeed, some intended actions do not involve means or ends. Consider

---

[8] It might be argued that the two individual ends are not the same in that necessarily I have as an end not only that the sniper die, but that I kill him. (And likewise for your individual end.) (See Searle 1983, esp. chap. 4.) But my example is intended to be illustrative only; it serves this purpose even if it does not correctly describe reality. On the other hand, if this claim is true, it will cause me to revise my account of collective ends; strictly speaking they will consist of a set of different individual ends to the effect that each have as an end not only that some state of affairs obtain, but that he contribute in part to the realization of that state of affairs. However, this revision to the content of collective ends would not be fatal to my account. In any case I am already committed to the claim that ends bring with them means in the sense that an agent performs the means in the belief that it is the means, or part of the means, to his end.

a gratuitous act of arm raising. I intentionally raise my arm but for no purpose; I just do it, albeit intentionally. I have no *end* in so raising my arm. Moreover, I have no *means;* I do not raise my arm by means of, for example, a pulley. Rather, my arm is under my direct control, and intending to raise it is sufficient for it to be raised.

Fourth, CET relies on a fourfold distinction between ends, intentions, beliefs, and desires, but makes use only of ends, intentions, and beliefs.[9] So CET does not have as constitutive elements affective attitudes such as desires or preferences. Having a desire (or preference) is not the same thing, on this view, as having an end. Ends, like intentions, are conative states. On the other hand, in distinguishing between ends and affective attitudes such as desires, the claim is not that there are ends that are neither directly nor indirectly the object of some motivating affective state such as a desire.

Fifth, CET, as outlined above, constitutes a core theory of joint action. But this core theory can be extended to cover a range of different cases of joint action in respect of which the following points can be made (cf. Miller 1992a):

(1)    There are many types of joint action in which it is not the case that the performance of a contributory action by any of the participating agents is dependent on the performance of contributory actions by *all* of the other participating agents.

(2)    The actions X, Y, and so on performed by participating individual agents might be of the same type. Each agent might have to perform the same kind of action. Further, the "action" might not even be a single discrete action. It might be a set of actions of the same or different types, or it might be an activity or even a whole enterprise.

(3)    The collective end might not be a state of affairs but rather a process. And this end might relate to the actions performed to realize it as a consequence or a result or as a whole to its parts.

(4)    The realization of the collective end can itself be simply a means to some further end, or it can be an end in itself, or it can be both means and end.

---

[9]  In fact, I distinguish between two sorts or "intending": trying and intending proper. The latter but not the former entails a belief that one can succeed in the action "intended." This kind of distinction is a familiar one in the literature. See, for example, Bratman (1987, 136). It is, of course, also true that the end of some intentional action can itself become an intended action. See Searle (1983, chap. 1).

(5) The collective end can be a lower-order collective end or a higher-order collective, that is, a collective end with respect to other collective ends; for example, the members of the executive of a political party might have as a collective end to reinforce the existing collective end of members of the party to build solidarity among the members.

(6) Higher-order collective ends can be what David Schmidtz refers to as maieutic ends: "ends that are achieved through a process of coming to have other ends" (Schmidtz 1994, 228). For example, the members of the board of directors of a company might have as a collective end to settle on the collective long-term goals of the company. These ends to be chosen are final ends; they are not to be chosen for the sake of some other ends, but they are nevertheless, not yet settled on.

(7) The collective end can be consciously held or unconscious.[10] More specifically, the collective end can be one the participating agents need to keep in mind while they are performing the actions that are the means to that end; or it might be an end that the agents will realize only if they concentrate wholly on the means, such as the end of happiness. Relatedly, collective ends can be implicit or explicit (expressed to oneself or others, normally linguistically), and latent (e.g., participants are asleep) or activated (actions are currently being performed as a means to the collective end).

(8) The actions constitutive of joint action can be performed at the same time and place, or at different places at the same time, or at the same place at different times, or at different places and times. Indeed, the actions of the individuals can be separated by thousands of miles and/or hundreds of years, for example, building the Great Wall of China.

(9) The actions constitutive of joint action can be interactive – in the sense that in the performance of each individual action the agent adjusts his action to the action of the other, such as dancing – or noninteractive (in this sense).

(10) Joint action typically, although not necessarily, involves either direct communication (of some sort or other) between each individual and every other individual, or indirect communication between the

---

[10] Unconscious ends are not necessarily "open" in any stronger sense than that there is mutual belief with respect to them, and beliefs can be unconscious.

individuals – A communicates with B, and B with C, but A does not
communicate with C.[11]

### 3. CONVENTIONS, RULES, AND NORMS

We can distinguish between different, albeit connected and overlapping, *generic* kinds of joint action and activity, including communicative, economic, educative, sexual, and religious activity. The repetition
over time, and duplication in space, of any one of these different kinds
of generic joint activity can give rise to a more or less connected, and
more or less continuous, stretch of joint activity that can be termed a
*sphere of activity* (Miller 2001, chap. 6). So the ongoing series of economic transactions across Germany constitutes a sphere of activity.
(Michael Walzer has developed the related idea of a sphere of justice;
see Walzer 1983.)

Spheres of activity (by stipulative definition) are regulated by *conventions*. They thereby take on different specific forms according to the specific conventions that structure them. Often, although not necessarily,
they are also regulated by explicit rules, including laws. And they are
also often – but again, not necessarily – regulated by social norms. Here
I need to distinguish between rules, conventions, and social norms.
(I offer detailed accounts of these social phenomena, and the differences between them, in Miller 2001.) In doing so I necessarily operate
with stipulative definitions that to some extent run counter to one or
more of the conflicting patterns of common usage. The term *rule* in particular is used to refer to a miscellaneous group of social regularities in
action and, for that matter, principles of thought.

I stipulate that a *rule* is a (typically explicitly formulated) directive
issued by some authority or other to undertake a certain course of action
in certain recurring situations. So laws are a species of rule enacted by
governments. A convention is a regularity in action performed by a set
of individual agents and directed to a collective end. (For a detailed
definition and defense thereof, see Miller 1986a, 1992a, 2001 chap. 3.)
Somewhat more precisely, conventions are *joint procedures*, where a procedure is (roughly speaking) a habit, the automatic repetition of an action
in a recurring situation. So a joint procedure is a procedure that is jointly
followed because it realizes a collective end.

---

[11] See Cohen and Levesque for a contrasting account (1991, 506).

Moreover, on this conception conventions *qua* conventions are normatively neutral – other than in the minimal sense involved in instrumental rationality. Conventions are normatively neutral notwithstanding the fact that agents can be held to have failed to conform to any given convention. On this account a conventional regularity in action does not constitute a *standard of behavior* to which agents *ought* to conform. Naturally, an agent by not conforming might fail to realize the collective end that he has, the end that is realized by conformity to the convention. However, that would be a mere failure of instrumental rationality.

So conventional actions are not necessarily the content of directives issued by authorities. Nor are they necessarily explicitly formulated anywhere. Thus, driving on the left-hand side is a convention in Australia, although not in Germany; it is a regularity in action among Australians, which secures the collective end of avoiding car collisions. As it happens, this convention is also a law, although it might not have been.

Social norms are regularities that are also norms (Miller 1997a, 2001b, chap. 4); agents believe that they have a duty to conform or that they otherwise *ought* to conform. Such norms include ones respecting and enforcing rights. Here the "ought" is not that of mere instrumental rationality; it is not simply a matter of believing that one ought to conform because it serves one's purpose. Some conventions and most rules are also norms in this strong sense. For example, the convention and the law to drive on the left is a norm; people feel that they ought to conform. This strong (and wide) sense of "ought" *includes* – but is not exhausted by – the so-called *moral* ought. Members of some social groups feel strongly about, for example, *aesthetic* requirements; accordingly, the aesthetic "ought" underpins some of their norms of action.

## 4. ORGANIZATIONS

Organizations consist of an (embodied) formal *structure* of interlocking roles (Miller 2001b, chap. 5). An organizational role can be defined in terms of the agent (whoever it is) who performs certain tasks, the tasks themselves, procedures (in the above sense), and conventions. Moreover, unlike social groups, organizations are individuated by the kind of activity that they undertake and by their characteristic *ends*. So we have governments, universities, business corporations, armies, and so on. Perhaps governments have as an end or goal the ordering and leading of societies, universities the end of discovering and disseminating knowledge, and so on. Here it is important to emphasize that these ends are, first, collective ends and, second, often the latent and/or implicit (collective) ends of individual institutional actors.

A further defining feature of organizations is that organizational action typically consists of, what has elsewhere been termed, a *layered structure of joint actions* (Miller 1998a, 2001b, chap. 5). One illustration of the notion of a layered structure of joint actions is an armed force fighting a battle. Suppose at an organizational level a number of joint actions ("actions") are severally necessary[12] and jointly sufficient to achieve some collective end. Thus the "action" of the mortar squad destroying enemy gun emplacements, the "action" of the flight of military planes providing air cover, and the "action" of the infantry platoon taking and holding the ground might be severally necessary and jointly sufficient to achieve the collective end of defeating the enemy; as such, these "actions" taken together constitute a joint action. Call each of these "actions" level-two "actions," and the joint action that they constitute a level-two joint action. From the perspective of the collective end of defeating the enemy, each of these level-two "actions" is an individual action that is a component of a (level-two) joint action: the joint action directed to the collective end of defeating the enemy.

However, each of these level-two "actions" is already in itself a joint action with component individual actions; and these component individual actions are severally necessary and jointly sufficient for the performance of some collective end. Thus the individual members of the mortar squad jointly operate the mortar to realize the collective end of destroying enemy gun emplacements. Each pilot, jointly with the other pilots, strafes enemy soldiers to realize the collective end of providing air cover for their advancing foot soldiers. Further, the set of foot soldiers jointly advance to take and hold the ground vacated by the members of the retreating enemy force.

At level one there are individual actions directed to three distinct collective ends: the collective ends of (respectively) destroying gun emplacements, providing air cover, and taking and holding ground. So at level one there are three joint actions, namely, the members of the mortar squad destroying gun emplacements, the members of the flight of planes providing air cover, and the members of the infantry taking and holding

---

[12] Here there is simplification for the sake of clarity. For what is said here is not strictly correct, at least in the case of many actions performed by members of organizations. Rather, typically some threshold set of actions is necessary to achieve the end; moreover the boundaries of this set are vague.

ground. However, taken together these three joint actions constitute a single level-two joint action. The collective end of this level-two joint action is to defeat the enemy; and from the perspective of this level-two joint action, and its collective end, these constitutive actions are (level-two) individual actions.

It is important to note that on this (stipulative) definition of organizations they are, *qua* organizations, non-normative entities. In this respect they are analogous to conventions, as we have defined conventions. So being an organization is not of itself something that is ethically good or bad, any more than being a convention is in itself ethically good or bad.[13] This can be consistently held while maintaining that organizations, as well as conventions, are a pervasive and necessary feature of human life, being indispensable instruments for realizing collective ends. Collective ends are a species of individual end; but merely being an end is in itself neither morally good nor morally bad, any more than being an intention or a belief is in itself morally good or morally bad.

Although this definition of an organization does not include any reference to a normative dimension, most organizations do as a matter of contingent fact possess a normative dimension. As was the case with conventions, this normative dimension will be possessed (especially, although not exclusively) by virtue of the particular moral/immoral ends (goods) that an organization serves, as well as by virtue of the particular moral (or immoral) activities that it undertakes.[14]

Further, most organizations possess a normative dimension by virtue (in part) of the *norms* governing the constitutive organizational roles. More specifically, most organizations consist of a hierarchical role structure in which the tasks and procedures that define the individual roles are governed by norms; and in hierarchical organizations some of these norms govern the relations of authority and power within the organization. It is not simply that an employee in fact undertakes a particular set of tasks, or tends to comply with the directives of his employer. Rather, the employee undertakes those tasks and obeys

---

[13] The terms "good" and "bad" are being used here in a relatively wide sense so as to embrace a range of objective goods, as opposed to things that are merely believed to be good, or simply wanted or aimed at. Such objective goods are principally ethical or moral goods. (The terms "ethical" and "moral" are being used interchangeably.) But they also include, for example, aesthetic goods.

[14] Here it is not necessary to distinguish objectively from subjectively felt moral considerations. Suffice it to say that social norms necessarily embody subjectively felt moral considerations, but not necessarily objectively correct ones.

the directives of his employer, by virtue of the social and other norms governing the employee's (and employer's) roles, and the relations of authority and power that exist between these roles. The employee believes that someone in his position has a duty to perform the tasks in question, and believes that the employer has a right to issue directives to his employees. Moreover, this belief is shared and acted on by the other employees (and employers) and is held by each conditionally on its being held by the others. In short, the behavior of the employees and employers is governed by *social norms*.

It should also be noted that the social norms governing the roles and role structures of organizations are both formal and informal. If formal, then they are typically enshrined in explicit rules, regulations, and laws, including laws of contract. For example, an employee not only believes that he ought to undertake certain tasks and not others, but these tasks are explicitly set forth in his contract of employment. As mentioned above, informal social norms to a greater or lesser extent comprise the *culture* of an organization.

Organizations with the above detailed normative dimension are *social institutions* (Giddens 1984; Parsons 1982). So – and as already mentioned – institutions are often organizations, and many systems of organizations are also institutions.

## 5. JOINT INSTITUTIONAL MECHANISMS

A feature of many social institutions, whether they be of the organizational or nonorganizational variety, is their use of *joint institutional mechanisms* (Miller 1992a, 1995a, 2001b, chap. 1).[15] Examples of joint institutional mechanisms are the device of tossing a coin to resolve a dispute, voting to elect a candidate to political office, use of money as a medium of exchange, and, more generally, exchange systems such as markets for goods and services.

Joint institutional mechanisms consist of (a) a complex of differentiated but interlocking actions (the input to the mechanism), (b) the result of the performance of those actions (the output of the mechanism), and (c) the mechanism itself. Thus a given agent might vote for a candidate.

---

[15] The term "social mechanism" is used in a variety of senses, but especially to refer to underlying causal processes that produce recurring social outcomes and mechanism models that seek to explain the emergent effects of collective behavior. See Mayntz (2004).

He will do so only if others also vote. But, further, there is the action of the candidates, namely, that they present themselves as candidates. That they present themselves as candidates is (in part) constitutive of the input to the voting mechanism. Voters vote *for candidates*. So there is interlocking and differentiated action (the input). Further, there is some result (as opposed to consequence) of the joint action: the joint action consisting of the actions of putting oneself forward as a candidate and of the actions of voting. The result is that some candidate, say, Barack Obama, is voted in (the output). That there is a result is (in part) constitutive of the mechanism. That to receive the most number of votes is to be voted in, is (in part) constitutive of the voting mechanism. Moreover, that Obama is voted in is not a collective end of all the voters. (Although it is a collective end of those who voted for Obama.) However, that the one who gets the most votes – whoever that happens to be – is voted in is a collective end of all the voters, including those who voted for some candidate other than Obama.

Money, markets, and other systems of exchange are also a species of joint procedural mechanism. Such exchange systems coordinate numerous participants seeking to exchange one thing for another thing, and to do so on a recurring basis with multiple other participants. For participants A, B, C, D, and so on and exchangeable token things w, x, y, z, and so on (possessed by A, B, C, D, etc., respectively), the individual end of each participant, say, A, on any single instance of a recurring exchange enabling situation, such as a marketplace, is to exchange w for something (x or y or z, etc.) possessed by B or C or D, and so on; similarly for B and C and D, and so on. Moreover, on any such occasion at, or near, the point of exchange two participants, say, A and B, will have a collective end; thus A and B each has the collective end that A and B exchange w and x on this occasion. Here the realization of the collective end constitutes a joint action; however, it is a joint action – and its constitutive collective end – in the service of the individual end of each participant.

The whole coordinated set of these single joint actions of exchange constitutes the output of the joint mechanism, that is, that A exchanges w for x with B, C exchanges y for z with D, and so on. Naturally, the *particular* configuration of joint actions (individual exchanges) that results on some occasion of the recurring situation is not aimed at by anyone; for example, it is not a collective end of A or B that C and D exchange y and z. However, that there be *some* coordinated set of exchanges is the point or collective end of the system; certainly the regulators and designers of the system have or had this as a collective end, and even the participants all have this as a collective end, even if unconsciously. The latter point is evidenced by attempts on the part of participants to remedy defects or problems with the system, for example, by communicating to all participants any change in the location of the points of exchange.

Since the occasions for exchange are instances of a recurring situation, each participant has a *standing* individual end with respect to a single open-ended set of future recurring such occasions for exchange, that is, that on each of these occasions he or she, say, A, will receive some relevant thing from B or from C, and so on. Likewise, each of the participants has a *standing* collective end with respect to a single open-ended set of associated future joint actions of exchange of some relevant thing with B or C, and so on. Finally, each of the participants has a *standing* collective end with respect to a single open-ended *set of sets of coordinated multiple* future joint actions of exchange; that is, each has a collective end with respect to the results of the future workings of the joint mechanism, namely, that there be on each future occasion of the recurring situation some coordinated configuration of joint actions of exchange.

Note that an exchange system is institutionalized when it is "regulated" by social norms – and typically by enforceable formal regulations and laws – as a consequence of its constitutive joint actions and/or collective ends having moral significance. This might be as a result of competition between participants for scarce items that provide benefits to their possessors, for example, social norms of fair competition, promises to hand over the scarce item at the jointly decided exchange rate, or social norms not to "steal" items in the possession of others (Chapters 2 and 10).

## 6. ACTING *QUA* MEMBER OF A GROUP/ *QUA* OCCUPANT OF AN INSTITUTIONAL ROLE

As mentioned above, there is allegedly a problem for individualist accounts of joint action provided by actions performed by individuals *qua* members of a group and (relatedly) *qua* occupants of an institutional role (Miller 2007c). This objection is put by Searle (see above), but also by Margaret Gilbert and by Frederick Schmitt (Schmitt 2003, 147–50).

The notion of acting *qua* member of a group is often quite straightforward because the group can be defined in terms of the collective end or ends which the group of individuals is pursuing. Consider a group of individuals building a house. Person A is building a wall, person B the roof, person C the foundations, and so on. To say of person A that he is acting *qua* member of this group is just to say that his action of building the wall is an action directed toward the collective end that he and the other members of the group are seeking to realize, namely, a built house.

Notice that the same set of individuals could be engaged in different collective projects. Suppose persons A, B, C, and so on in our above example are not only engaged in building a house but also – during their holidays – in building a sailboat. Assume that A is building the masts, B the cabin, C the bow, and so on. To say of A that he is acting *qua* member of this group is just to say that his action of building the masts is an action directed toward the collective end that he and the other members of the group are seeking to realize, namely, a built boat. Accordingly, one and the same person, A, is acting both as a member of the "house building group" (G1) and as a member of the "boat building group" (G2). Indeed, since A, B, C, and so on are all and only the members of each of these two groups, the membership of G1 is identical with the membership of G2.

Moreover, when A is building the wall he is acting *qua* member of G1, and when he is building the mast he is acting *qua* member of G2. But this phenomenon of one agent acting as a member of different groups in no way undermines individualism. Indeed, CET is able to illuminate this phenomenon as follows. For A to be acting *qua* member of G1 is for A to be pursuing – jointly with B, C, and so on – the collective end of building the house; for A to be acting *qua* member of G2 is for A to be pursuing – jointly with B, C, and so on – the collective end of building the boat.

Further, let us suppose that G1 and G2 each have to create and comply with a budget; G1 has a budget for the house and G2 has a budget for the boat. The members of G1 and G2 know that they must buy materials for the house and the boat (respectively) and do so within the respective budgets. Assume that A, B, C, and so on allocate $50,000 to pay for bricks for the house. This is a joint action. Moreover, this joint action is one that A, B, C, and so on have performed *qua* members of G1. G1 is individuated by recourse to the collective end of building the house, and the proximate (collective) end of buying bricks is tied to that group, G1, and to its ultimate end of building a house. Accordingly, A, B, C, and so on are not in buying the bricks acting *qua* members of G2. For G2 is individuated by the collective end of building a boat, and A, B, C, and so on do not *qua* members of G2 have any plans to build their boat from bricks!

Thus far we have focused on the notion of acting *qua* member of a group. However, we need to focus on the related notion of acting *qua* occupant of an institutional role. Clearly the two notions are related. The notion of acting *qua* occupant of a role is simply that of performing the tasks definitive of the role (including the joint tasks), conforming to the conventions and regulations that constrain the tasks to be undertaken, and pursuing the purposes or ends of the role (including the collective ends).

Note the relevance here of the above-introduced notion of a *layered structure of joint actions*. As described above, a layered structure of joint actions is a set of joint actions, each of which is directed to a further collective end; so it is a macro-joint action comprised of a set of constituent micro-joint actions. This account of a layered structure of joint actions can be supplemented by recourse to concepts of conventions, social norms, and the like, and especially by recourse to the explicitly normative notions of rights, obligations, and duties that are attached to, and in part definitive of, many organizational roles (Miller 2003a). It is not simply that organizational role occupants *regularly* jointly act in certain ways in preference to others, or in preference to acting entirely individualistically; rather, they have institutional duties to so act and – in the case of hierarchical organizations – institutional rights to instruct others to act in certain ways.

At any rate the point to be made here is that my account of the notion of acting *qua* member of a group in terms of acting in accordance with collective ends can be, and should be, complicated and supplemented by the normative notions of rights and duties to accommodate various different kinds of acting *qua* member of an organized group, including acting in hierarchical roles such as that of prime minister, for example. So role occupants such as Tony Blair take on the tasks definitive of the role. More specifically they take on the institutional rights and duties definitive of the role, and some of these institutional rights and duties are also moral rights and obligations. Accordingly, it makes sense to say of Tony Blair that he has this and that moral obligation *qua* prime minister but not necessarily *qua* father or husband.

## 7. CONCLUSION

In this chapter the individualist teleological account of social institutions has been elaborated. This theory provides the theoretical platform for much of what follows in this book. At the core of the teleological account of social institutions is the Collective End Theory of joint action and, therefore, the theoretical concept of a collective end. Other key theoretical notions introduced here are subelements of social institutions. They include conventions, rules, social norms, layered structures of joint action, and joint mechanisms. In the following chapter I turn explicitly to the normative dimension of social institutions.

# The Moral Foundations of Institutions

## 1. THE VARIETIES OF SOCIAL INSTITUTION

Self-evidently, social institutions have a multifaceted normative dimension, including a moral dimension.[1] Moral categories that are deeply implicated in social institutions include human rights and duties, contract-based rights and obligations, and rights and duties derived from the production and consumption of collective goods.

Collective goods of the kind under discussion have – as stated in the Introduction – three properties: (1) they are produced, maintained, or renewed by means of the *joint activity* of members of organizations or systems of organizations, that is, by institutional actors, (2) they are *available to the whole community*, and (3) they *ought* to be produced (or maintained or renewed) and made available to the whole community because they are desirable goods and ones to which the members of the community have an (institutional) *joint moral right*.

Such goods are ones that are desirable in the sense that they ought to be desired (objectively speaking), as opposed to simply being desired; moreover, they are either intrinsic goods (good in themselves) or the means to intrinsic goods. They include, but are not restricted to, goods in respect of which there is an institutionally prior moral right, such as security.

Roughly speaking, on my account, aggregated needs-based rights, aggregated non-needs-based human rights, and other desirable goods generate collective moral responsibilities that provide the ethico-normative basis for institutions, for example, business organizations in competitive

---

[1] An earlier version of the material in this section and the following section appeared in Miller (2003a).

markets, welfare institutions, police organizations, and universities, which fulfill those rights (see Section 3).

For example, the aggregate need for food generates a collective moral responsibility to establish and maintain social institutions, such as agri-businesses, the members of which jointly produce foodstuffs; once the relevant institutions are established, then the needy have a joint moral right, and ought to have a joint institutional right, to the food products in question. Accordingly, the needy have a right to buy the food products (they cannot be excluded from purchasing them), or, if they are unable to do so, then the products ought to be provided to the needy free of charge.

I note that in modern economies there is a derived moral right to paid work, that is, a right to a job (some job or other), because (other things being equal) without a job one cannot provide for one's basic needs (and one's family's needs) and one cannot contribute to the production, main-tenance, and renewal of collective goods, such as via taxes. Naturally, if no paid job can be made available to some person or group, then they may have no moral right to one, but if so, then (other things being equal) they will have a moral right to welfare.

I also note that in many cases social institutions do not, strictly speak-ing, produce collective goods; rather, they only make a necessary contri-bution to their production (or maintenance or renewal) – for example, police organizations contribute to the maintenance of security.

As pointed out in the Introduction, some quite fundamental moral rights, values, and principles are logically prior to social institutions, or, to be more precise, logically prior to social institutions that are also orga-nizations, or systems of organizations – bearing in mind that some other institutions, such as human languages, are not social institutions in this sense.

Basic human rights, such as the right to life (including, but not restricted to, the right not to be killed), the right not to be physically or psychologically disabled (by, for example, chopping off of one's limbs or by enforced lobotomy), the right not to be tortured, the right not to be incarcerated (whether in a cave, a cage, or a modern prison), and the right to freedom of thought and communication are logically prior to social institutions.

Indeed, these basic human rights provide the raison d'être (by my lights, collective end) for a number of social institutions. (In Part B of this book I argue the specifics of this claim in relation to particular institu-tions.) Consider, for example, police institutions (Chapter 9). The police role consists in large part in protecting persons from being deprived of their human rights to life, bodily security, liberty, and so on; the police do so by the use, or threatened use, of coercive force.

Naturally, the institution of the police is different from other institutions that are either not principally concerned with protecting human rights or, if they are, do not necessarily rely on coercion in their work on behalf of human rights. Take welfare institutions (Chapter 7). There is a human right to a subsistence living, and aiding the deprived is a fundamental purpose of welfare institutions. However, aiding the deprived does not necessarily or routinely involve the use, or threat of the use, of coercive force. Thus welfare institutions are different in kind from policing institutions, although both are grounded in large part in prior human rights.

Now consider business organizations operating in competitive markets (Chapter 10). Many business organizations do not have the protection of human rights or the fulfillment of needs-based rights as a primary purpose; nor should they. On the other hand, human rights are an important *side constraint* on business activity. Human rights can function as side constraints because they are moral rights of great strength; indeed, their strength is such that they can justifiably be enforced. So they are not to be confused with relatively weak moral rights, such as the rights generated by promises made in relation to morally unimportant matters, for example, my right that you return to me my pen that you borrowed and solemnly promised to return; such rights are not necessarily justifiably enforceable. Moreover, human rights are not amenable to a process of simple addition; one individual's right to life, for example, is not half as strong as, or worth half the value of, the aggregated rights to life of two individuals (Miller 2008b, chap. 5). Accordingly, business organizations should not engage in activities that violate the human rights of workers or other members of the community. Moreover, as already noted, business organizations provide jobs and, therefore, indirectly – via salaries and wages – enable managers and workers to provide for their basic needs, such as for food, clothing, and shelter.

As argued in Chapter 1, Section 5, markets (narrowly construed) are simply a species of joint procedural mechanism. Such exchange systems coordinate numerous participants, each of whom is seeking to exchange an item they possess for an item they have as an end to possess; moreover, most participants are seeking to exchange on a recurring basis and (over time) with multiple other participants. Markets are defined in terms of individual and joint actions serving, respectively, individual and collective ends.

Again, as argued in Chapter 1, Section 4, organizations (narrowly construed) – including business organizations – are layered structures of joint action and, as such, are defined in terms of complexes of individual and joint actions serving (respectively) individual and collective ends.

Here it is important to recall that joint procedural mechanisms and layered structures of joint action – and, therefore, markets and organizations – are, *qua* markets and *qua* organizations, non-normative entities. So being a market or an organization is not of itself something that is ethically good or bad, any more than being an action is in itself ethically good or bad.[2] This is so notwithstanding that markets and organizations are a pervasive and necessary feature of human life, being indispensable instruments for realizing collective ends.

Typically, markets (in my narrow sense) are embedded in a context of buyers and sellers with desires (but not necessarily needs), on the one hand, and moral right, duties, and commitments on the other: for example, ownership of a good, a commitment to provide a particular good, or service in exchange for payment. Moreover, once there are buyers and sellers competing with one another (sellers with other sellers, buyers with other buyers, and buyers with sellers), then the moral issue of fairness arises. In short, competitive markets are social institutions. They have a normative dimension and are governed by social norms.

Similarly, as argued in Chapter 1, Section 4, although an organization (in my narrow sense) is a morally neutral entity *qua* organization, most organizations are in fact social institutions possessed of a normative dimension and governed by social norms. For example, when a business organization becomes a hierarchical organization with contractually based (in part) relations of authority and power between employer and employee, then moral issues pertaining to the infringement of individual autonomy arise and are resolved, at least in part, by social norms (Chapter 3).

Business organizations operating in competitive markets have collective ends; however, these ends are multifarious. Although some business organizations operating in competitive markets serve aggregated needs (e.g., private schools provide basic education) or provide other

[2] I use the terms *ethical* and *moral* more or less interchangeably and construe ethical or moral actions as being objectively so. Moreover, actions that are morally or ethically good might be so by virtue of being the means to produce goods that are good in some wider sense (in addition to being ethically or morally good). For example, it might be the case that something that is essentially an aesthetic good, e.g., a work of art, nevertheless morally ought to be produced.

collective goods (e.g., private art galleries contribute to the transfer of cultural heritage by displaying the works of past masters), many serve only aggregated desires (e.g., for ice cream).

From the perspective of normative institutional theory – and given their enormous potential for realizing moral and other value-driven purposes, such as meeting aggregated needs for basic foodstuffs, clothing, or medicines – business organizations operating in competitive markets can, and should, be viewed instrumentally, and the ends that they serve, or could serve, prioritized. Indeed, as I shall argue in Part B, many existing business organizations operating in competitive markets should be given direction from, if not redesigned in the light of, normative institutional theory. Media organizations and financial markets are cases in point (Chapter 10).

On the other hand, it is not inconceivable that some social institutions that do *not* currently operate in a competitive market should be redesigned so that they do thus operate, and for the purpose of ensuring that they better serve their defining collective ends. Hence the existence of privately funded universities in the United States arguably has strengthened the university sector as a whole and, thereby, enhanced the collective goods that universities exist to produce (Chapter 8).

As is by now quite evident, I do not claim that all, or even most, business organizations in competitive markets ought to serve directly some collective moral purpose or other collective good, albeit many do; indeed, I reject this claim. Nor am I suggesting that most such business organizations do not embody a variety of moral or ethical values; clearly they do, including the exercise of freedom, the facilitation of the exercise of moral rights to property, and the promotion of a work ethic.

Rather, I am asserting that business organizations and markets per se do not have inherently valuable collective ends that are internal to them, but, nevertheless, they are instrumentally valuable social forms that should be used to realize collective moral purposes and other collective goods, as required. Moreover, some of these moral purposes are *indirectly* achieved; so we need to distinguish between social institutions that have as their *direct* collective end the production (or maintenance or renewal) of a collective good and those that have such a collective good(s) only as an *indirect* end. Thus business organizations provide jobs and pay their employees wages that are in turn used, both to provide for the basic needs of these employees and their families and, via taxes, to contribute to the production, maintenance, and renewal of collective goods, such as security, public health and education, and so on.

My instrumentalist view of markets stands in stark contrast with a view that has come to be referred to as market fundamentalism (Soros 2008). Specifically, market fundamentalism holds to the view that the moral right to property is such that it overrides aggregated needs-based rights and other collective goods. Given the pervasiveness of market fundamentalism, and its inconsistency with the perspective that I am offering here, let me offer further discussion beginning with the centerpiece of market fundamentalism, namely, the moral right to property.

The moral right to property is actually a bundle of moral rights – indeed, a set of such bundles, such as intellectual property rights or land rights – some of which are use rights, others exclusion rights, and still others transfer rights. None of these moral rights are *absolute* rights; arguably, there are no absolute moral rights – but, if there are, these are not among them. Rather, each of these rights requires a justification, that is, the provision of some rational moral basis; and identifying this basis, or, rather, bases, reveals the moral defeasibility of private property regimes. These use, exclusion, and transfer rights have three kinds of moral basis.

The first kind of moral basis is, roughly speaking, "I found it first and there was no prior owner to it." This moral basis is both a relatively weak moral basis, for example, it is trumped by needs-based human rights, and a relatively rare one in modern settings, given, for example, the comprehensive property rights coverage of the framework of nation-states and their constitutive social institutions. Historically it is also overstated; for example, European powers did not find America, Australia, Africa, and other continents first and claim it for themselves in the absence of any prior owners – rather, in effect, they stole the various lands in question from indigenous peoples.

The other two moral bases are of much greater importance. They are natural (as opposed to institutional) moral rights, specifically, need (e.g., use of land to grow food) and contribution to production – the philosopher John Locke's "mixing of one's labor" with material gives rise to a moral right to the resulting product. However, neither of these two moral bases supports market fundamentalism.

For one thing, they both provide strong support for *legal* property rights sometimes being overridden by needs-based moral rights and (potentially) by the moral rights of productive workers.

For another, needs-based property rights and/or producer-based property rights are consistent with a variety of legal property regimes including, crucially, collectivist property regimes. Consider, for example, a socialist-style property regime in which property, including access to the use of land and its products, use and exchange of manufactured goods, and intellectual property rights, were allocated in part on the basis of need and in part on the basis of productive contribution. I am not here advocating socialism, in any of its forms; far from it. Rather, I am merely pointing out that the only two compelling moral bases for property rights are consistent with collectivist property arrangements, as well as private property ones. Accordingly, arguments in favor of private property frameworks as superior to collectivist property ones will turn on instrumentalist considerations – specifically, on my account, on their respective (actual and potential) contribution to the provision of collective goods (in my sense, not in a specifically socialist sense of that term).

It might be thought that property rights based on contribution to production in particular ground transfer rights; and it is transfer rights that in large part underpin market fundamentalism. Certainly the burden of the case in favor of market fundamentalism rests on transfer rights. But transfer rights are the weakest link in the market fundamentalist's argumentative chain.

From the fact that I might have produced something or, indeed, might otherwise own something – for instance, I discovered the cure for HIV/AIDS or own the land through which a river runs – it simply does not follow that I can use or not use it as I see fit, and exclude or not exclude others from it. For example, I do not have a moral right to pollute the river that runs through my land so that downstream users become ill and die; nor does the fact that I have bought the arable land in question give me the moral right to infuse it with toxic substances and, thereby, render it unusable by future generations. Again, I cannot decide to hide my cure for HIV/AIDS from all others so that it is not available to save the lives of millions.

More specifically, from the fact that I might have certain use and exclusion rights to something that I have produced, it does not follow that I have the right to transfer all those rights to someone else or that, if I do, the transferred rights have the same stringency as they had when they attached to me as the originator of the product in question. For example, I morally ought not to be allowed to transfer my ownership rights to a large tract of rural land in a remote part of the country to would-be foreign buyers known to support terrorist groups by providing training grounds for them in remote rural areas. Again, the author of a book transfers various economic rights to the publisher. However, there are certain rights that the author retains and, I suggest, ought to retain, for example, the right to be known as the author and not to have the work altered by the publisher. Accordingly, there could be no objection to a law that prevented someone from falsely claiming the authorship of a book, even if the actual author had agreed to this.

So much for market fundamentalism. Let me now return to some further implications of my own account.

In the context of competition for scarce resources, other things being equal, the realization of the collective goods definitive of social institutions ought to override any other roles they might have in relation to the satisfaction of (aggregated) desires. For example, the building and staffing of hospitals should take priority over the setting up of ice cream parlors; and, where a business organization (e.g., a media company) has, normatively speaking, a collective end that is also a collective good in my sense (e.g., as an element of the Fourth Estate), then this collective end ought to override purely commercial considerations. Indeed, in such cases commercial considerations should be in the service of these larger moral purposes. On the other hand, commercial viability, profitability, and the like are important concerns; after all, the larger moral purposes that the businesses in question exist to serve will not be realized if the business goes bust. Moreover, the private property rights in play in such contexts (e.g., rights of shareholders) need to be respected for the same reason (as well as by virtue of their status as moral rights, albeit ones that are overridden by needs-based human rights, for example).

More generally, my instrumentalist conception of business organizations operating in competitive markets has the implication that markets and their constitutive organizations ought to be designed, regulated, and held accountable on the basis of their (direct or indirect) contribution to collective goods; profits ought to be regarded merely as proximate ends, collective goods as ultimate ends. Similarly, the internal structure of business organizations, including corporate governance structures, and the like ought to be designed in the light of the (direct or indirect) contribution of these organizations to collective goods. In short, I am insisting that the much vaunted invisible hand of markets be made to deliver on its promises, including by way of appropriate incentive structures that are regulated into existence (Chapter 10).

Obviously, business organizations per se need to be sharply distinguished from inherently morally objectionable social institutions, such as slavery. But there is a conceptual distinction in play here that is in need of further clarification.

Slavery is an *inherently* morally objectionable social institution that mobilizes physical force and ideology in the economic interests of the slave owners and at the expense of the human rights of the slaves. Moreover, historically, slavery was often underpinned by business organizations operating in competitive markets; indeed, slavery has constituted a de facto, and often de jure, extension of property rights so as to include human beings as property to be bought and sold.

Thus some markets, such as slave markets or the market in heroin, are morally objectionable, some are morally neutral, such as the market in chocolate bars, and some are morally worthy, such as markets in life-saving drugs.[3]

On my *descriptive* teleological account, all business organizations, or systems of such organizations, operating in competitive markets – and market-based slavery in particular – are social institutions. After all, in every case they are constituted by a structure of roles and associated tasks directed toward collective ends; moreover, these roles, tasks, and ends are subject to social norms, and other morally significant social forms (however morally repugnant these might be in the case of slavery).

However, by the lights of my *normative* teleological account of social institutions, the direct or indirect collective end(s) of any given institution is a collective good. In addition, there ought to be moral constraints on institutional activities, for example, human rights constraints. Accordingly, on my normative teleological account an inherently morally objectionable institution such as slavery is defective *qua* social institution. The point is not that some institutions of slavery are defective by virtue of not living up to their constitutive "moral" standards or not realizing their ends as institutions of slavery. On the contrary: all institutions of slavery are *necessarily* morally defective by virtue of living up to these standards and realizing these ends, that is, simply by being institutions of slavery. Let us say that institutions of slavery are defective *qua* species of social institution.

Now consider a private school that has morally objectionable features, for example, the children are abused by the teachers. This school is defective *qua* school (but not *qua* species of social institution). Let us say that such schools are morally defective *qua* instances of the particular species of social institution that they are, that is, *qua* schools.

---

[3]  It is also the case that to the extent that a business organization provides a paid job that enables employees to provide for their needs, and that of their families, and also generates tax revenue for the provision of collective goods, then it is morally worthy.

## Institutional Moral Rights

Notwithstanding the above, many moral rights, duties, values, princi-ples, and so on are *not* logically prior to social institutions. Consider in this connection the moral right to vote, the moral right to a fair trial, the right to buy and sell land, and the moral right to a paid job; the first right presupposes institutions of government of a certain kind (demo-cratic government), the second criminal justice institutions of a certain kind (e.g., courts of law that adjudicate alleged crimes), and the third and fourth economic institutions of a certain kind. Let us refer to such institution-dependent moral rights as "institutional moral rights" (as opposed to natural moral rights).

Evidently, institutional moral rights depend in part on rights-generating properties possessed by human beings *qua* human beings, but also in part on membership of a community or of a morally legitimate institution, or occupancy of a morally legitimate institutional role.

As noted in the Introduction, such institutional moral rights and duties include ones that are (a) derived at least in part from collective goods and (b) constitutive of specific institutional roles, such as the rights and duties of a fire officer (see Section 3). They also include moral rights and duties that attach to all members of a community because they are dependent on institutions in which all members of the community participate, for example, the duty to obey the law of the land, the duty to contribute to one's country's national defense in time of war, the right to vote, the right of access to paid employment in some economy, the right to own land in some territory, the right to freely buy and sell goods in some economy. These moral rights and duties are institutionally relative in the following sense.

Even if they are in part based on an institutionally prior human right (e.g., a basic human need, the right to freedom), their precise content, stringency, context of application (e.g., jurisdiction), and so on can be determined only by reference to the institutional arrangements in which they exist and, specifically, in the light of their contribution to the col-lective good(s) provided by those institutional arrangements. So, for example, a property regime, if it is to be morally acceptable, must not only reward the producers of goods, for example, by protecting the ownership rights of the producers of goods to the goods that they pro-duce (e.g., would-be consumers cannot steal their goods), it must also ensure that consumers are benefited and not harmed (e.g., producers are required to meet health and safety standards). More particularly, a property regime, if it is to be morally acceptable, must satisfy the requirements of institutionally prior human rights; specifically, it must ensure that the needs-based rights of consumers are fulfilled (e.g., producers are required to compete under conditions of fair competition, or are otherwise constrained, to ensure that their products are available at prices the needy can afford).

We need to make a further distinction between (a) institutional moral rights and (b) institutional rights that are not moral rights. The right to vote and the right to stand for office embody the human right to autonomy in the institutional setting of the state; hence to make a law to exclude certain people from having a vote or standing for office, as happened in apartheid South Africa, is to violate a moral right. But the right to make the next move in a game of chess, or to move a pawn one space forward, but not, say, three spaces sideways, is entirely dependent on the rules of chess; if the rules were different, (e.g., each player must make two consecutive moves, pawns can move sideways), then the rights that players have would be entirely different. In other words, these rights that chess players have are *mere* institutional rights; they depend entirely on the rules of the "institution" of the game of chess (Searle 1995). Likewise, (legally enshrined) parking rights, such as reserved spaces and one-hour parking spaces in universities, are *mere* institutional rights, as opposed to institutional *moral* rights.

I will now consider in more detail the moral rights and collective goods that underpin social institutions.

## 2. JOINT RIGHTS, COLLECTIVE GOODS, AND INSTITUTIONS

### Needs-Based Rights

Each member of a community has individual needs for food, water, shelter, and the like, and a derived set of needs-based human rights.[4] However, it is only when a certain threshold of aggregate need (or, for example, aggregated rights violations) exists that the establishment of an institution takes place; agribusinesses or welfare institutions, for example, are not established because a single person's need for food has not been realized (Chapter 7). When such a threshold of unmet aggregate

---

[4] There are moral bases for human rights other than needs. For criticism of need-based theories of human rights see Griffin (2008).

need exists, there is a collective moral responsibility to engage in joint activity to fulfill the aggregate need in question. Accordingly, a cooperative enterprise is, or ought to be, embarked on that has as a collective end the provision of goods to the needy, many by means of the joint activity of the participants in the enterprise; that is, an institution producing a collective good has been, or ought to be, established (see Section 3).

There is a threefold distinction to be made between the desired, the desirable, and the needed; something can be desired without being desirable, and desirable without being needed. Here I stress the importance of the distinction between needs and desires. As David Wiggins argues (Wiggins 1991), needs are not simply a class of strong desires. If I desire to have x and x is y, then I do not necessarily desire to have y. Assume, for example, that x is a glass of water and y is a glass of $H_2O$, but I do not know that water is $H_2O$. Now consider needs. If I need x (water) and x is y (water is $H_2O$), then I need y ($H_2O$). Unlike "desire," "need" is not an intentional verb, and, unlike desires, what I need depends on the way the world objectively is, as opposed to how I think it is (Wiggins 1991, 6). As Wiggins also points out (9), categorical needs, such as for food, should not be confused with, and are not reducible to, mere instrumental needs: for example, I need $2 (as a means to buying an ice cream). Merely instrumental needs are not categorical needs, nor are they in the service of categorical needs; rather, instrumental needs are simply the means to realize desires.

An important feature of a categorical need of a person is that it must be fulfilled, if harm to the person is to be avoided (Wiggins 1991, 9). This noncontingent connection between needs and harms is in part reflective of the fact that many needs and, specifically, basic human needs, are relative to constitutive properties of human beings. Being the kind of organisms that we are, human beings need, for example, a flow of oxygen; indeed, we cannot survive without it. Importantly, human needs are relative to human well-being – relative, that is, not simply to human survival, but to human flourishing. This is not to say that any condition that contributes to human flourishing is a need. But it is to say that unless certain human needs are met – including some needs that are not strictly necessary for survival – humans cannot flourish; children, for example, need to be reared in a relatively safe and caring environment if they are not to suffer long-term psychological harm.

The noncontingent relation between needs and harms and, more specifically, the relativity of human needs to human flourishing implies that needs, or at least human needs, are ethico-normative in character

(Wiggins 1991, 11). Hence to fulfill someone's human need is *pro tanto* a good thing to do, and to deprive someone of their human need is *pro tanto* a bad thing to do. Indeed, under certain conditions human needs generate moral rights and correlative moral obligations. Whether or not a human need generates a moral right to the thing needed will depend on the extent of the harm suffered if the need is not fulfilled, the existence of someone who could meet the need and do so at little cost to him- or herself, and so on. Moreover, not all needs that morally ought to be fulfilled are such that the person or persons with the need have a moral right that it be fulfilled. In short, some categorical needs generate moral rights, but others do not. However, all categorical needs are such that they morally ought to be met, if this is possible and at a relatively small cost.

Needs are relative to circumstance (Wiggins 1991, 11), albeit some needs, such as for water, are relative to unalterable and/or invariable circumstances, while this is not so in the case of other needs, such as the need for a dentist. Finally, some, but by no means all, needs generate moral rights and obligations. Suppose I have a need for food and water but am unable to provide for these needs of mine. If so, perhaps I have a right that you provide me with food and water, if you are able to do so at little cost to yourself. On the other hand, if I have a need for friendship, it does not follow that I have a right to your friendship, even supposing that you could provide it at little cost to yourself.

## Joint Moral Rights

Let me now consider one way in which certain human rights, notably the individual human right to autonomy (Griffin 2008), can underpin social institutions and constitute collective goods. In the kind of case I have in mind human rights underpin social institutions via joint moral rights, and do so in a particular way. Let me explain.

Consider the right to political secession. Arguably, the Kurds in Iraq have a right to secede. But, if this is a right, it is not a right that some Kurdish person has as an individual. After all, an individual person cannot secede. The right of the Kurds to secede – if it exists – is a right that attaches to the individual members of the Kurdish social group, but does so jointly. Similarly, the related right of the Kurds to exclude others from their territory, if it exists, is a joint right; some Kurdish person acting as an individual does not have a right to exclude, for example, would-be immigrants.

Now consider the right to political participation. Each Canadian citizen has a moral right to participate in political institutions in Canada; non-Canadians do not have a right to such political participation in Canada. Moreover, the right to political participation of each Canadian is dependent on the possession of the right to political participation in Canada of all the other Canadians; Canadians have a joint moral right.

Such joint rights need to be distinguished from universal individual human rights. Take the right to life as an example of a universal individual human right. Each human being has an individual human right to life. However, since one's possession of the right to life is wholly dependent on properties one possesses as an individual, it is not the case that one's possession of the right to life is dependent on someone else's possession of that right.[5]

Notice that joint rights can be based in part on properties individuals possess as individuals. The right to participate in political institutions is based in part on membership of a political and legal community, and in part on possession of the individual human right of autonomy.

Consider the right to vote. This is an individual, institutional moral right. Nevertheless, it is based in part on the prior individual human right to autonomy. In a social or political setting requiring collective or joint decision making this individual human right is transformed into an individual institutional moral right to vote via a joint right: the joint right to political participation. Indeed, properly speaking, the individual institutional moral right to vote is itself a joint right; each has a right to vote only if each of one's fellow bona fide members of the political community in question likewise has a right to vote.

Here there are four related points to be made. First, the institution, say, representative government, is not based on an aggregate of individual human rights, but rather a joint moral right – a joint moral right that is in turn in part based on the individual human right of autonomy. (Note that although many joint moral rights are institutional rights, many are not, for instance, the natural joint right of noninstitutionally based producers to their product.) Second, the exercise of the joint right of political participation is an end in itself; it is not simply a means to some further end (although in fact it is also a means to other ends; see

---

[5] Joint rights also need to be distinguished from conditional individual rights. By mutual consent A might have a right to fish in B's river on condition that B has a right to hunt in A's woods. However, neither A nor B has a joint right; rather, each has a conditional individual right. For one thing, the content of A's right brings with it no essential reference to the content of B's. For another, A can unilaterally extinguish B's right, as B can A's.

Chapter 12). Third, the exercise of the joint right to political participation is a collective end; it is an end that is realized by the actions of many, and not by one person acting alone. Finally, it is a collective end that morally ought to be realized (by virtue being the fulfillment of moral rights), and that is enjoyed in being realized; so it is a collective good.

In fact, the institution of representative government is grounded in a number of collective goods. Representative government not only has as a collective end to embody, or give expression to, the joint right to political participation, but also to provide various other collective goods, for example, the coordination and regulation of other social institutions (the education system, the health system, the criminal justice system, the financial system, etc.), to ensure that they realize their (respective) collective ends (Chapter 12).

As we have seen, political participation is joint activity that morally ought to be performed. Moreover, it is joint activity that is constitutive, both of the collective end-in-itself that it serves, and of the collective good that it is; the producers are the consumers, so to speak. In this respect political institutions differ from, say, welfare institutions. The latter institutions are instruments in the service of prior needs-based rights, rather than an expression or embodiment of those rights. Accordingly, the producers are not necessarily the consumers.

## Aggregated Moral Rights and Collective Goods

Let me now explain how it is that the realization of aggregated needs-based rights, and of other aggregated moral rights, are collective goods in my sense, that is, jointly produced (or maintained or renewed) goods that ought to be produced (or maintained or renewed), and that are, and ought to be, made available to the whole community since they are desirable goods and ones to which the members of the community have a joint moral right.

As already argued, the realization of such aggregated rights is achieved by joint activity – or, at least, is achieved partly by joint activity; joint activity – and specifically, institutional activity – is typically only a necessary, not a sufficient, condition for the realization of aggregated moral rights. The maintenance of public health, for example, relies only in part on hospitals and other institutions; it also relies, for example, on general adherence to social norms of cleanliness, eating nutritious foods, and so on.

It should also be pointed out that social institutions (especially business organizations operating in competitive markets), which meet aggregate needs, or otherwise realize (or contribute to the realization of) aggregated moral rights, often go well beyond the provision of such collective goods and realize parallel aggregated desires; consider, for example, the retail food industry in some economy that aggressively markets and sells a much larger quantum of basic foodstuffs, such as dairy products, than is actually needed and, thereby, indirectly exacerbates an obesity problem in the population.

As one might expect of something claimed to be a collective good, the fulfillment of aggregated rights is not something that is available to only one person. Of course, the fact that it is *aggregated* rights that are in question makes this trivially true. Moreover, since it is moral rights that are in question, then each and every rights bearer ought to have available to them the good to which he or she has a right; hence the good ought to be made available to the whole community.

However, the enjoyment of rights is typically thought to be an individual affair; and, indeed, in many respects it is. If, for example, my right to individual freedom is fulfilled, then I enjoy the exercise of *my* right and no one else enjoys the exercise of *my* right (even if they enjoy the exercise of their own). It is also true that the exercise of my right to freedom (at least in part – see below) is logically consistent with the inability of others to exercise their respective rights to freedom, for instance, if I am Robinson Crusoe and everyone else lives in an authoritarian state.

It is, of course, a commonplace of political philosophy that the establishment of government and the rule of law is instrumentally necessary for the preservation of the freedom of each of us, albeit under the restriction not unduly to interfere with others; the alternative, as Hobbes famously said, is the state of nature, in which life is nasty, brutish, and short. However, I want to make a somewhat different point; there is another reason that most of us rely on the fulfillment of the rights to freedom of others to enjoy adequately our own freedom.

Specifically, I cannot engage in (freely performed) *joint* activity with others if they cannot exercise their rights to freedom. For example, I cannot freely participate in elections unless others can also do so; hence the absurdity of my voting in an election in which all the other votes were cast in accordance with the instructions of the dictator of my country. Again, I cannot freely engage in buying and selling transactions in a so-called free and competitive market unless others can do likewise; hence the absurdity of my offering goods for sale at price x, when buyers are required by law (in a socialist state, for example, that for some reason makes an exception of me) to buy those goods at price y.

As I have argued in this book, joint action is (in part) constitutive of all institutions, political, economic, and otherwise. Accordingly, unless I am the one, or one of the ones, who is in control of the actions of others – including determining their participation in joint activity – then my freedom is (literally, and not merely figuratively) diminished to the extent that the freedom of others is. So the fulfillment of one person's right to freedom is importantly connected, directly or indirectly – via a pervasive network of joint institutional activity – to the fulfillment of the rights to freedom of many other persons. So the right to freedom of action is *in part a joint* right to engage in freely performed *joint* action; specifically, in institutional settings it is in part a joint right.[6]

As we have seen, the fulfillment of aggregated moral rights to freedom is not only morally desirable, it is in part dependent on joint institutional activity, such as that undertaken by governments and others under the rule of law. However, as we have also seen, the right to freedom is in part a joint right (at least in institutional settings). Accordingly, the fulfillment of aggregated moral rights to freedom is a collective good.

What of aggregated needs-based rights – the right to basic foodstuffs and shelter, for example? In modern economies these aggregated needs are fulfilled by means of joint activity, for instance, by business organizations in competitive markets. So these morally required goods, that is, fulfilled (aggregated) needs-based rights, are *jointly produced;* so they meet this defining condition for being a collective good. What of their enjoyment? In what further respects, if any, does the enjoyment of aggregated needs-based rights meet the defining conditions for being a collective good?

As we saw is the case with aggregated rights to freedom, the fact that the fulfilled needs-based rights in question are *aggregated* makes it trivially true that the members of the community in general enjoy these rights. Likewise, since it is moral rights that are in question, then each and every rights bearer ought to have available to them the good to which he or she has a right. Again, if my right to basic foodstuffs is fulfilled, then I enjoy the exercise of *my* right, and only I enjoy the exercise of *my* right (even if others also enjoy the exercise of theirs). It is also true that the exercise of my needs-based rights to basic foodstuffs, shelter, and so on is logically consistent with the inability of others to exercise their respective rights to these goods, for instance, if I am a successful subsistence farmer living

---

[6] Indeed, I hold that the right to freedom of action is in part a joint moral right in interpersonal and social settings more generally, i.e., any context involving joint action.

in a failed state. Moreover, others can exercise their needs-based rights without my doing so, for instance, if the needed goods are only available in a market and I cannot afford to pay for them while others can.

Nevertheless, each of us, albeit indirectly, relies on the fulfillment of the needs-based rights of others to enjoy adequately our own needs-based rights. The reason for this is twofold.

First, in modern societies most individuals rely on social institutions, such as agribusinesses or manufacturers of building materials, operating in competitive markets, to produce the foodstuffs and other necessities to fulfill their needs-based rights. Indeed, even if they were disposed to do so, few modern individuals are even capable of producing sufficient food, clean water, adequate shelter, medicine, and the like for themselves; few of us living in modern societies are, or could easily become, subsistence farmers.

Second, most individuals rely on business organizations operating in competitive markets to provide paid jobs that (a) enable them to pay for the basic necessities of life and (b) generate taxes to fund a variety of other collective goods necessary for the production and distribution of these basic necessities, for instance, transport, communications, research and training, and other infrastructure.

So there is a complex structure of direct, and indirect, interdependence (as opposed to one-way dependence) and overlap between the needy and those who fulfill their needs. For example, there is direct interdependence between agribusinesses and the paying consumers of basic foodstuffs; and there is indirect interdependence between the former and all the other organizations that pay their employees and, thereby, enable them to become paying consumers of basic foodstuffs.

For our purposes here, an important feature of this complex structure of economic interdependence and overlap is the indirect interdependence between the bearers of needs-based rights themselves, that is, the consumers of basic necessities; they rely on one another economically to maintain the agribusinesses and other companies that provide their basic necessities. Accordingly, in modern economies, speaking generally, if one person's needs-based right to food, shelter, and the like is fulfilled, then so are the relevant needs-based rights of many other persons.

This de facto indirect web of economic interdependence between the bearers of needs-based rights does not, of course, necessarily encompass *all* the members of a community; for example, there might not be any dependence of the employed on the unemployed. Nevertheless, under conditions of full employment (or near full employment in conjunction with welfare payments to the unemployed) and sufficient production of basic necessities to meet the needs of all, then this de facto indirect web of economic interdependence will encompass all members of the community; the web of economic interdependence will be complete.

This web of economic interdependence is, of course, not of such a kind that the meeting of the needs of a single person is a necessary or sufficient condition for the meeting of the needs of any other single person, let alone of all other persons taken in aggregate. Rather, the interdependence between individuals, between small subsets of the whole community, and between individuals and small subsets is partial and incremental. Roughly speaking, the larger the subset, the greater the dependence on it of its members (taken individually) and of individuals and subsets outside it; and the less dependent it is on any particular subset outside it (or on any small subset of itself).

Each and every member of the community has a needs-based right to the basic necessities of life. Accordingly, if the de facto web of economic interdependence is complete – and there are adequate production levels – then the needs-based rights of all will be fulfilled. Moreover, such a completed web of economic interdependence will parallel a deontic structure of interdependent (aggregated) needs-based rights. The (aggregated) needs-based rights in question are interdependent by virtue of being joint rights. Let me explain.

As mentioned above, a needs-based right is not per se a jointly held right; it follows that an aggregate of needs-based rights is not necessarily a set of jointly held rights. However, a needs-based right and, likewise, an aggregate of needs-based rights are such only in the context of the possibility of their fulfillment (either by the rights bearers themselves, or by others); one cannot have a right to something if it is impossible (logically or practically) for it to be provided.

The context in question, that is, a well-functioning modern economy, is one in which aggregated needs-based rights are fulfilled (and realistically can only be fulfilled) by economic institutions characterized by a completed web of economic interdependence among the consumers of basic necessities, that is, the bearers of the needs-based rights in question. But in that case – given that rights exist only if it is possible for them to be fulfilled – then the needs-based rights in question are *joint* rights.[7]

---

[7] The notion of possibility in play here needs to be furthered specified. Thus, it might not be possible today, but possible tomorrow; surely this would not mean one did not have a right today. Again, something weaker than logical possibility is called for. Thanks to Christian Barry for drawing my attention to this kind of problem.

One member of the community in question has a right to basic necessities only if others do, and vice versa. The institutional arrangements in question are not such that they could provide for one person, or even a small group of persons; they are designed to provide for aggregate needs, that is, for large groups of consumers. Since it is not possible to provide for one person (or even a small group), that person cannot have a right to the basic necessities independent of others having this right. That is, the right of any one person to the basic necessities is a jointly held right; the needs-based rights in question are joint rights.

I have defined collective goods as jointly produced goods that ought to be produced and made available to the whole community, because they are desirable goods and ones to which the members of the community have joint moral rights. The fulfillment of aggregated needs-based rights is a collective good in this sense.

In the remainder of this section I consider a class of putative collective goods that, nevertheless, appear to be goods to which members of the community do not have a joint moral right. Such goods include the ones made available by art galleries, museums, and public parks. Access to museums, for example, is evidently a collective good in *some* sense; however, arguably, it is not something to which people have a prior moral *right*. Incidentally, many business organizations in competitive markets produce such collective goods, such as privately owned art galleries do; I return to this point below.

However, we need to be careful to distinguish between a *prior* moral right that a good be brought into existence (or continue in existence) and a moral right to a good in the circumstance that the good does in fact exist; the latter does not entail the former. Accordingly, I grant that there is no *prior* moral right that art galleries, museums, parks, and the like be established (or continued in existence). Nevertheless, I hold that once established (other things being equal), there may well be a moral right of access to them, indeed, a moral right jointly possessed by all members of the relevant communities. Needless to say, the joint moral right in question is a good deal weaker than, say, the human right to life or to freedom.

For example, I take it that there is a joint moral right of access to art galleries that display the works of past masters (as opposed to the works of, say, minor contemporary artists). Typically the current membership of some society or culture are members of a diachronic society or culture, that is, one that exists intergenerationally. As such, they are entitled to have access to their history, including the important communications and artistic achievements of past members; indeed, an analogous argument can be made in relation to human civilization as a whole. Of course, from this right to access to, say, the works of past masters it does not follow that there ought not to be an entrance fee to the relevant galleries; but it does follow that those who cannot afford to pay ought, nevertheless, to have access. So although the moral basis of some institutions is a prior (aggregated) moral right, the moral basis of others is a collective good in respect of which there are no *prior* moral rights (albeit there are joint moral rights to these latter goods once they exist).

It might be argued against this that many such goods are produced by private individuals and groups; how could a privately produced good to which there is no *prior* moral right be a good to which the members of the community – as opposed to the producers of the good – have a joint moral right? The short answer is that the good in question is a collective good, that is, it is desirable that it exist and that there be general access to it; its desirability (as opposed to its simply being desired) is the reason for producing it.

It is true that when a collective end is a collective good in my favored sense, then there are two sets of claimants in respect of that good. There are those that produced the good; they have a joint right to the good by virtue of having produced it. Then there are those who have a joint moral right to it; they are the ones for whom the good was, or ought to have been, produced, for instance, visitors to museums.

It might be thought that the property rights of the joint producers of the good in question, say, a privately funded museum, trump any joint moral claim that might be pressed by the consumers of the good, should a conflict arise. This, of course, would not show that the latter do not have a joint right; merely that it is overridden by the joint right of the producers. But in any case the claim that the rights of producers trump the claims of consumers is not necessarily true. For one thing, the number of consumers who are not rights bearers might be far greater than the number of rights bearers: for example, the aggregate of relatively weak individual claims of hundreds of thousands of museum visitors might morally outweigh the joint moral right of the two owners of a museum. For another thing, there might be other important moral considerations in play that restrict ownership rights: for example, the historical and cultural value of the museum pieces might be such that the joint producers of the museum might forfeit their joint rights to the museum pieces if they fail adequately to protect, preserve, and make them available to the members of the cultural group in question.

### 3. COLLECTIVE MORAL RESPONSIBILITY AND INSTITUTIONAL DUTIES

In the last section we considered three different moral justifications for the establishment of institutions, namely, aggregate need, prior joint moral rights, and collective goods not based on prior moral rights (let us refer to the latter as non-rights-based collective goods). So much for the (so to speak) demand side of social institutions: rights and goods. Now let us turn to the supply side: the responsibilities and duties of the producers.

To simplify matters I will work with collective responsibilities to assist that are generated by needs-based rights, including ones deriving from harmful natural occurrences. Let us begin with the duty to aid, such as the duty to save a drowning man, A. Here the assumption is that the person, B, is able to assist at little or no cost to him- or herself. Moreover, he or she is uniquely able to assist, or at least is salient among those who are able to assist. Accordingly, the drowning man is in need of assistance – he will die if not assisted – and someone, namely, B, can assist him at little cost to themselves. So the drowning man, A, has a needs-based right to assistance from B. Notice that B's duty to assist correlates with A's right to be assisted.

Now assume that there are a number of persons, B, C, and D, each of whom could assist A, and do so at little cost to themselves. In that event A has a needs-based right to assistance from B or C or D – B, C, and D being the only individuals able to assist A at little cost to themselves – and B has a correlative moral duty to assist A (if neither B nor C has not done so); and C and D have similar correlative moral duties.

By comparison with individual noninstitutional moral duties to aid, there is a very large set of institutional moral duties to assist. The latter are attached to a wide variety of institutional roles, for example, doctors, nurses, firefighters, police, psychiatrists, and social workers.

The question that now arises concerns the moral basis for the existence of such moral duties that are also institutional duties, that is, institutional moral duties. The members of a fire crew, for example, each have a positive moral institutional duty to put out an incipient grass fire in the bush that – given the very high temperature and strong winds – will, if not extinguished, develop into a full-scale bush fire that will destroy property, and perhaps even lead to loss of life. Here it is not simply that the members of the fire crew, and indeed anyone else, would be doing a good thing if they put out the grass fire. Indeed, unlike ordinary members of the public, the members of the fire crew are morally *required* to extinguish the fire; it is their morally required institutional duty to extinguish the fire. So now the question to be asked is: What is the moral basis for this institutional duty?

It might be thought that the institutional duty is based on a promise. Each member of the fire crew has made a promise to put out fires (a promise he has presumably made on the condition that he will be suitably remunerated). However, promises are an implausible basis for such duties. Although some doctors, for example, may take the Hippocratic Oath, occupants of many of these institutional roles do not take any oaths or make any promises. More importantly, they would still have these institutional duties even if it turned out that they did not make any promises to perform the actions in question. Thus, a firefighter who recklessly left a fire to burn would not be able to escape moral condemnation or disciplinary action on the grounds that he never made anyone any promises to fight fires.

Another kind of answer to this question is based on the idea that creating reasonable expectations of benefits generates moral obligations to provide those benefits (Gert 2004). Once a person actually takes on a role to, say, assist those who are ill, reasonable expectations are generated on the part of the ill that their illnesses will be treated. As a consequence a doctor comes to have a duty to treat those who are ill. However, intentionally creating expectations that one will assist is not sufficient to generate a moral obligation to assist, given that there is no prior moral obligation to assist.

Consider a community in which there is only one winemaker. The winemaker has no moral obligation to assist a community to realize its aggregated desire to consume wine by making and selling wine, albeit in fact the winemaker does make and sell wine to the community. Accordingly, the members of the community reasonably assume that they will continue to be able to procure wine from the winemaker, albeit at a price. Now assume that the winemaker decides that he will continue to make wine, but in smaller quantities and only for select customers – customers who understand and fully appreciate wine, as distinct from ordinary drinkers. Accordingly, the reasonable expectations of many former customers – the nonconnoisseurs – are dashed. Moreover, since there is no other winemaker to whom they have access, these customers suffer various harms, notably deprivation of pleasure. Notwithstanding the deprivation of pleasure caused by his actions, surely the winemaker does not have a *moral duty* to make and sell wine to ordinary drinkers.

Certainly, given he now stocks only expensive, high-quality wine, he is discriminating against the ordinary drinkers in favor of the connoisseurs. But this discrimination is not arbitrary; indeed, it has a rational justification in terms of his personal interest in high-quality wine and those who appreciate it.

I conclude that the creation by a role occupant of reasonable expectations that he or she will provide benefits does not generate a moral duty to so provide those benefits. In the case of our finicky winemaker surely no one, not even his disappointed former customers, would claim that because of his actions he should be, for example, subject to a public protest or boycott, let alone to some form of disciplinary or punitive action, such as a financial penalty. Evidently there is nothing to publicly protest about, for the reason that he has done nothing morally wrong. And since he is certainly not liable to disciplinary action or punishment in particular, then presumably he has not breached any morally required institutional duty.

Thus far we have not found a plausible justification for institutional moral duties. Let us return to our bushfire scenario. Suppose that there are no firemen in the vicinity. Indeed, the only people in the areas are a group of bushwalkers from a well-known philosophy department in New Hampshire. No single member of the group could put out the small grass fire, but if they act jointly they can do so without risk to themselves, or indeed any great inconvenience. Moreover, they know that there is no way for them to warn the local community of the impending danger, should they refrain from extinguishing the fire. Presumably – given their awareness of the near certainty of a conflagration if they do not intervene – the members of the group have a collective moral responsibility to do so (and the members of the community a moral right that they do so). To see this, assume that the group, under the sway of a defective moral theory, decides that they have no such obligation and, in the spirit of savoring the raw power of nature in its elemental outback state, seeks a suitable vantage point from which to view the inevitable spectacular firestorm with its attendant large-scale destruction of life and property.

Notwithstanding any sympathy one might have with the desire of our erstwhile American friends to observe, understand, and analyze the unique phenomenon that is the Australian bushfire, we would be inclined to blame these philosophers for failing to do what we believe they were morally obliged to do. I note that in some jurisdictions in the world the failure of individuals or groups to assist in these sorts of circumstance renders those individuals and groups liable for punishment.

So the needs – indeed, needs-based moral rights – of individuals and groups for various forms of assistance that can be adequately rendered only by groups generates collective moral responsibilities on the part of groups to so assist.

So far so good; but what of *institutional* moral duties? In many cases such collective responsibilities to assist can most effectively be discharged by establishing institutions and associated institutional roles; crucially, the constitutive duties of such institutional role occupants are to provide the needed assistance: for example, members of fire brigades have an institutional duty to put out fires.

Moreover, these institutional duties are also moral duties. For these institutional duties derive from the relevant prior collective moral responsibility, such as to avert the destruction of life and property caused by fires.

In summation, fires cause death and destruction, and the consequent aggregated needs-based moral rights to protection from fires generates a collective moral responsibility to fulfill these aggregated rights. This collective moral responsibility is typically discharged by establishing an institution that has as its collective end to avert the destruction of life and property caused by fires; this collective end is also a collective good: for instance, it is jointly brought about, it morally ought to be brought about. The constitutive duties of the institutional role occupants of this institution are determined by, and derived from, the collective end, such as the duty of a fireman to put out fires derive from this collective end. Moreover, the collective moral responsibility to avert the harms caused by fires (i.e., to realize the collective end) devolves to the relevant institutional actors, such as the members of fire brigades; it is now their special, joint *moral* – and not simply institutional – duty to fight fires.

Members of a given group may have collective moral responsibilities toward the membership of that very group, that is, the group of which they are members. However, this is not necessarily the case. Consider the millions of people in the world living below the poverty line. Is there a collective moral responsibility on the part of the members of affluent countries to assist the poor? There is; the collective responsibility of the affluent is based on the aggregated needs-based rights of the poor to assistance. How is this collective responsibility to be discharged? It is to be discharged by establishing/redesigning relevant institutions and/or government policies, such as reforming harmful trade policies or taxing the rich to provide for the poor (Chapter 7).

Again, consider cross-generational responsibilities. The current generation of Australians has a collective moral responsibility to address problems of climate change that, if unaddressed, will harm future generations. As is the case with the other collective responsibilities, this collective moral responsibility to future generations is most effectively discharged through the establishment of appropriate institutions and associated roles, such as the Murray Darling Commission.

Having explored in general terms the normative character of social institutions, let us now turn in the final section of this chapter to a more specific normative aspect of institutions, namely, their conformity or lack of it with principles of justice (as opposed to moral rights or morality in general). My concern here will be with different types of principles of justice, such as distributive versus penal, the scope of principles of justice, such as global justice, and the application of principles of justice to institutions (as opposed to individuals *qua* individuals).

## 4. JUSTICE

Justice is an important normative aspect of many, if not all, social institutions.[8] Market economies, salary and wage structures, tax systems, judicial systems, prisons, and so on are all to be evaluated in part in terms of their compliance with principles of justice.

Here it is important to distinguish the concept of justice from, on the one hand, the related concept of a right – especially a human right – and from goods, such as well-being and utility, on the other hand. Self-evidently, well-being is not the same thing as justice. However, there is a tendency to conflate justice and rights. Nevertheless, the concepts are distinct; or at least justice in a narrow relational sense should be distinguished from the concept of a right. Genocide, for example, is a violation of human rights – specifically, the right to life – but it is not necessarily, or at least principally, an act of injustice in the narrow relational sense. A person's rights can be violated, irrespective of whether or not another – or indeed everyone else – has suffered a rights violation. However, injustice in the relational sense entails an unfairness as between persons or groups; injustice in this sense consists of the fact that someone has suffered or benefited but others have not (and there is no adequate justification for this state of affairs). Although the concept of a right and the concept of justice (in this sense) are distinct, violations of rights are typically acts of injustice and vice versa.

---

[8] An earlier version of the material in this section appeared in Miller (2007a).

Moreover, the concept of justice is itself multidimensional. Penal justice (sometimes referred to as retributive justice), for example, concerns the punishment of offenders for their legal and/or moral offences, and is to be distinguished from distributive justice. Hence it is a principle of penal justice, but not distributive justice, that the guilty be punished and the innocent go free.

Distributive justice is essentially a relational phenomenon to do with the comparative distribution of benefits and burdens as between individuals or groups, including the distribution of rights and duties but not restricted to the distribution of rights and duties, for instance, the injustice of excluding blacks from voting in elections to determine the national government in apartheid South Africa or of lower wages being paid to women than those paid to men for the same work. (These are also instances of rights violations.)

On the view of distributive justice being propounded here, justice is but one moral value and distributive justice but one dimension of justice. Accordingly, it is always an open question whether or not some action or policy required by the principles of distributive justice is morally required *all things considered.*

Distributive justice is an important aspect of most, if not all, social institutions; the role occupants of most institutions are the recipients and providers of benefits, for instance, wages, consumer products, and the bearers of burdens, such as allocated tasks, and, accordingly, are subject to principles of distributive justice. Moreover, arguably some institutions, perhaps governments, have as one of their defining collective ends to ensure conformity to principles of distributive justice in the wider society. However, distributive justice does not appear to be a *defining* feature, collective end, or otherwise, of *all* social institutions. By this I do not mean that some social institutions are unjust, such as the institution of slavery, although clearly many are. Rather I am referring to the fact that a number of social institutions, such as the English language or even the institution of the university, are not *defined* – normatively speaking – in terms of justice, but rather by some other moral value or values, such as truth. Communication systems, such as human languages, are arguably defined in part in terms of the end of truth, but not in terms of justice; hence, a communicative system would cease to be a communication system if its participants never attempted to communicate the truth, but not if its participants failed to respect principles of distributive justice, for example, in terms of the number of occasions on which particular speakers were allowed to speak.

The principles of distributive justice can be applied at an individual level, at an intra-institutional level, at a societal level, and at a global level. If principles of distributive justice are applied at an individual level, then the question arises as to the scope of the application: Is it, for example, the individuals who happen to occupy a neighborhood, the individuals who comprise a society, the individuals who comprise the human race, or some other demarcated set of individuals?

Moreover, if the principles of distributive justice are applied at an institutional level, then an analogous question arises in relation to the scope of the application: Is it, for example, a particular institution or a structure of institutions? If the latter, is it the institutional structure of a society or the global institutional structure? Famously, John Rawls addressed and privileged the question of the distributive justice of the structure of institutions in a given (liberal democratic) society (1972, 1999). Arguably, this is a somewhat narrow focus, whatever one thinks of the specific account of distributive justice that Rawls elaborated in relation to the structure of institutions at the societal level. Why is it not, for example, important to focus on the application of principles of distributive justice in relation to the global structure of, say, political and economic institutions? At any rate, our concern here is with the application of the concept of distributive justice at the institutional level (although not necessarily only with respect to the structure of institutions within a given society, let alone liberal democratic society). The contrast here is between the institutional level and the individual level. However, it is important to determine what this distinction consists of.

Justice is a moral (relational) property and as such, I suggest, is only properly applied either to the actions of *individual* human beings or to the relations between *individual* human beings, including their relative wealth, status, and power.[9] More specifically, a social entity or relation between social entities is not per se just or unjust, notwithstanding that in ordinary speech social entities and their relations to one another are said to be just or unjust; for example, the United States is sometimes said to be an unjust society. Rather, claims ascribing justice or injustice to social entities and/or their relations are translatable into claims regarding the actions of, and relations between, individual human beings: for example, the distribution of income between the individual citizens of the United States is unjust.

---

[9]  I am not concerned here with the possibility of human-like nonhumans, such as rational and morally sentient Martians.

Given this individualistic conception of justice (and of moral properties more generally), how is a distinction to be maintained between the application of principles of distributive justice at an institutional level, on the one hand, and at an individual level, on the other? Quite simply, by helping ourselves to the concept of an institutional-role occupant (and the relations, actions, and effects on role occupants *qua* role occupants).

Institutional-role occupants are individual human persons. However, they are individual human persons who happen to occupy one or more institutional roles, including in contemporary nation-states the role of citizen. As such, they have certain institutional rights and duties, in the manner adumbrated in earlier sections of this chapter.

Accordingly, an institution is in some respect or on some occasion unjust in one of two main ways: intra-institutionally unjust and externally institutionally unjust. An institution is in some respect or on some occasion *intra-institutionally* unjust if a role occupant of this institution *qua* role occupant of this institution (a) stands in an unjust relation to some other role occupant within this institution *qua* role occupant of this institution or (b) performs an action that is unjust to some role occupant of this institution *qua* role occupant of this institution. For example, a company in which the CEO's salary is 50 times the wage of the lower-echelon workers is prima facie unjust in respect of its system of rewards.

An institution is in some respect or on some occasion *externally unjust* if a role occupant of this institution *qua* role occupant of this institution (a) stands in an unjust relation to some other non–role occupant of this institution or (b) performs an action that is unjust to some non–role occupant of this institution: for example, the members of a parliamentary cabinet jointly decide to remove the minimum wage level in the interests of economic growth, notwithstanding that this policy will further impoverish the least well-off.

Accordingly the unjust actions of, and unjust relations between, ordinary human beings are actions and relations at the individual *non-institutional* level by virtue of not being acts of, and relations between, individuals *qua* institutional-role occupants. Thus if a group of wealthy entrepreneurs buy a large (but allowable) number of tickets to soccer matches in some national league and then sell them at grossly inflated prices to wealthy soccer fans (again, this is allowable), then arguably there has been an injustice to the relatively impoverished soccer fans who would otherwise have been able to afford these tickets and attend the matches of their beloved home teams. However, these are not acts of injustice at the institutional level, because a one-off joint action of a number of entrepreneurs does not constitute an institution, and so there are no persons acting *qua* institutional actors in this injustice.

Notice that on this account of the distinction between the institutional and the individual levels of just/unjust actions and relations, if a role occupant (acting *qua* role occupant) treats some *non–role occupant* unjustly, then this is, nevertheless, an injustice at the institutional level. So if the members of an apartheid government refuse to enact legislation giving the vote to (currently disenfranchised) blacks, then this is an institutional injustice.

Note also that on this way of drawing the distinction it does not matter whether the institution in question is an intra-societal institution, for instance, an institution within a nation-state, or an extra-societal, including global, institution, such as the United Nations.

On the other hand, this way of drawing the distinction between the individual and the institutional level of the application of principles of distributive justice assumes that some relevant institution has been established. However, it is possible that there are in fact no institutions designed to deal with some pressing issue of distributive justice and, therefore, no institutional-role occupants to rectify the injustice. Surely, it might be argued, such an injustice is an injustice at the institutional level. I suggest that such cases are not cases of the injustice of institutions per se, but rather of the injustice of *the absence* of institutions. Such cases point to the need to make a threefold, rather than a merely twofold, distinction in this area: (1) injustice at the individual level, (2) injustice at the institutional level, (3) injustice at the individual level that is of such magnitude as to warrant the establishment of an institution.

It might further be argued that a crucial factor in all this has been ignored, namely, *groups* of individuals, for example, socioeconomic classes or ethnic and gender-based groups (Miller 2001b, chap. 6). The application of principles of distributive justice at the institutional level is, or ought to be, in large part the application of such principles not so much to individuals per se, but to groups whose members are known to be, say, systemically discriminated against. Doubtless, much injustice is group based. To the extent that institutional actors are themselves guilty of group-based injustice – for example, politicians whose policies discriminate against indigenous people, employers who exploit young workers in terms of pay and conditions – then this is a matter of injustice at the institutional level, as this notion has been characterized above. However, there is a further point at issue here.

Group-based injustices can exist primarily at the individual level rather than primarily at the institutional level. Some groups of individuals might have significant advantages in the competition for scarce goods, such as wealth, power, and status, by virtue of their greater initial wealth, their access to social networks, and so on. That is, they have no *formal* institutional advantages. Moreover, it is not self-evident that a given institution, such as a corporation, university, medical, or legal profession, is unjust simply by virtue of the fact that some groups enjoy informal and highly generic advantages in relation to the competition for access to and progress within the institution in question; surely it is too much to insist that every institution must ensure complete equality of opportunity if it wants to avoid the charge of injustice.

However, it might be argued that this line of argument fails to accommodate group-based injustices of the kind in question. Indeed, the Rawlsian difference principle might be invoked at this point; the system of institutional arrangements within a society taken as a whole should work to the advantage of the least advantaged.

In response to this, I suggest that such group-based injustices, if injustices they be, are not necessarily injustices at the institutional level, but rather might well be injustices at the individual level. Nevertheless, they might be injustices at the individual level that are of such a magnitude that they need to be addressed institutionally. However, they are not injustices in respect of which there is no relevant remedial institution in existence. Rather, existing institutions, especially governments, are presumably obliged to formulate appropriate policies to deal with such group-based injustices. Such policies might include death duties and/or tax scales with very high marginal rates of taxation at the top end of the scale.

On the other hand, if such group-based injustices are in fact the result of the practices or structures of institutions (taken individually or collectively) within the society, then they would constitute injustices at the institutional level. For example, if the quality of educational preparation necessary to become a doctor or lawyer was in fact available only to the very rich, then arguably the educational institutions themselves are unjust, that is, there is injustice at the institutional level. In many societies socioeconomic group-based injustices exist at both the individual and the institutional levels. That is, relevant institutions are both failing to take steps to redress prior group-based injustices at the individual level and are further exacerbating those injustices by adding another layer of injustice at the institutional level.

There is a category of institutions in respect of which the distinction between group-based individual injustices and injustices at the institutional level collapses, namely, institutions that have as one of their defining purposes to redress large-scale distributive injustices in the wider society, that is, governments.

The assumption here is that the institutional (collective) ends of government – or at least of the state, including the government but also state-based agencies coordinated by government, such as police organizations and welfare institutions – go beyond protecting human rights to, for example, life and liberty; and also go beyond providing the necessary means to the realization of those rights (e.g., basic health, education, and conditions of law and order that enable citizens to pursue their various individual and collective projects). For, as we have seen, the concept of a right, especially a human right, needs to be distinguished from the concept of justice, including distributive justice; and the realization of human rights is a more pressing moral imperative than compliance with the principles of distributive justice.

On the other hand, minimalist conceptions of the institution of government might stop short of advocating a major role for government in applying principles of distributive justice in the wider society.

A further question that arises here pertains to the putative obligation of governments to protect the human rights of citizens of other states (or for that matter, noncitizens). Arguably, all individuals and institutions, including governments, have a moral obligation to protect human rights, for instance, not to violate the right to life or liberty. And some of these human rights evidently include positive rights to security and the provision of basic necessities, such as food and water. Some have argued that there are no such obligations on the part of governments, other than to their own citizens. This view might prove difficult to sustain, given that the principle not to infringe a human right applies universally, and given that the notion of a human right cannot be restricted to so-called negative rights, that is, cannot be restricted to rights not to be interfered with (see Section 3).

Perhaps ironically, a conception of the institution of government that is minimalist in respect of the *nature* of its obligations – that is, government exists only to protect the human rights of its citizens – might generate (presumably unwittingly) maximalism in respect of the *scope* of those obligations – that is, other things being equal, the government has an obligation to protect the human rights of all, whether they be its citizens or not. Naturally, other things are not equal: for example, there are practicalities and a certain division of labor in respect of the protection of the human rights of different groups. Australia, for example, cannot presumably be expected to protect the human rights of the Tibetans, given the relative power of China vis-à-vis Australia. On the other hand, Australia might be reasonably expected to intervene to protect the human rights of the East Timorese.

Some (Blake 2001) have argued (a) that a liberal democratic government has a moral obligation to ensure respect for the human rights of its own citizens and others alike, but has moral obligations only to ensure that its own citizens comply with principles of distributive justice (specifically, the – controversial – Rawlsian difference principle) and (b) that the reason for this is that its own citizens alone are legitimately subject to the coercive authority of the government. The latter claim is open to question (Anderson 1999). No doubt citizens subject to the coercive authority of a government have a moral right to political rights, for example, a right to vote and to stand for political office; they relinquish a degree of their individual autonomy in favor of a degree of jointly held autonomy (as well as – at least – protection of their human rights, and law and order). However, it is difficult to see why citizens being subject to the coercive authority of a government (willingly or, for that matter, unwillingly) generates a moral obligation on the part of the government in question to apply principles of distributive justice – specifically, the controversial Rawlsian difference principle – to the interactions between the citizens.

On the other hand, arguably, the coercive authority of government does generate a moral obligation on the part of government to enforce respect for (inherently, justifiably enforceable) contracts between citizens that are freely entered in to. For the latter are expressions of the autonomy of citizens, and in accepting the coercive authority of the government, citizens have relinquished a further aspect of their individual autonomy, namely, their individual rights to enforce certain of the contracts that they freely enter in to (namely, justifiably enforceable contracts).

More generally, insofar as individuals outside the state, whether acting individually or jointly, are morally justified in using coercive force in the service of their human rights, other moral rights, principles of justice, and for other important moral reasons, then – given the individuals in question have surrendered their capacity to use coercive force to the state – the state is (at least, in principle) entitled to use coercive force in the service of precisely the same set of moral considerations. This is, of course, not to say that these are the only moral reasons that might justify the state's use of coercive force; however, any additional moral considerations would need to be considered on their merits.

In conclusion, a final point about liberal democratic governments and distributive justice. There is at least one important principle of distributive justice that arises in the context of collective enterprises (joint action); namely, that, other things being equal, the benefits produced by joint actions should flow back to those who performed the joint action. In fact, as we saw earlier in the chapter, other things being equal, the producers of such a benefit have a joint moral right to it by virtue of being joint producers of it. Nevertheless, the benefit in question is distributed; so let us speak of a rights-based principle of distributive justice.

Let us assume that inevitably citizens of a given polity participate in collective enterprises, whereas this is not necessarily the case for individuals who are not citizens of the same polity. (In the contemporary globalizing world this assumption is increasingly implausible; but let us grant it for the sake of argument.) Surely this principle of distributive justice, if any, should be enforced by governments in relation to their own citizens but not in relation to noncitizens. Perhaps. At any rate, one key test of this proposition is whether or not individuals would be morally entitled to enforce such a principle of distributive justice in the absence of government. If the answer is in the affirmative, that is, individuals have a "natural" right to enforce this principle of distributive justice, then presumably governments have a right to enforce it; after all, as we have seen above, according to liberal democratic theory individuals relinquish to government whatever preexisting moral rights to enforcement they might have had.

What if the answer to our question is in the negative; does it follow that the government has no moral right to enforce this principle of distributive justice? Not necessarily. For one thing, enforcement of such a principle of distributive justice is not necessarily the violation of a human right; if it were, this would be a moral constraint on governmental action in this regard. For another thing, in the context of a liberal democratic state citizens can make legitimate joint decisions – via their representative governments – that are simply unavailable to them when they are functioning as lone individuals; and one of these joint decisions might well be to enforce such a principle of distributive justice in their society on the grounds that it is a weighty moral principle, the enforcement of which is morally required.

Now consider – as is in fact the case – a world in which many joint economic enterprises are in fact trans-societal, such as multinational corporations. Naturally, the citizens of different societies (polities) – or at least their representative governments – might also make a joint decision to (jointly) enforce this principle of distributive justice in relation to trans-societal joint economic enterprises involving citizens from both polities; for example, wages in a poor society would need to reflect the contribution of the wage earner to the overall benefits produced by the multinational corporation. And if the citizens are committed on moral grounds to the enforcement of this principle of distributive justice in relation to *intra*societal economic interactions, it is difficult to see why they should not be likewise committed to it in *trans*-societal economic interactions.

## 5. CONCLUSION

In this chapter I have elaborated an account of the general normative character of social institutions based on my individualist, teleological model, and according to which social institutions have a multifaceted normative dimension with multiple moral sources, including human needs, human rights, promise making (itself an institution), and deontic properties derived in part from the collective goods that are the raison d'etre of institutions. Collective goods are jointly produced by institutional actors and are, and ought to be, available to the whole community, because they are desirable goods, ones to which members of the community have (institutional) joint moral rights.

On my account the moral values of human life, human freedom, and the moral duty to assist other humans in need, for example, are logically prior to social institutions. Indeed, the fulfillment of prior aggregated moral rights is the defining collective end of some institutions and give direction to others. I have also discussed distributive justice as it pertains to institutions. In the next three chapters I turn to three key theoretical normative issues that arise for social institutions, namely, individual autonomy in institutional settings (Chapter 3), collective responsibility (Chapter 4), and institutional corruption (Chapter 5). These issues pertain, respectively, to the rights, abilities, and powers of individual institutional actors, the moral basis of the duties of institutional actors, and the decline of institutions. I begin with individual autonomy.

# 3

## Individual Autonomy

### *Agency and Structure*

## 1. INSTITUTIONAL STRUCTURE AND INDIVIDUAL AGENCY

As noted in the Introduction, it is convenient to conceive of social institutions as possessed of five dimensions, namely, activity, structure, function, culture, and sanctions.[1] However, it needs to be kept in mind that this is potentially misleading because, as we saw above, there are conceptual differences between functions and ends. On some accounts, function is a quasi-causal notion (Cohen 1978, chap. 9); on others, it is a teleological notion, albeit one that does not necessarily involve the existence of any mental states (Ryan 1970, chap. 8).

Although the structure, function, and culture of an institution provide a framework within which individuals act, they do not fully determine the actions of individuals. There are a number of reasons why this is so. For one thing, rules, norms, and ends cannot cover every contingency that might arise; for another, rules, norms, and so on themselves need to be interpreted and applied. Moreover, changing circumstances and unforeseeable problems make it desirable to vest individuals with discretionary powers to rethink and adjust old rules, norms, and ends, and sometimes elaborate new ones.[2]

Inevitably the individuals who occupy institutional roles are possessed of varying degrees of discretionary power in relation to their actions. These discretionary powers are of different kinds and operate

---

[1] The material in this chapter on agency and structure is in large part derived from Miller (2007a).
[2] On the other hand, radical revision, especially in relation to legitimate and central institutional purposes, might destroy an institution. Some think the contemporary Western university is under threat by virtue of a process of radical revision of academic purposes in favor of economic ones.

at different levels. For example, senior- and middle-level public servants have discretion in the way they implement policies, in their allocations of priorities and resources, and in the methods and criteria of evaluation of programs. Indeed, senior public servants often exercise discretion in relation to the formulation of policies. Consider that Gordon Chase, the New York Health Services Administrator, conceived, developed, and implemented the methadone program in New York in the early 1970s, notwithstanding political opposition (Warwick 1981, 93). Lower-echelon public servants also have discretionary powers. Police officers have to interpret rules and regulations, customs officers have the discretionary power to stop and search one passenger rather than another, and so on.

Traditionally, members of the so-called professions, such as doctors, lawyers, members of the clergy, engineers, and academics, have enjoyed a very high degree of individual autonomy, notwithstanding their membership in, and regulation by, professional associations. In recent times they have increasingly been housed in large, bureaucratic, hierarchical organizations in which their professional autonomy has evidently diminished somewhat (Chapter 6). Indeed, the working population more generally is increasingly employed by large, bureaucratic, hierarchical organizations, whether corporations or public-sector organizations – so much so, that arguably the central threat to individual autonomy in modern societies is no longer governments but rather corporations and nongovernment public-sector organizations (Campbell and Miller 2004).

Certain categories of individual institutional actors have discretionary powers and a reasonable degree of autonomy in the exercise of their institutional duties. However, it is not only the individual actions of institutional actors that are not fully determined by structure, function, and culture. Many joint or cooperative actions that take place in institutions are not determined by structure, function, or culture. For example, a senior public servant might put together a team of like-minded people, and they might pursue a specific agenda not determined by, and even in part inconsistent with, the prevailing institutional structure, function, or culture.

It should also be noted that legitimate individual or collective discretionary activity undertaken within an institution is typically facilitated by a rational internal structure – including role structure – by rational policy- and decision-making procedures, and by a rational institutional culture. By rational, it is here meant internally consistent, as well as rational in the light of the institution's purposes. Arguably, the corporate culture in many contemporary corporations, such as Enron, is not rational in this sense. In particular, a culture of greed, recklessness, and breaking the rules is – from the standpoint of this rationality, as opposed to the rationality of some self-interested factions within these organizations – inconsistent with a hierarchical organizational structure preoccupied with accountability. Accordingly, it is likely that many (individual and collective) discretionary judgments will be ones that do not contribute to the realization of the institution's purposes, even if they do facilitate the narrow self-interest of individuals and factional elements.

Aside from the internal dimensions of an institution, there are its external relationships, including its relationships to other institutions. In particular, there is the extent of the independence of an institution from other institutions, including government. One thinks here of the separation of powers between the legislative, executive, and judicial institutions in the United States and elsewhere.

It should be noted that, strictly speaking, independence is not the same thing as autonomy, but is rather a necessary condition for it. An institution possessed of independence from other institutions might still lack autonomy if it lacked the kinds of rational internal structure and culture noted above. Indeed, internal conflicts can paralyze an institution to the point where it becomes incapable of pursuing its institutional purposes. A university, for example, might enjoy independence from outside institutions, including government, but might be paralyzed by internal conflict between staff and students. Such conflict might take the form (in part) of ongoing demonstrations that disrupt classes, and thereby prevent lectures and tutorials from being held.

Granted that institutional actors have a degree of discretionary power, nevertheless they are constrained by institutional structure, and specifically the role structure, of the role that they occupy. As is often pointed out, institutional structure also enables the action of institutional actors. Police officers, for example, have significant powers not possessed by ordinary citizens.

However, a question arises as to the nature of the relationship between institutional structure and the agency of institutional actors. More specifically, a question arises as to whether or not one of these is logically prior to the other (or neither is). Thus some theorists, such as Émile Durkheim, are held to conceive of structure as sui generis in relation to individual agency (Durkheim 1964); and, indeed, at least in the case of structuralists such as Althusser, explanatory of human "agency" (Althusser 1971). The proposition of structuralists such as Althusser is that institutional structure (in the sense of a structure of social roles and social norms – conceived by Althusser in Marxist terms) is a basic, nonreducible feature of reality, and the actions, values, self-conceptions, and the like of individual human agents must conform to these structures because, properly understood, human agency is in fact constituted by these structures. An individual human agent is simply the repository of the roles and values of the institutions in which the agent lives his or her life. Other theorists, for instance, arguably Max Weber (Weber 1949) and methodological individualists, conceive of institutional structure as simply an abstraction from the habitual and interdependent actions of individual institutional actors. Social reality is wholly comprised of individual human agents and their ongoing, patterned interactions; there is no social structure as such. (Theorists such as Durkheim occupy a mid-position according to which there is both sui generis structure and nonreducible agency; such theorists now confront the problem of potential conflict between social structure and individual human agency – which overrides which and under what circumstances?)

In relation to this issue, Anthony Giddens has attempted to reconcile the felt reality of individual agency with the apparent need to posit some form of institutional structure that transcends individual agency (Giddens 1976, 1984).

According to Giddens, structure both is constituted by human agency and is the medium in which human action takes place (Giddens 1976, 121). This seems to mean, first, that structure is nothing other than the repetition over time of the related actions of many institutional actors. So the structure consists of (1) the habitual actions of each institutional agent, (2) the set of such agents, and (3) the relationship of interdependence between the actions of any one agent and the actions of the other agents. But it means, second, that this repetition over time of the related actions of many agents provides not just the context, but also the framework, within which the action of a single agent at a particular spatiotemporal point is performed. Structure *qua* framework constrains any given agent's action at a particular spatiotemporal point. (In addition, and as Giddens is at pains to point out, structure *qua* framework enables various actions not otherwise possible: for example, linguistic structure enables speech acts to be performed.)

This seems plausible as far as it goes; however, we are owed an account of the interdependence between the actions of different agents. On a teleological account of institutions this interdependence is in large part generated by the ends of the institutions.

Here we need to remind ourselves of a characteristic feature of institutions, namely, their reproductive capacity. Institutions reproduce themselves, or at least are disposed to do so. On the teleological account of institutions, this is in large part because the members of institutions strongly identify with the institutional ends and social norms that are definitive of those institutions, and therefore make relatively long-term commitments to institutions and induct others into those institutions.

However, it has been suggested by Roy Bhaskar and others that this reproduction of institutions is the unintended result of the free actions of institutional actors in institutional settings (Bhaskar 1979, 44). By way of support for this proposition, Bhaskar claims that people do not marry to reproduce the nuclear family or work to reproduce the capitalist system.

The first point to be made by way of response to Bhaskar is that even if the reproduction of an institution was an unintended consequence of the intentional participation of agents in that institution, it would not follow that those agents did not have various other institutional outcomes as an end. For example, members of a business might have the maximization of profit (an institutional outcome) as an explicit collective end, even if the reproduction of the company (another institutional outcome) was not intended by anyone.

The second point is that having an outcome as an implicit and/or latent collective end is not equivalent to individually explicitly intending to bring about that outcome. (An implicit collective end is one that is being pursued, but not consciously or in accordance with some explicit expression – normally linguistic – to that effect. A latent collective end is one that is being pursued, but not at that precise time: for example, not when all the members of the organization are asleep at night.) But it is implicit and/or latent collective ends that are in question, not individual explicit intentions. What is the evidence for the former in relation to Bhaskar's chosen examples?

It is plausible to assume that in the typical case of a nuclear family in a contemporary Western setting the couple married to (i.e., having as a collective end to) establish and maintain a single nuclear family; indeed, such a couple tries also to ensure that their adult children in turn establish and maintain nuclear families. Moreover, in their interaction with members of other families and with potential fathers, mothers, husbands, and wives, let us assume that the married couple in question express – often explicitly –their own commitment not only to their own nuclear family, and to the present or future nuclear families of their adult children, but also to nuclear families in general. Further, where appropriate and possible, such a married couple – let us assume – often assists members of other families to establish and maintain their own nuclear families. Arguably, these fairly plausible assumptions, if they obtain, taken in combination constitute empirical evidence that each member of the large set of such typical married individuals has – jointly with each or most of the other members of the set – an implicit and (much of the time) latent collective end to reproduce the institution of the nuclear family.

Similarly, assume that the owners and managers of a company work to maintain the existence of their company and – through training, recruitment, and so on – to ensure that it continues beyond their retirement or resignation. Moreover, assume that, in their ongoing interaction with customers and with other businesses, they knowingly – and in the case of sales and marketing personnel, intentionally – establish and maintain specific economic relationships. More generally – let us assume – they express, often explicitly, not only their commitment to their own business, but to the market system in general. Further, let us assume that where appropriate and possible, they assist in the maintenance and further development of that system, such as by voting for a market-oriented political party. Now consider a set of such companies. Arguably – given these fairly plausible assumptions – each owner and manager of any of these companies has – jointly with the others – an implicit and (much of the time) latent collective end to reproduce the market system.

Further, there are institutions, such as schools and churches, and policy-making bodies, such as governments, that are explicitly engaged in the enterprise of reproducing a variety of social institutions other than themselves. They contribute to the reproduction of various social institutions by propagating the "ideology" of these institutions, but also by advocating and, in the case of government, by implementing specific policies to ensure the reproduction of these institutions.

Doubtless, unintended consequences – or, more precisely, consequences not aimed at as an end – have an important role in the life and for that matter, the death, of institutions. Such consequences might include ones produced by evolutionary-style causal mechanisms, or ones involved in so-called hidden hand mechanisms. (Albeit, as we saw above, hidden hand mechanisms are often the product of deliberate institutional design by governments, regulators, and other policy makers, and so their consequences are in a general sense aimed at by the designers, if not by the participating institutional actors themselves.)

More specifically, habitual action is a necessary feature of individual and collective – including institutional – life, and each single action performed on the basis of a habit contributes in turn, and often unintentionally, to the maintenance and reinforcement of that habit. So the fact that institutional actors necessarily act in large part on the basis of habit means that many of their actions unintentionally contribute to the reproduction of the institution. However, this is consistent with a teleological account of social institutions – since, as noted above, there are outcomes other than institutional reproduction, and many of these are outcomes that are clearly aimed at. Moreover, it is consistent even with a teleological explanation of the reproduction of social institutions, because the establishment and periodic justificatory review of habits are themselves susceptible to teleological explanation.

In this section we have addressed the so-called agent-structure question and defended a broadly individualist and teleological account of structure. Arguably, many social institutions produce collective goods (as defined in Chapter 2); indeed, we saw in Chapter 2, on teleological (and, for that matter, functional) accounts, institutions exist to do so. However, in resolving the agent-structure question in favor of a modest form of individualism we have not thereby necessarily rescued the concept of individual autonomy. To be sure, individual agency is no longer threatened by sui generis social structures that are wholly constitutive of it. However, it does not follow that individual autonomy is not comprised by sociality and, in particular, by influential social institutions, whether these are conceived as broadly individualist and teleological in character or not.

## 2. INSTITUTIONS AND INDIVIDUAL AUTONOMY

This section is concerned with the relationship between the autonomy of the individual human agent and social institutions, and specifically with an alleged problem for individual autonomy arising from social institutions.[3] The problem stems from the fact that individual agents are necessarily influenced, indeed conditioned, by the social institutions that they inhabit. Individual agents make choices within a preexisting framework of social institutions, including hierarchical organizations comprised in part of relationships of authority and power. The attitudes

---

[3]   The material in this section is in large part derived from Miller (2003b). On this general issue see Benn (1988, 169, 179, 194–8, chap. 12); Dworkin (1988, chap. 10); Benson

of individual agents, including their desires and beliefs, are dependent on social attitudes, such as approval and disapproval. Moreover, the very abilities of individual agents to make appropriately autonomous responses to these social institutions and associated attitudes – abilities such as the ability to reason, or to imagine alternative possibilities to the ones socially presented to them – are themselves socially provided, conditioned, and constrained. In short, what and who an individual agent is, and which choices he or she makes, is necessarily in large part a function of his or her past and present institutional environments. Does not this fact undermine the possibility of individual autonomy?

Human beings do not, for the most part, freely decide whether or not to be the kinds of creatures that want to eat, or to have sex, or to communicate with one another; they must eat to live, and they are by nature sexually oriented, and communicative.

The fact that human beings have a range of basic needs and natural inclinations does not undermine the possibility of their being autonomous; rather, it places constraints on their decision making. Human beings need to eat, but what, when, how, how much, and so on is very much a matter of individual and collective choice. And one element of collective choice is choice of conventions; it is a matter of (often rational) collective choice whether this convention rather than some alternative convention is established for the purpose of realizing a given end.[4]

Nor does the fact that some of these needs or inclinations are essentially interpersonal, such as communication and sex, mean that the shared ends that they give rise to somehow constitute a threat to the individual autonomy of the agents pursuing those ends. Once again, whom one has sex with, when and what one communicates, and the like are very much matters of individual, interpersonal, and collective choice. Moreover, an important element of collective choice in all this is the choice of conventions in relation to ends that derive from basic interpersonal needs and inclinations. Consider here the collective choice of linguistic conventions in relation to the interpersonal need for communication.

What of grasping the validity of objective moral principles? Human beings do not freely decide that murder or rape is morally wrong; rather,

---

(1991); Christman (1991); Kekes (1989, chap. 5, 111–12); May (1996, 18–20); Mackenzie (2001).

[4] I do not mean to imply that a choice between conventions is necessarily an arbitrary choice. Sometimes such collective choices are arbitrary, but this is by no means necessarily the case. See Miller (2001b, chap. 3). Nor do I mean to imply that rational choices always result from explicit – as opposed to implicit – processes of reasoning.

they make a (correct) judgment that this is so. This judgment is truth aiming and can be said to be "free" only in this somewhat limited sense. The fact that judgments, including many, if not all, moral judgments, ought to be constrained by the truth does not somehow compromise or diminish the autonomy of the person making those judgments – any more than the need to be constrained by scientific facts diminishes the autonomy of scientists engaged in scientific work.

Indeed, being able to make correct moral judgments is a necessary condition for moral agency, and therefore for being an autonomous moral agent. By my lights, a being who was not disposed to make correct moral judgments – and act on them – would not be a moral agent, and therefore would not be an autonomous moral agent.

Moreover, a rational, moral agent who, nevertheless, frequently infringed fundamental moral principles – either because he or she made incorrect moral judgments or because he or she chose to ignore his or her correct moral judgments – would not be acting as an autonomous moral agent. The autonomy of such an agent is significantly diminished by the fact that he or she frequently, and in fundamental ways, acts against his or her nature as a moral agent. Such an agent would be a grossly immoral agent, as opposed to a nonmoral agent. If an immoral agent is not acting freely, but acting, say, under inner compulsion, then he is not acting autonomously. On the other hand, if an immoral agent is acting freely, then he is, nevertheless, not necessarily acting autonomously. In particular, if he is a grossly immoral agent, then he is not acting autonomously; rather, he is acting, so to speak, with license.

On the other hand, even autonomous moral agents make some false moral judgments, and sometimes fail to act on their correct moral judgments. Suppose a moral agent makes an important false moral judgment that is inconsistent with a prevailing (objectively correct) social norm. Or suppose the agent makes the correct moral judgment, but nevertheless fails to act on it; she knowingly does wrong. Is there not now a conflict between the autonomy of the individual agent and compliance with morally correct social norms? No doubt there is a conflict; I am not suggesting that being autonomous entails making correct moral judgments all the time and always acting on one's correct moral judgments. Rather, the point I am making is that given the objective character of at least most important moral issues, there is no in-principle inconsistency between individual autonomy and social norms. In theory, they can, and ought to, coincide; autonomous individuals and reflective societies can, and ought to, agree on moral truths.

It might be responded to all this that the real problem with social
norms, as distinct from objective moral principles grasped by autonomous moral agents, is that social norms – whether they embody objective
moral principles or not – constitute a coercive imposition on the individual members of social groups and social institutions.

The notion of coercion being used here is somewhat opaque, but there
is no doubt that social norms can have a coercive function, for example,
a social norm according to which the so-called untouchables in India are
treated as inferior.[5] Specifically, members of a class, social group (be it
racially, sexually, culturally, economically, or otherwise delineated), or
occupants of a particular type or level of organizational role sometimes
act jointly, albeit informally and even unconsciously, to exercise power
over members of another class, social group, or set of role occupants.
Social norms that express hierarchies of status and manifest power relationships can play a key role in this regard, for instance, social norms
governing the relations between blacks and whites in apartheid South
Africa. However, the question is whether this is a necessary feature of
social norms. I suggest that it is not. Here we need to distinguish two different kinds of issue. The first issue pertains to induction into a moral
community conceived as a set of social institutions. It is a necessary – but
not a sufficient – condition for an individual human being initially grasping the validity of moral principles that they are inducted as a child into
some moral community. But it would not follow from this that the principles were coercively imposed on the individual, that the individual did
not come to grasp the truth of the principles, or that he does not later in
life freely conform to the principles. Rather, the learning environment
provided by the moral community and, in particular, by social institutions, such as the family and educational institutions, is a necessary condition for the individual initially coming to grasp moral principles, as an
initial grasp of mathematical principles might require a teacher.

Another kind of issue concerns the continued conformity of rational,
moral adults to the current social norms of the social institutions that
they inhabit. With respect to many moral principles, it is plausible that
a necessary – but not sufficient – condition for the continued conformity of one autonomous agent is the continued conformity – together
with the persistence of the associated moral attitudes – of the other
occupants of the social institutions in question. There are a number of

---

[5] See Stanley Benn (1988, chap. 12) for a taxonomy of social groups in relation to degrees
of social control.

reasons why this might be so, three of which I will explain and illustrate below. However, the general point to be made is that from the fact that an agent's conformity to a moral principle is in part dependent on the conformity to that moral principle on the part of others, and/or on the existence of relevant associated moral attitudes in others, it does not follow that the moral principle has been coercively imposed on the agent, and that therefore the agent's autonomy is diminished or otherwise compromised.

The first of the above-mentioned reasons is as follows. Sometimes the failure of others to conform to a moral principle provides a reasonable excuse, and perhaps an adequate moral justification, for one's own non-conformity. If others tell lies to me, or break promises to me, or steal from me, does not this give me an excuse for doing likewise? After all, if I continue to comply with principles of truth telling, or promise keeping, or respect for property when others do not, I will be exploited and I might even suffer great harm. Surely turning the other cheek is not in all such circumstances a moral requirement.

So with respect to some moral principles, it is necessary that others conform to them, if I am reasonably to be expected to do so. Accordingly, when I conform in a context of general conformity – and conform in part because others conform – I may well be acting reasonably, and (other things being equal) autonomously. Certainly there is no reason to think that my conformity to such moral principles is necessarily the result of coercion. I conclude that the fact that my continuing conformity to a social norm is in part dependent on the continuing conformity of others does not necessarily diminish my autonomy.[6]

The second of the three reasons why the conformity and moral attitudes of others might be a necessary condition for my own conformity can be explained and illustrated as follows. Sometimes other agents' disapproval of a given moral agent's nonconformity to a moral principle is a necessary condition for the conformity of that moral agent to that moral principle. (Or, at least, other agents' disapproval of the agent's nonconformity and approval of his conformity is a necessary condition for the agent's conformity.) Assume that the agent in question generally acts in accordance with moral principles, and assume that he believes

---

[6] Naturally, if nonconformity to social norms is such that the very existence of a moral community is called into question, then it might no longer be possible to function as a moral agent, and therefore as an autonomous moral agent. In this respect individual autonomy, at least for social beings, is dependent on general conformity to central moral principles. See the last section of this chapter.

conformity to this particular moral principle is the right thing to do. Nevertheless, the agent might be tempted to infringe this principle, and some other moral principles, and might actually infringe all of these moral principles, were it not for the disapproving attitudes of other agents. Consider certain kinds of corruption.

Suppose the agent in question is given a very demanding position of great political power, but one with a meager financial reward. Suppose, further, that he is occasionally offered bribes to ensure that government tenders on offer go to one of a number of foreign contractors. He knows that it is morally wrong, but he also knows that accepting foreign bribes is not unlawful – so he will go unpunished – and that his wrongful actions will go undiscovered. Moreover, his life, and that of his family, will be made a great deal easier if he accepts the bribe. He also resents having to work so hard and under such great pressure for so little reward. He feels inclined to start taking the bribes on offer. At this point he remembers that others would strongly disapprove of his accepting a bribe, and he does care what other people think of him. Of course, since his actions will go undiscovered, he will never in fact have to suffer their disapproval. However, he worries about what they would think of him, if they knew what he had done. For he is not seeking misplaced approval; nor is his fundamental concern to avoid justified disapproval. Rather, he desires justifiably to be approved of and justifiably to avoid being disapproved of. Accordingly, he refuses the bribe.

In the above scenario, the agent's belief that accepting bribes is wrong, taken in conjunction with his desire both for the justified approval of others and to avoid their justified disapproval, is sufficient to cause him to refuse the bribe. Here one contrast is with an agent who does what is morally right only because it is morally right, and thus entirely independently of what the attitudes of others might be. What others might think or not think of its actions in itself makes no difference to its actions. (Of course, it cares what others might do to it as a result of their attitudes to it.) Perhaps such a moral agent is autonomous; however, I suggest that it is not a recognizable (autonomous) human agent.[7] Human beings are social animals, and care deeply about what others think of them. Accordingly, obliviousness to the moral approval and disapproval of others cannot be a necessary condition for the moral autonomy of human beings.

---

[7] Perhaps it is something like what those of a Kantian persuasion have in mind when they speak of rational, moral agents.

Another contrasting agent to the one in the above-described scenario is an agent who cares about what others think of them, but who lacks a certain self-awareness. Assume that this second contrasted agent believes that taking bribes is morally wrong and is influenced by this consideration, but – like the agent in the original scenario – this agent is even more strongly influenced by the temptations afforded by the bribe, given bribe taking is not unlawful he will go unpunished, and so on. However, assume that there is an important difference between this agent and the one in the original scenario. This agent decides to take the bribes. He does so because he thinks that his desire for the moral approval of others, and his aversion to their moral disapproval, will be satisfied, just so long as he is not found out; and he knows that he will not be found out.

Here we need to get clear what the precise nature of the attitude of moral approval and moral disapproval is. The whole point of the attitude of moral approval is that the person approved of has done what is morally right, and vice versa for the attitude of moral disapproval. So person A morally approves of person B for the reason that person B does what is right. Accordingly, if B desires A's moral approval, then B desires not only that A approve of B because A believes that B does what is right; B also desires that A approve of B because A *knows* that B does what is right. Naturally, if A falsely believes that B does what is morally right, then A will morally approve of B. However, the point is that B will not have secured what B desired. For B knows that he, B, has not done what is right, and that therefore A's attitude of approval is not the kind of approval that he, B, desires; B desires to be approved of because he has in fact done what is right.[8]

Now let us return to the second agent we contrasted with the agent in our original scenario. Recall that this second contrasting agent desires both moral approval and to avoid moral disapproval. However, on the basis of our discussion of the nature of moral approval and disapproval,

---

[8]  Perhaps there are desires for approval (and to avoid disapproval) that are possessed, irrespective of whether or not the approval (or disapproval) is justified. (In my view, these would not be desires for *moral* [dis-]approval.) If so, and if the desire of the agent in our scenario were this kind of desire, then the realization of this agent's desire would not be affected by his belief that he had done wrong; for such a desire is realized if, and only if, the agent is approved of by others. If the agent in our scenario had this kind of desire, then it may well be rational for him to take the bribes on offer. For he would not have a conflict between taking the bribes and acting on his desire to be approved of. (There would still be a conflict with his belief not to do wrong, but that was outweighed, in our scenario, by other considerations.) On the other hand, if the agent in our scenario had a genuine desire for *moral* approval (and to avoid moral disapproval), then there would be a conflict between this desire and his taking the bribes. For this desire

we can now see that he will not fully or adequately realize his desire. For although he does not see this at the time of his decision to take the bribes, his desire is not simply to be an object of moral approval (and to avoid being an object of disapproval); rather, it is a desire to be an object of moral approval (and to avoid being an object of moral disapproval) because he has, in fact, done what is right, and avoided doing what is wrong. So this agent, unlike the agent in the original scenario, lacks a certain reflective self-awareness in relation to the nature of his desire for moral approval and the avoidance of moral disapproval.

The agent in the original scenario cares about what others think of him; he desires their moral approval. But he is also reflectively self-aware in relation to this desire; he knows what it is that he really desires in this regard. What is the significance of this for the relationship between individual autonomy and the (dis-)approval of others?

I have described a certain kind of moral agent who is susceptible to corruption, but who, nevertheless, is able to resist corruption in part because of his belief that corruption is morally wrong, and in part because of his desire justifiably to be morally approved of and justifiably to avoid being disapproved of. So this agent cares what others think of him to the extent of being influenced by their moral approval and disapproval; in this he is at one with most human beings. Yet the fact that this agent in this way cares what others think of him does not diminish his autonomy, and certainly it does not show that he has been coerced by others. For the moral attitudes of other agents constitute only a necessary, but not a sufficient, condition for his moral probity. Moreover, the performance of the morally significant action of refusing to take the bribes – the action in part motivated by his desire for others' moral approval and the avoidance of their moral disapproval – is actively mediated by his awareness of the nature of this desire of his. This kind of action-guiding self-awareness is indicative of autonomous moral agency.

I conclude that the existence of social norms sustained in part by the moral approval and moral disapproval of others is quite consistent with individual autonomy, and therefore that the individuals who conform to those norms are by no means necessarily coerced into so doing.

Let me now explain and illustrate a third and final reason why the conformity and moral attitudes of other agents might be a necessary

---

could not be adequately and fully realized if he takes the bribes. Rather, his taking of the bribes would sour the enjoyment he used to experience as a result of the moral approval of others. Accordingly, it may well be rational for him to refuse the bribes.

condition for a given agent's conformity. The agent in question might not even reasonably have a belief in certain moral principles, in the absence of conformity to those principles by other agents, and in the absence of those agents' ongoing expressions of disapproval of nonconformity.

Consider a traditional community in which there is an abhorrence of engaging in homosexual practices. Everyone believes that engaging in homosexual practices is morally wrong, even the minority who feel inclined to engage in them. Now assume that the beliefs of the community in relation to homosexual practices are incorrect; there is nothing morally wrong with these practices. Further, assume that over time these beliefs will be challenged on the basis of rational scrutiny, and, indeed, will eventually be overturned. Naturally, mutual belief in, and continued conformity to, a set of moral principles may at times require reflection, explicit widespread discussion, and public communication; what might be required from time to time is a kind of explicit collective reaffirmation of the group's moral principles. Likewise, the abandonment of certain hitherto accepted moral principles may involve such ongoing processes of collective discussion and decision.

At any rate, in the anti–homosexual practices phase it does not even occur to most heterosexually inclined persons to question their abhorrence of homosexual practices. For although that abhorrence is partly socially instilled, it is also in part sustained by the fact that it is psychologically conducive – they themselves find the sexual advances of members of the same sex somewhat repellent. No doubt the majority should question their moral beliefs in regard to homosexual practices, but they do not; and it is understandable why they do not. In our example a necessary, but not sufficient, condition for the (incorrect) moral belief of almost any individual member of the community is the (incorrect) moral beliefs of most of the other members of the community. Nevertheless, the autonomy of the majority (heterosexually inclined) members of the community is not diminished by virtue of their incorrect moral beliefs about homosexual practices. To see this, consider the homosexual minority. By contrast with the heterosexual majority, the autonomy of the homosexual minority is diminished by the prevailing social norms. Specifically, the social norms are an obstacle to the sexual self-expression of the minority homosexually inclined group.

The basic point to be extracted from our explanatory discussions and illustrations is that social norms taken individually do not necessarily threaten individual autonomy. For any given social norm need only be such that the moral attitudes and conformity of others is a necessary, but not a sufficient, condition for one's own moral attitude and conformity. However, the question remains as to whether an individual's autonomy is threatened by social institutions, that is, structured sets of roles and social norms. Let us turn to the most obvious kind of institutional threat to individual autonomy, namely, hierarchical institutions.

## 3. INSTITUTIONAL HIERARCHIES

As we have seen, organizations consist of an (embodied) formal structure of interlocking roles.[9] And these roles can be defined in terms of specialized tasks governed by procedures and conventions. Moreover, unlike social groups, organizations are individuated by the kind of tasks that their members undertake, and by their characteristic functions or ends. So we have governments, universities, business corporations, armies, and so on. Perhaps governments have as an end or goal the ordering and leading of societies, universities the end of discovering and disseminating knowledge, and so on.

### Hierarchies of Power

Most societies at most times have made use of, and been comprised in part of, organizations. Moreover, the structure of organizations has varied enormously. Some are extremely hierarchical with an emphasis on formal (rules and structures) as well as informal (via conventions and social norms) control of the individual behavior and attitudes of their members. Military organizations have traditionally been of this kind. It is often claimed that Japanese organizations, including corporations and government departments, are also of this sort, although with the qualification that employees are looked after and treated well as long as they conform to prevailing conventions and norms and obey their superiors. Other organizations, such as Western universities, have been more collegial in character.

As noted above, the workforce in contemporary societies is increasingly employed by large, bureaucratic, hierarchical organizations such as corporations and public-sector organizations. Accordingly, the interactions that individual human beings have, whether as consumers, employees, or ordinary citizens, is increasingly with organizations, rather than other individuals, and these interactions are characterized by lopsided power

---

[9]  See Harre (1979, 37–43) for an account of structure. See also Miller (2001b, chap. 5).

relationships; the relatively powerless individual human being confronts a large, well-resourced, and much more powerful organization.

Large, bureaucratic, hierarchical organizations not only possess power by virtue of their financial and personnel resources, they also possess power by virtue of their legally backed hierarchical authority in relation to their employees in particular. Moreover, the institutional structure of modern societies is such that for most citizens there is no realistic alternative to interacting with large, powerful organizations in most institutional settings, including the marketplace as consumers and employees. Clearly, in modern societies these organizations constitute an in-principle threat to individual autonomy. This threat is implicitly recognized in the establishment of trade unions, minimum wages for workers, consumer protection agencies, and so on.

However, although governmental and nongovernmental institutional authorities wield power, they are also dependent on collective acceptance.[10] As a consequence, institutional authorities are vulnerable; for example, once people choose not to obey a government's directives, for example, it is finished; it simply ceases to function or exist as a government. Nor is the point here simply that, say, rulers cannot exercise their right to rule, if their right to rule is not collectively accepted, although this is in fact the case. Rather, a ruler does not even possess a right to rule unless she is able to exercise authority over her subjects.

The actions of those in authority constitute in large part the exercise of power. As such, these actions of authorities are an in-principle threat to individual autonomy, albeit one that depends for its order of magnitude on a variety of factors, including the possibility of subordinates engaging in their own organized, collective action. Indeed, arguably this in-principle threat might cease to exist under certain conditions, for example, if the institutional authority is subject to consensual democracy.

As we have seen, the power of institutional authorities is dependent on collective acceptance. To this extent institutional power is potentially constrained by autonomous individuals acting collectively. However, collective acceptance might be passive in a sense of passivity consistent with the nonexistence of autonomy. Moreover, even if a majority actively

---

[10] Language does not in this way depend on collective acceptance. For an account of the dependence of language on "collective acceptance," and specifically on conventions, see Miller (2000a).

accepts some authority – that is, they exercise their autonomy in accepting the authority – it might still be the case that a minority do not.

As is well known, institutional mechanisms have been developed to deal with this problem of respect for individual autonomy in the context of hierarchical organizations. Democratic processes are perhaps the most important category of such institutional mechanisms. The basic idea is a very familiar one. It involves each individual autonomously participating in the democratic process, and deciding to abide by the outcome of that democratic process, such as voting for a particular leader and accepting the outcome of the vote.

Insofar as individuals autonomously choose to participate in organizational hierarchies – and, therefore, have viable alternatives – or insofar as individuals autonomously accept, say, democratic decision procedures, and those democratic decision procedures permeate organizational hierarchies, then organizational hierarchies are not necessarily inconsistent with individual autonomy. Rather, they are simply a species of joint decision-making procedures. However, they are joint decision-making procedures in which although each individual exercises his or her autonomy jointly and equally with others in respect of some issues, each does not do so equally with respect to all matters (or at least does so only indirectly via some subgroup with a greater share of power). However, to reiterate, in contemporary societies (at least), organizational hierarchies, such as large public- and private-sector bureaucracies, are unavoidable, and are not subject to pervasive democratic decision-making procedures. Accordingly, individual autonomy is compromised. Moreover, individual autonomy is also compromised in nondemocratic nation-states, and even in democratic nation-states – because in the contemporary world, at least, there is no real option but to live in a nation-state, and thereby to be subject to governmental control.

## Hierarchies of Status

Thus far we have been speaking of institutional hierarchies of power; we have not discussed hierarchies of status. Hierarchies of status are an important feature of hierarchical institutions in that they reflect and reinforce the hierarchical authority and power structures constitutive of these institutions.

Status hierarchies, like organizational hierarchies, are dependent on collective acceptance; indeed, they are produced, sustained, and in part constituted by collective attitudes of approval. Status hierarchies, but not necessarily organizational power structures, depend on mobilizing attitudes of approval and the desire to be approved. The attitude of approval here used is a generic one embracing admiration and the desire to be admired, respect and the desire to be respected, and even envy and the desire to be envied; it is not simply the narrow notion of moral approval.

The attitudes of approval that are constitutive of status hierarchies have a certain structure of interdependence. Here we need to distinguish interdependence of attitude from interdependence of action. One agent does not perform some action X on condition the other agents perform X. Rather there is interdependence of attitude: that is, one agent approves of some agent A or some action X (performed by A) on condition the other agents approve of A or X. Let us refer to such a structure of interdependence with respect to the attitudes of approval within some social group as collective approval.

This interdependence of attitude needs also to be distinguished from the collective interdependence of attitudes and actions. In the latter case an agent performs an action X on the condition that everyone, including himself, approves of his X-ing – the agent is motivated by a desire to meet his own expectations of himself, as well as the expectations of others. This is not collective approval in the required sense.

One of the most important aspects of the desire for social approval is the desire for high status, including the high status attaching to upper-echelon roles in institutional hierarchies; and one of the most important effects of social approval is high status, including the high status that attaches to occupancy of upper-echelon roles in institutional hierarchies. Individuals seek the high status attaching to the institutional role of president of the nation, high court judge, CEO of a corporation, or Oxford University professor because they want to be approved of, and to possess such a high status *is* to be socially approved of; indeed, it is to be collectively approved of in our above sense. Conversely, the high status attaching to these institutional roles is sustained by collective approval, that is, by the fact that individuals who gain these positions are the objects of interdependent attitudes of approval for so doing.

Institutionally based status hierarchies – and, therefore to an extent, institutional power – can be reinforced or undermined by moral beliefs. Priests, for example, have traditionally enjoyed a position high in an institutionally based status hierarchy. However, this high institutionally based status of priests is heavily dependent on the moral beliefs of Roman Catholics, such as that priests are moral leaders; thus the coming to light of numerous cases of sexual abuse on the part of priests has threatened this status hierarchy and plunged the Catholic Church into a deep institutional crisis.

More generally, a person's reputational status in a community typically depends to some extent on the beliefs members of the community have about his or her moral probity; hence in many communities criminals are shunned, and those who work for the common good are admired. This relationship between reputational status and ethical "performance" is one that can be exploited to achieve the collective ends of institutions, such as when politicians pursue the common good, albeit motivated in part by a desire to enhance their reputations and, thereby, stay in office. (See Chapter 6 for a detailed discussion of this issue and related joint mechanisms, such as reputational indices for corporations.)

On the other hand, approval-based status and morality can be antithetical. This is perhaps most evident in the case of totalitarian leaders. Consider, for example, the adulation of the genocidal maniac Hitler on the part of the crowds at the Nuremberg and other rallies.

Untrammeled pursuit of the high status attaching to upper-echelon institutional roles, and the concomitant adulation of those who already have this high status by virtue of their occupancy of these roles, can amount to a form of servility on the part of both pursuers and adulators; a subjugation of self to collective approval (as well as to institutionally based power). Consider the adulation of billionaire corporate leaders among those in the business community and, for that matter, the wider society. The Australian billionaire media and casino tycoon, and notorious "high roller," Kerry Packer, for example, was given a state funeral when he died. On the other hand, the dependence of high status on changeable collective attitudes makes those with high status vulnerable to their erstwhile adulators. Billionaire Wall Street bankers are held in much less regard during the current global financial markets' "meltdown" than they were before it. Before the crisis they were envied in many quarters as highly intelligent, hugely successful, market actors whose financial wizardry should not be overregulated, let alone curtailed; now they are simply greedy, if not criminal, speculators who have brought the financial system to its knees and whose activities should have been subject to intrusive oversight and regulation, if allowed at all.

Status-based adulation, and its associated servility, is at odds with individual autonomy. The most obvious mode of protection of individual autonomy from corrosive status hierarchies is a commitment to certain objective moral principles on the part of the individuals who make up, or interact with, the relevant institutions and with their associated status hierarchies: specifically, a commitment to the principle of the equal worth of human beings in respect of their capacity for autonomous decision making. This principle, and related objective moral principles, can come to be social norms in institutional settings: social norms that diminish institutionally based status hierarchies and, thereby, constrain institutional power and thus protect individual autonomy. Naturally these moral principles may need to be deliberately designed in to institutional structures if they are to take root as social norms and, thereby, limit status addiction. The democratization of the structures of business corporations is one such design option (Lane 2004).

## 4. THE THREAT OF THE PAST

The social institutions that condition the actions of individual persons predate and postdate the actions, interactions, and, indeed, lives of particular generations of individual persons. Accordingly individual persons are not simply inducted into a social world; they are inducted into a sociohistorical world (Miller 2001b, introduction). Does the historicity of social institutions threaten individual autonomy?

Individuals are inducted into the social forms and other social ideas of the past – including socially communicated theories, quasi theories, and moral narratives. But these social forms and social ideas do not constitute a monolithic structure; rather, they comprise a miscellany of sometimes competing conventions, norms, institutions, and socially conditioned theories and narratives. Moreover, the residue of the past consists of more than social forms and social ideas; it also contains the ideas, memories, and handed-down skills that derive from the individual – as opposed to collective – lives of past generations. For example, a mother might have had personal moral experiences particular to herself, which she might make known to her daughter, but not to others. Or the unique ideas of a great philosopher might become known to future generations of thinkers.

And there is this further point. Individuals do not confront the residue of the social forms of the past as atoms; they confront it – or rather participate in it – jointly. It does not follow from this that any given generation of individuals can simply abandon these social forms – far from it. However, it does follow that these social forms are to a greater or lesser extent subject to change, and in some instances rejection, and that they are often changed and rejected in accordance with more or less rational processes. At any rate, these processes of change do not involve actions other than the actions of individual human beings. Further, these processes consist in large part of the joint activity of individual actors.

An important corollary of this conception is that much joint activity takes place over an extended period of time, and, specifically, intergenerationally. The building of the Great Wall of China and the development of the literary form of the novel are in each case intergenerational joint projects. More generally, most important institutions involve intergenerational joint projects. Consider universities or governments or hospitals.

The historicity of social action, and specifically of social institutions, does not seem, at least in principle, to threaten individual autonomy, any more than the existence of present social action and social institutions threatens it; social actions and social institutions, whether residues of the past or newly arrived, are essentially manifestations of joint activity. As such, they do not constitute an in-principle threat to autonomy. But here we need to take a closer look at the impact of past decisions on present ones.

In this connection I want to draw attention to two constraints on practical reasoning in accordance with historically established social institutions, and therefore on the actions of autonomous moral agents (Miller 2001b, 151–9).

The first constraint on practical reasoning arises in relation to participation in long-term projects, including historically established institutional enterprises.

An agent living in a moral community[11] typically contributes to a variety of long-term projects that (a) realize collective, and not simply individual, ends[12] and (b) are historically established and intergenerational in character. Notable among such long-term projects are historically established institutional enterprises that realize not only individual ends, but also, more importantly, collective ends that are pursued (at least in part) because they are believed to be morally worthy ends; such ends include collective goods (as defined in Chapter 2). Consider in this connection a school teacher, a doctor in a hospital, a police officer, or a worker in the clothes industry. And consider a taxpayer or a voter or a parent.

---

[11] My use of the term *moral community* in this book is in contrast with non-moral community, as opposed to immoral community.

[12] Roughly speaking, a collective end is an individual end more than one agent has, and that is such that, if it is realized, it is realized by all, or most, of the actions of the individuals involved. See Chapter 1; see also Miller (2001b, 57).

Michael Bratman has considered rationality in relation to long-term projects, albeit not collective long-term projects, and therefore not intergenerational collective projects. Bratman has successfully argued, in relation to the future-directed intentions involved in long-term projects, that it might be rational for an agent with such intentions not to reconsider one of those intentions, even though it might be rational to reconsider that intention, and indeed change it, from an all things considered external viewpoint (Bratman 1987, chap. 6).[13] The general point here is that finite agents that are long-term planners need to build a degree of stability into their future-directed intentions or ends if they are to achieve them; they need to focus on the means to the end, rather than constantly questioning the rationality or wisdom of the long-term end itself, or embarking on a different project that would realize a different end. So there is a presumption in favor of maintaining, rather than abandoning, long-term ends and projects.

In light of Bratman's point, and given that historically established institutional enterprises are a species of long-term project, there is a presumption in favor of an agent who is participating in a historically established institutional enterprise not to abandon that enterprise.

However, there will be restrictions on the choices of participants in (intergenerational) institutional enterprises that might not exist, or exist to the same extent, in individual, long-term projects. In the case of collective projects, the participation of any given agent is dependent on the participation of the other agents; so if the other agents abandon the project, then typically the given agent has no choice but also to abandon it. Moreover, in the case of institutional enterprises in particular, usually a would-be participant necessarily embarks on the project after it is already in progress; she participates in a project that is at a stage, and in

---

[13] The notion of an all things considered external viewpoint is by no means unproblematic, even when we are speaking of a single agent at a particular time and in respect of a specific future project. When we consider collective projects, then we have multiple agents, and therefore multiple all things considered external viewpoints; and when we consider intergenerational collective projects, then we have multiples of multiple agents and external viewpoints. Moreover, with such projects we have multiple agents, both at a given time and over intergenerational time, all of whom are engaged in interdependent decision making with at least some of the other agents. Accordingly, we have multiple all things considered external viewpoints, each of which has to take into consideration the things being taken into consideration by the other external viewpoints. At this point, we start to lose our grip on the notion of an all things considered external viewpoint. Perhaps we invoke God! At any rate, for my purposes here all I need to do is gesture at the intuitive and vague *idea* of an all – or most – or many-things-considered external viewpoint.

a condition, not of her own choosing. In addition, since an institutional project is a collective project, typically any given agent cannot determine the precise nature and direction of the project; for the agent is only one among a possibly very large number of contributors.

These above-mentioned general points seem to hold for intellectual institutions, as well as other institutions. On the other hand, intellectual institutions need to allow greater individual freedom within them than is the case for some other institutions (Chapter 8).

Before embarking on a long-term individual project, a rational individual agent will go through an intensive process of reason-based decision making, and specifically a process that looks at the individual actions that she will be performing and the individual ends that she will realize. However, as we have seen above, once a single agent has decided to embark on such a project, the agent ought to have a presumption in favor of not abandoning it. This presumption in favor of continued participation in any such project or enterprise can be offset by rational and moral considerations: for example, the end or goal of the project can no longer be achieved, or the end or goal of the project has come to be seen as less important than some other ends that would be realized by other projects; but there is, nevertheless, a presumption to be offset.[14]

Moreover, for the same reasons as apply in the case of a single, rational agent, a given set of individual agents, once they have embarked on a long-term collective project, ought to have a presumption in favor of not abandoning the project. Accordingly, each of the member agents of the set of agents ought to have a presumption *qua* member of the set of agents participating in that collective project in favor of not abandoning the project. Thus, members of a historically established institutional enterprise, such as a legal system, ought to have a presumption against abandoning that institution. This presumption in favor of continued participation can be offset by rational, including moral, considerations; but there is, nevertheless, a presumption to be offset.[15]

---

[14] So from time to time during the course of a long-term project a rational agent will engage in a reconsideration of the project and their participation in the project. At such reconsiderations one of the questions raised would be whether or not the presumption in favor of not abandoning the project has been offset. Such reconsiderations ought to be relatively infrequent, given the costs they incur.

[15] Of course, the institution, over time, can be transformed in sometimes very significant ways, if that is desirable.

The existence of this presumption amounts to a constraint on each agent's practical reasoning in relation to their continued participation in both long-term individual and long-term joint projects, including historically established institutional enterprises.

But notice that we have now identified two aspects of the presumption in favor of agents not abandoning long-term collective projects, including institutional enterprises. For the presumption is possessed by any given participating individual agent *qua* individual agent performing individual actions in pursuit of individual ends, albeit in the context of a collective enterprise; but it is also possessed by each participating individual agent *qua* member of the set of agents participating in the collective enterprise. The presumption against an individual agent – *qua* individual agent pursuing individual ends – abandoning the collective project might be offset by some other consideration particular to her: for instance, she has a personally rewarding individual project to pursue. However, it would not follow from this that the collective project ought to be abandoned – far from it. More specifically, it would not even follow from this that the individual agent in question ought to abandon the collective project. For *qua* member of the set of participating agents, perhaps she ought not to abandon the collective project; perhaps she is making a valuable contribution to an important collective end. In that case the individual would find herself in a dilemma. There is no reason to think that she would not be able to resolve the dilemma; after all, she remains one agent, albeit one agent who functions as an agent performing actions in the service of individual ends, as well as an agent performing (sometimes the same) actions in the service of collective ends. Nevertheless, there may well be a dilemma to resolve.

This first constraint on an agent's practical reasoning does not threaten her individual autonomy. To be sure, individual autonomy is diminished if the range of historically established institutions that individuals can choose from is highly restricted. Consider a simple society without art, music, or any developed intellectual traditions or institutions. Moreover, agents who want to engage in long-term joint projects, including historically established institutions, will have to pay a price of sorts; they will not at all times be in possession of an all things considered good and decisive rational justification for their participation in any given project – indeed, from an all things considered external viewpoint it might be that they should abandon the project; they will be dependent on the contributions of others; they will have to join the institution when it is at a stage and in a condition not of their choosing; and any given individual cannot determine the nature and direction of an institutional enterprise. But for this price they receive the benefit of being able to complete and contribute to larger projects, and thereby realize, and contribute to the realization of, much greater ends than would otherwise be the case.

Indeed, it is typically in the context of long-term joint enterprises, especially historically established institutional enterprises, that the greatest achievements are made. Consider the cathedrals built in Europe in the Middle Ages. Or consider the contribution of a notable scientist to the understanding of problems in, say, physics. Surely when agents participate in such enterprises their autonomy is often thereby enhanced, rather than necessarily diminished. For, on the one hand, they may well achieve individual ends beyond what they would otherwise have been able to achieve, such as the exercise of their creative ability as a craftsman or physicist, and on the other hand, they may well contribute to a collective end of enormous significance, such as the construction of one of the highest expressions of collective aesthetic, moral, and spiritual value, namely, a famous cathedral, or a theoretical framework that illuminates a range of profound and long-standing intellectual questions in relation to the nature of the physical universe.

The second constraint on practical reasoning that I wish to draw attention to arises in connection with whole structures of historically established social norms. This constraint arises from the fact that any given agent's conformity to a given set of social norms is by definition to a considerable extent dependent on the conformity, and the moral attitudes, of the past and present others who conform, or conformed, to those social norms. Here it is important to stress that any given moral agent involved in diverse interactions with other moral agents conforms not simply to one or two social norms, but rather to a large and complex structure of social norms. Moreover, for finite creatures such as human beings, such a structure of social norms is necessarily in large part intergenerational in character; when it comes to the establishment of a complete, or near complete, structure of social norms governing individual and interpersonal actions, each new generation cannot simply begin anew.

Nevertheless, this conformity to a historically established structure of social norms might still seem to be an irrational addiction to the past, and therefore a threat to individual autonomy. So it is important to get clear what exactly the constraints on autonomy are in this regard. Here a number of points need to be made.

First, a single rational agent (at least in theory) could reconsider with a view to revision, or even abandonment, any one of the moral principles he or she adheres to, while continuing to conform to the other principles.[16] However, he or she could not revise and abandon all or most of these principles at the same time on pain of losing his or her individual self-identity – moral identity being a necessary condition for the self-identity of most human beings.[17] The same point holds for a set of rational agents jointly reconsidering the moral principles that they adhere to as members of a moral community; in theory any one principle could be revised, and even abandoned, but not the totality simultaneously.

Second, a single, rational, human agent could not – even over a significant period of time – individually reconsider and revise, let alone abandon all, or even most, of the moral principles that they originally adhered to, on pain of not being able to continue to cooperatively interact with the fellow members of their moral community.

Third, the members of the moral community (at least in theory) could – over a significant period of time – jointly (rationally) reconsider, revise, and even abandon large fragments of the structure of moral principles that they adhere to.

In short, a historically established framework of social norms embodied in the social institutions of a community operates as a (multifaceted) constraint on the practical reasoning of the rational members of that community. On the other hand, within that constraint, or those constraints, individuals, especially individuals acting jointly, are free to make significant changes over time to this historically established framework. Naturally, specific structures of social norms may well undermine individual autonomy, for example, structures of norms in slave societies.[18] However, it seems that there are other actual, or at least possible, societies in which the structures of social norms embody a high

---

[16] I say "in theory" because I am assuming that the consistent infringement of one moral principle might not necessarily impact on an agent's capacity to comply with other moral principles. But this is doubtful, at least in relation to many moral principles, e.g., refraining from killing people.

[17] So I take it that if a functioning human person was able to abandon all their moral principles today, then tomorrow he would no longer be a functioning human being; moral principles are central to a moral agent's identity, and like the planks on Aristotle's ship, they cannot be replaced all at once. Naturally, a person could move from one moral community to another, and there could be important differences between the two communities. However, if the differences between the two communities are too profound, then the person may not be able to make the switch successfully. On the other hand, if the switch was gradual – given a good deal of overlap between possible human moral communities – then a switch might be relatively painless.

[18] For many people in such "moral," i.e., immoral, communities, individual autonomy may well be impossible.

degree of individual freedom, egalitarianism, reflective rationality, and so on, and that in these societies at least, individual autonomy is alive and well. Accordingly, it seems reasonable to conclude that historically established frameworks of social norms – embodied in social institutions – are not in principle inconsistent with individual autonomy.

If it is still insisted that any historically established framework of social norms necessarily diminishes individual autonomy, then the following response is available. Given that individual human beings (a) have to be inducted into some structure of moral principles and (b) desire to live in communities, and need, therefore, to conform to some structure of institutionalized social norms, the only coherent notion of autonomy for human agents is one that takes an historically established institutional framework of social norms as a background condition for their individual and interpersonal action. Such a framework of social norms is an enabling condition for the existence of an autonomous human moral agent seeking to engage in individual and interpersonal action; it is not necessarily a threat to it. Immanuel Kant uses the image of a bird to make this kind of point: "The light dove cleaving in free flight the thin air, whose resistance it feels, might imagine that her movements would be far more free and rapid in airless space."[19] Just as air is necessary for birds to fly, so a structure of historically established institutionalized social norms is necessary for autonomous human beings to live as human beings.[*]

## 5. CONCLUSION

In this chapter the principal concern has been with individual autonomy in institutional settings. I have addressed the so-called agent-structure question and defended a broadly individualist and teleological account of institutional structure according to which structure is not some sui generis "entity" existing independently of the actions of the individual human agents who are constrained by it; rather, structure is itself simply the repetition over time of the interdependent actions of many agents – actions directed toward collective ends.

---

[19] Kant (1943, 6). This point is not undermined by Robinson Crusoe scenarios. The point about Robinson Crusoe is that he continued to desire social interaction, e.g., with Man Friday or with his former society, and he continued to rely on social forms, e.g., language, and social activities, e.g., reading, to maintain his existence.

[*] Thanks to Andrew Alexandra and Fred Schmitt for helpful comments on the last two sections of this chapter.

Moreover, it has been argued that although the character of individual agents and their choice of actions are necessarily in large part a function of their past and present institutional environments, this fact does not undermine the possibility of individual autonomy.

Having considered individual autonomy in relation to social institutions in this chapter, in the next chapter we turn to the detailed treatment of another important normative concept that is deeply implicated in social institutions, namely, collective moral responsibility.

# 4

# Collective Moral Responsibility

In this chapter I discuss one of the key moral concepts that, as we saw in Chapter 2, underpins social institutions, namely, collective moral responsibility.[1] As we have seen above, aggregated needs-based rights, for example, generate the institutional rights and duties of the members of welfare institutions via collective moral responsibility. I elaborate and defend an individualist account of collective moral responsibility, that is, one that ascribes moral responsibility only to individual human beings, as opposed to collective entities.[2] Moreover, this account of collective moral responsibility presupposes the teleological account of joint action and social institutions elaborated in Chapters 1 and 2. On this individualist, teleological conception collective entities, such as social groups and organizations, have collective moral responsibility only in the sense that the individual human persons who constitute such entities have individual moral responsibility, either individually or jointly; collective entities as such do not have moral responsibility.[3] Note that individualism in this sense is entirely different from the view that collective entities are reducible to individual human persons – an ontological claim that I reject. I begin by outlining my individualist, teleological account of collective moral responsibility.[4] However, the burden of the chapter is my attempt to extend this account to enable it to accommodate a variety of different species of collective moral responsibility.

---

[1] Thanks to Andrew Alexandra, Dean Cocking, and Daniel Cohen for helpful comments on this chapter.

[2] An earlier version of the material in this section appeared in Miller (2006a).

[3] For an influential collectivist account, see French (1984). For arguments against collectivist accounts, see Miller (1997b), and Miller and Makela (2005).

[4] In this section I offer a revised version of an account I have propounded in a number of places. See Miller (1998a, 2001a, 2001b, chap. 8, 2006a).

## 1. COLLECTIVE MORAL RESPONSIBILITY

We can usefully distinguish four senses of collective responsibility.[5] I will do so in relation to joint actions.[6]

As we saw in Chapter 1, roughly speaking, two or more individuals perform a joint action if each of them intentionally performs an individual action, but does so with the true belief that in so doing they will jointly realize an end that each of them has. Having an end in this sense is a mental state in the head of one or more individuals; however, it is an end that is not realized by one individual acting alone; that is, it is a collective end. For example, you and I lifting a bank safe onto a truck is a joint action, because you lift one side and I the other; each of us lifts his side truly believing the other will lift his, and each of us has as an end that the bank safe be situated on the truck.

Agents who perform a joint action are responsible for that action in the first sense of collective responsibility, that is, they intentionally performed the action and did so for a reason. Here responsibility is being used in a morally and institutionally neutral sense. Accordingly, to say that they are collectively responsible for the action is just to say that they performed the joint action. That is, they each had a collective end, each intentionally performed their contributory action, and each did so because each believed the other would perform his contributory action, and that therefore the collective end would be realized.

It is important to note that each agent is individually responsible for performing his contributory action, and responsible by virtue of the fact that he intentionally performed this action, and the action was not intentionally performed by anyone else. Of course, the other agents (or agent) *believe* that he is performing, has performed, or is going to perform the contributory action in question. But mere possession of such a belief is not sufficient for the ascription of responsibility to *the believer* for the performance of the individual action, that is, the other agent's action. What are the agents *collectively* responsible for? or, what amounts to the same thing here, What are the agents *jointly* responsible for? The agents are collectively or jointly responsible for the realization of the collective *end;* the realization of the collective end results from their performance of their contributory actions. In our bank safe lifting example, each person

---

[5] On the notions of joint and collective responsibility see, for example, Zimmerman (1985) and May (1987, chap. 4).

[6] Miller (1992a, 2001b, chap. 2).

is individually responsible for lifting his side of the bank safe, and the
two agents are collectively or jointly responsible for bringing it about that
the bank safe is situated on the truck.

   If the occupants of an institutional role (or roles) have an institutionally determined obligation to perform some joint action, then those individuals are collectively responsible for its performance, in our second
sense of collective responsibility, that is, collective *institutional* responsibility.[7] Here there is a *joint* institutional obligation to realize the collective
end of the joint action in question. In addition, there is a set of derived
*individual* obligations; each of the participating individuals has an individual obligation to perform her contributory action.[8] (The derivation
of these individual obligations relies on the fact that if each performs his
or her contributory action, then it is probable that the collective end
will be realized.)

   There is a third sense of collective responsibility, namely, the responsibility of those in authority; this is a species of institutional responsibility. Suppose the members of the cabinet of the parliament of country
A (consisting of the prime minister and his or her cabinet ministers)
collectively decide to exercise their institutionally determined right to
increase taxes, and direct the tax office to implement this decision. The
tax office does what it was ordered to do. The cabinet is collectively institutionally responsible for the tax increase by virtue of the fact that each
of the members of cabinet – jointly with the other members – agreed that
there was to be a tax increase. (This form of collective decision making is
an instance of what I call a joint institutional mechanism. See below.)

   What of the fourth sense of collective responsibility, collective *moral*
responsibility? Collective moral responsibility is a species of moral responsibility. Roughly speaking, an agent is morally responsible for an action if
the agent was responsible for the action in the neutral sense, that is, the
agent intentionally performed the action and did so for a reason,[9] and
the action was morally significant. There are a number of ways in which
an action might be morally significant. They include that the action is

---

[7] There is an artificial sense of institutional responsibility that is not at issue here, e.g., the
   ascription of legal responsibility or liability to collective entities such as corporations.
[8] Naturally, the individual role occupants also have institutional obligations that are not
   derived from joint institutional obligations.
[9] The reason was causally efficacious in the right way, as was the intention. See Davidson
   (1973). I do not want to get bogged down in debates concerning the precise nature of
   moral responsibility and, more specifically, the relation between moral responsibility
   and determinism.

intrinsically morally good or bad the goal or end of the action is morally good or bad, and the (foreseen or reasonably foreseeable) consequence of the action is morally good or bad.

Moreover, collective moral responsibility is a species of joint responsibility. Accordingly, each agent is individually morally responsible, but conditionally on the others being individually morally responsible: there is interdependence in respect of moral responsibility. This account of collective moral responsibility arises naturally out of the account of joint actions.

Thus we can make the following claim about moral responsibility: If agents are collectively responsible for a joint action or the realization of a (foreseen or reasonably foreseeable) outcome consequent upon the performance of a joint action, in the first, second, or third senses of collective responsibility, and the action or outcome is morally significant, then – other things being equal[10] – the agents are collectively *morally* responsible for that action or outcome and – other things being equal[11] – ought to attract moral praise or blame, and (possibly) punishment or reward for the joint action or for bringing about the outcome.

Note that I am respecting the threefold distinction between (1) the rightness or wrongness of an action, (2) the moral responsibility of an agent (or agents) for that action and/or (potentially) its outcome, and (3) the blameworthiness or praiseworthiness of the agent (or agents) for the action and/or its outcome. Note also the distinction between the (so to speak) internal outcome of a joint action and its external outcome (or outcomes). The internal outcome is the state of affairs, the coming into existence of which is the realization of the collective end of the joint action. The external outcome is any further consequence of the joint action, consequences that are not in this way constitutive of the

---

[10] Other things might not be equal, e.g., the agents might be psychopaths and, as a consequence, have diminished moral responsibility or perhaps even no moral responsibility at all.

[11] As with the preceding clause, other things might not be equal, e.g., the agents might have an excuse moral or justification for performing a joint action, the performance of which would otherwise have been blameworthy. Here I am assuming that the excuse in question does not diminish their moral responsibility, nor does it justify their action. Suppose, for example, that I decide not to do my duty and attend an appropriately scheduled, moderately important, university committee meeting because a good friend whom I have not seen for a long time unexpectedly arrives in town on a business trip and wants me to take her to lunch during the period in question, there being no other opportunity for us to meet on this particular visit. I am fully morally responsible for my action, and my action is not morally justified; nevertheless, surely I have an excuse. See also the examples in Section 6 below.

joint action. In what follows, the context will make it clear whether I am speaking of the internal or the external outcome of a joint action; nevertheless, the distinction needs to be kept in mind.

What are agents who perform morally significant joint actions collectively morally responsible for? Other things being equal, each agent who intentionally performs a morally significant *individual* action has *individual* moral responsibility for the action. So in the case of a morally significant joint action, each agent is *individually* morally responsible for performing *his contributory* action, and the *other* agents are *not* morally responsible for his individual contributory action. But, in addition, the contributing agents are *collectively* morally responsible for the outcome or *collective end* of their various contributory actions. To say that they are collectively morally responsible for bringing about this (collective) end is just to say that they are *jointly* morally responsible for it.

As is the case with joint action, joint responsibility involves interdependence, albeit interdependence of responsibility, as opposed to interdependence of action. In the case of joint responsibility, each agent is individually morally responsible for realizing the relevant collective end, but conditionally on the others being individually morally responsible for realizing it as well.

Having thus elaborated what I take to be the central notion of collective moral responsibility, I now want to turn to a number of problems that arise in relation to collective moral responsibility for actions. The first of these concerns an individual's causal contribution to a morally significant joint action.

## 2. MAKING A DIFFERENCE

Some have suggested that an agent cannot be held morally responsible for an outcome if his action did not make any difference to the existence of that outcome; the outcome would have taken place whatever the individual did, or did not do.[12] The idea is that unless an agent's action is a necessary condition for that outcome, then the agent cannot be held morally responsible for it. But suppose two hit men simultaneously shoot a third man, killing him. Suppose further that each of the two bullets was sufficient to kill the man, so neither bullet was necessary. Accordingly, neither shooter's action made any difference, and so, on the view before us, neither is morally responsible for the man's death.

---

[12] For example, Hardin (1988, 156–7).

This is an absurd conclusion. Clearly each is guilty of murder: that is, not only does each have a degree of moral responsibility for killing the man, but each is *fully* morally responsible for killing the man. This is so notwithstanding the fact that neither one performed an action that was a necessary condition for the outcome. So one can be held morally responsible – indeed, fully morally responsible – for an outcome if one's action is either a necessary or a sufficient (or a necessary and sufficient) condition for the outcome.

Now consider the following collective action situation in which the outcome of the collective action is overdetermined by the actions of the agents involved. Suppose that each of five men inflicts a single stab wound on a sixth man, John Smith, intending to kill him. Assume the stabbings are simultaneous. Smith dies from his wounds; however, three stab wounds would have been causally sufficient to kill him. That is, three stab wounds are individually causally necessary, and jointly causally sufficient, to kill Smith. Therefore, no single stab wound (of the five) is either causally necessary or sufficient for Smith's death. So although each of the men performed an action, a stabbing, that was causally necessary and sufficient for *wounding* Smith, not one of the five men performed an action that was either causally necessary, or causally sufficient, for Smith's *death*. So each of the men is individually morally responsible for *wounding* Smith, but what about the moral responsibility for *killing* him? It might be thought that if a person has not performed an action that was either causally necessary or sufficient for a person's death, then that person cannot be held responsible for the person's death. So none of the five men is responsible for Smith's death. But if none of the five is responsible, then presumably no one is responsible. For the cause of Smith's death was the stab wounds, and these were made by the five men.

Notwithstanding the above claimed lack of individual moral responsibility, it might be held that the five men were *collectively* morally responsible for Smith's death. But even this appears to be false, because only the actions of three of the men were necessary for Smith's death. So at best we are entitled to conclude that (an unspecified and perhaps unspecifiable) three of the five men were collectively responsible for Smith's death, but no individual was responsible. This conclusion is very unpalatable indeed. For one thing, it sets up an unbridgeable gap between collective responsibility and individual responsibility; a collective can be morally responsible for an outcome, even though none of its members are.[13] For

---

[13] Although some theorists, e.g., Hardin (1988), are prepared to bite the bullet.

another, it licenses the commission of immoral acts, so long as they are collective actions involving overdetermination; individual perpetrators are not morally responsible for heinous crimes, so long as they commit those crimes collectively, and their actions overdetermine the outcome.

We first need an analysis of the kind of collective actions at issue. We have one at hand – my above described account of joint actions. So we can conceive of such cases of collective action as actions directed to a collective end; in our example, the collective end is the death of Smith. Each of the five men has the collective end as an end. Moreover, each of the five performs the act of stabbing as a means to the collective end he has.

Further, the actions of the five agents are *interdependent:* that is, each performs his contributory action if he believes the others will perform theirs, and each does so only if he believes this. Why are the actions interdependent? They are interdependent by virtue of the existence of the collective end possessed by each of the five agents, and toward the realization of which each of the individual acts is directed.

So there is a collective end, and there is interdependence of action: that is, each stabbed only on condition the others stabbed. So the full set of five acts of stabbing can be regarded as *the means* by which the collective end was realized; and each act of stabbing was a *part of* that means. Moreover, in virtue of interdependence, each act of stabbing is an integral part of the means to the collective end. Since killing someone is morally significant, I conclude that all five agents are jointly – and therefore collectively – *morally* responsible for killing Smith. For each performed an act of stabbing in the service of that (collective) end, Smith's death, and each of these acts of stabbing was an integral part of the means to that end. Moreover, each agent can be held *fully* morally responsible for Smith's death; the moral responsibility of each is not diminished by the fact that each of the others is also morally responsible.

The example demonstrates that an individual's action need neither be a necessary nor a sufficient condition of an outcome for the individual to be fully morally responsible for that outcome. If an individual makes a causal contribution to an outcome, and does so in the service of an intention or end to realize that outcome, then this is sufficient – other things being equal – for the individual to be fully morally responsible for that outcome.

It is important to distinguish between agents who are full participants in a joint action and who bear full moral responsibility for it, and agents who merely assist with the joint action and have only diminished moral responsibility for it. Consider a version of the stabbing scenario in which, in addition to the five persons who stabbed Smith to death, there is a sixth person who sold the knives to the killers and who knew what the knives would be used for. The knife seller has made an indirect, and lesser, causal contribution to the outcome. The causal chain that begins with the act of knife selling and terminates in the death of Smith is mediated by the acts of stabbing; and the acts of stabbing play a much more central role in Smith's death than the act of selling the knives does. Moreover, the knife seller did not have an *intention* or (individual or collective) *end* that Smith be killed. Therefore, the knife seller has significantly *diminished* moral responsibility for Smith's death.

There are some joint actions in which many of the participants do not make a *direct* causal contribution to the realization of the collective end. Consider a firing squad scenario in which only one live round is used, and it is not known which member of the squad is firing the live round. The soldier with the live round is (albeit unknown to him and his fellow firing squad members) *individually* causally responsible for shooting the prisoner dead; no other member of the firing squad makes a *direct* causal contribution to the death of the prisoner. However, the members of the firing squad are *jointly* morally responsible for its being the case that the prisoner has been shot dead. How so? There is a morally significant joint action, namely, the joint action of bringing it about that the prisoner has been shot dead – albeit shot dead by only one of the soldiers. Each soldier, jointly with the other soldiers, shoots at the prisoner in the belief that his bullet might be the one to kill the prisoner, and having as a collective end that the prisoner be shot dead. Moreover, by virtue of having this collective end, each soldier shoots if the others shoot, and no soldier shoots unless the others do. So if the soldiers with blanks in their guns had not fired, then the soldier with the live round in the chamber of his gun would not have fired, and the prisoner would not have been killed. In this kind of case, the fact that only one of the soldiers directly caused the death of the prisoner does not make a great deal of moral difference. If, for example, the prisoner were an innocent man, then each of the members of the firing squad would be, jointly with the others, guilty of wrongful killing. On the other hand, the soldier who actually fired the live round, if he discovered this, may reasonably feel somewhat more responsible than the others. He would do so by virtue of the fact that he, but not the others, *directly* caused the death; it was his bullet that killed the prisoner.

There are some morally significant joint actions in which each of the participating agents makes a very small causal contribution and in which the collective end is an end only in an attenuated sense. In many of these cases, each participant has substantially diminished moral responsibility for the outcome.

Consider fundraising for a charity. Suppose two million people are each asked to donate one dollar to raise one million dollars to build a new wing for a children's hospital. (The organizers rightly believe it is probable that at least one in two people will donate if asked.) The donors are engaged in a joint action of sorts, and the outcome aimed at is morally significant. Therefore they are, at least to some degree, collectively morally responsible for the outcome. On the other hand, the moral responsibility does not rest solely with the donors; the organizers have an important share in the moral responsibility. Moreover, each of the donors made only a very small contribution and at little cost to themselves – unlike each of the individual organizers. Further, each of the donors had the end, to raise one million dollars, only in an attenuated sense. For one thing, each would not mind too much if the hospital wing was not built, and their dollar was not returned to them; the "end" is weakly held, and so the means to realize it should, and does, involve only a very minimal cost. For another thing, none of the donors has this "end" as an end that is an integrated element of the overall structure of ends he or she is pursuing; for example, this "end" is not a means to another important end.

What are we to conclude from this? Since each agent provides only a tiny fraction of the overall one million dollars contributed, and since each has raising the one million dollars as an end only in an attenuated sense, then each cannot have full natural responsibility for the outcome; at best, each has a minor share in whatever extent of natural responsibility the donors jointly have for the outcome. Therefore, other things being equal, each donor has substantially diminished *moral* responsibility for the outcome. Moreover, given the natural responsibility in question is collective or joint natural responsibility – and given the outcome is morally significant – then each agent has (substantially diminished) moral responsibility for the outcome, jointly with the other agents.[14]

The *ceteris paribus* clause in relation to the diminished responsibility of the donors exists in part to signal the existence of a range of considerations that prevent a diminution in moral responsibility *automatically* following a reduction in an agent's share of natural responsibility. One such

---

[14] In fact, the donors are only responsible, *jointly* with the organizers. But this makes little difference to the point I am making.

consideration is the existence of a relevant institutional responsibility, especially an institutional responsibility designed to serve an important moral purpose. For example, an institutional-role occupant who fails in his institutional duty by making what is only a tiny causal contribution to some morally untoward outcome, nevertheless, might be held *fully institutionally* responsible for the outcome and, as a result, *fully morally* responsible for the outcome; or at least he might enjoy only a minor diminution in moral responsibility, and certainly not a moral diminution commensurate with his very minor share of natural responsibility for the outcome.

Consider a group of a hundred sailors in a wooden ship. The sailors know it is a serious legal offence to steal nails by extracting them from the ship's woodwork, and that any sailor doing so can be held fully legally liable for any adverse consequences. The sailors know that this law derives from the fact that, if undertaken on a large scale, extracting nails can weaken the structure of the ship, causing it to sink. Notwithstanding this law, each of the hundred sailors extracts a single nail from the ship's woodwork, but each does so in ignorance of the actions of the others. The unforeseen consequence of their actions is that the ship sinks. In this scenario each sailor might reasonably be held *fully* institutionally responsible for the ship having sunk, and suffer a commensurate punishment. Given that each sailor is fully institutionally responsible for the sinking of the ship, and given that this is morally significant, then perhaps each ought to be held *fully* morally responsible for this outcome. At best, each sailor should enjoy only *partly diminished* moral responsibility for the sinking of the ship, notwithstanding the fact that each makes only a tiny causal contribution to the outcome.

### 3. COLLECTIVE RESPONSIBILITY IN ORGANIZED GROUPS

The second problem to be discussed arises in the context of the actions of organized groups and organizations. Typically, such organized groups and organizations consist in part of institutional-roles with their attendant rights and duties. Moreover, institutional-role structures are often hierarchical, and hence involve relations of authority and power.[15]

---

[15] So a lower-echelon role occupant may have diminished moral responsibility for their action, given they were acting under orders. However, acting under orders does not thereby extinguish one's moral responsibility for one's actions. Naturally, whether or not a subordinate has diminished moral responsibility, or even no moral responsibility, for a wrongful action done under orders depends on the action in question. If the

The analysis of the actions of organized groups and organizations requires the notion of a layered structure of joint actions introduced in Chapter 1.[16]

As we saw in Chapter 1, an illustration of the notion of a layered structure of joint actions is, in fact, an army fighting a battle. At level one we have a number of joint actions. The members of, say, the infantry move forward on the ground. The members of, say, a mortar group pound the enemy positions with mortar fire. Finally, air support is provided by a squadron of fighter planes. So there is a series of level-one joint actions. Now, each of these three (level-one) joint actions is itself describable as an *individual* action performed (respectively) by the different groups, namely, the action of killing the enemy by mortar fire, protecting the advancing troops by providing air support, and moving forward to take and hold the ground occupied by the enemy. However, each of these "individual" actions is a component element of a larger joint action directed to the collective end of winning the battle. For each of these individual attacks is part of a larger plan coordinated by the military leadership. So these "individual" actions constitute a *level-two* joint action directed to the collective end of winning the battle.

Accordingly, if all, or most, of the individual actions of the members of the military were performed in accordance with collective ends, if the performance of each of the resulting level-one joint actions were themselves performed in accordance with the collective end of winning the battle, and if the actions were morally significant, then, at least in principle, we could ascribe joint moral responsibility for winning the battle to the individual members of the infantry platoon, mortar squad, and fighter pilot squadron. So agents involved in complex, morally significant, cooperative enterprises can, *at least in principle*, be ascribed collective, that is, joint, moral responsibility for the outcomes aimed at by those enterprises.

As we saw above, institutional obligations are often joint obligations and, as such, can reinforce prior joint *moral* obligations or transform a supererogatory action into a moral obligatory one.[17] Thus, if two surfers jointly intervene to save the life of a large man drowning in heavy seas,

action is murdering someone, then, I suggest, the subordinate has full moral responsibility; if the action is minor damage to property on the part of a soldier during wartime, then, I suggest, the soldier has diminished moral responsibility.

[16] Miller (1998a, 2001b, chap. 5).
[17] They can also diminish or extinguish moral obligations previously attached to non-institutional actors, but now attached to institutional actors. Perhaps all citizens had a moral obligation to put out serious fires before the establishment of fire-fighting organizations.

this might be a supererogatory joint action. However, if the two surfers are lifeguards on duty, then the same joint action might be jointly institutionally obligatory and, therefore, jointly morally obligatory.

Moral dilemmas can arise when *institutionally based* moral obligations and *noninstitutional* moral obligations conflict. In a variation on Sartre's famous example, Should a young soldier, Pierre, go to war or stay home and look after his very sick mother?[18] *Qua* soldier, Pierre has an institutionally based moral obligation to go to war. But such is his love for his mother that he reasonably feels morally obliged to look after her. Be that as it may, our issue is not the one of finding a solution to the Pierre's moral dilemma. Rather, the point is that such moral dilemmas arise for individual human persons, such as Pierre, and involve only *individual* moral obligations. In this and like scenarios there is no apparent need to posit a moral obligation that attaches to a collective entity such as, for example, the French army per se.

Now, suppose the members of a platoon of soldiers are jointly engaged in a firefight against a group of well-intentioned guerrillas engaged in a morally unjustified revolutionary war. Assume that the soldiers discover in the course of the bloody ongoing encounter that the revolutionaries consist in large part of their close relatives, such as brothers and sisters, as well as their friends. *Qua* soldier, each has a jointly held *moral* obligation – an institutionally based jointly held moral obligation – to use lethal force against the members of the guerrilla group. But how can members of a group be reasonably expected to kill their own sisters, brothers, and friends? Once again, our concern here is not to find a solution to the *moral* dilemma. Rather, the point is that such moral dilemmas arise for individual human persons, such as the members of the platoon, and involve only *jointly held* moral obligations. In this and like scenarios there is no apparent need to posit a moral obligation that attaches to a collective entity such as, for example, the army of the state per se.

## 4. JOINT INSTITUTIONAL MECHANISMS AND COLLECTIVE RESPONSIBILITY

As we saw in Chapter 1, joint actions can also be distinguished from joint mechanisms.[19] Joint mechanisms consist of (a) a complex of

---

[18] Sartre (1948, 35–8).
[19] See Miller (1992a, 2001b, chap. 5).

differentiated, but interlocking, individual actions (the input to the mechanism), (b) the result of the performance of those actions (the output of the mechanism), and (c) the mechanism itself. For further details concerning joint mechanisms see Chapter 1. The point to be stressed here is that joint mechanisms are to be understood in purely individualist terms, specifically, in terms of the collective end theory of joint action.

Some joint mechanisms are *institutional* mechanisms. One such example is voting for public officials. Another has also been mentioned, namely, a parliamentary cabinet making a decision to raise taxes. Here the cabinet makes a decision that each member has agreed to. Naturally, some members of the cabinet may privately disagree with the decision. However, ultimately, they all agree to publicly accept that decision; which is to say that each agrees *qua* member of the cabinet. Here the notion of acting *qua* occupant of a role (see Chapter 1) is simply that of performing the tasks definitive of the role (including the joint tasks), conforming to the conventions and regulations that constrain the tasks to be undertaken, and pursuing the purposes or ends of the role (including the collective ends).[20] Accordingly, each member of the cabinet is *institutionally* responsible, jointly with the others, for the decision to raise taxes. Moreover, given the moral significance attaching to raising taxes, each member of the cabinet is *morally* responsible, jointly with the others, for the decision to raise taxes. This is so, notwithstanding the fact that some members might believe that it is immoral to raise taxes and, as a consequence, might have strenuously argued against this course of action. These members face a moral dilemma of the kind we discussed above. They can resolve the dilemma by making the decision to set aside their privately held belief in favor of the majority view of the cabinet; in effect, *qua* cabinet member, each individually endorses the decision that taxes be raised. If, on the other hand, some member of the cabinet cannot, *qua* member of the cabinet, accept the decision to raise taxes, then her position *qua* member of the cabinet becomes untenable; so she must resign from the cabinet.

Indeed, it might be that most, or even all, of the members of the cabinet believe that it is immoral to raise taxes, and yet all, or most, vote for taxes to be raised. However, even if this is the case, each cabinet member remains, *qua* cabinet member, *institutionally* responsible, jointly with

---

[20] For more on the analysis of the notion of acting *qua* member of a group, or *qua* role occupant, see Miller (2007c).

the other members, for the decision to raise taxes; and, given the moral significance of taxes being raised, each cabinet member is likewise *morally* responsible, jointly with the others, for this outcome.

My individualist notion of a joint mechanism is also able to handle examples in which an institutional entity has a representative who performs an individual action, but it is an individual action that has the joint backing of the members of the institutional entity. Consider, for example, an industrial union's representative, George, who is engaging in wage negotiations with a company on behalf of the union membership and is authorized to accept any wage offer above a certain threshold that has been predetermined by the union membership. George rejects the company's offer of $X because it is below the threshold. At one level of description, George performs an individual action of rejection, namely, the individual action describable as George rejecting the offer. At another level of description, the union membership has jointly rejected the offer. How so? There is a joint institutional mechanism that involves input from the union membership and output from George. The mechanism itself consists of George's action (the output of the mechanism) counting as the joint action of the members of the union (the input of the mechanism). What is this relation of "counts as"? It is simply the relation of authorization or, more specifically, of delegated authority.

## 5. COLLECTIVE RESPONSIBILITY FOR OMISSIONS

In this section I explicitly consider collective moral responsibility for omissions. Consider a scenario in which a boat at sea is sinking and dozens of its passengers (who are war refugees) are about to drown. The bystanders are the members of the crew in an adjacent, but somewhat distant, boat. Here there are large numbers of people whose lives are at immediate risk, and there is one group of bystanders, and only one group, who could successfully intervene; moreover, they could do so without significant cost to themselves.

The first question that arises in relation to this scenario is: Who, if anyone, ought to intervene? In some rescue scenarios involving multiple agents, the action of one agent could save the life or lives at risk. In such cases each bystander has an individual, but conditional, moral obligation. Each has an obligation to perform the rescue on the condition that none of the others do so. So if someone performs the rescue, then the others have not failed to discharge their individual moral obligations. On the other hand, if no one performs the rescue, then each has failed to discharge their individual moral responsibility.[21] In short, we have interdependence of individual moral responsibility to intervene, although not joint moral responsibility to intervene.

However, in the scenario under consideration this is not the case. Rather, let us assume that a collective decision is required on the part of the bystanders in the adjacent (potential) rescue boat to sail sufficiently close to the sinking boat, and then assist the drowning passengers to board their boat. What is needed is the performance of a *joint* action involving *all* of the bystanders. Let us further assume that although this collective action is considered by the bystanders (e.g., arguments are put for and against the desirability of the passengers being rescued), they make a collective decision *not* to intervene, and do so having as an end that the passengers in the sinking boat not be prevented from drowning; the crew of the boat in question despise refugees.

Here we have a species of joint action, namely, intentional joint inaction. Although each of the bystanders refrains from acting, each does so in the service of a collective end, that is, the end that the drownings not be prevented from occurring, or, at least, not be prevented from occurring by the bystanders (maybe they would not prevent a third party from rescuing the drowning passengers, if such a party existed). Accordingly, there is individual moral responsibility on the part of each of the bystanders for their refraining to act, and there is joint moral responsibility for failing to prevent the drownings. So the members of the crew are collectively morally responsible for failing to prevent the drownings in the manner of collective moral responsibility set forth in the first section of this chapter.

In a second version of the rescue scenario, the members of the crew might individually intentionally refrain from doing anything to contribute to effecting the rescue; for example, no one strongly argues to their fellow crew members that the crew jointly ought to assist; but there is no collective decision not to intervene. There is no collective end; rather, each individually decides not to intervene because it is too much bother to intervene. Although there is no collective end, the members of the crew know (they have common knowledge; see Lewis 1969) that the passengers will drown, unless they act jointly to rescue them. Accordingly, if

[21] I accept the existence of positive rights, such as the right to security and subsistence. Such rights give rise to individual and collective responsibility. For the case in favor of positive rights, and an explanation of how rights generate responsibilities, see Shue (1996).

the crew does not act, then they have collectively *allowed* the passengers to drown.

Arguably, the members of the crew are less morally culpable in the second version than in the first. In the first they had nonprevention of the drownings as a collective end – and argued against anyone in favor of rescuing the drowning passengers – whereas in the second they did not; they simply knew that the passengers would drown if they did not intervene.

On the other hand, even in the first version the members of the crew do not contribute causally to the drownings as would be the case in the following third version of the scenario. In this third version the refugees are actually passengers of the rescue boat, but they are passengers who have been swept overboard by a large wave, are clinging to the sides of the boat, and are calling on the members of the crew to assist them to get back on board. However, concerned at being behind schedule, the members of the crew collectively decide to set sail at full speed with the result that the passengers clinging to its sides are unable to continue to do so, and drown as a consequence. Clearly, the members of the crew have caused harm, and have done so either as a means to a collective end or, at least, in the full knowledge that they were doing so. That the members of the crew cause the harm to the passengers is morally significant; hence greater moral culpability attaches to them than attaches to the members of the crew in the first (and, obviously, second) version of the scenario. However, this third version does not involve a collective *omission;* so let us return to the first and second versions.

Let us now assume that in the second version of the scenario one crew member decides to try to do something on his own, hoping that others will join in and assist him. However, they do not, and his efforts are to no avail. Naturally, there is no obligation on the part of any single crew member to do anything if they know that the others are not going to do likewise; for in that event the end would not be realized. So each is under a moral obligation to contribute to the rescue effort on condition, and only on condition, that the others do.

It is important to distinguish this kind of case from ones in which each will intervene if and only if the others do, but each does not have as an end to effect the rescue; rather, each has, say, the individual end to avoid bringing about a situation in which the others intervene, but he does not. This latter situation is a case of having the individual end of not being the odd person out; but this is not the same as promoting a collective end of saving the lives of the drowning passengers.

In our rescue scenario the following ascriptions of moral responsibility are warranted. First, a given bystander is *individually* morally responsible for failing to individually intervene to effect the rescue, if (a) the passengers did in fact drown, (b) that bystander intentionally refrained from individually intervening to assist in the prevention of the drownings, even though the other bystanders did intervene, or that bystander would have intentionally refrained from intervening, if the others had intervened, and (c) the intervention of that bystander, taken in conjunction with the intervention of the other bystanders, would have been sufficient to prevent the drownings, and at little or no cost to the bystanders.

Second, the members of the crew are *collectively* morally responsible for failing to prevent the drownings if[22] (a) the passengers did in fact drown, (b) the members of the crew individually intentionally refrained from intervening, (c) each of the crew members' intervening (having as a collective end to save the lives of the passengers) would have resulted in the prevention of the drownings, (d) each of the crew members would still have intentionally refrained from intervening with the collective end of preventing the drownings, even if the others had intervened with that end.

Notice that on the above definition the members of the crew are collectively morally responsible for failing to prevent the drownings, irrespective of whether they had this outcome as a collective end or merely collectively allowed it; albeit, as mentioned above, less moral culpability attaches to the latter than to the former. It should also be noted that, other things being equal, if a given crew member is *not individually* morally responsible for failing to individually intervene to prevent the drownings, then that crew member does *not* share in the *collective* moral responsibility for failing to jointly intervene to prevent the drownings.[23]

The rescue scenario illustrates the individual moral obligation to assist others whose lives are at immediate risk if one can do so at little or no cost to oneself and if there is no one else available to assist. It also illustrates the joint moral obligation on the part of members of groups to cooperate to assist others whose lives are at immediate risk if the members of the group can do so at little or no cost to themselves and if there is no other group (or for that matter individual) able to do so.

---

[22] Note that here, and in the Pony Express example below, I am only offering sufficient conditions for collective moral responsibility for omissions.

[23] Other things might not be equal. For example, the individual might be locked up, and hence unable to intervene, even if she wanted to. It might be argued that if so, then the person does not have a full share in the collective responsibility for nonintervention.

These individual and joint moral obligations to rescue are in some jurisdictions legally enshrined; for instance, in international law ships have a legal duty to assist other ships that are sinking. If so, there are a set of individual and joint *institutional* obligations to reinforce the preexisting individual and joint *moral* obligations.

Let me now consider an example of collective moral responsibility for joint omission in the case of *sequential* omissions, that is, a set of omissions, each member of which is completed before the next begins.

One paradigm of sequential joint *action* is a relay. Suppose A, B, C, and D are members of the USA Olympic 4 × 400 meter relay team. Each participant runs 400 meters and passes a baton to his fellow relay member. This is joint action; but it is joint action in which the constitutive individual actions are performed *sequentially* rather than simultaneously. The agents have a collective end, to complete the running of the relay, and they each believe that the other members have done, are doing, or will do their parts.[24] If this collective end has moral significance, then each of the participants is – jointly with the others – morally responsible for this outcome. This might be so if, for example, a large company has agreed to make a large donation to charity if the USA team wins the relay. Although the members of the relay team might be collectively morally praiseworthy if they win the relay and thereby ensure that the large charitable donation is made, it is doubtful that they are blameworthy if they do not. So this case does not involve individual or collective *moral* responsibility for omission.

For the purpose of exploring the notion of collective moral responsibility for omissions, let us consider a somewhat different version of the relay scenario, namely, the Pony Express scenario. Assume that the "relay" is run by 10 men on horseback, and involves the passing of important mail from one participant to the next; the collective end is the delivery of the mail to the final destination. Assume further that the Pony Express is an institution in which the institutional-role occupants – the riders – have a collective institutional responsibility to realize this collective end. So each rider has a derived, individual institutional responsibility to ride for one day and deliver the mail to the next stop. Once again, the delivery of the mail involves a joint sequential action, and, given the morally

---

[24] *Contra* some theorists, e.g., Bratman (1992), the members of the relay team do not intend the actions of the other members. How could the last runner, for example, intend the action of the first runner, given the latter action took place in the past and the last runner became so only during the second runner's lap? See Miller (2001b, 80).

significant collective end, each of the riders is – jointly with the others – morally responsible for the outcome: the successful delivery of the mail to its final destination.

Given this institutionally based moral responsibility, any one of the riders who failed without adequate justification to deliver the mail on his sector would be morally responsible for an omission. Moreover, in so doing he would ensure that the collective end was not realized. However, the other riders would not be similarly morally responsible if they were ready and willing to deliver the mail across their sectors – or, indeed, had already done so. So there is individual, but not collective, moral responsibility for an omission.

Now consider a *joint* omission on the part of the riders. The riders would be collectively morally responsible for an omission if they collectively and intentionally brought it about that, for example, 10 separate mail deliveries were not made. Assume that this is in fact what happens, and that the means by which they achieve this outcome is by agreeing to an arrangement whereby each rider takes a turn in not turning up to work, knowing that the participation of each is a necessary condition for the mail getting through. Each knows which day he is not to turn up to work, although not which day any one of the others is not to turn up. Moreover, each knows that if he turns up for work, he will have no option but to deliver any available mail.

The Pony Express riders are *collectively* morally responsible for failing to deliver the mail on each of the 10 occasions if (a) the mail was not in fact delivered on these 10 occasions, (b) the riders have an institutionally based joint moral responsibility to bring it about that the mail is delivered to its final destination on each occasion, (c) each of the riders delivering the mail in his sector on each occasion (having as a collective end the delivery of the mail to its final destination) would have resulted in the delivery of the mail to its final destination on each occasion, (d) each rider individually intentionally refrained from delivering the mail in his sector on one occasion, and did so having as an end that the mail would not reach its final destination on that occasion and, given the arrangement with the other riders, on the other nine occasions.[25]

Finally, it should be noted that, other things being equal, if a given rider is *not individually* morally responsible for failing to deliver the mail

---

[25] Each rider has the collective end that the mail not reach its final destination on each of the 10 occasions. Each also has an individual end that the mail not reach its final destination on that one occasion when he does not turn up to work.

in his sector on the one occasion on which his failure is necessary in the circumstances to prevent the mail's getting through to its final destination, then that rider does *not* share in the *collective* moral responsibility for failing to deliver the mail to its final destination on that occasion and on the other nine occasions (given that *ex hypothesei* he was not individually morally responsible for failing to deliver the mail in his sector on any of these other nine occasions).

## 6. AGAINST THE COLLECTIVIST CONCEPTION OF MORAL RESPONSIBILITY

In this section I turn to a theoretical issue that arises in relation to the moral responsibility of institutional actors for institutional wrongdoing.[26] On the view that I have presented above it is only individual human persons that are morally responsible for institutional moral wrongdoing. However, there is a view which seeks to attribute moral responsibility to institutions per se (and, more generally, to collectives per se). I need to resist this collectivist conception. I will do so here by considering and rejecting three institutional scenarios offered in support of the collectivist conception by David Copp (2007). Elsewhere I have offered detailed rebuttals of Copp (Miller 2007e), French (Miller 2001b), Gilbert (Miller and Makela 2005), and other collectivists.

Copp frames the issue in terms of what he refers to as the Collective Moral Autonomy Thesis (CMA). CMA breaks into two parts: The first part is the thesis that (O), "it is possible for a collective to have a moral obligation to do something even if no (natural) person who is a member of that collective has a relevantly related moral obligation – an obligation, as we might say, to take part in bringing it about that the collective fulfils its obligation"; the second part is the thesis (R)

> It is possible for a collective to be morally responsible for having done something (that is, to deserve a specific moral response for having done it, such as praise or blame) even if no (natural) person who is a member of that collective is morally responsible (or deserves the same kind of response) for having done something relevantly related – for having taken a part, as we might say, in bringing it about that the collective did the relevant thing.

Copp nowhere offers an account of what he terms "collectives," but he includes social institutions such as armies, states, and universities.

---

[26] An earlier version of the material in this section appeared in Miller (2007e).

Moreover, his three key scenarios are to do with institutions, namely, a government, a prison, and a university.

In this context it is important to stress that to sustain CMA, Copp must provide clear examples of collectives that possess *moral* obligations and are the bearers of *moral* responsibility; after all, it is uncontroversial that some collectives, such as corporations, have *institutional*, including legal, obligations and are the bearers of *institutional*, including legal, responsibility. Moreover, the collectives in question must not themselves be susceptible of individualist analysis such that it turns out that some individual human beings have the moral obligations and/or moral responsibility in question, albeit not the individuals Copp had initially nominated. For example, in Copp's opening example of individual bombers who (he claims) do not have an all things considered obligation not to bomb the city, there is a collective who does have such an obligation, namely, the government. However, the government is a collective susceptible to individualist analysis, for example, in terms of the prime minister and his or her cabinet. Moreover, once this analysis is performed, then individual human beings, such as the prime minister, are available as possessors of the relevant all things considered moral obligations and bearers of the associated moral responsibility.

Copp's notion of moral responsibility is essentially a backward-looking notion to be applied to past and present morally significant actions – and as such associated with praise and blame – and not to be confused with the essentially forward-looking notion of moral responsibility in play in examples such as "Parents are morally responsible for seeing to it that their children are well fed" and "The mechanic is morally responsible for seeing to it that the car brakes are fixed properly." Perhaps the latter forward-looking sense of moral responsibility is a special case of moral obligation, for example, "Parents have a moral *obligation* to see to it that their children are well fed." This forward-looking notion of moral responsibility is akin to and, in some cases, derived from institutional responsibility; for example, police officers have an institutional and a moral responsibility to arrest offenders.

Further, I take it that the notion of moral responsibility in play here is pretheoretic in character; no particular theory of moral responsibility is being presupposed. Of course, some theorists identify the concept of moral responsibility with the concept of blameworthiness/praiseworthiness (or with the more general concept of deserving of a positive or negative response, including but not restricted to blame or praise).[27] Doubtless, *in general* if someone is morally responsible for some act, then the person will be blameworthy (in the case of a morally wrong act) and praiseworthy (in the case of a morally right act). However, it is controversial – and, as mentioned above, in my view false – that for someone to be morally responsible simply consists in their being blameworthy or praiseworthy. On the face of it a person can be morally responsible for an action without being either blameworthy or praiseworthy. Consider the case of someone who is asked if he will murder his mother and father in return for a payment of $1,000. He refuses to do so. He is morally responsible for having done the morally right thing; so he is not blameworthy. On the other hand, he is surely not worthy of praise merely because he refused to murder his own parents for a relatively small amount of money. So he is morally responsible for his action, but neither blameworthy nor praiseworthy.

Now consider a different but related example. In this second example the man is not offered any money to kill his mother and father; rather, he will be killed unless he kills two innocent strangers. He is under a moral obligation not to kill the two innocent strangers, and, presumably, this overrides his moral right to preserve his own life; so all things considered he ought not to kill the two strangers. On the other hand, if in fact he does kill the two strangers, he will be morally excused for doing so, given his moral right to preserve his own life. Self-evidently, he is not praiseworthy; after all, he did the wrong thing. Nor is he blameworthy, however, given that he is morally excused for performing the action. Yet the man is morally responsible for his action of killing the two strangers and, thereby, preserving his own life. For he correctly believed that the action was morally wrong all things considered, and he could have chosen to do what was morally right; he was not, for example, overcome with fear. It is just that he decided on reflection to act in accordance with his

---

[27] Copp opts for this more general concept in the revised version of his paper. However, it is not clear that this does not simply create further problems for him. For the notion of being deserving of a positive/negative response is close to being vacuous; in particular, it is now unclear whether the positive/negative responses in question have any specifically moral character. Thus I like X is a positive response to X and may well be warranted. But liking X is not necessarily a moral response; after all, X might be the teller of a funny joke. But surely a person is not necessarily *morally* responsible for every funny joke that they make; funny jokes do not necessarily have any moral significance, even if (being funny) they are deserving of a positive response. At any rate, I want to maintain not only a distinction between moral responsibility and blameworthiness/praiseworthiness, but also a distinction between moral responsibility and deserving of a negative/positive response.

own self-interest rather than his moral obligation. At any rate, my main
point is that Copp is not entitled to assume that the concept of moral
responsibility is to be identified with the concept of blameworthiness/
praiseworthiness.[28] So his arguments in favor of CMA cannot rely on this
assumption.

### Example 1: Kidnapping and the Prime Minister

In this example the prime minister (PM), say, Gough Whitlam (a former
PM of Australia), is taken hostage by an outlaw group who threaten to
kill the PM unless the PM authorizes the release of a dangerous prisoner (Copp 2007). The government morally ought, all things considered, to refuse to release the prisoner, because if this demand is acceded
to, many other groups will adopt similar tactics. Moreover, according to
Copp, the PM has a *pro tanto* moral obligation not to release the prisoner.
However, notwithstanding the PM's (claimed) *pro tanto* moral obligation
not to release the prisoner, the PM has an excuse for doing so, namely,
self-preservation.

Here I need to invoke the distinction made in Chapter 1 between
relativizing it to this example, Gough Whitlam *qua* prime minister and
Gough Whitlam *qua* some other role occupant or Gough Whitlam *simpliciter,* that is, Whitlam the individual human being. *Qua* PM in a government obliged to pursue the public interest in the context of present
and possible future hostage situations, Whitlam has an *all things considered* moral obligation not to release the prisoner; on the other hand,
as a human being whose life is presently threatened, Whitlam has a
moral right to self-preservation. Now, Whitlam is both PM (and as such
a member of the government) and a human being whose life is threatened; accordingly, the question arises as to what *he Whitlam* should do,
all things considered. Now let us assume (as in effect Copp does) that
whereas Whitlam's right to self-preservation does not override his obligation not to release the prisoner, it is morally excusable for him to release
the prisoner in these circumstances.

On the analysis I have just offered, *contra* Copp, the example does
not support his proposition that it is possible for a collective to be all-in
morally liable to a moral response (morally responsible all things

---

[28] Or, for that matter, the related but more general notion of deserving of a negative/
positive response.

considered) even if no member of the collective is all-in morally liable to that response for having done something relevantly related. Assume that Whitlam in his capacity as PM in fact releases the prisoner (by signing the appropriate release orders). Given that Whitlam correctly believed that the all things considered moral obligation of the government – and, therefore, his all things considered moral obligation *qua* PM – was to refuse to release the prisoner, Whitlam *qua* PM did what he knew to be morally wrong. Moreover, he could have chosen to do what was the morally right thing for him as PM to do. So Whitlam is morally responsible (as opposed to blameworthy) for committing what it was morally wrong for him as PM to do, to release the prisoner.

What of the government of which the PM is a member? Is the government morally responsible? In Copp's example, aside from the PM, no member of the government (or anyone else for that matter) could have done anything to prevent the prisoner being released; aside from anything else, they did not know, and could not reasonably have known, what was going on. Accordingly, the individual members of the (executive arm of the) government, that is, the cabinet ministers, could not have prevented the prisoner being released, and, therefore, to this extent they are not morally responsible (and, therefore, not blameworthy). (For simplicity, I will at this point treat the government as comprised of the PM and cabinet rather than, for example, all the government members of the legislature.) So, *contra* Copp, the government per se is not morally responsible (and, therefore, not blameworthy); rather, the PM alone bears moral responsibility for the act. Accordingly, perhaps the PM should be dismissed from office by, say, the Queen or, in the case of Australia, the Governor-General (as indeed happened in the case of Whitlam, albeit for very different reasons). At any rate, the example as analyzed does not support Copp's view. For the government is not morally responsible (and, therefore, not blameworthy) for having released the prisoner; moreover, a member of the collective (the PM) *is* morally responsible (as opposed to blameworthy) for having released the prisoner, that is, for having done something relevantly related.

This analysis is consistent with Whitlam's action of releasing the prisoner being morally excusable (and, therefore, Whitlam not being blameworthy), given that it was an act of self-preservation. (Again, note the distinction between being morally responsible for an action and being morally blameworthy for performing it.) As we have seen, Whitlam failed to discharge his all things considered moral obligation not to release the prisoner and was morally responsible for failing to do so. However, that he acted to preserve his life constitutes a moral excuse. So, I am in agreement with Copp that Whitlam committed a morally excusable, morally wrong act; that is, Whitlam is not blameworthy.

The analysis is also consistent with the government, that is, the PM and the members of the cabinet, being held *institutionally responsible* – as opposed to morally responsible – for the release of the prisoner. It might be that there is an institutional arrangement in place to the effect that in such cases the PM is necessarily to be taken to be acting on behalf of the government, that is, the cabinet including the PM; accordingly, the entire membership of the cabinet as well as the PM might be required to resign (or otherwise held to account for failing to discharge their collective institutional responsibility). Here I note that institutional responsibilities and liabilities do not necessarily track moral responsibilities and liabilities. Consider in this connection strict liability in law; an employer might be held strictly liable for the behavior of her employee, notwithstanding the morally exemplary behavior and attitude of the employer.

Indeed, even if we make the quite different (and implausible) assumption, namely, the assumption that the government simply is the PM (Copp seems at one point to be suggesting this), that is, Whitlam *qua* PM is the government, then the analysis is also consistent with the government being morally responsible for failing to discharge its all things considered moral obligation.[29] For the government, that is, Whitlam *qua* PM, is morally responsible for failing to discharge Whitlam *qua* PM's all things considered moral obligation. Is Whitlam *qua* PM blameworthy for not doing his duty? Certainly, Whitlam *qua* PM may reasonably be held liable for his failure to do his duty, for instance, tried and sentenced to imprisonment. However, Whitlam the PM is also Whitlam the man whose life is under threat, and it is unclear whether the concept of blame can sufficiently disaggregate these aspects of a single moral agent; blameworthiness, unlike moral obligation, qualifies

---

[29] I am assuming that the government is an *embodied* role: i.e., if the PM's job is vacant, then, properly speaking, there is no government (although there might be a caretaker government, for example). Accordingly, on this admittedly implausible view that the government simply is the PM, then it would in fact be critical to keep the PM from being killed, because strictly speaking there would be no government unless and until a replacement PM was found. This is, of course, one of the problems of absolute monarchies and the like. Copp at one point appears to countenance the possibility of a government being an unembodied role (or perhaps set of roles). This really would be an abstractionist view of institutions! At any rate, it is, to say the least, implausible that abstract entities can have moral properties; not to speak of agency.

agents not actions. But for the same reason it is equally unclear whether the government, that is, Whitlam *qua* PM, is blameworthy. At any rate, the general point to be made here is that on this rendering of the example there is no collective entity possessed of any moral property not possessed by an individual human person; this is because the collective entity, namely, the government, *is* an individual person, namely, Whitlam *qua* PM.

Copp offers a second version of the prime minister example. However, in this second version it is not the life of the PM that is under threat but rather that of his daughter; it is the PM's daughter who has been kidnapped.

The moral obligation of Whitlam *qua* father is to release the prisoner and save his daughter. (Here the institutional *role* of father might be invoked; alternatively, one might invoke a father's particularistic, personal, and emotionally held moral obligation to his daughter.) On the other hand, the institutionally based moral obligation of Whitlam *qua* PM is not to release the prisoner, but rather to sacrifice the life of the citizen who also happens to be his daughter. If the PM opts to release the prisoner, he is morally responsible for failing to do his duty as PM; presumably, at the very least he would need to resign. (And if he is acting on behalf of the government as a whole, that is, the members of the cabinet including the PM, then perhaps they are all jointly institutionally and morally responsible; accordingly, the other members of the cabinet should also resign.) If Whitlam chooses not to release the prisoner, then he is morally responsible for failing to do his duty *qua* father to save the life of his daughter. He has to choose between two evils, and whichever option he chooses, he is morally responsible for it.

There are moral obligations and (forward-looking) moral responsibilities that an institutional-role occupant might possess *qua* role occupant. However, in addition to these there are moral obligations and (forward-looking) moral responsibilities (both *pro tanto* and all things considered ones) that the occupant of the role might possess, but that do not arise by virtue of his or her role occupancy; rather, they arise by virtue of some other institutional role the person happens to occupy or by virtue of something other than occupancy of an institutional role, for example, by virtue of being a human being. Accordingly, we need the notion of a bearer of moral obligations such that the obligations in question include, but are not restricted to, institutional role obligations – which is to say that we need the idea of an individual human being who might or might not occupy any given institutional role. If we use proper names such as "Whitlam" to refer to individual human beings (names as so-called rigid designators), then we can ascribe moral obligations (both role-based and non–role-based obligations) to Whitlam *simpliciter* (and to other thus named individual human beings). Thus it is Whitlam *simpliciter* – as opposed to Whitlam *qua* PM or Whitlam *qua* father – who has a moral obligation not to kill the innocent. And it is Whitlam *simpliciter* who might have a role-based moral obligation at time t1 but not at time t2, because Whitlam *simpliciter* is not *defined* as the occupant of this (or these) institutional role(s).

A moral obligation all things considered that a person has *qua* role occupant might conflict with a moral obligation that the person has *qua* some other role occupant, or with some non–role-based moral obligation. Accordingly, there might arise the further question as to what the moral obligation of the person all things considered is. Indeed, this is precisely what is taking place in Copp's Kidnapping the PM's Daughter example (as well as in his Kidnapping the Prime Minister version of this example). So Whitlam *qua* PM has a moral obligation all things considered not to release the prisoner. However, Whitlam *qua* father has a moral obligation to save the life of his daughter. Accordingly, Whitlam *simpliciter* now has a further moral question in relation to what he ought to do all things considered. Copp claims that the answer to this further question – the question, what ought Whitlam to do, all things considered – is that Whitlam ought to release the prisoner. I don't want to dispute this. (Although it is not entirely clear to me why Copp thinks that when Whitlam's own life is threatened – as in version 1 of the example – his obligation to refuse to release the prisoner is not overridden, whereas when the life of his daughter is threatened his obligation to refuse to release the prisoner is overridden.) Rather, I want to point out that this is different from the answer to the same question addressed to Whitlam *qua* PM. Moreover, I want to insist that there are two distinguishable moral questions in play, both of which are questions about what ought to be done all things considered. However, the first question is addressed to Whitlam *qua* PM, the second to Whitlam *simpliciter*.

Accordingly, the reply to Copp is that the government has an all things considered moral obligation not to release the prisoner, but Whitlam *qua* member of the government, that is, *qua* PM, *has* a relevantly related all things considered moral obligation, indeed, precisely the same all things considered moral obligation, namely, the obligation not to release the prisoner. So the example does not support CMA.

## Example 2: The Prison Board

In this example, all (Bob, Alice, and Ted) but one member (Carol) of the Board of Governors of a prison vote against a proposal that, morally speaking, they ought to have endorsed. The twist is that each member of the board had a supposed excuse for voting as they did. Copp's principal concern here is with moral responsibility; specifically, he wants to endorse the conclusion that the board is morally responsible all things considered for the outcome, but none of the individual members are morally responsible (all things considered) for it.

By my lights, if the members of the board meet the conditions for being jointly institutionally responsible for the decision, and the decision is morally significant, then – other things being equal – they are, *qua* board members, jointly morally responsible for the outcome. Assume that the decision is morally significant. What of their institutionally based moral responsibility?

Here there are a variety of putative excuses. Suppose a member argues strongly against the joint decision (Carol), or was not in attendance, say, because of an emergency (Bob). If so, then the member can dissociate herself from the board's joint decision, such as by resigning or by stepping down pending the reversal of the decision or issuing a public statement dissociating himself from the decision. If the member does not dissociate herself from the decision, then, in effect, she has accepted it and, therefore, the institutional and moral responsibility that flows from it. In the example, as described, Carol and Bob each accepted the board's decision. Accordingly, Carol and Bob are each institutionally and morally responsible for the adverse outcome of the board's decision.

Second, suppose the board's decision-making process has a design fault: for example, members vote by pushing a button on a panel, but the recording device does not count the votes correctly. Presumably the members of the board are not institutionally responsible for ensuring the good working order of such equipment and, therefore, not morally responsible for voting outcomes that are incorrectly generated in this way. This kind of design fault is not involved in this example as it is described.

Third, suppose two members (Ted and Alice) have an arrangement such that each takes turn in doing the research, and such that the one who has not done the research relies on the other person's research. Suppose that this arrangement goes awry, and each of these members makes a bad decision based on the false belief that the other had done the research. Presumably, this is not an *institutionally* acceptable excuse, because it is up to the member to see to it that her decision is based on the actual results of good research. Moreover, each could have done so, for example, if each had done his own research or checked to ensure what the actual research results were. So each is institutionally and morally responsible for the board's decision. Accordingly, Alice and Ted are each institutionally and morally responsible for the adverse outcome of the board's decision.

I conclude that in the prison board example, as described, the board is morally responsible for the adverse outcome and, *contra* Copp, each member is morally responsible for the adverse outcome. Is the board blameworthy but none of its members morally blameworthy? Presumably, *some* of the members of the board are blameworthy. For example, Alice and Ted are blameworthy in relation to the board's voting outcome because they should not have had their informal practice of relying on the research of the other.

It is consistent with this to hold that Carol in particular is not blameworthy; after all, she voted in favor of the increased security measures, and it might be that all things considered she ought not to dissociate herself from the decision; for example, perhaps in the scheme of things the decision in question is not all that important, and she cannot reasonably dissociate herself from every decision the board makes that she voted against.

Naturally, the example could be redescribed in such a way that each member of the board did not have moral responsibility all things considered for the adverse outcome. One such redescription is that offered by a design fault of the kind mentioned above. However, in this kind of example the collective, the board, is not institutionally or morally responsible.

A second such redescription is one in which each of the members of the board has a valid *moral* excuse for their actions, but none escapes institutional responsibility. On my account the board and its members would not be morally blameworthy, even though they were institutionally responsible. Would they, nevertheless, be morally responsible?

Perhaps, perhaps not; this depends on the nature of excuses. Excuses, such as in the case of the PM in Copp's earlier examples, render a person blameless without negating the person's moral responsibility. Perhaps "excuses" negate moral responsibility and, therefore, render the person blameless as well. So it is quite coherent to hold that the prison board is both institutionally responsible and morally responsible, but blameless.

Moreover, in cases of the latter kind, by the lights of my individualist account of collective moral responsibility, the prison board being morally responsible is equivalent to the members of the prison board being collectively, that is, jointly, morally responsible.

My general suggestion here in relation to blameworthiness in particular is that to the extent that we are inclined not to blame any of the individual members of collective entities for some untoward outcome of their actions, we are inclined not to blame the collective entity. Thus in the prison board example if we really believe each has an acceptable moral excuse – even Ted and Alice – then we will ascribe institutional and moral responsibility to the board, but stop short of blaming it. This suggests that the moral blameworthiness of the prison board really is – *contra* Copp – nothing beyond the blameworthiness of its members. At any rate, my initial point stands, namely, that Copp has not provided, as he needs to, a clear example in which the board is morally blameworthy, but none of its members are.

## Example 3: The Tenure Committee

In Copp's scenario, a university's tenure committee consists of three persons, A, B, and C, and it has to determine whether or not candidate Borderline should be granted tenure. The university's standard for tenure is excellence in each of the three areas of research, teaching, and service. The university's procedure (P1) for determining whether this standard has been met is for each member of the committee to vote on whether she believes the candidate is excellent in all three areas: if there is a majority in favor, then tenure is granted; if not, then it is denied. However, in this instance, A, B, and C each believe there are only two areas in which Borderline is excellent; so each votes to deny tenure, and, consequently, the university denies tenure. The twist is that with respect to each area, such as research, a majority believes Borderline is excellent. Accordingly, if the procedure had been to vote on each area (P2), then Borderline would have been deemed to be excellent in all three areas and would have been granted tenure. Let us assume, as Copp does, that P2 is a good procedure for ensuring the university's standard for tenure is met and that P1 is flawed.

As it happens, I do not accept a number of Copp's key claims in relation to the moral obligations, and attendant responsibility and blameworthiness, of the university, and those of the members of the tenure committee.

Since P1 is a flawed procedure that is delivering an unjust outcome to Borderline, the university has a *pro tanto* moral obligation to adopt a new procedure, for example, P2, and overturn the tenure committee's decision to deny tenure to Borderline. For the same reason the tenure committee, and the individual members of the tenure committee, have a *pro tanto* moral obligation not to deny tenure to Borderline. On the other hand, since at the time in question P1 is the officially sanctioned procedure, the university, the tenure committee, and its members have a *pro tanto* institutional obligation – and consequent moral obligation – to comply with it.

Let us assume, *pace* Copp, that the university has a moral obligation, all things considered, not to refuse tenure to Borderline; the *pro tanto* obligation to avoid an unjust outcome based on a flawed procedure overrides the *pro tanto* obligation to comply with the existing official procedure. What of the members of the tenure committee? Other things being equal, each has a moral obligation, all things considered, not to refuse tenure to Borderline; the members each have the same *pro tanto* moral obligations as the university, and there is, thus far, every reason to believe that these moral obligations have the same moral weight for the members of the committee as they have for the university. In particular, the fact that P1 is the officially sanctioned procedure does not absolve the members of the tenure committee from any moral responsibility for acting in accordance with that procedure, given that the procedure is a flawed one that is producing an unjust outcome, that is, given the assumption made by Copp in constructing the tenure committee scenario.

My conclusion is that, *contra* Copp, the moral obligations, both *pro tanto* and all things considered, of the university and of the members of the tenure committee mirror one another.

Both the university and the members of the tenure committee have a moral obligation, all things considered, not to deny tenure to Borderline. Consequently, if either did so, then (again, *contra* Copp) each would be morally responsible for failing to discharge their respective moral obligations. The same point holds in respect of the blameworthiness of the university and of the members of the tenure committee.

Now, it might be that the two conflicting *pro tanto* obligations in question do not have the same moral weight for the members of the tenure committee that they have for the university. For example, the university might have an obligation to overturn the results of its procedures when they are revealed to be flawed; whereas this might not be an obligation, or might not be as strong an obligation, for the members of the tenure committee. However, if so, this is because the university and the tenure committee are for certain purposes different collectives with different, albeit overlapping, sets of obligations and responsibilities.

Specifically, procedures for awarding tenure are not established by the tenure committee, nor does the tenure committee have responsibility for overturning unfair decisions properly made in accordance with the procedures; rather, these matters are the responsibility of, say, a second committee of the university. So the part of the university that is responsible for the procedures being what they are and for overturning unfair decisions is not the same part of the university that is responsible for making individual decisions as to tenure on the basis of those procedures. But in that case the tenure committee scenario is not a scenario of the kind that Copp needs because it does not involve a collective and the members of that very same collective; rather, it involves two distinct collectives, two distinct committees.

On the other hand, if there is no second committee that is responsible for establishing the procedures for tenure, and for overturning the procedurally correct but unfair decisions of the tenure committee, then presumably the university leadership, such as the senate or the vice-chancellor, is morally responsible for failing to establish such a committee (or functionally equivalent mechanism). In these circumstances the tenure committee *is* morally required to subject the procedures it is using to close moral scrutiny and to see itself as the court of last appeal; in these circumstances the tenure committee has a *pro tanto* obligation to overturn the results of its procedures when they are revealed to be flawed. After all, if it does not, who will?

As it happens, Copp focuses on a particular alleged moral difference between the university and the members of the tenure committee (Copp 2007). He argues that each member of the tenure committee considered individually did not have an all things considered obligation not to deny tenure, notwithstanding that each had a *pro tanto* reason not to deny tenure to Borderline (the same *pro tanto* reason the university had, namely, that this was an unjust outcome based on a flawed procedure). Copp introduces an additional alleged moral consideration in favor of this claim: that "none of them believed that Borderline had achieved excellence in all three of the required areas." That is, each member of the committee considered individually had a reason to deny tenure above and beyond the failure of the candidate to meet the conditions for tenure under procedure P1, namely, that each believed that Borderline had not achieved excellence in all three areas; accordingly, each member considered individually did not have an all things considered obligation not to deny tenure. However, this fact should not be given any moral weight by the members of the tenure committee, assuming that all believe that P1 is a flawed procedure that has delivered an unjust outcome to Borderline. For it is the unacceptability of the procedure (P1) (by virtue of its inability to deliver a just outcome) that is in question, not the judgment of any individual member of the tenure committee in relation to Borderline's lack of excellence in all three areas.

Perhaps Copp intends here to be giving weight to the fact that *all* of the members of the tenure committee judged that Borderline was not excellent in all three areas: that is, each member considers not simply that he does not think that Borderline is not excellent in all three areas but that all the members of the committee think as he does. But that would be tantamount to retracting the proposition that P1 was in fact deeply flawed; it would be to suggest that P1 – the procedure that delivered its verdict on tenure on the basis of whether each member of the committee believed Borderline was excellent in all three areas – was actually a reasonable procedure after all. Clearly this maneuver is not acceptable, because it flies in the face of a central assumption of the example.

A final point to be made here is that even if it was allowable for each of the members of the tenure committee to give moral weight in their decision to their knowledge that it was their common belief that Borderline was not excellent in all three areas, this would not necessarily generate a different all things considered moral obligation for the committee members than that obligation the university is under. For presumably the university should now likewise attach moral weight to the fact that none of the members of the tenure committee believed that Borderline was excellent in all three areas.

Moreover, if the tenure committee is actually constitutive of the university with respect to the latter's decision making on tenure – there being no other committee to hear appeals, for example – then the university would in fact be according such weight simply by virtue of the tenure committee deciding to do so.

And if the university ought *not* to attach the same weight that the tenure committee ought to attach, then this must be because it is a different collective – say, a committee of appeal or a vice-chancellor with the power to overrule the tenure committee's decision – from the collective constituted by the members of the tenure committee: that is, for this purpose the university is not identical with the tenure committee, and the two collectives have, to some extent, disparate obligations and responsibilities.

So we return yet again to the conclusion that Copp's scenario is not a scenario of the kind he needs, because it is not a scenario that involves a collective and the members of that very same collective for the purposes at hand.

## 7. CONCLUSION

In this chapter I have focused on a moral notion that is fundamental to understanding the normative dimension of social institutions, namely, collective moral responsibility. Many social institutions are, or ought to be, established by virtue of a specific collective responsibility we have to one another or to others. Moreover, within any given social institution, institutional actors have collective moral responsibilities to one another and to noninstitutional actors. In this chapter I have outlined an individualist account of collective moral responsibility based in part on the collective end theory of joint action elaborated in Chapter 1. I have also argued for the following claim in relation to collective moral responsibility: If agents are collectively responsible for a joint action or the realization of a (foreseen or reasonably foreseeable) outcome, in the first (institutionally and morally neutral), second (institutional), or third (institutional authority with respect to another person) senses of collective responsibility, and the joint action or outcome is morally significant, then – other things being equal – the agents are collectively *morally* responsible for that action or outcome and – other things being equal – ought to attract moral praise or blame, and (possibly) punishment or reward, for the action or for bringing about the outcome. Further, I have tested this account by applying it to a wide range of cases of collective responsibility. Finally, I have also rebutted a range of counterexamples put forward by David Copp in his elaboration of a competing nonindividualist account.

# 5

# Institutional Corruption

In earlier chapters we discussed various normative aspects of social institutions including human rights (such as individual autonomy) in institutional settings, the application of principles of distributive justice to institutions, and the collective moral responsibility of institutional actors. Another extremely important normative aspect of social institutions is corruption. If illegitimate social institutions can compromise individual autonomy and other human rights, corruption can undermine legitimate social institutions. In the chapters following this one I consider various forms of corruption in specific institutional settings. Here my concern is to articulate a theoretical understanding of the notion of institutional corruption. In doing so, I make use of my above-elaborated individualist, teleological account of social institutions.

## 1. VARIETIES OF INSTITUTIONAL CORRUPTION

The causes and effects of institutional corruption, and how to combat corruption, are issues that are increasingly on the national and international agendas of politicians and other policy makers.[1] For example, the World Bank has relatively recently come around to the view that economic development is closely linked to corruption reduction (World Bank 1997). Again, the FBI is currently investigating numerous suspected financial crimes in the U.S. financial services sector in the wake of the current spate of corporate collapses and bailouts in the investment banking and insurance sector. By contrast, the *concept* of corruption has not received much attention (but see Part 1, "Terms, Concepts and Definitions," of Heidenheimer and Johnston 2002). Existing conceptual

[1] An earlier version of the material in this chapter appeared in Miller (2005).

work on corruption consists of little more than the presentation of brief definitions of corruption as a preliminary to extended accounts of the causes and effects of corruption and the ways to combat it.[2] Moreover, most of these definitions of corruption are unsatisfactory in fairly obvious ways.[3]

Consider one of the most popular of these definitions, namely, "Corruption is the abuse of power by a public official for private gain."[4] No doubt the abuse of public offices for private gain is paradigmatic of corruption. But when a bettor bribes a boxer to "throw" a fight this is corruption for private gain, but it need not involve any public office holder; the roles of boxer and bettor are usually not public offices.

One response to this is to distinguish public corruption from private corruption, and to argue that the above definition is a definition only of public corruption.[5] But if ordinary citizens lie when they give testimony in court, this is corruption; it is corruption of the criminal justice system. However, it does not involve abuse of a public office by a public official. And when police fabricate evidence out of a misplaced sense of justice, this is corruption of a public office, but not for private gain.

In the light of the failure of such analytical-style definitions it is tempting to try to sidestep the problem of providing a theoretical account of the concept of corruption by simply identifying corruption with specific legal and/or moral offences.

However, attempts to identify corruption with specific legal/moral offences are unlikely to succeed. Perhaps the most plausible candidate is bribery; bribery is regarded by some as the quintessential form of corruption (Noonan 1984; Pritchard 1998). But what of nepotism? Surely it is also a paradigmatic form of corruption, and one that is conceptually

---

[2] For example, Klitgaard, Maclean-Abaroa, and Parris (2000, 2) define corruption as "misuse of office for personal gain." For a recent review of the general literature on corruption see Jonathan Hopkins (2002).

[3] An important exception here is the more sophisticated analytical account offered by Dennis Thompson of political corruption in his 1995 book, *Ethics in Congress: From Individual to Institutional Corruption.*

[4] For one of the most influential statements of the abuse of public office for private gain definitions see Joseph Nye (1967, 417–27).

[5] Thompson (1995, 7, 195) distinguishes between individual and institutional corruption; the latter involves infringements of institutional norms – rather than just principles of ordinary morality – by the occupants of institutional roles. However, Thompson remains committed to the conventional definition, albeit only as a definition of institutional corruption – as distinct from individual or private corruption. He says, "Like all forms of corruption, the institutional kind involves the improper use of public office for private purposes" (1995, 7).

distinct from bribery. The person who accepts a bribe is understood as being required to provide a benefit to the briber, otherwise it is not a bribe; but the person who is the beneficiary of an act of nepotism is not necessarily understood as being required to return the favor.

In fact, corruption is exemplified by a very wide and diverse array of phenomena of which bribery is only one kind, and nepotism another. Paradigm cases of corruption include the following. The commissioner of taxation channels public monies into his personal bank account, thereby corrupting the public financial system. A rogue trader speculates unsuccessfully on international financial markets with very large amounts of money that he neither owns nor is authorized to use, thereby causing the collapse of the investment bank that employs him. A political party secures a majority vote by arranging for ballot boxes to be stuffed with false voting forms, thereby corrupting the electoral process. A police officer fabricates evidence to secure convictions, thereby corrupting the judicial process. A number of doctors close ranks and refuse to testify against a colleague who they know has been negligent in relation to an unsuccessful surgical operation leading to loss of life; institutional accountability procedures are thereby undermined. A sports trainer provides the athletes he trains with banned substances to enhance their performance, thereby subverting the institutional rules laid down to ensure fair competition. It is self-evident that none of these corrupt actions are instances of bribery.

Further, it is far from obvious that the way forward at this point is simply to add a few additional offences to the initial "list" consisting of the single offence of bribery. Candidates for being added to the list of offences would include nepotism, police fabricating evidence, cheating in sport by using performance-enhancing drugs, fraudulent use of travel funds by politicians, and so on.[6] However, there is bound to be disagreement in relation to any such list. For example, law enforcement practitioners often distinguish between fraud, on the one hand, and corruption, on the other.[7] Most important, any such list needs to be justified by recourse to some principle or principles. Ultimately, naming a set of offences that might be regarded as instances of corruption does not obviate the need for a theoretical, or quasi-theoretical, account of the concept of corruption.

---

[6] Arguably some forms of nepotism are not also forms of corruption. See Adam Bellow (2003).

[7] For an attempt to make out this proposed distinction see G. J. Rossouw (2000, 886–9).

As it happens, there is at least one further salient strategy for demarcating the boundaries of corrupt acts. Implicit in much of the literature on corruption is the view that corruption is essentially a legal offence, and essentially a legal offence in the economic sphere.[8] Accordingly, one could seek to identify corruption with economic crimes, such as bribery, fraud, and insider trading. To some extent this kind of view reflects the dominance of economically focused material in the corpus of academic literature on corruption. It also reflects the preponderance of proposed economic solutions to the problem of corruption. After all, if corruption is essentially an economic phenomenon, is it not plausible that the remedies for corruption will be economic ones?[9]

But many acts of corruption are not unlawful. That paradigm of corruption, bribery, is a case in point. Before 1977 it was not unlawful for U.S. companies to offer bribes to secure foreign contracts; indeed, elsewhere such bribery was not unlawful until much later.[10] So corruption is not necessarily unlawful. This is because corruption is not at bottom simply a matter of law; rather, it is fundamentally a matter of morality.

Second, corruption is not necessarily economic in character. An academic who plagiarizes the work of others is not committing an economic crime or misdemeanor; and she might be committing plagiarism simply to increase her academic status. There might not be any financial benefit sought or gained. Academics are more strongly motivated by status, rather than by wealth. A police officer who fabricates evidence against a person he believes to be guilty of pedophilia is not committing an economic crime; and he might do so because he believes the accused to be guilty and does not want him to go unpunished. Economics is not necessarily involved as an element of the officer's crime or as a motivation. When police do wrong they are often motivated by a misplaced sense of justice, rather than by financial reward. Again, a person in authority motivated by sadistic pleasure who abuses her power by meting out cruel and unjust treatment to those subject to her authority is not engaging in an economic crime, and she is not motivated by economic

---

[8] This is implicit in much of Susan Rose-Ackerman's influential work on corruption. See Rose-Ackerman (1999).

[9] See Rose-Ackerman (1999) for this kind of view. See Barry Hindess (2001) for a contrary view.

[10] See the Foreign Corrupt Practices Act of 1977, Public Law 95–213 (5305), December 19, 1977, United States Code 78a, Section 103. See also Organization for Economic Co-operation and Development (OECD) Convention against Bribery of Foreign Public Officials in International Business Transactions of 15th February 1999.

considerations. Many of those who occupy positions of authority are motivated by a desire to exercise power for its own sake, rather than by a desire for financial reward.

Economic corruption is an important form of corruption; however, it is not the only form of corruption. There are noneconomic forms of corruption, including many types of police corruption, judicial corruption, political corruption, academic corruption, and so on. Indeed, there are at least as many forms of corruption as there are social institutions that might become corrupted. Further, economic gain is not the only motivation for corruption. There are a variety of different kinds of attractions that motivate corruption, including status, power, addiction to drugs or gambling, and sexual gratification, as well as economic gain.

We can conclude that the various currently influential definitions of corruption, and the recent attempts to circumscribe corruption by listing paradigmatic offences, have failed. They failed in large part because the class of corrupt actions comprises an extremely diverse array of types of moral and legal offences.

That said, *some* progress has been made. At the very least, we have identified corruption as fundamentally a moral, as opposed to legal, phenomenon. Acts can be corrupt even though they are, and even ought to be, legal. Moreover, it is evident that not all acts of immorality are acts of corruption; corruption is only one species of immorality. Consider an otherwise gentle husband who in a fit of anger strikes his adulterous wife and accidentally kills her. The husband has committed an act that is morally wrong; he has committed murder, or perhaps culpable homicide, or at least manslaughter. But his action is not necessarily an act of corruption. Obviously the person who is killed (the wife) is not corrupted in the process of being killed. Moreover, the act of killing does not necessarily corrupt the perpetrator (the husband). Perhaps the person who commits a wrongful killing (the husband) does so just once and in mitigating circumstances, and suffers remorse. Revulsion at his act of killing might cause such a person to embark thereafter on a life of moral rectitude. If so, the person has not been corrupted as a result of his wrongful act.[11]

An important distinction in this regard is the distinction between human rights violations and corruption. Genocide is a profound moral wrong, but it is not corruption. This is not to say that there is not an

---

[11] Nor does there appear to be any institution or institutional process that has been corrupted, e.g., the institution of marriage.

important relationship between human rights violations and corruption; on the contrary, there is often a close and mutually reinforcing nexus between them (Pearson 2001). Consider the endemic corruption and large-scale human rights abuse that have taken place in authoritarian regimes, such as that of Idi Amin in Uganda and that of Suharto in Indonesia. And there is increasing empirical evidence of an admittedly complex causal connection between corruption and the infringement of subsistence rights – there is evidence, that is, of a causal relation between corruption and poverty. Indeed, some human rights violations are also acts of corruption. For example, wrongfully and unlawfully incarcerating one's political opponent is a human rights violation; but it is also corrupting the political and judicial processes.

Thus far, examples of different types of corrupt action have been presented, and corrupt actions have been distinguished from some other types of immoral action. However, the class of corrupt actions has not been adequately demarcated within the more general class of immoral actions. To do so, a definition of corrupt actions is needed, and specifically of actions that corrupt social institutions (Miller 2001, chap. 6). To this task we now turn.

## 2. FIVE HYPOTHESES CONCERNING THE CONCEPT OF INSTITUTIONAL CORRUPTION

In this section I discuss five hypotheses concerning the concept of institutional corruption.

### First Hypothesis: The Personal Character of Corruption

Persons are relevantly involved in all corruption, and in institutional corruption in particular.

Let us assume that there are at least two general forms of corruption, namely, institutional corruption and noninstitutional personal corruption.[12] Noninstitutional personal corruption is corruption of persons outside institutional settings. Such corruption pertains to the moral character of persons, and consists in the despoiling of their moral

---

[12] It may be that institutional corruption and noninstitutional personal corruption are not jointly exhaustive forms of corruption. In particular, there could be corruption of noninstitutional practices. If so, then this form of corruption will also involve persons. It might be argued that there can be noninstitutional corruption of practices in which

character. If an action has a corrupting effect on a person's character, it will typically be corrosive of one or more of a person's virtues. These virtues might be virtues that attach to the person *qua* human being, for instance, the virtues of compassion and fairness in one's dealings with other human beings. Alternatively – or in some cases, additionally – these virtues might attach to persons *qua* occupants of specific institutional roles, for example, impartiality in a judge or objectivity in a journalist.

Our concern here is only with institutional corruption. Nevertheless, it is plausible that corruption in general, including institutional corruption, typically involves the despoiling of the moral character of persons, and in particular, in the case of institutional corruption, the despoiling of the moral character of institutional-role occupants *qua* institutional-role occupants. To this extent institutional corruption involves personal corruption.

Note that personal corruption, that is, being corrupted, is not the same thing as performing a corrupt action, that is, being a corruptor. Typically, corruptors are corrupted, but this is not necessarily the case. Note also that corruptors are not simply persons who perform actions that corrupt, they are also morally responsible for this corruption. (As we shall see, there is one important category of corruptors that is an exception to this, namely, corruptors who are not morally responsible for being corrupted, yet whose actions are both an expression of their corrupt characters and also have a corrupting effect.) The precise nature of corruptors and their relationship to the corrupted is discussed in more detail below.

Note also in relation to personal corruption that there is a distinction to be made between possession of a virtue and possession of a disposition to behave in certain ways. Virtues consist in part of dispositions, but are not wholly constituted by dispositions. A compassionate person, for example, is disposed to help people. But such a person also experiences

---

no person corrupts and in which no person is corrupted, e.g., corruption of a noninstitutional practice without corruption of any participants in the practice. Perhaps the conventional practice in a community of neighbors watching out for one another's property when it is unintentionally left unsecured, e.g., a neighbor keeping an eye on the unlocked garage next door in case of thieves, is corrupted when a large minority of the members of the community can no longer be bothered to comply with this convention. Yet, presumably those who flout the convention are not thereby guilty of corruption and have not thereby been corrupted. After all, they are not under a moral obligation to comply; compliance is a supererogatory act. If so, then it seems that the practice has not been corrupted after all; rather, such cases are better thought of simply as partially abandoned practices than as corrupted ones.

certain emotional states and understands other people in a certain light; compassion involves nondispositional states. Moreover, a compassionate person has actually performed compassionate acts; he or she is not simply disposed to do so. Accordingly, although personal corruption may consist in part of the development or suppression of certain dispositions, for instance, in developing the disposition to accept bribes or in suppressing the disposition to refuse them, the development or suppression of such dispositions would not normally constitute the corruption of persons. Thus a person who has a disposition to accept bribes but who is never offered any is not corrupt, except perhaps in an attenuated sense.

Naturally, in the case of institutional corruption typically greater institutional damage is being done than simply the despoiling of the moral character of the institutional-role occupants. Specifically, institutional processes are being undermined, and/or institutional ends subverted. Here the institutional ends in question are the ultimate collective ends definitive of the institution, and/or the proximate individual and collective ends the realization of which facilitates those ultimate ends (Chapter 1). Needless to say, if the collective ends definitive of an institution are subverted, then to that extent the institution will fail to provide the collective good that is its raison d'être (see Chapter 2).

However, the undermining of institutional processes and/or ends is not a sufficient condition for institutional corruption. Acts of institutional damage that are not performed by a corruptor and do not corrupt persons are better characterized as acts of institutional *corrosion*. Consider, for example, funding decisions that gradually reduce public monies allocated to the court system in some large jurisdiction. As a consequence, magistrates might be progressively less well trained, and there might be fewer and fewer of them to deal with the gradually increasing workload of cases. This may well lead to a diminution over decades in the quality of the adjudications of these magistrates, and so the judicial processes are to an extent undermined. However, given the size of the jurisdiction and the incremental nature of these changes, neither the magistrates, nor anyone else, might be aware of this process of judicial corrosion, or even able to become aware of it (given heavy workloads, absence of statistical information, etc.). It seems that these judges have not undergone a process of personal corruption, and this is the reason we are disinclined to view this situation as one of institutional corruption.

One residual question here is whether or not institutional-role corruption could exist in the absence of the undermining of institutional processes and/or institutional ends. Perhaps it could not for the reason that an institutional role is defined in large part in terms of the institutional ends that the role serves as well as the institutional processes in which the role occupant participates in the service of those institutional ends. A possible counterexample might be that of a "sleeper": an official who accepts regular pay from a foreign spy agency but has not and perhaps never will be asked for any reciprocal service. At any rate, the close relationship between institutional roles, on the one hand, and institutional processes and ends, on the other, explains why institutional corruption typically involves both the despoiling of institutional role occupants *qua* institutional role occupants and the undermining of institutional processes and ends (Chapter 1, Section 6).

Finally, we need to formulate the first hypothesis precisely. The hypothesis is that, to be corrupt, an action must involve a corruptor who performs the action or a person who is corrupted by it. Although the corruptor and the corrupted might be the same person, this is not necessarily the case, and, indeed, there need not be both a corruptor and a corrupted; all that is required is that there be a corruptor or a corrupted person.

The first hypothesis expresses a necessary condition for an action being an instance of institutional corruption and, indeed, for its being an instance of corruption at all. This first hypothesis has turned out to be correct.

### Second Hypothesis: The Causal Character of Corruption

If a serviceable definition of the concept of a corrupt action is to be found – and specifically, one that does not collapse into the more general notion of an immoral action – then attention needs to be focused on the moral *effects* that some actions have on persons and institutions. An action is corrupt only if it corrupts something or someone – so corruption is not only a moral concept, but also a *causal* or quasi-causal concept:[13] that is, an action is corrupt by virtue of having a *corrupting effect* on a person's moral character or on an institutional process or end. If an action has a corrupting effect on an institution, undermining institutional processes or ends (individual and collective ends), then typically – but not necessarily – it has a corrupting effect also on persons *qua* role occupants in the affected institutions.

[13] This kind of account has ancient origins, e.g., in Aristotle. See Hindess (2001).

In relation to the concept of *institutional* corruption, the second hypothesis states (as a necessary condition) that an action is corrupt only if it has the effect of undermining an institutional process or of subverting an institutional end or of despoiling the character of some role occupant *qua* role occupant. This hypothesis asserts the *causal character of corruption*.

In this regard, note that an infringement of a specific law or institutional rule or norm does not in and of itself constitute an act of institutional corruption. To do so, any such infringement needs to have an institutional *effect*, for example, to defeat the institutional end of the rule, to subvert the institutional process governed by the rule, or to contribute to the despoiling of the moral character of a role occupant *qua* role occupant. In short, we need to distinguish between the offence considered in itself and the institutional effect of committing that offence. Considered in itself the offence of, say, lying is an infringement of a law, rule, social norm, and/or a moral principle. However, the offence is an act of institutional corruption only if it has some effect, for example, it is performed in a courtroom setting and thereby subverts the judicial process.[14]

A further point to be made here is that an act that has a corrupting effect might not be a moral offence considered in itself. For example, the provision of information by a corporate officer to an investor that will enable the investor to buy shares cheaply before they rise in value might not be a moral offence considered in itself; in general, providing information is an innocuous activity. However, in this corporate setting it might constitute insider trading and do institutional damage; as such, it may well be an act of corruption.

---

[14] Consider the following example in response to the second hypothesis. Q is responsible for counting votes in a precinct. He cheats and records more votes for candidate A, but this does not affect the election result – A wins, but A would have won anyway. It also has no effect on Q, as he is a bad person to begin with. On the causal account of corruption, Q has cheated; but has there been corruption? There are two relevant kinds of case. Suppose there are only two candidates, A and B, in the precinct and the vote count without cheating would have been *heavily* in favor of A anyway, i.e., the false recording of votes made no significant difference either in terms of the substantive outcome (A winning) or in terms of the margin of the win (A winning by a landslide). According to the causal account there has not been corruption – even if there was attempted corruption and the infringement of an institutional rule. This seems correct. On the other hand, if A would have won anyway, but only by a wafer-thin margin absent the false count – then the false vote counting has made a significant difference to the outcome, albeit only in terms of the relative number of votes for A and the electorate's consequent false belief that A was supported by an overwhelming majority. According to the causal account there has been corruption. Again, this seems to be correct.

A final point concerns the alleged responsibility for corruption of external noninstitutional actors in contexts in which there are mediating internal institutional actors. In general, an act performed by an external noninstitutional actor is not an act of institutional corruption if there is a mediating institutional actor who is fully responsible for the institutional harm. Consider an accountant who is besotted with a woman with expensive tastes. His obsession with the woman causes him to spend money on her that he does not have. Accordingly, he embezzles money from the company he works for. There is a causal chain of sorts from her expensive tastes to his act of embezzlement and the consequent institutional harm that his act in turn causes. However, she is not an institutional corruptor; rather, he is. For he is fully responsible for his act of embezzlement, and it is this act – and this act alone – that constitutes an act of institutional corruption. It does so by virtue of the institutional damage that it does.

It might be argued that although she did not corrupt any institutional process or end, she nevertheless corrupted him *qua* role occupant, for instance, by undermining his disposition to act honestly. But *she* has done no such thing. Rather, his disposition to act honestly has been undermined by himself, and specifically by his desire to please her coupled with his lack of commitment to the ethical and institutional requirements of his institutional role as an accountant.

Summing up, the second hypothesis states a necessary condition for an action being an instance of institutional corruption and, indeed, for its being an instance of corruption at all. This second hypothesis has turned out to be correct.

### Third Hypothesis: The Moral Responsibility of Corruptors

The third hypothesis states that an action is corrupt only if the person who performs it either intends or foresees the harm that it will cause – or, at the very least, could and should have foreseen it. Let us say that this further necessary condition expresses *the moral responsibility of corruptors*.[15]

As noted above, there is one important exception to the moral responsibility of corruptors hypothesis. The exception is that subclass of corruptors who are (a) corrupt, but not morally responsible for being so;

---

[15] Obviously, here I am working with a simplified definition of moral responsibility that does not take into account complications such as that a person might not be morally responsible if under hypnosis they knowingly perform a corrupt action.

and (b) whose actions are an expression of their corrupted characters and also have a corrupting effect.

We need to invoke our earlier distinction between acts of institutional corruption and acts of institutional *corrosion*. An act might undermine an institutional process or end without the person who performed it intending this effect, foreseeing this effect, or, indeed, even being in a position such that they could or should have foreseen this effect. Such an act may well be an act of corrosion, but it would not necessarily be an act of corruption. Consider our magistrates example involving a diminution over time in the quality of the adjudications of these magistrates. Neither government officials and other public servants responsible for resourcing and training the magistracy, nor the magistrates themselves, intend or foresee this institutional harm; indeed, perhaps no one could reasonably have foreseen the harmful effects of these shortcomings in training and failure to respond to increased workloads. This is judicial corrosion, but not judicial corruption.[16]

Because persons who perform corrupt actions (corruptors) intend or foresee – or at least should have foreseen – the corrupting effect their actions would have, these persons typically are blameworthy, but not *necessarily* so. For there are cases in which someone knowingly performs a corrupt action but is, say, coerced into so doing, and is therefore not blameworthy. So on this view it is possible to perform an act of corruption, be morally responsible for performing it, and yet remain blameless.

Moreover, we earlier distinguished between two species of corruptor. There are those corruptors who are morally responsible for their corrupt actions. And there are those corruptors who are not responsible for their corrupt character, but whose actions are (a) an expression of their corrupted character and (b) actions that have a corrupting effect.

Accordingly, we now have a threefold distinction in relation to corruptors: (1) corruptors who are morally responsible for their corrupt action and blameworthy, (2) corruptors who are morally responsible for their corrupt action and blameless, (3) corruptors who are not

[16] On the other hand, if the magistrates became aware of the diminution in the quality of their adjudications and chose to do nothing about it, then arguably the process of corrosion might have become a process of corruption by virtue of the corrupting effect it is having on the character of the magistrates *qua* magistrates. This example shows that there can be corruption of a person (the magistrate(s)) without a corruptor (assume the government and other officials are unaware of the problem of training and resourcing the magistracy). Naturally, if the resources were simply unavailable, then there would not be corruption on anyone's part, notwithstanding their knowledge of the harm being done.

morally responsible for having a corrupt character, but whose actions are (a) expressive of their corrupt character and (b) actions that have a corrupting effect. The existence of the third category of corruptors demonstrates that the third hypothesis is incorrect.

## Fourth Hypothesis: The Asymmetry between Corruptors and Those Corrupted

The fourth hypothesis concerns persons – in the sense of institutional-role occupants – who are corrupted. The contrast here is twofold. In the first place, persons are being contrasted with *institutional processes and ends* (individual and collective ends) that might be subverted. In the second place, those who are *corrupted* are being contrasted with those who *corrupt* (the corruptors).

Those who are corrupted have to some extent, or in some sense, allowed themselves to be corrupted; they are *participants* in the process of their corruption. Specifically, they have *chosen* to perform the actions that ultimately had the corrupting effect on them, and they could have chosen otherwise.[17] In this respect the corrupted are no different from the corruptors.

Nevertheless, those who are corrupted and those who corrupt may be different in respect of their intentions and beliefs concerning the corrupting effect of their actions. Specifically, it may not be true of those who allow themselves to be corrupted that they intended or foresaw or should have foreseen this outcome. This is especially likely in the case of the young and other vulnerable groups who allow themselves to be corrupted but cannot be expected to realize that their actions, or more likely omissions, would have this consequence.[18] Consider the case of children recruited into Hitler's Youth Movement (Hitler Jugend) who

[17] This holds even when people are corrupted through coercion, so long as they could have chosen to resist the coercion. On the other hand, if the action they performed was, for example, drug induced or otherwise not under their control, then they cannot be said to have chosen to perform it in my sense.

[18] Nevertheless, since it is possible to be corrupted without intending or foreseeing this – indeed, without the existence of any reasonable expectation that one would foresee it – one can be blameless for being corrupted in a way that one cannot be blameless for an act of corruption. This is because a putative act of corruption of an institutional process or purpose would not be – according to my account – an act of corruption, if the putative corruptor did not intend or foresee the corrupting effect of his action, and could not reasonably have been expected to foresee this corrupting effect. (Naturally, the act could still be an act of corruption if some person was corrupted by it.)

were inducted into the practice of spying on their classmates, teachers, and even parents, and reporting to the Nazi authorities any supposedly suspicious or deviant activities.

Moreover, even normally endowed adults who are placed in environments in which there are subtle and incremental, but more or less irresistible, inducements to engage in legal or moral offences can gradually and imperceptibly become corrupted. Consider a young police officer who has just started working in the narcotics area. Keen to "fit in," he foolishly accepts a minor "gift" of money from a senior police officer without knowing what it is for; he has committed a relatively minor legal infraction. Later on at a drunken party he reluctantly agrees to smoke a cannabis joint with some of his new colleagues (another minor legal infraction). Still later he is informed that the payment was his "cut" of an unlawful drug deal. This is done in the context of his being enthusiastically welcomed as "one of them," albeit the dire consequences of "ratting" on one's fellow police officers are also made clear. Confused and scared, he fails to report this unlawful payment; now he has committed a serious offence. The police officer is compromised, and compromised in a corrupt and intimidating police environment. He is on the proverbial slippery slope.

A corruptor of other persons or institutional processes can in performing these corrupt actions also and simultaneously be producing corrupting effects on him- or herself: that is, acts of corruption can have, and typically do have, a side effect in relation to the corruptor. They not only corrupt the person and/or institutional process that they are intended to corrupt; they also corrupt the corruptor, albeit usually unintentionally. Consider bribery in relation to a tendering process. The bribe corrupts the tendering process, and it will probably have a corrupting effect on the moral character of the bribe-*taker*. However, in addition, it might well have a corrupting effect on the moral character of the bribe-*giver*.

Here we need to distinguish between a corrupt action that has no effect on an institutional process or on another person, but that contributes to the corruption of the character of the would-be corruptor; and a *noncorrupt* action that is a mere *expression* of a corrupt moral character but that has no corrupting effect either on the agent or on anyone or anything else. In this connection consider two sorts of would-be bribe-givers whose bribes are rejected. Suppose that in both cases their action has no corrupting effect on an institutional process or other person. Now suppose that in the first case the bribe-giver's action of offering the bribe weakens his disposition not to offer bribes; so the offer has a corrupting effect on his character. However, suppose that in the case of the second bribe-giver, his failed attempt to bribe generates in him a feeling of shame and a disposition not to offer bribes. So his action has no corrupting effect, either on himself or externally on an institutional process or other person. In both cases the action is the expression of a partially corrupt moral character. However, in the first, but not the second, case the bribe-giver's action is corrupt by virtue of having a corrupt effect on himself.

I have argued that the corrupted are not necessarily morally responsible for being corrupted. I have also argued that typically corruptors are morally responsible for performing their corrupt actions. Accordingly, I have offered the hypothesis of an asymmetry between the corruptors and the corrupted. But what of those corruptors who are not morally responsible for their corrupt characters? Surely, at least in some cases, such people are not morally responsible for their corrupt actions, so strictly speaking – and contrary to our hypothesis – there is no asymmetry between the corrupted and the corruptors. This seems correct so far as it goes. However, some of those who are not morally responsible for having been corrupted are, nevertheless, morally responsible for not now trying to combat their corrupt characters. To that extent they might be held morally responsible for their corrupt actions, even if not for having been corrupted. Further, there is a difference between an action that corrupts and that is an expression of a corrupt character, and an action that has a corrupting effect but that is in no sense under the control of the person who performed it; for example, they did not intend to perform it, or their intention to perform it was caused by some agent external to themselves. For one thing, the former action, but not the latter action, is the action of a corruptor (as I have defined corruptors). Moreover, even if a person has a corrupt character and can do little about this, it does not follow that they have no control over the actions that are an expression of that character. Consider an official who finds it very hard to refuse bribes but who, nevertheless, tries to avoid opportunities in which he will be offered bribes. The upshot of this is that the hypothesis of an asymmetry between all corruptors and the corrupted may not hold up in anything other than an attenuated form. There is an asymmetry between the corrupted and those corruptors who are morally responsible for their actions: namely, the former are not necessarily morally responsible for being corrupted. However, some of those corruptors who are not responsible for being corrupted might not be responsible for their corrupt actions either. Accordingly, the fourth hypothesis is incorrect.

### Fifth Hypothesis: Institutional Corruption Involves Institutional Actors Who Corrupt or Are Corrupted

The fifth and final hypothesis to be discussed concerns noninstitutional agents who culpably perform acts that undermine legitimate institutional processes or ends. As concluded above, corruption, even if it involves the abuse of public office, is not necessarily pursued for private gain. Dennis Thompson also makes this point in relation to political corruption (1995, 29). However, Thompson also holds that political corruption, at least, necessarily involves abuse of public office. We have canvassed arguments that *contra* this view acts of corruption, including acts of political corruption, might be actions performed by persons who do not hold public office. However, we now need to invoke a distinction between persons who hold a public office and persons who have an institutional role. Citizens are not necessarily holders of public offices, but they do have an institutional role *qua* citizens, for example, as voters.

Consider the case of a citizen and voter who holds no public office but who, nevertheless, breaks into his local electoral office and falsifies the electoral role to assist his favored candidate in getting elected. This is an act of corruption; specifically, it is corruption of the electoral process. However, it involves no public office holder, either as corruptor or as corrupted. By contrast, consider a fundamentalist Muslim from Saudi Arabia who is opposed to democracy and who breaks into an electoral office in an impoverished African state and falsifies the electoral roll to facilitate the election of an extremist right-wing candidate who is likely, if elected, to polarize the already deeply divided community and thereby undermine the fledgling democracy. Let us further assume that the fundamentalist does so without the knowledge of the candidate, or, indeed, of anyone else. We are disinclined to view this as a case of corruption for two reasons: First, the offender is not an occupant of a relevant institutional role; he is not a citizen or even a resident of the state in question. Second, while the offender undermined a legitimate institutional process, namely, the electoral process, he did not corrupt or undermine the character of the occupant of an institutional role.

Accordingly, we can conclude that acts of institutional corruption necessarily involve a corruptor who performs the corrupt action *qua occupant of an institutional role* and/or someone who is corrupted *qua occupant of an institutional role*.

This enables us to distinguish not only acts of corruption from acts of corrosion, but also from moral offences that undermine institutional processes and purposes but are, nevertheless, not acts of corruption. The latter are not acts of corruption because no person in their capacity as institutional-role occupant either performs an act of corruption or suffers a diminution in their character. There are many legal and moral offences in this latter category. Consider individuals not employed by, or otherwise institutionally connected to, a large corporation who steal from or defraud the corporation. These offences may undermine the institutional processes and collective ends of the corporation, but given the noninvolvement of any officer, manager, or employee of the corporation, these acts are not acts of corruption.

### 3. THE CONCEPT OF INSTITUTIONAL CORRUPTION

In light of the discussion of the five hypotheses concerning the concept of institutional corruption, the following summary definitional account of institutional corruption is available:

An act X performed by an agent A is an act of institutional corruption if and only if:

(1)   X has an effect, Ep, of undermining, or contributing to the undermining of, some institutional process and/or (proximate (individual or collective) or ultimate (collective)) end of some institution, I, and/or an effect, Ec, of contributing to the despoiling of the moral character of some role occupant of I, agent B, *qua* role occupant of I;

(2)   At least one of (a) or (b) is true:

(a)   A is a role occupant of I, and in performing X, A intended or foresaw Ep and/or Ec, or A should have foreseen Ep and/or Ec;

(b)   There is a role occupant of I, agent B, and B could have avoided Ec, if B had chosen to do so.[19]

Note that (2)(a) tells us that A is a corruptor and is, therefore, either (straightforwardly) morally responsible for the corrupt action, or A is not morally responsible for A's corrupt character and the corrupt action is an expression of A's corrupt character.

---

[19] Regarding the definition, note that agent B could in fact be agent A. Regarding clause (1), note that agent A is not necessarily morally responsible for the effect Ep or Ec that his or her action X produces. Recall also that we are working with a simplified definition of moral responsibility.

According to the above account, an act of institutional corruption brings about, or contributes to bringing about, a corrupt condition of some institution. But this condition of corruption exists only relative to an uncorrupted condition, which is the condition of being a morally legitimate institution or subelement thereof. Aside from specific institutional processes and purposes, such subelements also include institutional roles and the morally worthy character traits that are associated with the proper acting out of these institutional roles.

Consider the uncorrupted judicial process. It consists of the presentation of objective evidence that has been gathered lawfully, of testimony in court being presented truthfully, of the rights of the accused being respected, and so on. This otherwise morally legitimate judicial process may be corrupted if one or more of its constitutive actions are not performed in accordance with the process as it ought to be. Thus to present fabricated evidence, to lie under oath, and so on are all corrupt actions. In relation to moral character, consider an honest accountant who begins to "doctor the books" under the twin pressures of a corrupt senior management and a desire to maintain a lifestyle that is possible only if he is funded by the very high salary he receives for doctoring the books. By engaging in such a practice he risks the erosion of his moral character; he is undermining his disposition to act honestly.

On this view, the corrupt condition of the institution exists only relative to some moral standards, which are definitional of the uncorrupted condition of that institution, including the moral characters of the persons in institutional roles. The moral standards in question might be minimum moral standards, or they might be moral ideals. Corruption in relation to a tendering process is a matter of a failure in relation to minimum moral standards enshrined in laws or regulations. On the other hand, gradual loss of innocence might be regarded as a process of corruption in relation to an ideal moral state.

If the process of corruption proceeds far enough, then we no longer have a corrupt official or corruption of an institutional process or institution; we cease to have a person who can properly be described as, say, a judge, or a process that can properly be described as, say, a judicial process – as opposed to proceedings in a kangaroo court. Like a coin that has been bent and defaced beyond recognition, it is no longer a coin; rather, it is a piece of scrap metal that can no longer be exchanged for goods.

The corruption of an institution does not assume that the institution in fact existed at some past time in a pristine or uncorrupted condition.

Rather, an action, or set of actions, is corruptive of an institution insofar as the action, or actions, have a negative moral effect on the institution. This notion of a negative moral effect is determined by recourse to the moral standards constitutive of the processes, roles, and purposes of the institution as that institution morally ought to be in the sociohistorical context in question. Consider a police officer who fabricates evidence, but who is a member of a police service whose members have always fabricated evidence. It remains true that the officer is performing a corrupt action. His action is corrupt by virtue of the negative moral effect it has on the institutional process of evidence gathering and evidence presentation. To be sure, in general in this institution, this process is not what it ought to be, given the corrupt actions of the other police in that particular police force. But the point is his action contributes to the further undermining of the institutional process; it has a negative moral effect as judged by the yardstick of what that process ought to be in that institution at that time.

In relation to institutions, and institutional processes, roles, and ends, I have insisted that if they are to have the potential to be corrupted, then they must be *morally* legitimate, and not merely legitimate in some weaker sense, for example, lawful. Perhaps there are nonmoral senses of the term *corruption*. For example, it is sometimes said that some term in use in a linguistic community is a corrupted form of a given word, or that some modern art is a corruption of traditional aesthetic forms. However, the central meaning of the term *corruption* carries strong moral connotations; to describe someone as a corrupt person, or an action as corrupt, is to ascribe a moral deficiency and to express moral disapproval. Accordingly, if an institutional process is to be corrupted, it must suffer some form of moral diminution, and therefore in its uncorrupted state it must be at least morally legitimate. So although marriage across the color bar was unlawful in apartheid South Africa, a priest, Priest A, who married a black man and a white woman was not engaged in an act of corruption. On the other hand, if another priest, Priest B, married a man and a woman, knowing the man to be already married, the priest may well be engaged in an act of corruption. Why was Priest B's act corrupt? Because it served to undermine a lawful, and morally legitimate, institutional process, namely, marriage between two consenting adults who are not already married. But Priest A's act was not corrupt. Why? Because a legally required, but morally unacceptable, institutional procedure – refusing to marry two consenting adults because they are from different race groups – cannot be corrupted. It cannot be corrupted because it was not morally legitimate to start with. Indeed, the legal prohibition on marriage across the color bar is in itself a corruption of the institution of marriage. So Priest A's act of marrying the black man and the white woman was not corrupt.[20]

A further point arising from this example pertains to the possibility of one institution (the apartheid South African government) corrupting another institution (the church in apartheid South Africa). Other things being equal, insofar as the priests (and other relevant institutional actors) in the church acted as Priest A did, that is, resisted the apartheid laws, the church as an institution would not have been corrupted. Moreover, the apartheid government's undermining of the institutional processes of the church did not in itself constitute corruption, because the government and its leaders are not per se – at least in a secular state – role occupants of the institution of the church. What of those priests who complied with the apartheid laws and did not marry mixed race couples? Here we need to distinguish mere compliance with the apartheid laws from embracing the laws. A priest might have complied with the apartheid law, but have done so only because no mixed race couple ever approached him to marry them. Presumably such a priest was neither a corruptor nor a person corrupted. What of a priest who actively supported the apartheid law by condemning such mixed race marriages as not legitimate in the eyes of God, denouncing the priests who performed them, and so forth? Presumably this priest has been corrupted, and – insofar as he is successful in his endeavors – he is a corruptor of the institution of marriage.

There are two residual points to be made in conclusion.

First, the despoiling of the moral character of a role occupant, or the undermining of institutional processes and ends, would typically require a pattern of actions – and not merely a single one-off action. So a single free hamburger provided to a police officer on one occasion usually does not corrupt and is not therefore an act of corruption. Nevertheless, a series of such gifts to a number of police officers might corrupt. They

---

[20] Consider the case of bribing a Nazi judge to enable a person guilty of a crime such as common assault, i.e., behavior that is rightly criminalized, to avoid punishment. On the view expressed here this could be a case of corruption, if the legal system in question is able to be segregated into morally legitimate and morally illegitimate fragments, and the judge was operating within the morally legitimate fragment.

might corrupt, for example, if the hamburger joint in question ended up with (in effect) exclusive, round-the-clock police protection, and if the owner intended that this be the case.[21]

Note here the pivotal role of habits. We have just seen that the corruption of persons and institutions typically requires a pattern of corrupt actions. More specifically, corrupt actions are typically habitual. Yet, as noted by Aristotle, one's habits are in large part constitutive of one's moral character; habits make the man (and the woman). The coward is someone who habitually takes flight in the face of danger; by contrast, the courageous person has a habit of standing his or her ground. Accordingly, morally bad *habits* – including corrupt actions – are extremely corrosive of moral character, and therefore of institutional roles and ultimately institutions.

However, there are some cases in which a single, one-off action would be sufficient to corrupt an instance of an institutional process. Consider a specific tender. Suppose that one bribe is offered and accepted, and the tendering process is thereby undermined. Suppose that this is the first and only time that the person offering the bribe and the person receiving the bribe are involved in bribery. Is this one-off bribe an instance of corruption? Surely it is, because it corrupted that particular instance of a tendering process.

The second residual point is that among instances of corruption there are ones in which corruptors are culpably *negligent;* they do, or allow to be done, what they reasonably ought to have known should not be done, or should not have been allowed to be done. For example, a safety inspector within an industrial plant who is negligent with respect to his duty to ensure that safety protocols are being complied with might be guilty of corruption by virtue of contributing to the undermining of those safety protocols.[22]

There are complexities in relation to corruption involving culpable negligence that are not necessarily to be found in other forms of corruption. Consider a company official who has a habit of allowing industrial waste products to be discharged into a river because this is the cheapest way to get rid of the unwanted products. But now assume that the official does so before the availability of any relevant scientific knowledge

---

[21] The owner's intention is not, of course, necessary for this to be a case of corruption; see the discussions of the first, third, and fourth hypotheses.

[22] And there is a further and related point to be made here. In general, corruptors corrupt, and the corrupted allow themselves to be corrupted, without adequate moral justification for so doing or allowing to be done.

concerning the pollution that results from such discharges, and before the existence of any institutional arrangement for monitoring and controlling pollution. It seems that the official is not necessarily acting in a corrupt manner. However, the same action might well be a case of corporate corruption in a contemporary setting in which this sort of pollution is well and widely understood, and antipollution arrangements are known to be in place in many organizations. While those who actively corrupt institutional processes, roles, and ends are not necessarily themselves the occupants of institutional roles, those who are culpably negligent tend to be the occupants of institutional roles who have failed to discharge their institutional obligations.

## 4. CONCLUSION

In this chapter I have provided a detailed analysis of the concept of institutional corruption and offered a definition of institutional corruption. In doing so I have discussed five hypotheses concerning institutional corruption: (1) the personal character of corruption, (2) the causal character of corruption, (3) the moral responsibility of corruptors, (4) the asymmetry between corruptors and those corrupted, (5) that institutional corruption involves institutional actors who corrupt or are corrupted. In so doing I have made use of the individualist, teleological theory, and its associated notions of collective ends, collective goods, and the like, elaborated in Chapters 1 and 2 to inform my theorizing.

This completes the theoretical part of this book. The remaining chapters consist of applications of the theoretical understandings developed in these first five chapters to specific institutions and various practical ethical problems confronting those institutions.

## PART B

# APPLICATIONS

# 6

# The Professions

## 1. DEFINING THE PROFESSIONS

On my individualist, teleological (normative) account, the members of the various professions are institutional role occupants and, as such, defined not only by recourse to their constitutive activities, but also by the collective ends served by these activities (Alexandra and Miller 1996), and, specifically, by the collective goods that they produce (or contribute to the production, maintenance, or renewal of), that is, jointly produced goods that are, and ought to be, produced and made available to the whole community because they are desirable and the members of the community have a joint right to them, for example, health, shelter, and justice. Thus surgeons engage in practices such as the cutting away of malignant tissue, and do so having as a (collective) end the preservation of health and, indeed, of life itself. Engineers design buildings, railways, and the like, and do so having as collective ends the provision of the needs-based right to shelter, the enabling of transport needed in a modern society, and so on. Similarly, the legal profession has as collective end the provision of a collective good to which all members of the community have a jointly held right, namely, justice.

Obviously some occupational groups that are not professions, nevertheless, provide collective goods. Firemen, for example, engage in activities such as hosing down buildings, and do so having as a (collective) end the extinguishing of fires; however, arguably, the occupational role of fireman is not a profession. So although the provision of a collective good is a necessary condition for being a profession, it is not a sufficient one. Shortly, I discuss the other defining properties of the professions.

Notice that some of these collectives goods produced by professions are ones to which members of a society have an institutionally prior

needs-based moral right, for example, the recovery of health resulting
from medical treatment or shelter provided by buildings. Other goods
produced by professions are *institutional* moral rights, that is, they presuppose an existing institution or framework of institutions. For example,
lawyers have as a collective end the administration of justice, and under
certain circumstances people have a need (as opposed to merely a desire)
for legal representation; but justice – insofar as it can be delivered by lawyers, judges, and the like – presupposes a set of laws that can be breached
or complied with, and many of these laws in turn presuppose other institutions; for example, corporate law presupposes corporations. Again,
under certain circumstances individuals and organizations have a need
(as opposed to a desire) for an auditor; but the profession of auditor
presupposes financial institutions and organizations with a financial
aspect. Indeed, the need for an auditor is itself a financially based need,
and one that the organization to be audited, say, a corporation or government department, might not desire. Nevertheless, there is a joint right on
the part of, for example, investors and ordinary citizens that certain organizations be subjected to an audit to determine their financial health.

I am concerned in this chapter only with the professions. Here the
paradigm cases include doctors, lawyers, and engineers. I have suggested that the first defining property of the professions is their pursuit
of collective goods (in my sense). These collective goods, as we saw in
Chapter 2, include (but are not restricted to), aggregated human rights,
institutional moral rights, needs, and rights-based needs.

A second defining feature of the professions concerns their relationship
to the markets in which they often operate. Here we need to distinguish
between the professions and what we might refer to as market-based
occupations. As noted above, the traditional professions include those
of lawyer, doctor, and engineer. Market-based occupations include shop-
keepers, chocolate manufacturers, the producers of TV soap operas,
and insurance salespersons, that is, those occupations whose primary
concern is to make a profit in the marketplace by selling a desired (but
not necessarily desirable) good to consumers. Thus a shopkeeper stocks
candy and sells it to consumers; in doing so he or she competes with
other sellers who are likewise trying to sell their goods to these same
potential consumers. The constitutive activity of the seller is the production and sale of goods (or simply the on-selling of goods produced by
others); however, his or her primary purpose in doing so is to make a
profit. Accordingly, the primary relationship between producer and consumer is an economic relationship, namely, that of seller to buyer. (The

professions are not, of course, the only non–market-based occupational groups; as we saw above, firemen, for example, are not members of a profession, but neither are they a market-based occupational group.)

By contrast with market-based occupational groups, the members of the professions, such as lawyers or doctors, do not engage in, or ought not to engage in, the constitutive activities of their professions primarily as sellers to buyers; the purely economic relationship of seller to buyer is, or ought to be, a secondary consideration. The economic relationship of seller to buyer is secondary to the needs of the client and, more broadly, to the requirement to provide the collective good definitive of the particular profession in question. Thus, in the case of doctors running their medical practices as businesses, the health needs of patients ought to take precedence over profit maximization; again, lawyers' duties to their clients and, more generally, their duties to the court ought to take precedence over the maximization of the profits of the legal firms in which the lawyers in question are partners. In short, the clients of members of a profession are not simply customers; indeed, this is demonstrated in part by the existence of one of the constitutive features of the professional-client relationship, namely, fiduciary duties, including duties of care.

This is, of course, not to suggest that members of the professions do not at times, and, indeed, in whole sectors of a given profession, fail to discharge their primary professional obligations as a consequence of, for example, commercial pressures. Regrettably, the failure of the so-called gatekeepers, that is, lawyers and auditors, has been a feature of periods in which there are widespread corporate collapses and corruption scandals (Chapter 10). Again, consider the negligence of engineers in the infamous *Challenger* space shuttle disaster in the United States, and the words that reverberate to this day: "think like a manager not like an engineer" (Davis 1998).

However, these failings merely underscore the importance of members of the professions understanding and discharging their professional obligations, including in the face of countervailing commercial and other pressures.

I have argued that the existence of a professional-client relationship is the second defining property of the professions – and one that ought to take precedence over the seller-buyer relationship that typically obtains between members of a profession and their clients. What of other defining features?

A third defining feature of the professions is their possession of expert knowledge not normally possessed by those outside the profession, for instance, of medicine in the case of doctors. If members of a profession, say, lawyers, are adequately to realize the ends of their profession (justice), then they need to possess expert technical knowledge (of the law). In contemporary societies this expert technical knowledge is in large part acquired by studying a degree at a university.

A fourth defining feature of the professions is professional autonomy. If members of a profession, say, lawyers, are adequately to realize the ends of their profession (justice), then they need to possess not only expert technical knowledge (of the law) but also a capacity to exercise discretionary judgment – including discretionary ethical judgment – in the application of this knowledge. Accordingly, they require a high degree of professional autonomy not necessarily required by other occupational groups. I return to this issue below.

A fifth, and final, defining feature of the professions pertains to their institutionalization. A profession, such as a doctor, a lawyer, is an institutional role. Strictly speaking, the term *profession* refers to a set of such institutional-role occupants. However, in contemporary societies, at least, the profession of, say, doctor is not simply a group of people who practice medicine. Rather, the members of a profession are also members of a social institution. Lawyers, for example, undertake their professional roles in the context of the legal system, comprised as it is of the law itself, the courts, law firms, and so on. Similarly, doctors undertake their professional roles in the context of a health system, comprised as it is of hospitals, surgeries, medical laboratories, and so on. Moreover, members of the professions are members of a professional body that is itself an institution, for instance, the American Medical Association or Engineers Australia. As such, their professional practice is regulated, they are required to have undergone a certified process of education and accreditation, and so on.

Many occupations that are not professions have some of the defining features of the professions. For example, garbage collectors jointly contribute to the provision of a collective good, namely, an environment free of health-threatening garbage. Nevertheless, they are not professionals in the required sense because, for example, they are not in possession of a body of expert knowledge. So the claim is that members of the professions possess *all* of the above properties, but members of other occupations do not.

Historically, the traditional professions have been distinguished from other occupations. However, recently the distinction has come under increasing intellectual and social pressure; the tendency is to assimilate the traditional professions to other occupations, and to regard any attempt to preserve the distinction as intellectually suspect, special pleading motivated by a desire to maintain a privileged position of prestige, power, and wealth.

My response to this is twofold. There are certain emerging professions, for instance, journalists and social workers. This is to be expected. When members of an occupational group come to possess the above-listed properties, then they have become a profession in the sense in question. And to the extent that members of the traditional professions cease to have these properties, then they will cease to be professions (or perhaps become debased or quasi professions). However, it remains the case that for any occupation reasonably and rightly to be counted as a profession, emerging or otherwise, it needs to possess – or to be in the process of coming to possess – the defining features of a profession. Moreover, it is important that those occupations that have, or ought to have, the various defining properties discussed above, such as professional autonomy and a professional-client relationship characterized by the duty of care, be marked off from those that do not and ought not; this is not a matter of looking after special interest groups, but rather of ensuring that the occupational groups in question provide the collective goods that the community needs them to provide.

Recently there has been a good deal of philosophical discussion focusing on the rights and duties of particular professions. These discussions have principally concerned specific ethical problems that confront members of particular professions. However, the normative context for these discussions is in large part the notion of a professional role with constitutive *special* rights and duties. To this issue I now turn.

## Professional Role Morality: Special Rights and Duties

As argued above, institutional roles in general, and the professions in particular, are constituted by institutional rights and duties that are also moral rights and duties. Many of these rights and duties are special in that those outside the profession do not have these rights and duties, for example, of a surgeon to operate on those in need. In the case of the professions, these rights and duties are typically rights and duties with respect to their clients, notably (as mentioned above) a duty of care; they are *special* rights and duties (Bradley 1927).

Christina Hoff Sommers (Hoff Sommers 1986) has argued that so-called impartialist moral theories, notably utilitarianism and Kantianism, fail adequately to accommodate special rights and duties (Collingridge and Miller 1997). She criticizes the Australian philosopher Peter Singer (Singer 1981) for an example of impartiality he gives, where he imagines himself about to dine with three friends when his father calls saying he is ill and asking him to visit.

According to Singer, to decide impartially I must sum up the preferences for and against going to dinner with my friends, and those for and against visiting my father. Whatever action satisfies more preferences, adjusted according to the strength of the preferences, that is the action I ought to take.

She is equally critical of the Kantian perspective of impartiality and its indifference to any particular relations to particular persons. She says that giving no consideration to one's kin commits

> the *Jellyby fallacy*. Mrs Jellyby, a character in Charles Dickens's *Bleak House*, devotes all of her considerable energies to the foreign poor to the complete neglect of her family. She is described as a "pretty diminutive woman with handsome eyes, though they had a curious habit of seeming to look a long way off. As if they could see nothing nearer than Africa." Dickens clearly intends her as someone whose moral priorities are ludicrously disordered. Yet by some modern lights Mrs Jellyby could be viewed as a paragon of impartial rectitude. (Hoff Sommers 1986, 442–3)

Hoff Sommers suggests that both Kantianism and utilitarianism have a common view of a moral domain comprising moral agents and moral patients. Within the moral domain the moral patients all exert equal ethical pull on the moral agents – the ethical pull of the starving relative is thus equal to that of the starving East African. The equal-pull thesis, which according to Singer is the only rational basis for ethics, entails the "principle of impartiality ... which is seen as liberating us from the biased dictates of our psychological, biological, and socially conventional natures (1981, 444). In reality, Hoff Sommers observes, the ethical pull of the starving relative and the East African are different. Hoff Sommers argues for the principle of differential ethical pull when it comes to the genus of special duties.

Hoff Sommers is correct to distinguish special duties from impartial duties, and to point to the problems for impartialist theories posed by partialist duties, including special duties. However, there is a further distinction that needs to be made, and that Hoff Sommers fails to make. Here filial obligations are salient: the moral obligations of adult children to their ageing parents.

According to Hoff Sommers, special positive obligations, including filial obligations, arise for a moral agent when the following conditions obtain:

> (1) In a given social arrangement (or practice) there is a specific interaction or transaction between moral agent and patient, such as promising and being promised, nurturing and being nurtured, befriending and being befriended. (2) The interaction in that context gives rise to certain *conventional* expectations (e.g. that a promise will be kept, that a marital partner will be faithful, that a child will respect the parent).

In the case of filial obligations, "the basic relationship is that of nurtured to nurturer, a type of relationship which is very concrete, intimate and long-lasting and which is considered to be more morally determining than any other in shaping a variety of rights and obligations."

A key question that needs to be asked of Hoff Sommers's account is what grounds the special positive obligations – including filial obligations? Are such obligations *purely* "conventional expectations"? Evidently not, and for two reasons. First, according to Hoff Sommers, these obligations are to some extent determined by the nurturing relationship between parent and child. Second, according to Hoff Sommers, these obligations are in part constitutive of an institution – the family – which institution is itself subjected to a universal deontological principle, namely, the principle of noninterference in the lives of others.

So by Hoff Sommers's lights, although filial obligations are conventional, they are to some extent determined by the (natural) nurturing relationship, and they are (ultimately) constrained by the universal deontological principle of noninterference.

Although Hoff Sommers's model of filial obligations in particular is interesting, it is, nevertheless, defective. It confuses *special institutional* duties with other partialist duties, namely, *agent-relative* duties and, more specifically, personal duties. It is, of course, the former that is of concern here.

Institutional roles, including perhaps the role of parent (albeit families are not social institutions of the kind under discussion in this book), give rise to special institutional duties. And, as we have seen, deontological and utilitarian theories have difficulty in adequately accommodating these. Indeed, it may well be that Hoff Sommers's Conventionalist model is an important contribution to understanding special institutional duties. However, what the Conventionalist model is unable to explain are filial obligations, understood not simply as instantiations of institutionally relative duties of adult children to their aged parents, but as obligations to particular persons *qua* particulars. An adult child does not have a felt obligation to his or her aged parent of the kind that, say, a doctor has to his patients. The difference lies in the essentially *personal* character of the obligation of an adult child to his or her aged parent. Institutional, including professional, special duties are essentially impersonal, but filial obligations are not, and Hoff Sommers's Conventionalist model is unable to accommodate this feature of filial obligations.

By contrast with such personal obligations, even ones in the context of the institution of the family, special institutional duties are impersonal in character. Nevertheless, they are partialist. Consider the lawyer's duties to her client. This is not an impartial duty (at least in the normal sense). Rather, it is a duty that the lawyer has only to her clients (which she does not have to others and which others, including other lawyers, do not have to her clients); moreover, it is a duty to defend the client even in the face of overwhelming evidence of guilt. Nevertheless, the duty is not personal in character, as is the case with an adult child and his ageing parent.

### Professional Autonomy

The autonomy of members of the professions is no doubt an intrinsic good; after all, individual autonomy, more generally, is an intrinsic good. However, professional autonomy is not quite the same thing as individual autonomy, and it needs special justification.

Professional autonomy concerns decision making within the sphere of the professional role in question. As such, it is both narrower and wider than that of individual autonomy that pertains to areas outside the professional role. Moreover, since professional autonomy is an *institutional* right, it is not possessed purely by virtue of properties one possesses as a human being, albeit it is obviously in part derivative from individual human autonomy.

A professional exercises professional autonomy in this sense (and is possessed of the corresponding kind of institutional authority; see Chapters 8 and 9) when his or her decisions and actions in relation to the professional matters at issue are "his or her call" – that is, he or she is the one to make the decision, and his or her decision cannot be overridden by a superior. A surgeon, for example, has to make a decision as to whether to operate, a decision that cannot be overridden by a hospital administrator.

Contrast this kind of authority with that possessed by, say, a personnel officer. The personnel officer may be given only very general instructions about hiring policy and exercise a good deal of discretion in the choices she actually makes. Nevertheless, her authority to employ new staff is delegated from a superior, who retains the right to withdraw it, and the right to overrule it in particular cases.

Professional autonomy tends to go hand in glove with professional liability. Thus the surgeon, and not necessarily the hospital, is the one to be sued if the surgeon makes a mistake. This is how it should be. If the surgeon is to be the one who makes the decision, then, rationally and morally, he ought to be the one who is held liable, if the decision is a bad one. Conversely, if the surgeon is to be held liable, then surely he must be the one given the right to make the decision.

As noted in Chapter 3, we need to distinguish the autonomy of an individual institutional actor from institutional autonomy, that is, the autonomy of the institution (or its leadership) vis-à-vis other institutions. In the case of professionals, the relevant institution would be the professional body, for example, the Law Society.

The ultimate justification for professional autonomy – as opposed to individual autonomy per se – is provided by the (collective) ends of the professional role in question.[1] Thus, surgeons ought to have professional autonomy just because this is the best way to maximize the health of patients, given the expertise and knowledge possessed by surgeons (but not by nonsurgeons).

Here I note the plausible view that human beings qua human beings have an inalienable moral right to refuse to kill or otherwise endanger the lives of fellow human beings, irrespective of the consent of the latter. If this is correct, then there are at least two bases for the autonomy of professionals when lives are at stake. One basis derives from the nature of the relevant institution, its institutional purposes, and the expertise of the professional practitioners in question. However, the second basis, as I have suggested, is a fundamental moral right: a moral right not to be required to kill another human being, or otherwise endanger their life, if one judges it to be wrong or otherwise unwarranted.

Thus far I have argued that the professions have a number of distinctive features that mark them off from other occupations. It must also be said that in recent times a number of the professions, notably lawyers and accountants, have come into disrepute in part as a consequence of their role in corporate scandals, such as Enron and the collapse of Arthur Andersen. Increasingly, accountants and solicitors, for example,

---

[1] Individual autonomy – as opposed to professional autonomy – is a human good to be maximized, other things being equal (Chapter 3).

are housed in large corporations and, as a consequence, subjected to commercial pressures of a kind that can compromise their professional integrity. This general issue of the corrosive effects of commercial pressures in the context of large corporations is an issue taken up in Chapter 9. It is, however, also relevant to the issue discussed in the next section, namely, integrity systems.

## 2. INTEGRITY SYSTEMS

Integrity systems can be contrasted with regulatory frameworks. A regulatory framework is a structured set of explicit laws, rules, or regulations governing behavior, issued by some institutional authority and backed by sanctions. It may serve to ensure compliance with minimum ethical standards (namely, those embodied in a law, rule, or regulation), but this is only one of its purposes. There are numerous laws, rules, and regulations that have little or nothing to do with ethics. An integrity system, by contrast, is an assemblage of institutional entities, mechanisms, and procedures, the purpose (collective end) of which is to ensure compliance with minimum *ethical* standards and promote the pursuit of *ethical* ideals.

Integrity systems for the profession will need to go beyond the ethical norms and ideals of good commercial practice. Specifically they will need to address the requirement that the professions are realizing their defining collective end, that is, serving the ends of justice, good health, and the like. Moreover, they will also need to ensure that professional rights are protected, professional duties discharged, and professional virtues exercised. For example, an adequate integrity system will protect professional autonomy while ensuring professional accountability.

But we need to get clearer about integrity systems. The term *integrity system* has recently come into vogue in relation to what is in fact a very ancient problem for organizations, occupational groups, and, indeed, whole polities and communities, namely, the problem of promoting ethical behavior and eliminating or reducing unethical behavior.

Here the term *system* is somewhat misleading in that it implies a clear and distinct set of integrated institutional mechanisms operating in unison and in accordance with determinate mechanical, or at least quasi-mechanical, principles. However, in practice integrity "systems" are a messy assemblage of formal and informal devices and processes, and they operate in often indeterminate, unpredictable, and sometimes even conflicting ways.

The term *integrity*, as used in the expression *integrity system*, is also problematic in that it appropriates a moral notion normally used to describe individual human agents and applies it to organizations and other large groups of individuals. Roughly speaking, individual human persons have integrity if (1) they possess the full array of central moral virtues, such as honesty, loyalty, and trustworthiness and (2) they exercise rational and morally informed judgment in their adherence to any given virtue, including when the requirements of different virtues might seem to come into conflict.

For example, persons with integrity would not allow themselves to act dishonestly out of a misplaced sense of loyalty, notwithstanding the importance of loyalty as one of the virtues possessed by a person with integrity.

By contrast with the notion of an individual person's integrity, integrity used in the context as I am employing it here of an integrity system for a profession applies to the representative bodies, for instance, the American Medical Association, and oversight bodies, for instance, the Office of the Legal Services Commissioner (in Australia) of the particular group, as well as to the large set of individual-role occupants within the profession and the organizations for which they work, for instance, hospitals and legal firms, and also to the structure, function, and culture of the group and its associated organizations, that is, to the profession as a social institution.

The integrity of a profession is in large part dependent on the individual integrity of its members, and therefore an integrity system is in large part focused on developing and maintaining the individual integrity of these members. Nevertheless, these groups are not simply the sum of its members, and so determining the integrity levels for these groups is not simply a matter of summing the levels of integrity of the individuals who happen to be its members.

In the first place, the individuals who comprise professions are role occupants, and the responsibilities and virtues required of them are somewhat different from, and in some respects greater than, those required of ordinary individual persons not occupying such roles. So, for instance, scrupulous attention to numerical detail might be a constitutive virtue of the role of an accountant but not of the role of a husband. And, of course, the technical competencies for which the lawyer, medical doctor, or engineer are responsible are not typically required of ordinary individual persons not occupying such roles.

Moreover, what counts as a professional responsibility or virtue, in terms of both technical and ethical competencies, varies greatly across different professional groups. The technical competencies for which the lawyer, medical doctor, or engineer are each responsible are not common *across* these groups. Similarly, the virtues are often role specific.

Although, arguably, the "zealous advocacy of one's clients' interests" might be a critical virtue to the role of a lawyer or barrister in adversarial legal systems, it is clearly not a critical virtue for the engineer. So what counts as integrity in an individual professional-role occupant is captured by neither what counts as integrity in an ordinary person nor what counts as integrity in some other occupational role. One important task, then, for specific professional areas is to determine what precisely the constitutive virtues of the individual-role occupant are and devise strategies to ensure that these virtues are developed and maintained in the members of that occupational or associational area.

In the second place, the integrity of a profession is not simply a matter of the integrity of the individual-role occupants who make it up. For the integrity of a profession is partly a matter of the structure, function, and culture of the profession *qua* institution. Consider structure, both legal and administrative. In a profession possessed of integrity the administrative processes and procedures in relation to, for example, promotion or complaints and discipline would embody relevant ethical principles of fairness, procedural justice, transparency, and the like.

Now consider function (collective ends). In a profession possessed of integrity the organizational goals actually being pursued would align closely with the collective ends, that is, collective goods, of the profession, such as the promotion of public safety for engineers or of human health for doctors, rather than purely commercial guidance. Finally, consider culture. In a profession possessed of integrity, the pervasive *ethos* or spirit, that is, the culture, would be one that was, for example, conducive to high performance, both technically and ethically, and supportive in times of need, but intolerant of serious incompetence or misconduct.

In looking at options to promote integrity and combat ethico-professional failures it is very easy to leap to a particular single "magic bullet" solution, like increasing penalties or giving more intrusive powers to investigative agencies, and doing so without considering the full array of implications, including the demonstrable (as opposed to hoped for) benefits (which of these measures has been tested and, as a consequence, is *known* to work?), and the costs in terms of resources, damage to ethico-professional *ethos*, and so on.

Moreover, "magic bullet" solutions are often offered in relative ignorance of both the actual nature and causes of the problems they are supposed to address. The truth is often in the detail.

So, for instance, many professions stand accused of being too tolerant of apparent cases of serious incompetence or corruption and of being so for self-interested reasons of protecting professional reputation. Moreover, these self-interested reasons come at the expense of the legitimate interests of consumers or the public. Although there may well be an apparent tolerance of serious incompetence or misconduct in some cases and although this may well come at the legitimate interests of the consumer or the public, it need not be because of reputational self-interested concerns nor aimed at deceiving the consumer or public.

There are at least two other significant factors commonly in play: namely, the difficulty of making judgments in some cases, especially "unique" cases, and, second, the highly litigious nature of the area. Unless, therefore, the nature of the problems, in particular their causes, are first identified, there is little hope of finding a solution to such problems.

Moreover, in attempting to determine the causes of unethical professional practices a number of preliminary questions need to be addressed. One set of questions pertains to the precise nature of the unethical practice at issue, and the context in which it occurs. What is the motivation? Are there, for example, as above, some compelling practical facts that explain the practice? What other pressures and opportunities might there be for the unethical practice in question? Another set of questions concerns the extent of the corruption or unethical practice: Is it sporadic or continuing, restricted to a few "rotten apples" or widespread within the area? Here, as elsewhere, rhetoric is no substitute for evidence-based conclusions.

Even when the answers to these questions have been provided there will arise further questions in relation to any remedies proposed. For example, any contemplation of mechanisms to redress ethico-professional misconduct that will require the expenditure of energy and resources – and may well impinge on individual freedom – needs to be justified in terms of the seriousness and extent of the misconduct to be successfully combated.

Second, and more importantly, understanding the causes of ethico-professional misconduct and failures and the tailoring of remedies to address them will involve considering and distinguishing between three sorts of motivation for compliance with moral principles.

One reason for compliance is the fear of punishment; hence the use, or threatened use, of the so-called big stick. So, for example, agent A does do not steal from agent B because A fears she will get caught and locked up. A second reason for compliance arises from the benefit to oneself. Hence the possible utility of the so-called carrot approach. So, for example, B pays B's workers reasonable wages because by doing so the workers are healthy, work productively, and B makes good profits. These two reasons are essentially appeals to self-interest. Taken in combination they constitute the "stick-carrot" approach much loved by many contemporary economists. However, there is a third reason for compliance. This is moral belief or desire to do what is right. A refrains from stealing because A believes that it is morally wrong to steal; B pays B's workers reasonable wages because B desires to be fair.

Here we need first to note the contrast between appeals to moral beliefs and appeals to self-interest. Acting from a concern to do what is right or good does not turn on whether or not it is one's self-interest. It may or may not be in one's own self-interest to be, say, honest or fair. Moreover, the notion of persons acting out of moral rectitude is completely at odds with the essentially manipulative approach of those who advocate *only* sticks and carrots.

That said, however, there are also important connections to be highlighted and promoted between "self-interest" and "moral interest" so that these conceptions are more in balance and integrated and less at odds. First, of course, the appeal to moral interest must be balanced by the appeal to self-interest. If, for example, it is at great cost to self to be, say, honest or fair, then one may have sufficient reason to not be honest or fair. Indeed, the reason need not be purely self-interested but also count as moral. So, for example, if it means my livelihood and that of my family, then I may have significant reasons from both prudence and morality to, say, steal.

It is evident that widespread and ongoing compliance typically requires appeals to self-interest (sticks and carrots) but also appeals to moral beliefs. Ideally, integrity systems should have penalties for those who do not comply, should enable benefits to flow to those who do comply, and should resonate with the moral beliefs of the people thus regulated; for example, laws and regulations should be widely thought to be just.

Thus, institutional design that proceeds on the assumption that self-interest is the only human motivation worth considering fails. It fails because it overlooks the centrality of moral beliefs in human life, and therefore does not mobilize moral sentiment. On the other hand, institutional design that proceeds on the assumption that self-interest can be ignored, and that a sense of moral duty on its own will suffice, also fails; it fails because self-interest is an ineradicable and pervasive feature of all human groups. (As argued below, deserved reputation has a pivotal role to play in the convergence of self-interest and ethical concerns.)

### 3. REACTIVE AND PREVENTIVE INTEGRITY SYSTEMS

Integrity systems can be thought of as being either predominantly reactive or predominantly preventive.[2] Naturally, the distinction is somewhat artificial, because there is a need for both reactive elements, for example, a complaints and discipline system, as well as preventive elements, for example, ethics training and transparency of processes, in any adequate integrity system. At any rate, integrity systems can be considered under the two broad headings, reactive and preventive.

### Reactive Integrity Systems

The reactive way of dealing with ethico-professional misconduct and corruption is the one that first comes to mind. The logic is direct: the activity is defined as one that is not acceptable; an individual engages in that activity and therefore, as a direct result, should be held to account for the misconduct and, if found guilty, disciplined in some way. The rationale for the reactive response for dealing with unethical behavior, including criminality and corruption, is threefold: offenders are held to account for their actions, offenders get their just deserts, and potential offenders are deterred from future offences.

Reactive mechanisms (i.e., institutional mechanisms; see Chapter 1, Section 4) for dealing with unethical behavior are fundamentally linear: setting out a series of offences (usually in legislation or regulations), waiting for an individual to transgress, then investigating, adjudicating, and finally taking punitive action. *Complaints and discipline systems* are basically reactive institutional mechanisms.

The weaknesses of the reactive approach are manifest. One obvious weakness is the passivity of the approach; by the time the investigators swing into action, the damage has been already done. Another problem stems from the fact that unethical behavior is often secretive; for instance, as mentioned above, professional associations may "close ranks" to protect the reputation of the group.

---

[2] This discussion is derived in part from Miller, Roberts, and Spence (2005, chap. 7).

Yet a further problem stems from the inadequacy of the resources to investigate and successfully prosecute, investigation and prosecution is resource intensive. Finally, if the chances of being caught or complained about are relatively slight due to under-resourcing, the deterrent effect is undermined, which in turn means there are an even larger number of offences and offenders for investigators to deal with.

Of course, the effectiveness of a reactive approach requires that significant detection mechanisms are available. Those who engage in ethico-professional misconduct then have at least two good reasons to fear exposure: first, detection may lead to legal or associational sanctions, such as fines, suspension, or expulsion from the industry, and, second, it may lead to moral sanctions emanating from work colleagues, community, and from significant others, such as friends and relatives. Nevertheless, there are a number of sources of information in relation to most forms of ethico-professional misconduct and corruption. One of the most important is fellow workers who may report such conduct or suspicious activity to superiors, or even blow the whistle.

## Preventive Integrity Systems

A preventive integrity system will typically embrace, or act in tandem with, a reactive integrity system. However, we can consider preventive mechanisms (i.e., institutional mechanisms) for dealing with ethico-professional misconduct independent of any reactive elements. If we do so, we see that they can be divided into three categories:

- Institutional mechanisms for promoting an environment in which integrity is rewarded, and, as a consequence, unethical behavior is discouraged; this is an attempt to reduce the desire or motivation to act unethically, so that opportunities for unethical behavior are not pursued or taken, even when they arise;
- The array of institutional mechanisms that limit (or eliminate) the opportunity for unethical behavior. Such mechanisms include corporate governance mechanisms such as separating the roles of receiving accounts and paying accounts to reduce the opportunity for fraud; and
- Those institutional mechanisms that act to expose unethical behavior, so that the organization, or community can deal with them. The term "transparency" may be used to characterize these mechanisms.

I accept that this threefold distinction is somewhat artificial, and that some institutional mechanisms will, in fact, come under more than one heading, and, indeed, that some, such as regulations, have both a reactive, as well as a preventive, role.

The first category in our breakdown of prevention mechanisms are those institutional processes that exist to promote ethical behavior. This category is made up of those components of an integrity system that engage with the individual's desire to do what is morally right and avoid what is morally wrong, and to be morally approved of by others for so acting. These institutional instruments include *codes of ethics* and *professional development programs*.

## 4. HOLISTIC INTEGRITY SYSTEMS

Thus far in the analysis of integrity systems, I have looked at integrity systems and mechanisms under the headings of reactive systems and preventive systems. It is evident that in most societies, jurisdictions, and indeed organizations, the attempt to combat unethical behavior involves both of the above.

That is, integrity-building strategies involve reactive systems as well as preventive systems, and within preventive systems there are mechanisms that promote ethical behavior, there are corporate governance mechanisms with, for example, antifraud or corruption functions, and there are various transparency mechanisms.

Moreover, it seems clear that an adequate integrity system cannot afford to do without reactive as well as preventive systems, and that preventive systems need to have all the elements detailed above. This suggests that there are two important issues. The first is the adequacy of each of the elements of the above systems, for example, how adequate is the complaints and discipline processes including the investigative capacity? Or how effective are the mechanisms of transparency? The second issue pertains to the level of integration and congruence between the reactive and the preventive systems; to what extent do they act together to mutually reinforce one another?

In this connection, it is worth noting that many jurisdictions have "watchdog" agencies. Such bodies are established by statutes that also define a range of offences, have powers to investigate, and refer matters to the courts for prosecution. However, it is notable that these watchdog agencies also involve themselves in prevention programs involving the development of preventive mechanisms; they no longer see their role as merely that of a reactive agency.

We should think of (better) integrity systems, therefore, as holistic in character and conceive of specific integrity-building mechanisms as elements of a holistic integrity system. In looking at the set of integrity building processes as a holistic system, we need, first, to remind ourselves what is presupposed by an integrity system.

First, and most obviously, there must be some shared moral values in relation to the moral unacceptability of specific forms of behavior, and a disapproval of those who engage in such behavior: that is, there needs to be a framework of accepted social norms.

Second, there needs to be a broadly shared conception in relation to what needs to be done (the institutional means) to minimize it (the collective end); for example, should it be simply criminalized or should the response include restorative elements?

Third, there needs to be present some capacity to create and implement institutional mechanisms that deal with the issue of unethical behavior and corruption, and this presumes some form of legal or regulatory system and organizational structure. Here considerations of efficiency and effectiveness are important.

Finally, there needs to be some source of authority whereby sanctions can be applied to individuals who engage in unethical behavior.

## 5. PROFESSIONAL REPUTATION

A key element in the establishment of effective integrity systems for occupational groups, organizations, and industries in general, and professional groups in particular, is the mobilization of reputation.[3] Naturally some groups and organizations are more sensitive to reputational loss (and the possibility of reputational gain) than others. Corporations and professional groups in the financial services sector, including bankers and auditors, are very sensitive to reputational loss. Those entrusted to make prudent decisions with other people's money are inevitably heavily dependent on a good reputation; similarly, for those entrusted to provide independent adjudications in relation to financial health.

When a high professional reputation is much sought after by members of an occupational group or organization, and a low one to be avoided at all costs, there is an opportunity to mobilize this reputational desire

[3] An earlier version of some of the material in this section appeared in Alexandra et al. (2006).

in the service of promoting ethical standards. Here the aim is to ensure that reputation aligns with actual ethical practice, that is, that an organization's or group's or individual's high or low reputation is deserved. The way to achieve this is by designing appropriate integrity systems. As we have seen above, key elements of an integrity system track compliance with regulations; for instance, accountability mechanisms ensure compliance with regulations (or, at least, expose noncompliance). The additional thought here is that key elements of an integrity system should track features of organizations and occupational groups that determine, or should determine, reputation. More explicitly, a reputational index could be constructed whereby an ethics audit awards scores in relation to specific ethical standards. In the remainder of this chapter I will sketch the broad outlines of such a reputational index.

Deserved reputation can provide an important nexus between the self-interest of corporations and professional groups, on the one hand, and appropriate ethical behavior toward consumers, clients, and the public more generally, on the other hand. More specifically, the deserved reputation of members of professional groups can provide such a nexus. Here there are three elements in play: (1) reputation, (2) self-interest, and (3) ethical standards such as compliance with technical accounting standards and avoidance of specific conflicts of interest, but also more general desiderata such as client/consumer protection. The idea is that these three elements need to interlock in what might be called a virtuous triangle.

First, reputation is linked to self-interest; this is obviously already the case – individuals, groups, and organizations desire high reputation and benefit materially and in other ways from it. Second, reputation needs to be linked to ethics in that reputation ought to be deserved; as already mentioned, the integrity systems are the means to achieve this. Third, and as a consequence of the two already mentioned links, self-interest is linked to ethics; given robust integrity systems that mobilize reputational concerns, it is in the self-interest of individuals, groups, and firms to comply with ethical standards (that are also professional standards). Here I reassert that self-interest is not the only or necessarily the ultimate motivation for human action; the desire to do the right thing is also a powerful motivator for many, if not most, people. Accordingly, the triangle is further strengthened by the motivation to do right.

In recent years the notion of a Reputation Index has gained currency in a number of contexts, especially in business and academic circles. The term seems to have a number of different senses. Sometimes it is used to describe a way of measuring the reputation that an organization actually has. Because reputation exists, so to speak, in the eye of the beholder, actual reputation does not always match deserved reputation. Accordingly, sometimes the term is used to describe a way of calculating the performance of an organization on the basis of which its reputation should be founded.

The first step in the process is to determine a way of accurately measuring the ethical performance of individual or organizational members of occupational and industry groups; this is an ethics audit.

Here I stress the importance of *objective* measures of ethical performance. The latter might include such things as results of consumer satisfaction surveys, gross numbers of warranted complaints and trends thereof, numbers of disciplinary matters and their outcomes, or outcomes of financial and health and safety audits (e.g., regarding electronic crime and corruption vulnerabilities). It would also include the existence of institutional processes established to assure compliance with ethical standards, for example, codes of ethics and conduct, financial and other audit processes, ethics committees, complaints and disciplinary systems, fraud and ethics units, ethical risk assessment processes, ethics and compliance officers, and professional development programs in ethics.

I note that although some of these institutional systems and processes might be legally required, this is by no means the case for all of them. In short, although reputational indexes include some indicators of compliance with those ethical standards (and associated processes of assurance) that are enshrined in law, they also include indicators of adherence to ethical standards that are above and beyond what is legally required. This is important given that (a) laws and regulation inevitably play "catch up" in relation to new and emerging ethical problems (including loopholes that are exploited by "creative" accountants and "legal engineers"), (b) it is both impractical and undesirable for all ethical standards and virtues to be embodied in laws and regulations – aspirational ethical goals are a case in point, and (c) ethical behavior and attitudes cannot simply be regulated into existence.

In addition to the ethics audit itself, there is a need for a process that engages with ethical reputation. Since ethical reputation should reflect the findings of the ethics audit, an ethical reputation audit should drive the relationship between de facto ethical performance (in effect, the deserved reputation) and actual reputation for ethical performance. The way to achieve this is by the participation of as many occupational members and industry organizations as possible in ethics audits, and by the widespread promulgation of the results of their de facto ethical performance (as determined by the ethics audit), including in the media. Naturally the results promulgated could be more or less detailed; they could, for example, simply consist in an overall rating as opposed to a complete description of the ethics audit results.

Reputational indexes give rise to a number of problems. There is the problem of devising acceptable, objective measures of ethical performance. Although ethical performance in a general sense is a somewhat nebulous notion, determining minimum ethical standards – that are, nevertheless, above and beyond legal requirements – and levels of compliance therewith is doable. Indeed, criminal justice and regulatory systems are devised in large part to prescribe objectively specifiable, preexisting, minimum ethical standards, for example, do not defraud or bribe; reputational indexes of minimum ethical standards simply take this process further by, so to speak, raising the ethical bar.

A greater problem is participation; what means are available to ensure the participation of occupational groups and organizations in reputational indexes? (Of course, in the case of those indices that simply measure compliance with legal requirements, there is no need to secure "participation"; the compliance failure is already in the public domain, and reputational indexes simply provide additional and more targeted publicity.) In relation to the problem of nonparticipation, there are a variety of responses, ranging from the mandatory use of reputational indexes by members of professional or industry groups (on pain of exclusion from the relevant professional or industry association) through to the provision of various kinds of incentive. The Professional Standards Council in Australia provides one kind of example for occupational groups. It offers capped liability as an incentive to occupational groups to participate in its ethico-professional standards programs.

A third, and still greater, problem is effectiveness. The use of reputational indexes can easily reduce into "tick-the-box" processes on the part of clever, well-resourced organizations seeking to avoid actual compliance with ethical standards in favor of engaging in elaborate exercises in window-dressing. Hence the need for meaningful ethical audits conducted by independent, adequately resourced, and professionally trained ethics auditors.

## 6. CONCLUSION

In this chapter I have applied my individualist, teleological model to the traditional and emerging professions. By the lights of that model these professions have as their defining collective end the realization of some collective good, for example, human health in the case of doctors.

I have also introduced the notion of an integrity system – an institutional system for enhancing integrity and reducing ethical misconduct and institutional corruption – and applied it to the professions. A key notion in play here is that of professional reputation and the so-called triangle of virtue.

The triangle has three elements: reputation, self-interest, and ethical requirements, such as particular ethico-professional standards, but also more general desiderata such as client/consumer protection and corruption prevention. These three elements need to interlock in the following way.

First, reputation is linked to self-interest; individuals, groups, and organizations desire high reputation and benefit materially and in other ways from it. Second, reputation needs to be linked to ethics in that reputation ought to be deserved; as already mentioned, the integrity systems are the means to achieve this. Third, given robust integrity systems that mobilize reputational concerns, it is in the self-interest of individuals, groups, and firms to comply with ethico-professional standards.

# 7

# Welfare Institutions

In this chapter I apply my individualist, teleological (normative) account of social institutions to welfare institutions or, at least, to one kind of welfare institution, namely, international institutions concerned with global poverty. I do so in the context of the assumption that, speaking generally, basic needs, such as for food, clean water, shelter, and medicines, are, and ought to be, provided for by nonwelfare institutions, notably, by business organizations operating in competitive markets. Nevertheless, given the manifest and ongoing failure on the part of such organizations, including in relation to global poverty, there is a need for welfare institutions. In addition, as will become evident below, there is a need to redesign markets, and market-based organizations, so that they are better able to provide for basic needs.

There are, of course, a plethora of welfare institutions concerned with the provision of a variety of types of welfare, including poverty alleviation, health care, aged care, unemployment benefits, and family allowances for children. Some of these welfare institutions provide targeted assistance, such as disability benefits; others provide general assistance, such as government financial assistance to the poor. Again, some of these institutions are to be understood as means by which the citizenry cater to the needs of their fellow citizens, such as those that are part of the so-called welfare state; other institutions cater to the needs of those who are not fellow citizens or otherwise members of the same state, for instance, nongovernmental organizations such as Oxfam providing assistance to the needy in developing countries. Moreover, in some cases the financial or other assistance provided has been generated by way of compulsory arrangements, for instance, income taxes or superannuation levied on salaries, and in other cases it has been freely given, for instance, charitable donations. Finally, the moral basis of these welfare institutions is evidently quite varied and complex. In many, perhaps most, cases the moral basis is a basic human need, such as the need for health care or the need for food. In many of these cases, as argued in Chapter 2, if the need is not met, severe harm, or even death, will result and, therefore, the needy may have, other things being equal, a derivable moral right (a needs-based right), and others a correlative (and enforceable) moral duty to meet the needs in question. Note that, as pointed out in Chapter 2, if A has a needs-based right to receive water from B or C or D – B, C, and D being the only individuals able to provide A with water at little cost to themselves – then B has a correlative moral duty to provide A with water (if neither B nor C has not done so), and C and D have a similar moral duty.

In other cases the moral basis is desert, for example, unemployment benefits paid only to those who have contributed to the scheme and/or worked for the organization (or nation-state?) that provides the benefits. In still other cases the moral basis is the right to compensation for harms suffered. Consider health care paid for by an organization to its workers whose ill health was the result of the work undertaken for the organization, such as payouts to medically discharged police officers.

Given the necessity to be selective, I have chosen to focus here only on international institutions concerned with the needs of people living in extreme poverty.

### 1. COLLECTIVE RESPONSIBILITY, INSTITUTIONAL DESIGN, AND THE DUTY TO AID

According to Peter Singer (relying on the World Bank figures) there are approximately one billion people in the world living in absolute poverty, and of the affluent persons in the world, each has an individual moral obligation to assist (Singer 2007).

Moreover, it is a very strong individual moral obligation; it has the same strength as the moral obligation that I have to save a drowning child in a pond adjacent to me if I can (Singer 1972). Further, it is a very demanding individual obligation in that my obligation is to give and keep giving to the threshold point at which either the great harm to others has been averted or the cost to me of giving is no longer comparatively insignificant. So even if I have given away most of my income to, say, Oxfam, I still have a moral obligation to continue giving, if my (by now) very modest income is, nevertheless, significantly above what is required to meet my basic needs; for, comparatively speaking, the cost to me of giving an additional amount of my very modest income is insignificant compared to the harm thereby averted, for example, saving one more starving child's life. I do not dispute the existence of a moral obligation on the part of the affluent to assist those living in absolute poverty; indeed, I believe that there is such an obligation. However, I do dispute the nature of the obligation (as expressed in the analogy with saving the drowning child) as well as Singer's view of its demandingness.

Let us consider the nature of the moral obligation to assist those currently living in absolute poverty (mainly in the so-called developing world). I will argue that the obligation in question is not an individual obligation per se, but rather a collective moral responsibility, albeit collective responsibility is, as argued in Chapter 4, a species of individual moral responsibility, namely, joint moral responsibility. The collective moral responsibility in question is grounded in the aggregate needs-based rights of those living in absolute poverty (Chapter 2). But let us first get clarity on Singer's analogy.

What is the analogy between giving to the needy and saving the drowning child supposed to be? In the case of the drowning child, I have a one-off, individual moral obligation to save the child. This is in part because my action is a necessary and a sufficient condition for the child's life to be saved; my single action, and my single action alone, will save the child. Do I have the same moral obligation to give, say, $20 to Oxfam today as I have to save the drowning child?

Surely this cannot be correct, because if I make a one-off payment to Oxfam I do not know that it will save any additional person; a large organization such as Oxfam with a budget in the hundreds of millions does not adjust its budgets and delivery schedules to the needy on the basis of $20 increments. Moreover, even if my $20 were to be earmarked for an additional child with, say, malnutrition (this is my arrangement with Oxfam), it will not necessarily save the child's life in the manner that I save the life of the drowning child. Children in absolute poverty typically face a range of ongoing threats to their life, and my $20 might only slightly prolong the child's life; the immediate threat from malnutrition is averted today only to have some disease, such as malaria, kill the child tomorrow. The implicit background assumption in the case of the drowning child is that the child when saved from drowning will return to a very different default state from the one facing the child in absolute poverty; specifically, the child saved from drowning will return to a situation in which she has adequate food and shelter, clean water, health care, and so on.

Finally, even if the $20 were to be earmarked for a particular child, and even if that child's life were to be saved for the long term because short-term malnutrition was the only threat to her life (perhaps malnutrition was the consequence of a one-off, disastrous crop failure), it was not *I* that saved her life; rather, I provided the money that enabled someone else to save her, for instance, the aid worker who fed the child over the requisite time period or the health worker who administered the vaccine or whatever. So it was the aid worker who saved the child, albeit my $20 paid for the food; so I am much more like the donor who paid for the life jacket that is thrown to the drowning child rather than I am like the passer-by who actually saves the drowning child.

So unlike in the drowning child case my action of giving $20 to Oxfam is not sufficient to save anyone's life (not for a short time, and certainly not for a long time); the actions of many other people are required, and required over a long period of time. But (again, unlike the drowning child case) nor is my one-off action necessary, because it is almost certainly the case that the same number of lives will be saved (for a long period of time) whether or not I give my $20. Indeed, it is far from probable that I will save even one life for a short period of time; certainly in most cases I do not *know* that my giving $20 today is a necessary condition for some-one's life being saved (for either a short time or for a long time).

I conclude that the proposed analogy between saving the needy and saving the drowning child is defective in two fundamental respects. First, unlike saving the drowning child – which requires an individual person to perform an individual action in accordance with his or her *individual* moral obligation – saving the billion in absolute poverty is to be understood as a situation calling for collective, interdependent, action on the part of many (perhaps millions, certainly thousands) in accordance with their *collective* moral responsibility to do so. Second, again unlike the saving the drowning child scenario, saving the billion in absolute poverty is a long-term project requiring a series of actions performed over a period of years on the part of each (or at least most) of the relevant persons; it is not a matter of a one-off action, even a one-off collective action. In short, there is a collective moral responsibility to save the billion in absolute poverty by means of long-term, collective action – indeed, institutional action (Shue 1996, chap. 5).

As argued in Chapter 4, collective moral responsible involves (1) a collective end (which is also a collective good, in this case the satisfaction of needs-based rights) to which the actions of the participating agents is directed, for example, eliminating the absolute poverty of a billion peo-ple and (2) a *jointly held* (individual) moral responsibility on the part of each agent to do their part toward realizing the collective end.

As already noted, unlike a (nonjoint) individual obligation, a jointly held obligation is an obligation that an individual has if, and only if, other individuals also have it. Moreover (again, unlike (nonjoint) individual obligations), it is an obligation that cannot be discharged by one individual acting alone. So even if a single person were to contribute sufficient funds or work-time to ensure that one or more children in absolute poverty were saved (for a long time) – as many aid workers in fact do – that would not of itself realize the collective end. Indeed, even to achieve that saving of lives requires the participation of a large number of other people.

Note also that what any given individual's part is depends on the overall collective action strategy – indeed, in the case of world poverty, a strategy of institutional design and implementation – and on what others are actually doing or are likely to do. Incidentally, this is consistent with an individual being morally obliged to do more than their *fair* share to realize the end; the duty to aid is ultimately derived from the needs-based *human rights* of the poor, and not from a principle of fairness (Chapter 2, Section 4).

Let us now turn to the question of the strength of my moral obligation to, say, pay $20 to Oxfam today. I suggest it is a very weak moral obligation, unlike my obligation in the drowning child scenario. On my collective action conception of the needs of the billion in absolute poverty, although the individual moral responsibility (jointly held with, let us assume, millions of others) is a strong moral obligation, it is an obligation to contribute over a long period of time. Thus, any individual's obligation to make a one-off contribution of $20 today *might be* very weak indeed; for it is what each contributes jointly with millions of others over the longer term to realizing the collective end to eliminate the absolute poverty of the billion that counts, unlike in the drowning child scenario. This is not to claim that there might not be occasions when a small group's, or even a single individual's (joint or individual, respectively), moral obligation to make a one-off contribution of $20 today might not be very strong; if, for example, the contribution in question in and of itself would in fact save lives. Rather, the point is that this prior (noninstitutional) collective moral responsibility of millions over a lengthy period of time (at least years, and probably decades) to meet the needs of the one billion living in absolute poverty is a highly diffuse moral responsibility; it is diffuse by virtue of the large numbers of the affluent who have this joint moral responsibility, as well as by virtue of the large number of occasions on which each person could contribute to discharging their own individual component of that jointly held responsibility.

That this obligation to pay $20 is considered in itself fairly weak is evidenced by the manifest absurdity of a policy of legally enforcing this obligation by, say, imprisoning any person who was found to have failed to make the $20 payment on a given occasion. By contrast, a criminal law by means of which the moral obligation to save a drowning child is enforced – a so-called good Samaritan law – is not manifestly absurd (even if such laws exist only in some jurisdictions). Whether or not there is, or could reasonably be, legal enforcement of a preexisting moral obligation is an important criterion of the strength of that moral obligation; hence, there is legal enforcement of the moral obligation not to kill an innocent person and, in some jurisdictions, legal enforcement of the moral obligation to save the life of a drowning person, if one can do so without risk to oneself. However, there could not reasonably be legal enforcement of the (assumed) obligation to make a one-off payment of $20 to Oxfam today.

On the other hand, there could be, in fact, there already is, legal enforcement of certain of our *collective* moral obligations to those in absolute poverty (as opposed to a one-off, individual moral obligation to give $20 to Oxfam); citizens of wealthy countries are legally required to pay taxes to ensure (among other things) that there are no persons in their societies in absolute poverty. The points to be made here are fourfold. First, the obligation to their needy fellow citizens is a jointly held *institutional* obligation that each affluent citizen has over the long term. Second, this collective institutional obligation is also a collective moral obligation. Third, the collective institutional obligation is a collective moral obligation by virtue of the prior noninstitutional, and highly diffuse, collective moral responsibility to assist the needy. Fourth, unlike in the case of the prior, diffuse collective responsibility to assist the needy, my (jointly held) individual (institutional and moral) obligation to pay taxes is rightly, and reasonably, enforced; that is, in effect, there are enforced payments by affluent citizens to their needy fellow citizens.

Accordingly, the problem faced by the billion in absolute poverty is a practical one. There is a prior, but diffuse, collective moral responsibility to assist the one billion living in absolute poverty, this collective responsibility being grounded in turn on their needs-based rights to assistance. However, this collective responsibility might only be able to be discharged adequately by establishing institutions of a particular kind, specifically, welfare institutions; that is, I am assuming welfare institutions are a necessary condition (but see the next section). Once established, individual citizens would have collective institutional obligations to assist the needy, for example, by way of "taxes" paid by affluent countries to poor countries; and these institutional obligations would also be collective moral obligations. In short, and putting matters somewhat simplistically, the practical problem is: What institutions need to be designed, or redesigned, to get affluent citizens of one or more (developed) countries to ensure the needs of citizens in developing countries are met?

We in the affluent world have (in aggregate, so to speak) a strong, but diffuse, prior collective moral responsibility to assist the needy in developing countries. However, the institutional mechanisms (and associated incentive structures and enforcement mechanisms) to enable us adequately to discharge this collective moral responsibility evidently do not yet exist or, if they do exist, do so in a defective form. Hence our immediate (derived) collective responsibility is to develop, or refashion, such institutional mechanisms – including free market mechanisms, for instance, free trade – in the context of an overall strategy to realize the collective end of eliminating the absolute poverty of the one billion. (This is, of course, consistent with continuing to support aid agencies; indeed, such agencies are presumably a part of any realistic strategy to realize the collective end.)

Let me return now to the demandingness of the (jointly held and long-term) individual obligation to assist the needy. Singer is an impartialist in relation to moral requirements. In the context of the issue of the obligations of the affluent to the world's poor, impartiality has been frequently discussed in relation to one's obligation to one's family or community, as opposed to one's obligations to strangers on the other side of the planet. As it happens I do not accept that my obligations to assist strangers on the other side of the planet are as strong, other things being equal, as my obligations in respect of my family, or even my community. However, I do not have the space to press this point here. I do, nevertheless, in passing note that one effect of the rejection of impartialism is to reduce the extent of the demandingness of my obligation to assist the needy outside my family, and outside my community.

I want to pursue the issue of impartialism vis-à-vis my responsibilities to assist *myself*, as opposed to any obligations others might have to assist me. Accordingly, I put forward the following moral principle: I am morally obligated to self-assist in relation to my basic needs for food, water, clothing, shelter, and health, and, other things being equal, this obligation is prior to any obligation on the part of others to assist me. (Other things might not be equal: for example, I might be starving myself to death as a form of protest.) Thus if I am in need of food, I must first take steps to provide myself with food before asking for handouts from others. So, in the first instance, the needy of the world morally ought to look to themselves. It is only if they cannot help themselves that they are morally entitled to assistance from others. Naturally, self-support might in turn rely on, for example, redesigning international trade arrangements that are currently unfair to the needy in developing countries, for example, current EU and U.S. agricultural subsidies to their own producers.

Accordingly, the principle of impartiality that, morally speaking, I stand to myself exactly as I stand to others is false, for I have moral responsibilities with respect to myself that are prior to the responsibilities that others have to me, for example, the responsibility to provide for my basic needs.

What are the implications of this partialism with respect to the obligation to self-assist for our moral obligations to the one billion in absolute poverty? At one level the implications are scant, assuming that they cannot deal with their problem without assistance. So there is a collective moral obligation to assist the one billion to eliminate their absolute poverty. However, there are some implications for the demandingness of our obligation in this regard. First, any giving we do must be in the context of assisting them to assist themselves; their responsibility (individually and collectively) for themselves in this regard is greater than ours. Second, we do not have to accept – indeed, we should reject – Singer's proposition that each of us has an obligation to keep on giving to the threshold point at which (assuming the harm to others has not been averted) the cost to me of giving is no longer comparatively insignificant. For this proposition rests on the principle of impartiality. If the moral benefit to you of my assisting you morally outweighs the moral cost to me, then, given the impartiality principle, I should assist you.

The implication of the rejection of the impartiality principle is that it is now – at least in principle – possible for an affluent person to draw the line in terms of their contribution to the absolute poor. They could do so on the basis of a different principle such as the principle that one ought to assist the needy right up to the point at which there is a significant moral cost to themselves, that is, a significant moral cost to themselves in absolute terms (albeit not in comparative terms). For example, as Garrett Cullity has suggested (Cullity 2006, chap. 9), it might be at the expense of spending a reasonable amount of time with one's friends or family, or it might mean one is not able to develop one's talents as, say, a philosopher.

Notwithstanding the above, it remains the case that the affluent have a strong, if diffuse, collective moral responsibility to assist the one billion living in absolute poverty, and to do so by designing, or redesigning, global institutions under which citizens and/or institutional actors have collective institutional obligations that are also collective moral obligations. Moreover, given that the needs and attendant severe harms in question, for instance, death as a result of starvation, are needs-based human rights, then this collective responsibility is sufficiently strong to underpin *enforceable* collective institutional/moral obligations.

This is consistent with holding that the billion living in absolute poverty do not have a needs-based human right to assistance, in the unlikely event that these needy are able to self-assist (individually or collectively) but are irrationally choosing not to do so, or the event that the affluent are unable to assist (or unable without considerable moral cost to themselves).

It is also consistent with holding that a violation of such a positive human right, that is, intentionally refraining from doing one's moral duty by rendering assistance, might be less morally wrong than many violations of negative moral rights, for example, murdering someone by shooting him, and more morally wrong than others, for example, an unprovoked assault causing broken bones.

Finally, it needs to be noted that enforcement admits of degrees; a rights-based law, for example, can be enforced by police use of lethal force or only by their use of nonlethal force. Different degrees of enforcement are appropriate for rights violations at different levels of seriousness; violations of property rights, for example, do not typically warrant police use of lethal force.

## 2. INTERNATIONAL WELFARE INSTITUTIONS

In a number of published works, notably his *World Poverty and Human Rights* (Pogge 2008), Thomas Pogge has sought to reframe the moral problem of global poverty as it has been presented by Singer and others. In the first place, and congruent with my conceptualization of the issue, he has sought to focus attention on institutions rather than on individuals per se. Accordingly, the issue becomes one of institutional design or redesign of, say, the World Trade Organization's treaty on global trade (Pogge 2008, 20) rather than that of trying to determine what financial contribution each of us in the affluent countries ought to make to contribute to the alleviation of world poverty. In the second place, Pogge has argued, in effect, that our obligations (duties, in his terminology) – the collective obligations of the governments and citizens of the world's rich countries – to the world's poorest are not principally positive obligations to assist, but rather negative obligations not to harm. Pogge does not deny the existence of positive obligations to assist, but, rather, in a spirit of ecumenism brackets them so that he can argue his case for the violation of negative rights. In any case, he holds that we in the rich countries are violating our negative obligations not to harm, and that if we desisted from these violations, then the plight of the world's poorest would be substantially eliminated (Pogge 2008, 26).

Although, no doubt, ecumenism is politically helpful in many contexts, I am not sure how appropriate it is here. From my own perspective it concedes too much moral ground to the violation of negative rights while unacceptably ignoring the gross immorality involved in violating some positive rights (albeit in Pogge's hands only as an argumentative – and political [?] – strategy). As was pointed out in Chapter 2, the violation of a negative right is not necessarily a particularly egregious violation, and negative rights are not necessarily justifiably enforceable. If, to use a variation on one of Pogge's examples, you promise to water my potted plant while I am on holiday but fail to do so, you have violated my right not to be harmed by the making of false promises. But this is a violation of a relatively trivial right. It would be absurd to equate this violation with, for example, failing to assist the drowning child – to return to Peter Singer's example; and the idea that you should be charged with the offence of, say, harmful breach of a potted plant promise and locked up, or otherwise suffer the coercive imposition of some punishment and/or compensation, is likewise absurd.

In relation to certain institutional moral rights and concomitant duties in particular, it is far from clear that positive rights have less moral strength than negative ones. Elsewhere (Miller 2007d), I have argued that certain positive rights, such as human rights to basic food or medicines, once institutionalized, generate *justifiably enforceable* institutional moral rights. Thus if a corrupt government is refusing to provide available medicines to its disease-afflicted, dying citizens, then, other things being equal, the latter may well be justified in using force to appropriate the needed medicines, if there are no nonviolent options available.

It might be suggested that such institutionalized moral rights are in reality negative rights. But this is not so. The suggestion, for example, that the harm consequent on a failure to keep a promise is an infringement of a negative right because the promisor has created an expectation that the promised action will be performed is not relevant here. For as we saw in Chapter 2, Section 3, institutional duties are not based on promises or expectations; rather, they are based on collective moral responsibilities that are, in the types of case in question, in turn based on aggregated needs-based rights, that is, positive human rights.

At a more fundamental conceptual level, as James Griffin points out (Griffin 2008, 166), the very distinction between positive and negative rights is problematic. One way to violate the right to liberty, for example, is to refrain from providing the necessary basic education to enable a person to develop in ways that would enable them to have a reasonable set of options in a modern society and, thereby, exercise their liberty.

It is also important to get clarity on the notion of harm in play here. I take it that by harming Pogge essentially means the following: (1) culpably causing serious harm and (2) violating some negative moral right(s) of the person harmed. Accordingly, one must cause the harm, either intentionally, or in the knowledge that one was doing so – or, at the very least, one ought to have known that one was doing so. Moreover, the negative rights in question must consist of some suitably circumscribed set of human rights; it would not, for example, consist of merely being unfair or in breaking a promise.

Below I argue that Pogge's strong claim is in need of qualification in two main respects. First, I suggest that our collective moral obligations as citizens, or members of the governments, of rich countries to the world's poorest are mixed; depending on which global institutional arrangement and which poor population is in question, they consist in part of moral obligations to refrain from violating negative rights, but they also consist in part of other obligations, including positive ones. Second, the nature and strength of the alleged collective obligations not to harm in question stand in need of analysis and differentiation from, on the one hand, the collective negative moral obligation not to commit crimes such as the Nazi mass murder of the Jews and, on the other hand, the collective positive obligation to provide a greater level of assistance to the needy than is currently the case by introducing enforceable institutional arrangements that are feasible alternatives to the ones currently in place, for instance, by requiring the rich nations to pay a somewhat higher level of tax to fund welfare benefits for the poor nations.

Regarding the former kind of case, the Nazis had a conscious, definite, and explicit collective end to eliminate the Jewish race; they established organizational structures and processes to achieve this end, and they went some considerable way toward realizing their genocidal aim. The members of the governments of rich nations are not engaged in any such conscious and intentional collective project of harming the world's poorest; the rich nations are not *deliberately* killing the world's poorest on a massive scale. Pogge makes this very point himself (Pogge 2007, 52). So Pogge's claim is that the rich countries are violating the negative rights of the world's poorest, not by deliberately causing harm to them, but by knowingly doing so (or at least we ought to know that we are doing so).

Pogge's argument rests on three premises: (1) under current global economic institutional arrangements, 2.53 billion or 39.7 percent of the world's population live in absolute poverty (using a poverty line that is less strict than the one used by Singer above), and 18 million die per annum as a result of poverty-related causes (Pogge 2008, 2); (2) these global institutional arrangements are coercively imposed on the poor by the rich countries acting in collaboration with the corrupt, authoritarian governments of the poor countries; (3) there are feasible alternative global institutional arrangements under which this poverty and the attendant deaths would be more or less eliminated, and at minimal economic cost to the affluent living in rich countries.

Accordingly, concludes Pogge, the affluent living in rich countries are collectively morally responsible for negative rights violations that harm the poor and, specifically, for the fact that 2.5 billion (or thereabouts) live in absolute poverty and that 18 million (or thereabouts) die each year from poverty-related causes. For example, Pogge claims (Pogge 2008, 18) that the WTO treaty is an institutional arrangement that is unfair to poor nations in its terms, and that it harms the world's poorest on a massive scale. Further, says Pogge, the rich countries of the world have coercively imposed the WTO treaty on poor countries, and, therefore, the members of their governments (at least) are collectively morally responsible for causing the harm that it does to the world's poorest (and, thereby, breaching their negative duties not to harm). According to Pogge (Pogge 2008, 22): "It is undeniable that our governments, by pressing this WTO Treaty on the rest of the world, have foreseeably taken out millions of poor persons who otherwise would have survived."

Let me first turn to the notion of collective responsibility that Pogge invokes. As should by now be evident, I am in complete agreement with Pogge's attempt to shift the focus from individual actions per se to institutional arrangements and, as a consequence, to put the emphasis on collective, as opposed to individual, moral responsibility.

However, the notion of collective responsibility in play is in need of further specification. Accordingly, I invoke my account of collective responsibility as joint responsibility. Here it is important to keep in mind the distinctions that I have made above, and in detail in Chapter 4, between collective responsibility for an outcome in the institutionally and morally neutral sense of having performed a joint action that caused the outcome (collective *causal* responsibility), collective *institutional* responsibility, and collective *moral* responsibility; neither causal responsibility nor institutional responsibility necessarily implies moral responsibility. Moreover, collective moral responsibility is itself in need of differentiation. Agents can be collectively morally responsible for their omissions as well as for their actions; and they can be collectively morally responsible for an untoward outcome in the sense that they were the ones who were primarily responsible for bringing about the outcome, or in the weaker sense that they provided some assistance to others so that the others could bring about that outcome. Agents can be collectively morally responsible in the sense that they deliberately and jointly brought about some untoward outcome, or in the weaker sense that they knew that this outcome would be the consequence of their deliberately performed joint action, or in the still weaker sense that they ought to have known that this outcome would be the consequence of their action.

Further, the collective responsibility of agents involved in Pogge's institutional examples exists at a number of levels. Consider the WTO treaty.

These levels include the membership of national trade delegations who negotiated the details of the WTO treaty, the membership of national governments who ratified it, and citizenry who voted in the governments who ratified it. Moreover, I analyze these various levels and their relations by means of my notions of a joint action and of a layered structure of joint action (Chapter 1). Thus the membership of one trade delegation performed, and is collectively morally responsible for, advocating the particular terms of trade that they advocated; call this a level 1 joint action. Given there were many such trade delegations, there were many such joint actions. Further, the memberships of the various trade delegations performed, and are collectively morally responsible for, the joint action of negotiating the particular terms of (the relevant parts) of the WTO treaty; call this a level 2 joint action, because it presupposes the various level 1 joint actions performed by each of the delegations considered individually. Likewise, the relevant members of the various governments performed, and are collectively morally responsible for, the level 2 joint action of bringing into existence the WTO treaty as an institutional arrangement; the relevant members of each government also performed, and are morally responsible for, one or other of the constitutive level 1 joint actions of ratifying the WTO Treaty.

As far as any putative collective moral responsibilities of citizens whose governments have ratified the WTO treaty, and like global institutional arrangements, are concerned, matters are somewhat more complicated. In representative democracies the government has to enact trade and related policies, and ratify, or not, specific trade arrangements; typically the citizens themselves cannot do these things. Moreover, the large voting populations in contemporary democracies cannot be assimilated to organizational structures, such as an administrative organ of government, or to small-scale directly participatory bodies, such as the cabinet in a Westminster-type system of government. Therefore, notions of collective responsibility that might apply to such organizations, or to such small structured groups, do not necessarily apply to the large populations of representative democracies. So the alleged moral responsibility of a democratic government that has instigated and ratified a trade treaty that is extremely harmful to large numbers of the world's poorest – assuming this to be the case – does not in any straightforward way translate into moral responsibility of the same kind, or order of magnitude, on the part of the citizenry who voted that government into office and who benefit from these treaties. This is, of course, not to say that the citizenry of representative democracies do not have some degree of collective moral responsibility for any such harmful actions of their governments done in their name; clearly they often do, but it may well be indirect (via the government and other institutions), diffuse, and attenuated (depending on a variety of factors, including the extent of public knowledge of the particular governmental policy in question and its effects). Incidentally, any collective responsibility the citizenry of rich countries might have in relation to the harmfulness of particular government policies in relation to the world's poorest is not to be equated with their more general collective responsibility to ameliorate the plight of the world's poorest; citizens of the world's rich countries know, or should know, that millions of the world's poorest are starving and that they can collectively do *something* about it, for instance, by increasing aid.

Let me now turn directly to the second general respect in which Pogge has sought to reframe the moral problem of global poverty, namely, by arguing that the principal source of the problem lies in negative rights violations consisting of harmful and coercively imposed institutional arrangements put in place by the affluent nations of the world, such as the WTO treaty. This claim seems to me to be in need of qualification on a number of counts.

Absent the coercive imposition of current global institutional arrangements (I return to this issue below) I would put the following moral frame on the predicament of the many millions living in absolute poverty and dying each year from poverty-related causes. Here I assume, for the sake of argument, that Pogge is correct in claiming that most of this poverty and death would have been avoided if the rich nations of the world had made modifications to global institutional arrangements, such as the WTO treaty, and in claiming that the rich nations could have made such modifications at no great cost to themselves. Given these assumptions, by my lights those living at severe risk of dying from poverty-related causes have a needs-based positive moral right to assistance from the rich nations; and the members of the governments (at least) of these rich nations have a concomitant moral duty to make the required modifications to the global institutional arrangements in question. Moreover, if these needs are not fulfilled, then the poor will necessarily suffer severe harm, if not death. So, assuming the members of the governments in question are aware of, or ought to be aware of, the plight of the poor, the feasibility of these life-preserving modifications to global institutional arrangements, and their moral duties in this regard, then these persons are, other things being equal, collectively morally responsible for the continued existence of the state of affairs in which the poor suffer the harms in question. However, this is not to say that the members of the rich governments are *causing* the harm and, therefore, have a negative duty to desist from harming. (Nor is it to say that they are primarily, or even minimally, collectively morally responsible for bringing that state of affairs into existence – albeit, as far as anything I have said here is concerned, the historical evidence might demonstrate that they were.)

Thus far I have been assuming that the current global institutional economic order was not coercively imposed. But what if, as Pogge claims, this global institutional order was in fact coercively imposed by the rich countries (acting with or without the collaboration of corrupt, authoritarian governments of poor countries)? Would the members of the governments of the rich countries (at least) now be collectively morally responsible for actively harming the poor (negative rights violation) – as opposed to simply being collectively morally responsible for allowing their poverty (and poverty-related deaths) to continue (positive rights violation)? Before answering this question we need to get clarity on the notion of coercive imposition in play here.

Assume that I imprison a man in the attic in my house for a month. Clearly I have violated his right to autonomy. Moreover I have incurred positive duties that I might not have had before imprisoning him; specifically, I now have a positive moral duty to ensure that he has adequate food, water, and so on – I have a duty of care. Moreover, if I do not provide adequate food, water, and the like, then, as Pogge says (Pogge 2007, 24), I have harmed him. I have harmed him by virtue of preventing him from having access to the basic necessities of life that he had access to before my intervention. So I have a negative moral obligation not to imprison him (violation of his right to autonomy); but I also have a negative obligation not to intervene to curtail his access to the basic necessities of life (violation of his right to life). This is evidently a paradigm case of what Pogge has in mind. But now we need to consider deviations from the paradigm.

First, we need to distinguish coercively imposed compliance with the terms of an arrangement that has been freely entered into from an arrangement that has itself been coercively imposed. So compliance with the terms of the WTO treaty, for example, might be coercively imposed by, for example, the use of trade sanctions. However, it would not follow from this that the WTO treaty had itself been coercively imposed.

Second, we need to distinguish coercively imposed arrangements from unfair agreements entered into as a consequence of lopsided power relationships. If the members of a trade delegation or government of some weak and poor country were in fact coerced into accepting or ratifying unjust and unreasonable terms of the treaty, then they may not be collectively blameworthy, nor even (depending on the degree of coercion) collectively morally responsible, for their action; indeed, it may even be that, as a consequence, the treaty ought not to be regarded as legally binding. Given the lopsided power relationships that obtain between the very poor and the very rich nation-states who are signatories to this treaty, and given the extraordinarily unfair terms that were accepted by some poor countries (*Economist*, Sep. 25, 1999, 89, quoted in Pogge 2008, 20), it might be argued that these terms were coercively imposed on the poor nations by the rich nations. However, inequality of power between contracting parties, and a resulting agreement that is unfair to the less powerful, does not necessarily imply coercion on the part of the powerful. Moreover, since unfairness is not, in and of itself, a rights violation, it is not necessarily the case that the unfair trade treaties in question constitute a negative rights violation.

In the light of these points, we can now see what Pogge needs to establish with respect to the alleged rich countries' imposition of the global institutional arrangements in question on the poor, namely, that (1) these arrangements have been *coercively* imposed by the rich countries on the poor populations (as opposed to being the result of a bargaining process between the more powerful, the governments of the rich countries, and the less powerful, the governments of the poor countries); (2) the agencies deploying the coercive force in question are in fact the governments of the rich countries, or perhaps the governments of the rich countries acting in concert with the governments of the poor countries – at any rate, as opposed to the governments of the poor countries acting alone – and they are deploying it in respect of the establishment of the institutional arrangements in question, and not merely by way of enforcing compliance with arrangements that have been freely entered into.

With these various points in mind, let us now turn to Pogge's central claim, namely, that there are many cases of coercively enforced global institutional arrangements that violate the negative rights of the poor, and that these are the principal cause of the problem of global poverty and poverty-related deaths.

There are certainly cases of enforced global institutional arrangements that harm the poor (as opposed to failing to assist them adequately). Consider the infamous Trade-Related Aspects of Intellectual Property Rights (TRIPS) agreement, which requires signatories to issue patents on pharmaceutical products and not simply on processes (as had been the case before 2005 in India in particular; see Pogge 2008, 226). When India signed on to TRIPS this had the effect of blocking the large-scale supply of life-saving medicines produced by Indian manufacturers of generic medicines to the world's poorest (Pogge 2008, 227). So there was an institutional arrangement in place that was assisting many of the world's poorest, and it was effectively destroyed by TRIPS. Clearly this is a case of indirectly harming the poor by destroying an institutional arrangement that is assisting them. TRIPS is a global institutional arrangement that is harmful in the extreme to the world's poorest and one that is coercively imposed on Indian manufacturers by the Indian government. Here coercive imposition is a necessary condition for the harm in question to be done; absent enforceable government legislation, the manufacturers would presumably have continued to supply generic medicines to the poor.

However, *contra* Pogge, the Indian government, but not the governments of rich countries, coercively imposed TRIPS on Indian manufactures of generic medicines for the poor. Nevertheless, the governments of the United States and other rich countries were collectively responsible for constructing and signing on to TRIPS, for succumbing to pressure from multinational pharmaceutical companies in doing so, and for putting pressure in turn on the Indian government to sign on to TRIPS. So there is a causal chain comprised of the deliberate actions of multinational companies, the relevant members of the governments of the rich countries in question, and the relevant members of the government of India. This causal chain terminates in the Indian manufacturers ceasing to produce cheap generic drugs for the poor and, as a consequence, large numbers of the poor dying from their poverty-related diseases. Presumably, the members of the pharmaceutical companies, and the members of the governments in question – and especially the members of the Indian government – were not *deliberately* aiming at harming the poor; but they must have realized that it would be a consequence of their joint actions. Accordingly, the relevant members of the multinational pharmaceutical companies, of the governments of the United States and the other rich countries, and of the Indian government are collectively morally responsible for causing the extreme harm to the world's poorest resulting from (the relevant parts of) the TRIPS agreement.

The question remains, however, whether such harmful global institutional arrangements are the principal cause of the problem, as Pogge contends. I suggest that it is unclear that *most* of the 2.5 billion living in absolute poverty, and the 18 million dying each year as a result of poverty, are doing so principally as a consequence of global institutional arrangements coercively imposed on the world's poorest nations by the world's richest nations acting in concert (at times) with corrupt, authoritarian governments of poor countries.

First, it is not obvious that most of those living in, and dying from, poverty in places such as Zimbabwe, Darfur, and Rwanda, for example, are doing so principally as a consequence of current global institutional arrangements, rather than principally as a result of domestic, home-grown conflict that is taking place more or less independently of these global arrangements. Here I note that the failure on the part of the governments of the United States, the United Kingdom, France, South Africa, and others to intervene efficaciously does not constitute actively harming; this is not to say, of course, that their nonintervention is not culpable failure to assist.

Second, many millions live in absolute poverty in powerful nation-states such as India and China. But India is a powerful democracy (not a weak or authoritarian state), and the Indian economy is not heavily dependent on world trade. Accordingly, the economic plight of the poor in India is in large part determined by internal domestic economic processes, structures, and government policies. So the claim that current global institutional arrangements are *coercively* imposed by rich countries on India and that this is a principal cause of poverty in India is implausible. Moreover, to the extent that global institutional arrangements are coercively imposed on India's poor, this is essentially because the Indian government – and no one else – has imposed them. Indeed, India is quite prepared to ignore international pressure from the United States and the EU when it suits. In the recent round of WTO trade talks (the Doha Development Round), for example, it was precisely India's refusal to accept U.S. and EU proposals that in part caused the failure to reach agreement; indeed, India claimed that it acted to protect the interest of its poorest farmers (Kilney 2008, 17).

As for China, it certainly coercively imposes institutional arrangements – including global ones – on its own citizens and, indeed, on other countries, such as Tibet; however, it is highly implausible that it is currently operating under global institutional arrangements that are *coercively* imposed on it. So as with India, if global institutional arrangements are coercively imposed on China's poor, then this is essentially because the Chinese government – and no one else – has coercively imposed them.

Insofar as the poverty in China is a result of coercively imposed institutional arrangements that destroy or undermine existing institutional arrangements, such as the above-described TRIPS agreement or, during the time of Mao's cultural revolution, the forced removal of, for example, doctors, nurses, and other health professionals from hospitals into jobs in the countryside as farm laborers (with the consequence that hundreds of thousands died from inadequate health care), then the relevant members of the governments in question are collectively morally responsible for actively harming their citizens. However, insofar as recent (legally enforceable) institutional arrangements in China and India, such as the introduction of elements of a free market system (e.g., the selling of stock and the ownership of businesses) in China after Mao, are assisting the poor by contributing to very high levels of economic growth, but doing so to a lesser extent than feasible alternatives, then the members of these governments are not necessarily collectively responsible for actively harming the poor; perhaps they are only collectively responsible for failing to assist the poor to the extent that they should be. (Many of these initiatives also have a harmful effect on the poor in particular, for example, as a consequence of environmental degradation in China.)

On the other hand, if in the authoritarian nation-state of China there are alternative economic institutional arrangements that foreseeably would greatly reduce absolute poverty and save the lives of millions, and if the Chinese government could relatively easily put these arrangements in place, if it chose to do so, then arguably to that extent the Chinese government is violating the negative rights of the people in question.

In this respect the situation in India is somewhat different and more complex by virtue of its being a representative democracy, and a somewhat shambolic one at that. Responsibility for the economic institutional arrangements in place in India – and any failure to implement feasible alternatives that foreseeably would greatly reduce absolute poverty and save millions of lives – attaches, at least in theory and to some extent in practice, to the citizenry at large – including hundreds of millions of Indians who are themselves impoverished, even if not living in absolute poverty – and not simply the government of India; however, the collective responsibilities of the citizenry at large in an impoverished, albeit developing, country such as India are indirect (via government and other institutions), diffuse, and attenuated.

In summation, Pogge has not established his strong claim that most of the 2.5 billion living in absolute poverty, and most of the 18 million who die annually from poverty, live in and die from their poverty primarily as a consequence of coercively imposed (by the rich countries), global institutional economic arrangements for which there are feasible alternatives: alternative institutional arrangements that would, if implemented, result in a cessation of this absolute poverty and poverty-related death currently visited on the poor by the rich. However, weaker versions of Pogge's claim might well be correct, and the following minimal claim is very hard to dispute: The members of the governments of rich democracies are, directly or indirectly, collectively morally responsible (to at least some degree and jointly with others) for a considerable proportion of the world's poverty, and poverty-related deaths, by virtue of failing to adjust global institutional arrangements in ways that would greatly reduce that poverty and those deaths – either by providing assistance to the world's poor or by refraining from violating their negative rights (or otherwise harming them) – and do so at minimal cost to themselves and their citizens.

## 3. REDESIGNING GLOBAL INSTITUTIONAL ARRANGEMENTS TO AMELIORATE GLOBAL POVERTY

In this final section I consider two specific global institutional arrangements discussed by Pogge. One is a current institutional arrangement in need of redesign, the second is an arrangement Pogge has designed and is hoping to have implemented.

As we have seen, sometimes poverty is greatly facilitated by current global institutional arrangements. Consider, for example, the so-called resource curse that blights countries such as Equatorial Guinea (Pogge 2008, 29; Wenar 2008). Natural resources, such as oil, generate enormous revenues from their sale abroad that are retained by the corrupt, authoritarian leaders of the countries in question; these revenues enrich both these leaders and their supporting elites at the expense of their impoverished citizenry. In effect, under current global institutional arrangements, the citizens of rich democracies buy stolen goods (natural resources that are the joint property of the impoverished citizenry of the states in question; Wenar 2008) and, thereby, causally contribute to the poverty in those countries. Moreover, there is a very obvious, feasible – indeed, more or less universally accepted – alternative institutional arrangement, namely, one in which property rights are respected. In this scenario the rich countries, or at least the members of their governments, are knowingly, actively assisting the repressive governments of the poor countries in question to violate the property rights of their citizens and, thereby – via the consequent avoidable impoverishment of these citizens – violate their negative human rights. To this extent members of the governments of the rich countries in question are culpably causally implicated in these negative rights violations and, in particular, in the continuing poverty of those whose rights are being violated.

It might be argued that in the case of these countries blighted by the resource curse it is not the rich countries that are coercively imposing the arrangement; it is the corrupt, authoritarian governments that are coercively imposing these arrangements under which they in effect steal the property of their own citizens and sell this stolen property to the rich countries. True enough; nevertheless, it is the rich countries that are providing these authoritarian governments with the financial means (and, in some cases, the armaments) by which they can coercively impose the arrangement. So the members of the governments of these rich countries are collectively morally responsible (jointly with the members of the authoritarian government in question) for the fact that this arrangement is coercively imposed on the poor in that country.

So much for harmful global institutional arrangements that violate the negative rights of the poor. Let us now turn to helpful ones. Pogge makes a number of potentially useful contributions to redressing the problem of global poverty (Pogge 2008, chaps. 8 and 9). One such contribution is Pogge's proposed Health Impact Fund (Pogge 2008, 244–6).

Pogge has proposed a new institutional arrangement, the Health Impact Fund (HIF), to help combat poverty-related diseases, such as HIV/AIDS and malaria. Under this arrangement pharmaceutical companies would voluntarily agree to sell their medicines at cost to the disease-afflicted poor; hence the poor would be paying a relatively low price for medicines, namely, the cost of production and distribution. The profits to the companies would be paid out of the HIF on the basis of the contribution of their medicines to the reduction of the global disease burden; thus profits would be performance based. Funding for the HIF is to come from governments; however, the cost to taxpayers would be offset to some extent by the reduced cost of medicines. Pharmaceutical companies would also retain their patent rights on their medicines.

Under this arrangement the performance of individual companies is tied directly to the collective end of the institution, namely, the reduction in the global disease burden. To this extent the HIF is an exemplar of my normative, teleological account of social institutions. The collective end is certainly a worthy one, but what of the means, that is, the questions of efficiency and effectiveness? Some have argued, for example, that the most important way to reduce the global disease burden is by distributing currently available drugs, the patents of which have run out, in conjunction with the provision of clean water, adequate food, and the like (Selgelid 2008). There is also the question of the feasibility of the HIF, to which I now turn.

Here there are three obvious questions. First, why should companies defect to the HIF? Presumably some companies will defect because they calculate that they can produce medicines that make considerable impact on the global disease burden, and that the profits they could make by doing so are greater than those they are currently making by competing with other companies in the production of medicines for rich peoples' afflictions.

Second, can governments provide sufficient funds to enable the HIF to provide profits to companies? Governments will need only to provide sufficient funds to the HIF to cover the profits of the participating pharmaceutical companies (as opposed to their production and distribution costs) and only to the extent that the medicines produced by these pharmaceutical companies actually reduce the global disease burden. Governments *can* surely provide significant funding for this very important and pressing purpose; whether or not they will remains an unanswered, and unanswerable, question. On the other hand, if securing very large amounts of government funding proved to be a problem, then the access of pharmaceutical companies to the HIF could be restricted and the degree of access varied, depending on the amount of government funds available as "winnings" to participating companies.

Third, is it not difficult, and perhaps impossible, to measure with a high degree of accuracy the contribution of any given administered medicine to the reduction in the global disease burden? Indeed, it is very difficult; fortunately, it might not be necessary. What is necessary is that (1) there are some reasonably reliable indicators of the causal impact in terms of disease reduction of the medicines in question, such as measurable impact on the health of (suitable) individuals in clinical trials multiplied by number of individuals who use the medicine; (2) there is some precise (but not necessarily accurate) method of measuring impact that is acceptable to the pharmaceutical companies, such as measurable impact on the health of (suitable) individuals in clinical trials multiplied by (audited) sales figures; and (3) the method of measurement in (2) more or less tracks the indicators in (1), such as sales figures more or less track actual use. Naturally, the indicators and the measures used can be continuously refined, as more knowledge is acquired.

Condition (1) needs to be satisfied to ensure that the medicines being rewarded are actually contributing usefully to the reduction in the global disease burden, but greater accuracy than this is not required. Condition (1) is needed to ensure that the collective end of the HIF is actually being realized.

Condition (2) needs to be satisfied in order that the pharmaceutical companies have some precise standard against which to determine their relative and absolute profits; but as long as they can maximize profits by meeting this standard, they will not be too concerned if the standard is itself an imperfect indicator of their actual contribution to the reduction in the global disease burden. Condition (2) is required to enable the pharmaceutical companies to pursue their self-interest (profits); they must know exactly what winning and losing consists in, and be rewarded accordingly.

Condition (3) is required to ensure that the precise measure used to allocate profits more or less tracks the far less precise indicators of causal contribution to global disease burden reduction. Condition (3) is required to ensure that the companies' pursuit of profit (the *proximate* individual ends of the institutional arrangement) usefully contributes to the reduction in the global disease burden (the *ultimate* collective end of the institutional arrangement).

## 4. CONCLUSION

In this chapter I have considered the arguments of Peter Singer and of Thomas Pogge in relation to the obligation to assist (Singer) or not harm (Pogge) the global poor. I agree with both Singer and Pogge that the affluent have a moral obligation to the poor. I have argued in favor of Pogge, and against Singer, that the affluent have a strong, if diffuse, collective moral responsibility to the one billion living in absolute poverty, and to do so by designing, or redesigning, global institutions under which citizens and/or institutional actors have collective institutional obligations that are also collective moral obligations. Moreover, given the needs and attendant severe harms in question, for instance, death as a result of starvation, this collective responsibility is sufficiently strong to underpin *enforceable* collective institutional/moral obligations, assuming the latter obligations can be discharged at relatively little moral cost to the affluent, and that the needy are unable to self-assist (individually or collectively).

I further argue that Pogge has not established his strong claim that most of the 2.5 billion living in absolute poverty, and most of the 18 million who die annually from poverty, live in and die from their poverty primarily as a consequence of coercively imposed, global institutional economic arrangements for which there are feasible alternatives that would not harm the poor. However, weaker versions of Pogge's claim might well be correct.

Finally, I have briefly discussed Pogge's innovative proposal for the design of his Health Impact Fund to try to incentivize pharmaceutical companies to conduct more research into poverty-related diseases.

# 8

# The University

In this chapter I apply my individualist, teleological (normative) account to the university as an institution, and in this context explore the normative notion of academic autonomy and its relation to freedom of intellectual inquiry.[1] In doing so I identify certain bureaucratic and market-based influences that tend to have a corrosive – if not a corruptive (Chapter 5) – effect on the institutional processes, roles, and ends of the university. I begin with a brief introduction to the contemporary university.

## 1. THE HYBRIDIZATION AND TRANSMOGRIFICATION OF THE UNIVERSITY

Academic autonomy is a so-called traditional academic value. Other such values include institutional autonomy, collegial conceptions of governance, academic freedom, tenure,[2] and ownership of intellectual property, and the centrality of academics and of academic matters in the life of the university.

These values are part and parcel of a particular (normative) individualist, teleological model – call it the traditional model – of the university and the constitutive institutional role of the academic. Roughly speaking, on this model universities have as a collective end (Chapter 1) the acquisition, transmission, and dissemination of knowledge, both for its own sake as well as for the multifarious benefits that such knowledge brings to the wider community; in short, universities produce a collective good (Chapter 2). It is important to stress that knowledge in this context

---

[1] An earlier version of the material in this chapter appeared in Miller (2000b).
[2] Two useful collections in relation to this and related issues are Pincoffs (1975) and De George (1997).

must be broadly conceived so to embrace not only information,[3] but also understanding and the skills to acquire information and understanding, including the skills needed by the professions (Chapter 6).[4]

In some quarters it is held that this traditional conception is outdated and irrelevant, as are its associated values. I argue that broadly understood the traditional view (suitably recast in terms of my individualist, teleological theory) is both viable and superior to salient alternatives, such as the modern bureaucratic business corporation.

Evidently many universities in the English-speaking world – and certainly in the United Kingdom and Australia – are being pushed by government, bureaucratic, and market forces in the direction of a very different institutional model, namely, that of the large bureaucratic business corporation. One argument for this is that universities need to be privatized and corporatized so as to enable them to become more competitive and better able to contribute to the economy.

This kind of argument is open to question on a number of counts. First, universities, although they have a role in relation to the national interests of the communities that fund them, have wider supranational collective ends, such as the pursuit of knowledge for its own sake, the dissemination of that knowledge internationally, and the pursuit of knowledge in the service of human, as opposed to national, needs. Is the cancer or HIV/AIDS research undertaken in, say, the United States undertaken simply for the good of sufferers who happen to be U.S. citizens? Is research into global warming undertaken by Australians undertaken simply to benefit Australia? Here it is important to point out that the drive on the part of many universities to secure intellectual property rights for the purposes of commercialization and their own enrichment is problematic if it means that this will compromise their institutional obligations to produce collective goods in respect of which members of various communities have joint moral rights, the right to medicines being a case in point.

---

[3] Here I am assuming that a piece of information, i.e., a true belief, does not necessarily have any inherent value. In this respect it is akin to an action (Chapter 1, Section 3). On the other hand, it might be insisted that, other things being equal, a true belief has greater value than a false belief and that, therefore, true beliefs must have *some* value; if it be so insisted, then I will grant that true beliefs have value in this minimal sense. In this respect they are akin to realized intentions, i.e., actions, as opposed to failed intention.

[4] This view is more or less that proffered by John Henry Newman in his famous work *The Idea of a University* (1854). See also Jaspers (1960) and also Pelikan (1992).

Second, the assumption that the corporatization and privatization of universities is, in fact, ultimately, that is, in the long term, going to assist the economy is extremely doubtful. If the problem is economic competition and growth, surely it must be business organizations, the international financial system, government economic policy, and the like that are in need of rethinking and reform. Increasing student numbers without a commensurate increase in funding, for example, although it may well deliver short-term efficiencies, ultimately tends to be, in the case of universities – as opposed to low-level training colleges – corrosive of educational standards as well as research quality and, therefore, of universities as institutions. Moreover, in the long term the best contribution universities can make to the economy is surely by way of original (including fundamental as well as applied) research and high-quality student education.

Third, notwithstanding the rhetoric, many of the recent developments in British and Australian higher education sector amount simply to bureaucratization, rather than the establishment of a set of efficient businesses functioning in a competitive market. This bureaucratization has taken the form in part of ongoing and ever-changing requirements to collect data, contrive mission statements, put in place (often counterproductive) accountability mechanisms, and satisfy bureaucratically defined quality audits. Such initiatives – whatever their initial impact – tend over time to lead to a loss of genuine efficiency in teaching and research. For one thing, they result in over-administration. For another, incessant changes in bureaucratic demands on academics breaches the first law of good administration, namely, stability of procedures and processes.

At any rate, thus far the result in the United Kingdom and Australia is the spawning of a hybrid institution comprising incongruous elements of the bureaucratic corporation (increasing bureaucratization but also market-focused practices and ideology), on the one hand, along with elements of the traditional university, on the other. The emergence of this hybrid beast both is corrosive of academic values and generates significant institutional confusion in relation to the appropriate culture, governance structure, and collective ends of universities.

Hybridization also has the effect of transmogrifying – in the sense of magically transforming – academic issues into resource, financial, market, and bureaucratic issues. This process is caused by, and in turn contributes to, the shift in the status of academics from autonomous professionals to industrial employees, and the concomitant shift in power from academics to administrators. Transmogrification also contributes to the erosion of academic values. For example, in Australia the undermining of institutional autonomy vis-à-vis government and market forces, taken in conjunction with the weakening of collegial processes and the watering down of academic tenure, reduces individual academic autonomy and, therefore, is likely over time to undermine freedom of inquiry in Australian universities.

If hybridization is problematic, full-blown corporatization – whatever its short-term economic benefits might be – would signal the death of the university as an institution. On the full-blown corporatization model, universities transmogrify into business operations, training full-fee-paying students for jobs and conducting research on a fully commercial basis for business and government. In place of universities we would have training colleges, servicing the immediate needs of the job market, and research centers, doing the bidding of whoever has the money to pay. This conception is ultimately incoherent. It is a conception fixated by short-term economic goals. Moreover, it is predicated on a misunderstanding of the nature and scope of human knowledge, the means by which it is acquired and transmitted, or of the importance of knowledge over the long term in the maintenance, reproduction, and transformation of societies, and the institutions and individuals that comprise them. The intellectual capital accumulated by generations of classicists, Asianists, physicists, philosophers, scientists, mathematicians, literary writers, historians, linguists, and for that matter economists – in Australia students are fleeing theoretical in favor of practical courses – ought not to be abandoned in the face of market forces representing the preferences of eighteen-year-olds and the current demands of, for example, the tourist industry. Ironically, the limitations, even in its own terms, of this economically fixated, near-sighted ideology are, as I write, being underscored by a global economic downturn that is adversely affecting tourism in particular.

Those who attack the traditional conception sometimes paint its supporters as Luddites unable to respond to a rapidly changing world. Here we need to differentiate issues. First, nothing I have said is inconsistent with the notion of a privately funded university. Whether or not an organization is a university is a matter of its activities, structure, culture, and collective ends, not its funding source. Naturally, the structure of funding can under certain conditions have a serious negative impact on the nature of universities, as described above. However, the point to be stressed here is that so long as a university realizes the collective good(s) that are definitive of universities and, in particular, ensures that commercial considerations are (all things considered) subservient to academic ones, then it does not matter whether it is privately or publicly funded.

Second, supporters of the traditional conception do not need to reject every particular new development that has taken place. There may well have been a need to strengthen the accountability of individual academics in relation to their teaching and research performance. Again, the new entrepreneurialism has assisted laudable new projects such as the provision of tertiary education to some occupational groups that need it and were formerly denied it. More generally, there is, and always has been, a need for interaction between universities and industry, the professions, and the wider community. Evidently, many universities have insulated themselves to an unacceptable degree from the wider community, and there has been a consequent need to invigorate these external relationships to ensure that the collective good, that is, knowledge, to which members of the wider community have a joint right is in fact being acquired, transmitted, and disseminated.

However, none of these *acceptable* new developments are inconsistent with the traditional model. For example, initiatives in higher education for police officers ought to be viewed as a continuation and extension of the traditional role of the university in professional education. Indeed, historically universities have proved themselves flexible, not only in respect of developing education programs for new professions, but also in relation to pursuing research in applied science and technology.

It has to be said that academics are to some extent responsible for the problems, or the extent of the problems, that they now confront. In Australia and the United Kingdom, in the face of attacks on institutional autonomy, collegiality, tenure, intellectual property, and so on, they seem to have fallen victim to a kind of collective paralysis. They have failed to speak out and failed to mobilize opposition. In some quarters of the humanities this is in part the result of an abandonment of these academic values. For example, many postmodernists are contemptuous of academic values such as truth, reason, knowledge, and individual academic autonomy (Freadman and Miller 1992).

To an extent academics have failed to rationally address some of the genuine academic issues – as opposed to artificially induced problems, such as competitive neutrality and enterprise bargaining – that confront universities, and one important result has been the transmogrification of these problems into resource, financial, and market problems to be dealt with by managers. One such academic issue is redundancies. Whether or not there ought to be redundancies in some area of the university is in large part an academic issue to do with the academic value and centrality of the area of intellectual inquiry in which redundancies are being proposed. The main effect of financial strictures ought to be to concentrate the collegial minds of universities on what the most academically important areas of inquiry are, and to seek to protect them by, for example, providing them compulsorily to students.

Another related problem concerns research. What ought to be the priority areas for research, and how much genuine intellectual progress is being made in these areas? This is a complex academic question that perhaps the collegial decision-making bodies of universities have not adequately addressed in the past, preferring to allow individual academics to go their own way and discipline groups to follow intellectual fashions. It might be that the intellectual specialization and compartmentalization resulting from the so-called explosion in knowledge, but also from the pluralist and competition-inducing structure of faculties and departments, might have worked against the possibility of especially large universities (multiversities) adequately dealing with this question. At any rate, the general result is that this important academic issue has been in large part transmogrified into a bureaucratic/competitive market issue. Universities are now busy competing with one another in a race that begins with a frenetic attempt to identify pots of money and second guess political agendas, and ends with an adjudication based on research dollars won and numbers of publications produced. The important institutional task of attempting to determine what sorts of research really need to be done and for whom, as well as genuinely assessing intellectual progress, is not being done adequately.

## 2. COLLECTIVE ENDS OF THE UNIVERSITY: FREEDOM OF INQUIRY AND KNOWLEDGE AS AN END-IN-ITSELF

The significance of academic values such as academic autonomy and collegiality are relative to a particular conception of the university as an institution and, more specifically, to a particular view of the collective goods produced by universities.

If the fundamental collective ends of the university are the acquisition of knowledge for its own sake, as well as the transmission of knowledge to students and its dissemination for the benefit of the community, for example, by way of its application in the production of agricultural, manufactured, and other goods, as well as in the preservation of cultural heritage, and the promotion of communal self-understanding, then we need to ask the conditions under which these ends could be realized. There are two general conditions, namely, freedom of inquiry and publication, on the one hand, and intellectual honesty and competence, on the other. It is obvious that without intellectual honesty and competence, knowledge will not be attained and disseminated. Self-deceivers, liars, and epistemological incompetents will not assist in the realization of so difficult and uncertain a goal as the acquisition of knowledge (in the sense of understanding), its transmission to students, and dissemination to the wider society. What of freedom of intellectual inquiry and publication?

There are two especially salient traditional arguments for freedom of intellectual inquiry, the first associated with John Stuart Mill, the second (loosely) associated with Immanuel Kant (Mill 1869; Kant 1785, 1979). (I do not mean to imply that these arguments are the only ones advanced by these philosophers, much less that the versions of them I propound below are precise renderings of the work of these philosophers.)

According to Mill, new knowledge will emerge only in a free market-place of ideas (Schauer 1981, 16–19). If certain ideas are prevented from being investigated or communicated, then the truth is not likely to emerge, because those suppressed ideas may in fact be the true ones. Since universities have as a collective end the acquisition of knowledge, presumably a university must in part consist of a free marketplace of ideas.

Let us look more closely at this argument, restricting ourselves to ideas in the sense of putative knowledge, for instance, hypotheses, unsubstantiated claims, interpretations, theories, requiring a complex process of reasoning and justification – the sort of knowledge pursued in universities. Here Mill appears to rely on a distinction between rational inquiry and justification on the one hand – a possibly solitary activity – and freedom of communication on the other.

This argument needs to be unpacked. I suggest the following rendering of it:

1. Freedom of communication is necessary for rational inquiry.
2. Rational inquiry is necessary for knowledge.

Therefore:

3. Freedom of communication is necessary for knowledge.

The argument is valid, and premise 2 is plausible in relation to the sort of knowledge pursued at universities. What of premise 1?

The justification for premise 1 is evidently that rational inquiry requires:

i.    A number of diverse views or perspectives (possessed by different persons and different interest groups)
ii.   A substantial amount of diverse evidence for/against these views (available from different sources)
iii.  Regarding i and ii, there is no single (a) infallible and (b) reliable authority.

Notice that Mill's argument for freedom of inquiry – understood as rational inquiry in a context of freedom of communication – is instrumentalist or means/end in its form. The claim is not that freedom of inquiry is good in itself, but rather that it is a means to another good, namely, knowledge. (It is then an open question – as far as Mill's argument is concerned – whether or not knowledge is an intrinsic good, or merely a means to some other good. By contrast, I have already assumed that knowledge is an intrinsic good.) To this extent the moral weight to be attached to freedom of inquiry is weaker than it would be by the lights of an argument that accorded freedom of inquiry the status of an intrinsic good or fundamental moral right.

The second argument for freedom of inquiry is not inconsistent with the first, but is nevertheless quite different. Specifically, it accords freedom of inquiry greater moral weight by treating it as having the status of a fundamental moral right. This second argument – or at least my own neo-Kantian rendering of it – relies on a wider sense of freedom of intellectual inquiry, one embracing not only freedom of thought and reasoning, but also freedom of communication and discussion (Kant 1979, 43–4; Dworkin 1979). The argument begins with the premise that freedom of intellectual inquiry thus understood is a fundamental human right.

Thus conceived, freedom of intellectual inquiry is not an individual right in the sense in which, for example, the right to life is. Although it is a moral right that attaches to individuals, as opposed to groups, it is not a right that an individual could exercise by him- or herself. Communication, discussion, and intersubjective methods of testing are social, or at least interpersonal, activities. However, it is important to stress that they are not activities that are relativized to certain designated social groups. In principle, intellectual interaction can and ought to be allowed to take place between individuals irrespective of whether they belong to the same social, ethnic, or political group. In short, freedom of intellectual inquiry, or at least its constituent elements, is a fundamental *human* right. Note that being a fundamental human right it can, at least in principle, override collective interests and goals, including national economic interests and goals.

If freedom of intellectual inquiry is a human right, then like other human rights, such as the right to life and to freedom of the person, it is a right that academics as humans possess along with all other citizens (and, for that matter, noncitizens). But how does this bear on the specific collective ends of the university to acquire, transmit, and disseminate knowledge?

Before we can answer this question we need more clarity on the relationship between the human right to freely engage in intellectual inquiry, on the one hand, and knowledge or truth, on the other.

The term *knowledge* as used in this context embraces not only information, but also understanding. Note also that to come to have knowledge in this sense, one must possess rational capacities, that is, capacities that enable not only the acquisition of certain kinds of information, but especially the development of understanding. Here the term *rational* is broadly construed. It is not, for example, restricted to deductive and inductive reasoning, much less to means/end reasoning.

Freedom of intellectual inquiry and knowledge, in this extended sense of knowledge, are not simply related as means to end, but also conceptually. To freely inquire is to seek the truth by reasoning. Truth is not an external, contingently connected end that some inquiries might be directed toward if the inquirer happened to have an interest in truth, rather than, say, an interest in falsity or (à la Derrida) playfulness (Freadman and Miller 1992, chap. 5). Rather truth is internally connected to intellectual inquiry. An intellectual inquiry that did not aim at the truth would not be an intellectual inquiry, or at least would be defective *qua* intellectual inquiry. Moreover, here aiming at truth is aiming at truth as an end in itself. (This is not inconsistent with also aiming at truth as a means to some other end.) In other words, an alleged intellectual inquiry that aimed at truth only as a means to some other end would not be an intellectual inquiry or would be defective *qua* intellectual inquiry, because for such a pseudo-inquirer truth would not be internal to his or her activity. Such a pseudo-inquirer is prepared to abandon – and, indeed, would have in fact abandoned –aiming at truth if, for example, it turns out, or if it had turned out, that the means to his or her end was not after all truth, but rather falsity (for this kind of point, see Dummett 1973, chap. 10).

Further, to engage in free intellectual inquiry in my extended sense, involving communication with, and testing by, others, is to freely seek the truth by reasoning with others. Intellectual inquiry in this sense is not exclusively the activity of a solitary individual; rather, it is a collective – or, better, joint – enterprise (see Chapters 1 and 2). Moreover, here reasoning is broadly construed to embrace highly abstract formal deductive reasoning at one end of the spectrum and informal (including literary) interpretation and speculation at the other.

There are, of course, methods of acquiring knowledge that do not necessarily, or even in fact, involve free inquiry, for instance, my knowledge that I have a toothache, or my knowledge that the object currently in the foreground of my visual field is a table, but these taken in themselves are relatively unimportant items of knowledge as far as universities are concerned. (Obviously other items of knowledge of the same species can be very important in the context of some intellectual inquiry, such as an inquiry into whether a recently developed drug eases pain or an inquiry into ordinary perception.)

Given that freedom of intellectual inquiry is a human right, and given the above-described relationship between intellectual inquiry and truth (or knowledge), we can now present our second argument in relation to freedom of intellectual inquiry. This argument in effect seeks to recast the notion of freedom of intellectual inquiry to bring out the potential significance for conceptions of the university of the claim that freedom of intellectual inquiry is a human right:

1.   Freedom of intellectual inquiry is a human right.
2.   Freedom of intellectual inquiry is (principally) freedom to seek the truth by reasoning with others.
3.   Freedom to seek the truth by reasoning with others is a fundamental human right.

This section began with the assumption that the university has as its fundamental purpose the pursuit of knowledge, both for its own sake and for the benefits such knowledge brings the wider society. Subsequent discussion has yielded the following additional plausible propositions. First, the kind of knowledge in question is attainable only by reasoning with others. Second, to engage in free intellectual inquiry is to seek truth (or knowledge) for its own sake. Third, freely seeking the truth (or knowledge) for its own sake, and by reasoning with others, is a fundamental human right.

Let us grant the existence of a human right to freely pursue the truth by reasoning with others. What are the implications of this right for universities and for academics' freedom of inquiry?

Given such a right of intellectual inquiry, it is plausible to conclude that the university is, at least in part, the institutional embodiment of that moral right, that is, the university is in part the institutional embodiment of the right to freely seek the truth by reasoning with others. That the university embody the right to freely seek the truth by reasoning with others is, of course, congruent with the (above-stated) collective end of a university to acquire, transmit, and disseminate knowledge for the benefit of the wider community. For not only is freely seeking the truth by reasoning with others congruent with the realization of the collective end of the provision of knowledge-based benefits to the wider community, it is a necessary condition for it. On the other hand, it is not a sufficient condition for it. Academics can all too easily seek the truth by reasoning with one another in an institutional cocoon: the so-called Ivory Tower. Hence the importance of academic engagement with other institutions, and with the wider community.

The notion of an institutional embodiment of a human right is multiply ambiguous.[5] For our purposes here, it is important to distinguish an institutional embodiment of a moral right from an institution, such that persons have a right that it be established and/or a right to be members of it or to have access to it. Citizens have a joint moral right that institutions of criminal justice, including courts of law, be established, and they have an aggregated needs-based right that schools be established and a joint right of access once they are established. But persons or citizens do not have a moral right that universities be established, or that once established everyone has a right of access to them, or even that universities ought to be established because they produce a good to which people have a moral right. Nevertheless, universities produce a desirable good, namely, knowledge – something that is both desirable in itself, and a means to other intrinsic goods. It is for this reason that universities ought to be established.

Moreover, once a justified decision has been made institutionally to embody a prior moral right – a decision that is not necessarily based on the existence of a right to have that institution established or a prior moral

---

[5] For one account of the manner in which the university as an institution embodies intellectual values by way of what he calls constitutive rules see Searle (1975).

right to the good it produces – then various things follow concerning the nature of that institution. One of the main things that follows is that the exercise of that (institutionally embodied) right by members of that institution ought to be facilitated and given special status and protection, and certainly not allowed to be infringed, either by other members of that institution or by external persons or groups.

Given that universities are (1) established to provide a collective good, namely, knowledge, both for its own sake and as a means to other benefits for the wider community, and (2) an institutional embodiment of the right of free intellectual inquiry, then there are at least four claims that seem warranted.

First, universities have been established as centers wherein independence of intellectual inquiry is maintained. This flows from the proposition that the university is an institutional embodiment of the moral *right* of the inquirers to freely undertake their intellectual inquiries. Universities are not, for example, research centers set up to pursue quite specific intellectual inquiries determined by their external funders. Nor should particular inquiries undertaken by academics at universities be terminated on the grounds that some external powerful group, say, government, might not find the truths discovered in the course of these inquiries politically palatable.

Second, the free pursuit of intellectual inquiry is not simply a right for academics, but also a duty. This follows from the fact that the university has been established to ensure that the right to intellectual inquiry is actually realized in practice. Failure to exercise this right would eventually lead to an inability to exercise it. The right would then cease to exist in any meaningful sense.

Third, universities must have a teaching function to enable the preservation, not only of knowledge, but also of the activity of free intellectual inquiry. Insofar as students go on to become academics, then knowledge and intellectual inquiry are preserved.

Fourth, universities have a duty to transmit intellectual skills and values to the wider community, and to disseminate scholarship and research to that community. Intellectual inquiry is not only a human right, it is an activity that produces external benefits. For example, knowledge is a means to other goods, including economic well-being. Accordingly, and notwithstanding the rights of academics to freely inquire, it is a requirement that, *qua* institution, a university discharge its obligation to bring it about that its intellectual activities take some direction from, and have a flow-through effect to, the wider community in terms of the production of external benefits; indeed, the members of the community have a joint right to these benefits.

It is worth noting here that insofar as students enter the wider community as, for example, members of the professions, the wider community benefits from knowledge and at least some of the methods and values of intellectual inquiry. Again, dissemination of research has obvious benefits to the community, including economic benefits.

On the view of the university under consideration, interference in the process of the free pursuit of knowledge in universities strikes at one of the fundamental collective ends for which universities have been established. Such interference could not be justified, for example, on the grounds that, whereas free inquiry might be necessary for the acquisition of knowledge in many instances, in some particular instance free inquiry was not leading to knowledge, and therefore in this case free inquiry could be interfered with without striking at the basic purposes of the university as an institution. To this extent the neo-Kantian argument affords greater protection of freedom of inquiry than does Mill's marketplace of ideas argument.

Moreover, the university, insofar as it pursues this end, can pursue it, even if so doing is inconsistent with the collective goals and interests of the community or government. In this respect the right of intellectuals to pursue the truth is akin to the right of the judiciary to pursue justice even in the face of conflicting collective goals and interests, including the national interest. The Mabo decision of the High Court of Australia to uphold certain land rights of Australian aboriginals might prove not to be in Australia's national economic interest. But insofar as judges were entitled as a matter of law and justice to recognize native title, then they were entitled to make the decision they made. Similarly, Australian academics researching political or ethical issues in, say, China or Indonesia have a right to publish that research notwithstanding the damage it might do to present diplomatic relations and economic prospects.

This is not to say that there might not arise some contingency, such as war, that would override the right or duty of an academic duty to speak the truth. For notwithstanding the importance of the human right of intellectual inquiry and its centrality to the institution of the university, freedom of intellectual inquiry in general, and of academic inquiry in particular, is not an absolute right. Specifically, it can be overridden if its exercise comes into conflict with other human rights, notably the right to life. Accordingly, if a contingency arose, such as war, then there may be a case for restraint on the part of academics in relation to publishing information that might assist the enemy state. Again, in the context of a threatened pandemic or a potential terrorist attack, then the duty of, say, a scientist to widely disseminate her findings could well be overridden. Doubtless, in relation to most academic research such contingencies are exceptions, and should be treated as such. Nevertheless, given the high risk to human life and health posed by misuse of scientific research, such biological research constitutes a special case. Censorship of academic research needs special justification. However, that justification is, in general terms, available in the areas in question, for instance, the high risk of misuse by terrorists of such research. Naturally, censorship of any specific research or research project will not only need some justification, it will need a *specific* justification that details the high risk of misuse of this specific research project outcome by terrorists: for example, the research outcome is a highly virulent, easily transmissible, and readily weaponized pathogen (Miller 2008b, chap. 6).

We saw above that, speaking generally, academics do not simply have a right to freely inquire, they have a duty to do so. In accepting an academic position, a person accepts an obligation to pursue the collective ends of the university as an institution, and a collective end of universities is free inquiry.

The duty to freely inquire has certain implications. For one thing, it will entail maintenance of an appropriate level of competence in the disciplinary area in question; and if for some reason an academic is no longer capable, psychologically or otherwise, of free inquiry in the disciplinary area in question, then they ought not to draw a salary provided for this purpose.

For another thing, this duty to freely inquire generates the further obligation to preserve knowledge and reproduce the rational capacities necessary for the preservation and extension of knowledge. In the final analysis, academics have an obligation to preserve, for example, classics as a field of study. And this duty to freely inquire brings with it the justification for certain kinds of institutional accountability mechanisms to ensure that this duty is satisfactorily discharged.

Importantly, academics not only have a right to inquire into, including to discuss and communicate, certain possibly controversial or otherwise difficult issues; they have duty to do so. The analogy with the judiciary is again relevant. In relation to the Mabo decision, the High Court judges not only had a right to make the decision that they made, but also a duty to do so, given the specific decision made was the one dictated by law and by justice. Again, academics inquiring into political or ethical issues in relation to Indonesia and China not only have a right, but also a duty to, as Edward Said puts it, "speak the truth to power" (1994, lect. 5). The fundamental obligation of academics is to the truth, as opposed to its consequences, as the fundamental obligation of judges is to justice and the law, and not to economic and other consequences. Moreover, insofar as consequences need to be taken into account, it is not the business of academics to give overriding weight to the interests of their country, or their community, or their university (for that matter). Certainly, it is not the business of academics to discount the human rights of East Timorese, or incarcerated Chinese dissidents, or, for that matter, the interests of members of other nations in a clean environment, or in the case of the Pacific Islanders, the preservation of coastal towns from rising sea waters.

Even if freedom of intellectual inquiry for academics is the institutional embodiment of a basic human right, the corresponding right for academics is somewhat specialized and raises a host of problems centering around the relationship of the individual academic to the university institution in which he or she is housed, the disciplinary group to which he or she belongs, and, of course, to the wider community. What is in question here is by no means simply the relatively individualistic notion of free intellectual inquiry that might be characteristic of the ordinary citizen in his or her community or even of the intellectual existing in a community outside of a university or like institutional context. Specifically, the right and duty of freedom of intellectual inquiry in universities immediately raises more detailed issues of so-called academic autonomy and academic freedom. To some of these I now turn.

### 3. ACADEMIC AUTONOMY

Freedom of intellectual inquiry among academics is a central element of academic autonomy. Academic autonomy also comprises the institutional autonomy of universities.

Autonomy is a philosophically problematic concept, and, indeed, an essentially contested one, as is its species, academic autonomy (see, e.g., Dworkin 1988). However, there are four relatively uncontroversial things that need to be said about autonomy – including both institutional autonomy and individual intellectual autonomy – for our purposes here (Chapter 3).

First, the existence of autonomy depends in part on independence from external control. So in the case of the intellectual autonomy of an individual, this requires (at least) the absence of unjustified customs, laws, and ideologies of a kind or prevalence that an individual could not reasonably be expected to resist. It would also require the absence of other individuals possessed of powers of control in respect of an individual that that individual could not reasonably be expected to resist. The latter might include powers of psychological intimidation or of indoctrination.

In the case of the autonomy of an institution, the requirement would be the absence of external coercion, or undue influence, including certain forms of financial influence. Obviously, universities during the Nazi or Eastern European communist periods lacked institutional autonomy in virtue of the coercive forces deployed by governments to ensure that they taught particular subjects. Again, the use of control-at-a-distance administrative mechanisms, such as those that ensure that research funds provided to publicly funded universities are for government-specified purposes only, is inconsistent with institutional autonomy in respect of research. A related kind of control-at-a-distance mechanism is one that devolves responsibility while maintaining control of funding. An example of this is enterprise bargaining in publicly funded Australian universities at this time.

Second, autonomy consists in part in the presence of various internal features. In particular, the autonomous intellect has the capacity and will to pursue truth by reasoning.

Institutional autonomy consists in part of the possession of structures and procedures for collective decision making that are both coherent with one another and rational in the light of the purposes of the institution. The process of hybridization mentioned above might tend to erode the autonomy of universities, for such hybridization tends to generate internal institutional incoherence. This incoherence is twofold. First, there can be an increasing lack of fit between university structures and procedures of governance, on the one hand, and their institutional purposes, on the other. Putting it simply, traditional collegial structures and processes can become emasculated, and universities can come to adopt more hierarchical top–down bureaucratic structures and processes. But the latter are inimical to the fundamental institutional purposes of universities, purposes such as free inquiry. Second, there can be an incoherence, and increasing tension, between the collegial structures within universities and the more hierarchical bureaucratic structures. Therefore, institutional autonomy is at risk.

Third, and relatedly, autonomy consists in part of the capacity and will to seek truth by reasoning in relation to one's own purposes, ends, dispositions, character, and so on. In short, the autonomous agent is self-reflective in a manner that is both preservative and rein-vigorating of the valuable features of the self, but also potentially self-transformative.

By analogy, institutions are not fully autonomous unless they are col-lectively self-reflective in relation to their purposes, structure, culture, and activities. Such institutional self-reflection is necessary to ensure that what is good and important is preserved and reenergized, but also to enable desirable transformation.

Fourth, individual autonomy presupposes an enabling framework of social forms, including conventions of language, accepted moral norms, and so on. For example, an individual person cannot think other than in a language, and cannot communicate other than in a community that adheres to moral principles of truth telling and of trust.

Freedom of intellectual inquiry presupposes an even richer enabling framework of conventions and norms, such as those governing the acqui-sition and testing of putative knowledge. Disciplined conformity to pro-cedures of testing, including peer analysis and criticism, and repetition of experiments by others, far from undermining free intellectual inquiry of the sophisticated kind undertaken in universities, is a condition for its existence. Daydreaming unmotivated by truth, but only by pleasure, is not free intellectual inquiry.

Once again by analogy with individual autonomy, institutional auton-omy presupposes an enabling framework of social forms and moral norms, and especially a framework of other institutions. This framework of other institutions has an enabling role with respect to a given institu-tion. For example, universities function, whether autonomously or other-wise, against a framework of other institutions such as schools, the legal and economic systems, and so on.

Having thus characterized in general terms the concept of autonomy, and the conditions for its existence, with special reference to both insti-tutional autonomy and individual freedom of intellectual inquiry, I want now to say something about the relationship between these, and the threats in particular to individual freedom of intellectual inquiry posed by particular social, political, and university environments. In what fol-lows there is a presupposition that the necessary background frame-work of socio-intellectual and institutional forms – referred to above as the fourth conditions for both individual autonomy and institutional autonomy (respectively) – are in place.

Let me first introduce a quote from the scientist cum philosopher Michael Polanyi:

> The existing practice of scientific life embodies the claim that freedom is an efficient form of organization. The opportunity granted to mature scientists to choose and pursue their own problems is supposed to result in the best utilization of the joint efforts of all scientists in a common task. In other words: if the scientists of the world are viewed as a team setting out to explore the existing openings for discovery, it is assumed that their efforts will be efficiently coordinated if only each is left to follow his own inclinations. It is claimed in fact that there is no other efficient way of organizing the team, and that any attempts to coordinate their efforts by directives of a superior authority would inevitably destroy the effectiveness of their cooperation. (Polanyi 1951, 34)

Polanyi's point is that each acts freely and independently, but does so, first, on the basis of the work of past (in this case) scientists, second, with constant reference and adjustment to the work of other contemporary scientists, and, third, (implicitly) in the overall service of a collective end of providing a comprehensive understanding of the phenomena in question. He emphasizes the importance of individual freedom in a context of interdependence (not simply dependence) in the service of a joint intellectual project. Although this description is brief, and there are no doubt differences between scientists and other academics, it is a useful general characterization of how high-quality academic work typically proceeds.

Given this characterization, and in the light of our discussion of autonomy, what can now be said about the relationship between autonomy and individual freedom of inquiry, and the ways in which they are or can be threatened?

The first point is that an oppressive or unduly interfering institutional environment – whether in the form of the university's administrative or academic hierarchy (oppressive structure), or in the form of peers (oppressive culture), or both – has the potential to undermine freedom of inquiry, and hence the possibility of attaining knowledge.

The second point is that the existence of an oppressive and unduly interfering internal university environment is very often brought about, or at least in part sustained, by the university's own lack of institutional autonomy vis-à-vis government or other external organizations. For example, in the recent experience of many Australian universities governmental interventionist policies have themselves triggered (usually successful) attempts on the part of senior administrators to more tightly control the activities of academics.

The third, and consequent, point is that freedom of inquiry is threatened in a university that (1) has itself little institutional autonomy vis-à-vis government and/or business, and that has (2) (a) a hierarchical noncollegial internal structure and/or oppressive internal culture and (b) limited protections for individual academics and for their control over their work, including weak forms of academic tenure, and lack of control of the dissemination of their work as a result of the undermining of ownership of intellectual property.

The above argument concerns itself with threats to academics' freedom of intellectual inquiry (and protections against those threats), irrespective of whether those threats emanate from within or without the university.

However, as the discussion of autonomy indicated, the removal of threats to freedom of inquiry is not sufficient for the exercise of the wider notion of individual academic autonomy. The conditions for freedom of inquiry are necessary if an academic is to possess individual academic autonomy, but they are not sufficient. To generate sufficient conditions we need to at least consider certain further conditions that we earlier described as internal. These features are both individual and institutional in character.

The first point to be made is that the preservation of the institutional autonomy of universities requires consistent university policies, stable administrative structures and procedures, and decision making that serves the purposes of the institution. In the absence of these internal institutional features academics will be unable to adequately undertake their teaching and research roles.

These internal institutional features are not simply administrative in nature. There is a need for coherence in relation to the subjects to be taught and the areas to be researched, and, indeed, at the university level, in relation to the disciplines to be established. This situation calls for collective rational reflection, negotiation, and (finally) agreement on the part of the knowledgeable via collegial structures. In relation to the establishment or maintenance of disciplines, decision making needs not only to be collectively rational in the narrow sense of realizing existing purposes and meeting coordination requirements, it also needs to be (collectively) critically self-reflective. For example, it should take place in part on the basis of judgments as to the foundational disciplines or skills or knowledge, such as (in my view) linguistic communication, literature, philosophy, critical reasoning, ethics, history, mathematics, and basic sciences.

The second point is that individual academics need to possess not only the relevant intellectual competence, but also the appropriate intellectual moral virtues, including intellectual honesty, scholarly diligence, the will to pursue the truth in the face of intellectual fashion and ideology, and so on.

Moreover, academics need to be critically self-reflective in relation to their intellectual work lest they fall into one or other of the twin traps of what might be termed "active ossification," on the one hand, or of "trivial technicality," on the other. The state of active ossification takes place when an academic continues with their scholarly or research work, but does so in a cocoon of their own making that the rest of the intellectual world has long since passed by. By contrast, the state of trivial technicality is often achieved by researchers who are "on the cutting edge" of some line of inquiry, but unfortunately it is an inquiry that is fundamentally trivial.

The third, and consequent, point is that in the absence of both sets of institutional and individual internal features, it is unlikely that academics will vigorously and competently pursue significant intellectual inquiries. If so, the fundamental collective ends of the university will not be realized, notwithstanding the existence of conditions of free inquiry.

## 4. CONCLUSION

In this chapter I have applied my individualist, teleological account to the university as an institution. I have argued that universities are (1) established to provide a collective good, namely, knowledge, both for its own sake and as a means to other benefits for the wider community, and (2) an institutional embodiment of the right of free intellectual inquiry. Here (2) is a necessary, but not a sufficient, condition for (1); specifically, academics can freely seek knowledge for its own sake without necessarily concerning themselves with the interests of the wider community. This is an infringement of the joint right of the wider community to the knowledge-based benefits potentially provided by universities. In this context I have also explored the normative notion of academic autonomy and its relation to freedom of intellectual inquiry. Specifically, I have argued that academy autonomy ultimately derives from the human right of intellectual inquiry – a joint right to freely seek the truth by reasoning with others. I have suggested that recent processes of bureaucratization and corporatization of universities in the English-speaking world have had a corrosive, if not a corrupting, effect on the university as an institution.

# 9

# The Police

## 1. THE COLLECTIVE END OF POLICING: PROTECTION OF MORAL RIGHTS

In this chapter I apply my individualist, teleological theory of social institutions to police institutions.[1] In addition, I discuss the institutionalization of a practice that is profoundly antithetical to, and corrosive and corruptive of, policing institutions, namely, torture.

I argue that, as with other social institutions, police institutions exist to realize a collective good (Chapter 2). The good in question involves an *aggregate* of moral rights (including human rights), namely, the moral rights of each and all of the members of some jurisdiction. Moreover, the good in question consists in the *protection* of this aggregate of moral rights. (Hence the antithetical nature of the practice of torture by police; as a violation of human rights it undercuts the principal institutional purpose of policing, on my account.) Further, rights protection is itself something to which members of the community have a joint right. In short, police officers jointly contribute to the aggregated rights protection of members of the community because the latter have a joint right to such protection.

The central and most important purpose, that is, collective end, of police work is the protection of moral rights, albeit this end, and

---

[1] See the *United Nations Code of Conduct for Law Enforcement Officials* (1979). Most of the articles in this code specify the human rights constraints on police officers. However, Article 1 stresses the duty to protect persons, and the commentary (under c) notes the duty of police to provide aid in times of emergency. An earlier version of the material in the first two sections of this chapter appeared in Blackler and Miller (2000). Another version appeared in Campbell and Miller (2004) and still another in Miller and Blackler (2005).

its pursuit by police, ought to be constrained by the law.[2] While police institutions have other important purposes that might not directly involve the protection of moral rights, such as to enforce traffic laws or to enforce the adjudications of courts in relation to disputes between citizens, or, indeed, themselves to settle disputes between citizens on the streets, or to ensure good order more generally, these turn out to be purposes derived from the more fundamental purpose of protecting moral rights, or they turn out to be (nonderivative) secondary purposes. Thus laws against speeding derive in part from the moral right to life, and the restoring of order at a football match ultimately derives in large part from moral rights to the protection of persons and of property. On the other hand, service of summonses to assist the courts is presumably a secondary purpose of policing.[3]

It is important to state – and, in some cases, restate – a number of things at the outset. Here as elsewhere in this book, I am putting forward a *normative* account of (in this case) policing, not a *descriptive* account; it is an account of what policing *ought* to be about, not what it has been or is about. Moreover, it is a normative theory of the *institution* of the police, that is, of the proper ends and distinctive means of the institution of the police. So it is not a theory about specific police methods or strategies; it is not a theory of, so to speak, best practice in policing. Accordingly, I will not here offer detailed arguments in relation to the disputes between "crime-fighter" and "peace-keeper" models of the role of police officers, or between "community-based" policing and "zero-tolerance" policing. That said, a normative theory of the institution of the police will have important implications for questions of police methods and strategies, although often these will not necessarily be straightforward or obvious.

Further, I am assuming a particular notion of moral rights, namely, the one outlined in Chapter 2 above. On this account moral rights are of two kinds. First, there are human rights: moral rights that individuals possess solely by virtue of properties they have as human beings, such as the right to life, the right not to be tortured, the right to freedom of thought, and the like.[4] Second, there are institutional (moral) rights: moral rights that

---

[2]  The material in this chapter before the sections on torture is a later version of that in
     Miller and Blackler 2005, chap. 1.
[3]  Naturally I acknowledge that many laws do not derive from moral rights, and that those
     that do often do not do so in any straightforward manner.
[4]  The intuitive idea is that there are certain properties that individual human beings
     possess that are at least in part constitutive of their humanity. Naturally there is room
     for dispute as to what these properties are; indeed, some putative properties might be
     criteria rather than defining properties. Moreover, although some putative properties,

individuals possess in part by virtue of rights-generating properties that they have as human beings, and in part by virtue of their membership of a community or morally legitimate institution, or their occupancy of a morally legitimate institutional role. Thus the right to arrest and detain someone for assault is a moral right possessed by police officers. This right is in part dependent on membership of a morally legitimate police institution, but it is also in part dependent on the human right of the victim not to be assaulted.

Moreover, I am assuming the following properties of moral rights. First, moral rights generate concomitant duties on others, for example, A's right to life generates a duty on the part of B not to kill A. Second, human rights, but not necessarily institutional moral rights, are justifiably enforceable; for example, A has a right not to be assaulted by B, and if B assaults or attempts to assault A, then B can legitimately be prevented from assaulting A by means of coercion.[5] Third, bearers of human rights in particular do not necessarily have to assert a given human right for them to possess it, and for the right to be violated; for example, an infant may have a right to life even though it does not have the ability to assert it (or for that matter to waive it).

On the view that I am advocating, while police ought to have as a fundamental purpose the protection of moral rights, their efforts in this regard ought to be constrained by the law. Insofar as the law is a constraint – at least in democratic states – then my view accommodates "consent" as a criterion of legitimacy for the police role.[6] However, in my view legality, and therefore consent, is only one consideration. For I am insisting that police work ought to be guided by moral considerations – namely, moral rights – and not simply by legal considerations. This enables me to avoid the problems besetting theories of policing cast purely in terms of law enforcement, or protection of the state, or even

e.g., the capacity to reason, are more salient than others, e.g., the capacity for bodily movement, I do not have a worked-out theory to offer. However, the main point to stress here is that the properties in question are ones that are held to have *moral* value, e.g., individual autonomy or life. This conception is consistent with a view of human beings as essentially social animals. See Miller (2003b).

[5] Note that I am here asserting a *normative* conceptual connection between *human* rights and enforcement. I am not making the more familiar (and controversial) claim that for something to be a moral right, it must be able to be enforced. Here it is also useful to distinguish between different orders of rights and duties. For example, the right to life gives rise to the duty not to kill, but also the duty to protect someone from being killed.

[6] I acknowledge that in common law countries the law reflects tradition, and therefore perhaps "consent" in another sense. See Kleinig (1996, chap. 2).

peace keeping.[7] Such theories are faced with the obvious problem posed by authoritarian states, or sometimes even democratic states, that enact laws that violate human rights in particular. Consider the police in Nazi Germany, Soviet Russia, or Iraq under Saddam Hussein. These police forces upheld laws that violated the human rights of (respectively) Jews, Soviet citizens, and Iraqi citizens (including Shi'ite Muslims' religious rights). By my lights, the officers in these police forces simultaneously violated human rights and abrogated their primary professional responsibility as police officers to protect human rights.

Finally, I reiterate that on the view that I am advocating, police engaged in the protection of moral rights ought to be constrained by the law, or at least ought to be constrained by laws that embody the will of the community in the sense that (a) the procedures for generating these laws are more or less universally accepted by the community, for example, a democratically elected legislature, and (b) the content of the laws are at least in large part accepted by the community, for example, they embody general policies with majority electoral support or reflect the community's moral beliefs.[8] So I am in part helping myself to a broadly contractarian moral constraint on policing, namely, the consent of citizens, although by our lights consent is not the raison d'être for policing; rather, it provides

[7] John Alderson at times seems to advocate a view close to the one that I am proposing. However, at other times he seems to be elaborating the view that human rights are merely side constraints on policing, rather than a raison d'être for police work (Alderson 1998, esp. chap. 1). By contrast, John Kleinig (1996, 27) offers a social peace-keeping theory, and as such is vulnerable to the objection that he leaves the way open for authoritarian policing in the name of social pacification. Naturally, Kleinig can qualify the social peace-keeping model by recourse to law. However, the problem is not thereby removed. For a legal system might itself simply be an instrument for authoritarian governmental control – as it was in Nazi Germany. In fact, Kleinig qualifies his social peace-keeping account by recourse to democracy (1996, 28). This still leaves open the possibility of social pacification in the service of the tyranny of the majority. What is called for is the constraint provided by some form of objective morality, e.g., moral rights.

[8] Here I am assuming that large fragments of a legal system can consist of immoral laws, and yet the system remain recognizably a legal system. See Dworkin (1998, 101). I am also assuming that for a legal system to express the admittedly problematic notion of the will of the community, it is at least necessary that the overwhelming majority of the community (not just a simple majority) support the content of the system of laws taken as a whole – even if there are a small number of individual laws they do not support – and support the procedures for generating laws, e.g., a democratically elected legislature (see Miller 2001b, 141–51). Finally, I am assuming that the fact that a party or candidate or policy or law secured (directly or directly) a majority vote is an important (but not necessarily decisive) consideration in its favor, and a consideration above and beyond the moral weight to be given to the existence of a consensus in relation to the value to be attached to voting as a procedure.

an additional (albeit necessary) condition for the moral legitimacy of police work (Cohen and Feldberg 1991, chap. 2). Moreover, I am refraining from providing police with a license to pursue their (possibly only individually) subjective view of what counts as an enforceable moral right. What counts as an enforceable moral right is an objective matter. Nevertheless, some particular person or group has to specify what are to be taken to be enforceable moral rights and what are not to be so taken; and in my view ultimately this is a decision for the community to make by way of its laws and its democratically elected government. Here I take it that in a properly constituted democracy the law embodies the will of the community in the sense adumbrated above. Moreover, we can further distinguish between local, regional, and national communities, especially in states that have subnational elected bodies such as local councils. This enables me to give substance to notions of community-based policing or partnerships between police and local communities. For at the subnational level, and especially the local level, it becomes feasible for police to consult and work with communities to address law enforcement issues in a consensual manner.[9]

Here there is an additional point to be made. The law concretizes moral rights and the principles governing their enforcement, including human rights as well as institutional moral rights. To this extent the law is very helpful in terms of guiding police officers and citizens in relation to the way that abstract moral rights and principles apply to specific circumstances. For example, there is a human right to life that can be overridden in accordance with certain moral principles, such as self-defense or defense of the lives of others. However, it is the laws governing the use of deadly force by police officers that provide an explicit and concrete formulation of these moral rights and principles, and thereby prescribe what is to be done or not done by police officers in specific circumstances.

In short, in my view police ought to act principally to protect certain moral rights, those moral rights ought to be enshrined in the law, and the law ought to reflect the will of the community. Should any of these conditions fail to obtain, then there will be problems. If the law and objective (justifiably enforceable) moral rights come apart, or if the law and the will of the community come apart, or if objective moral rights and the

---

[9] Moreover, community-based policing might reconstitute itself as problem-based policing, and thereby be more effective. See Goldstein (1990) and Barlow, Edward, and Brandl (1996, 86–9).

will of the community come apart, then the police may well be faced with moral dilemmas. I do not believe that there are neat and easy solutions to all such problems (see Heffernan 1985). Clearly, if the law and/or the citizenry require the police to *violate* moral rights, then the law and/or the citizenry will be at odds with the fundamental purpose of policing. Accordingly, depending on the circumstances, the police may well be obliged to disobey the law and/or the will of the community. On the other hand, what is the appropriate police response to a citizen violating someone else's objective moral right in a community in which the right is not as a matter of fact enshrined in the law, and the right is not supported by the community? Consider, in this connection, women's rights to, say, education under an extremist fundamentalist religious regime, such as the former Taliban regime in Afghanistan.[10] Under such circumstances an issue arises as to whether police are morally obliged *qua* police officers to *enforce* respect for the moral right in question. Again, I suggest that they may well be obliged to intervene to enforce respect for such a moral right.

Normatively speaking, then, the protection of fundamental moral rights – specifically *justifiably enforceable* (aggregate) moral rights – is a collective good to which the members of the community have a joint right, and it is the central and most important collective end of police work.

As it happens, there is increasing recourse to human rights legislation in particular in the decisions of domestic as well as international courts. This is an interesting development. However, it must also be pointed out that the criminal law in many, if not most, jurisdictions already in effect constitutes human rights legislation. Laws proscribing murder, rape, assault, and so on are essentially laws that protect human rights. So it is clear that whatever the historical importance of a "statist" conception of human rights – human rights as protections of the individual against the state – such a conception is inadequate as a *general* account of human rights. Human rights in particular, and moral rights more generally, also exist to protect individual citizens from their fellow citizens, and individual citizens from organizations other than the organizations of the state. Moreover, tort law is also relevant here; for example, tort law provides for compensation for the unintended infringement of human rights.

In this connection, please note that I do not say that the protection of (legally enshrined, justifiably enforceable) moral rights ought to be

---

[10] Regarding the role of the religious police of the Taliban in the Department of the Promotion of Virtue and Prevention of Vice, see Rashid (2001, chap. 8).

the *only* collective end of policing, merely that it ought to be the *central and most important* end, and that other important ends and roles derive from it. Here it is important to note that I am rejecting the dichotomy sometimes offered between police as law enforcers and police as peace keepers. Both roles are important, but our account shows why they are important. Law enforcement is important mainly because laws embody moral rights. Likewise, peace keeping is important in large part because disorder typically consists of, or is a prerequisite for, violations of moral rights, including rights to security of person and of property.

Moreover, there are numerous service roles that police play, and ought to continue to play, because they consist of, or facilitate, their central and most important role of protecting moral rights. Consider, in this connection, police assistance in relation to missing persons who might have come in harm's way, or assisting drunks who might otherwise harm themselves or be harmed.[11]

Nevertheless, I do not hold that police are, or ought to be, preoccupied with seeing to it that *all* moral rights are secured. Roughly speaking, police are, or ought to be, engaged in moral rights work to the extent to which the moral rights in question are ones that justify and potentially require the use of coercive force for their protection.[12] Some moral rights are not justifiably enforceable, for example, a wife's moral right to the sex her husband promised her when they got married. Other moral rights do not necessarily, or in general, require the use of coercive force for their protection. For example, a physically disabled person might have a moral right to appropriate access to public buildings such as libraries and government offices, and such access might necessitate the provision of ramps as opposed to stairs. But the securing of this right for the disabled might call for action only on the part of the local council; there might be no need for the police to be involved.

Here the distinction made by Henry Shue is relevant. Shue distinguishes between three sorts of duties that correlate with what he calls "basic rights" (Shue 1996, 52). These are the duties to (a) avoid depriving, (b) protect from deprivation, and (c) aid the deprived.

In relation to police work, (b) above, the duty to protect from deprivation, is especially salient. Police are typically engaged in protecting

[11] Note that on my view there are moral rights to assistance. So, a drunk person in danger of, say, collapsing on his way home and freezing to death in the Finnish winter would have a moral right to assistance. Indeed, coercive force might need to be used to prevent such a person from endangering himself.

[12] Though no doubt all *human* rights need protection from time to time.

people from being deprived of their right to life, liberty, or property. Note that police provision of rights protection is distinctive in part by virtue of police use of, or more often the threat of the use of, coercive force. This is not, of course, to suggest police always or even typically use coercive force, or threaten to use it; rather, the claim is that this recourse to coercion is a distinctive and routine feature of policing, and is in some sense "the bottom line" when it comes to realizing the proper ends of policing.

At any rate, the account of the institution of the police that I am offering promises to display the distinctive defining features of the institution of the police, namely, its use of coercive force in the service of legally enshrined moral rights. On this account the institution of the police is quite different from other institutions that are either not principally concerned with moral rights or that do not necessarily rely on coercion in the service of moral rights.

It might be argued that contemporary military institutions meet my definition of the institution of the police. Consider so-called humanitarian armed intervention in places such as Somalia, Bosnia, Rwanda, Kosovo, and East Timor. Whether or not each of these armed interventions was principally undertaken to protect human rights is a matter of controversy. At any rate, we make three points in response.

First, the nature and evolution of military and policing institutions is such that the lines have often been blurred between the two. For example, in the British colonies the police historically had a paramilitary role in relation to what was regarded as a hostile population, for instance, the Royal Irish Constabulary. Indeed, according to Richard Hill:

> Coercion by army and by police have always been distinguished by differences of degree, rather than kind, and through most of the history of policing there was no clear demarcation between the two interwoven strands of control situated towards the coercive extremity of the control continuum. ... Historically, constables were generally considered to be a reserve military body for mobilization by the state in potential or actual emergency; conversely soldiers were frequently called upon to conduct duties generally considered to be of a "policing" nature. (Hill 1986, 3)

But from this it does not follow that there are not good reasons for a *normative* theory of *contemporary* policing in liberal democracies to make distinctions between the fundamental role of the police and that of the military. Such reasons would include the well-documented and highly problematic character of paramilitary police forces, including in relation to the violation by such forces of individual moral rights, and the tendency for such forces to become simply the instrument of governments rather than the protectors of the rights of the community and the servants of its laws. Indeed, arguably it is precisely this malign tendency that is taking place in the United States, the United Kingdom, and other liberal democracies in the context of the so-called war on terrorism (Miller 2008b).

Second, although contemporary military forces may undertake humanitarian armed interventions from time to time, this is not, or has not been, their fundamental purpose; rather, national self-defense has avowedly been their purpose.

Third, to the extent that military institutions do in fact take on the role of human rights protection by means of the use of coercive force, then they are being assimilated to police institutions. It is no accident that recent humanitarian armed interventions are referred to as episodes of international *policing*.

There are some other objections to our account of the institution of the police. I try to deal with the most important of these later in this chapter. In the following section, I offer a brief account of moral rights and the cognate notion of social norms insofar as they pertain to policing. In the section after that, I present my theory of policing as the protection of legally enshrined moral rights by means of coercive force. In the section following that one, I deal with some residual issues arising from the use of harmful methods in policing, including methods that under normal circumstances would themselves constitute human rights violations. In the final section I consider the practice of torture ("third degree") as antithetical to policing.

## 2. MORAL RIGHTS AND SOCIAL NORMS

As already argued, moral rights – notably human rights – are a basic moral category; but they are far from being the only moral consideration. Here we note that moral rights comprise a relatively narrow set of moral considerations. There are many moral obligations that are not, and do not derive from, moral rights, such as an obligation to assist a friend who is depressed, or not to cheat on one's girlfriend.

The point of human rights is to protect some basic human value or values. On James Griffin's account, human rights arise from the need to protect what he calls "personhood" (Griffin 2008). At the core of his notion of personhood is individual autonomy. Certainly, autonomy is a basic human value protected by a structure of human rights. However,

I have some reservations about Griffin's account; specifically, it might turn out to be too narrowly reliant on autonomy. Perhaps the right not to be tortured does not simply derive from a right to autonomy; perhaps it derives, at least in part, from the right not to suffer extreme pain intentionally inflicted by another.[13] Although I have no worked-out account of human rights to offer here, my own sympathies lie with a pluralist account (Griffin 2008, 51) rather than Griffin's personhood account or David Wiggin's needs-based account (Wiggins 1991; Griffin 2008, 88).

More specifically, I want to suggest that there is a coherent notion of individual *identity* that (a) underpins certain human rights and (b) is not reducible to individual liberty or autonomy or, for that matter, to prior human needs.

According to the so-called Stolen Generation Report commissioned by the Australian government, in the nineteenth and twentieth centuries thousands of aboriginal children were taken from their families by Australian state welfare officials and police and placed in white Australian families or nonindigenous institutions (Human Rights and Equal Opportunity Commission 1997). The official reasons given included that these children were at risk or neglected, and that these white families or institutions could provide better care for the children. The report disputes the validity of these reasons.

Subsequently, many of these children who are now adults have come forward and expressed moral outrage at what happened to them; evidently the experience profoundly harmed them. It is now widely accepted that this policy was a violation of human rights. Let us accept that this is the case. The question that now arises is: By virtue of what property of parents and their children does this human right exist?

Presumably the right exists by virtue of an acknowledged deep relationship between parents and their children, and between siblings. To simplify, we will focus on the relationship between a mother and her young – say, five-year-old – child, a relationship that has both a biological and an emotional dimension.[14] If we focus on the child, as opposed to the mother, this relationship is, in fact, so central as to in part constitute the *identity* of the child. Small wonder, then, that removing young children from their mothers generated the degree of trauma that it in fact did.

---

[13] This is a point made by Tom Campbell in discussion.

[14] I am assuming that five-year-olds are old enough to have established a very strong particular interpersonal relationship – indeed, an identity-conferring interpersonal relationship – with their mothers, but too young to be autonomous in any meaningful sense.

However, the basis of the child's human right not to be removed from its mother can hardly be the child's autonomy. It is not the autonomy of the child that has been violated, because young children do not possess autonomy.

This suggests that we need to distinguish between individual autonomy and individual identity. Perhaps the term *autonomy* is sometimes used so as to embrace the notion of individual identity. If so, then we should distinguish between a "thick" and a "thin" sense of autonomy. An autonomous agent in the thin sense means something like a rational chooser; an autonomous agent in the thick sense means something like a rational chooser possessed of an individual identity, which identity the rational chooser takes into account in making his or her rational choices.

At any rate, whatever the correct theoretical account of human rights might be, we assume that Griffin is right to set out a relatively limited set of moral considerations as being human rights. These will include the right to life, to physical security, to freedom of thought, expression, and movement, and to freedom to form human relationships, including freedom to choose one's sexual partner. They will also include the right to a basic subsistence, so they will include rights to food, water, and shelter.

However, moral rights will include a range of rights that go beyond human rights, namely, institutional moral rights (Chapter 2, Section 2). As said above, these are moral rights that depend in part on rights-generating properties possessed by human beings *qua* human beings, but also in part on membership of a community or of a morally legitimate institution, or occupancy of a morally legitimate institutional role. Here we need to invoke the distinction made earlier between (a) institutional rights that embody human rights in institutional settings, and therefore depend in part on rights-generating properties that human beings possess as human beings (these are institutional *moral* rights), and (b) institutional rights that do not embody human rights in institutional settings (these are not necessarily institutional *moral* rights, but rather *mere* institutional rights).

A large question arises at this point as to the status of property rights. Are such rights institutional *moral* rights or *mere* institutional rights? It would seem that at least *some* property rights are institutional *moral* rights by virtue of being in part dependent on rights-generating properties that human beings have *qua* human beings. Specifically, some property rights depend on the rights-generating properties of (a) the need to have exclusive use of certain physical material, for instance, *this* food and water, and physical space, for instance, *this* shelter; and (b) individual or collective *labor*, including labor that *creates* new things, for instance, tools or ornaments that an individual or particular group has made. Some of these property rights might be individual rights, such as to personal effects, and some might be collective rights, such as to occupy a certain stretch of territory and exclude others from it. At any rate, I will assume that some property rights are institutional *moral* rights.

Some (but not all) moral rights, including many (perhaps all) human rights, are, or ought to be, embodied in the laws governing a community. This is most obvious in the case of many of the so-called negative rights, such as the right to life, the right to physical security, and the right to property. Murder, assault, rape, theft, fraud, and so on are criminal offences. Moreover, the police have a clear and central role to investigate and apprehend the perpetrators of these crimes – the rights violators – and bring them before the courts for trial and sentencing.

Obviously there are large fragments of the legal system concerned with matters other than criminality. For example, there are all manner of disputes of a noncriminal nature that are settled in the civil courts. These often involve important questions of *justice* that are not human rights issues. On the other hand, many of these disputes involve institutional moral rights, for example, who gets what part of the estate of some deceased relative, or of the property formerly jointly owned by a husband and wife now involved in divorce proceedings. Moreover, insofar as a dispute is, or gives rise to, an issue of justice, then moral rights are involved, at least in the sense that the disputants have a moral right to a just outcome.

To the extent that law enforcement by police is enforcement of moral rights, whether enforcement of criminal law or not, the police are undertaking their fundamental role (on my account). On the other hand, the police do have a legitimate role in relation to law enforcement, where the laws in question do not embody moral rights. This is a matter to which I return later in this chapter. Suffice it to say here that the law enforcement role of the police in relation to matters other than the enforcement of moral rights is, in my view, either a derived role or it is a secondary role.

It is also the case that in Anglo-Saxon countries in particular, there are some human rights that are not embodied in the law. Some of these are embodied in the law in some European countries. For example, in Australia, although it is a legal requirement that police assist someone who is drowning or starving, it is lawful for an ordinary citizen to refrain from providing such assistance. Yet the right to life is a human right, and therefore there is a concomitant moral obligation to assist someone who is drowning or starving, or at least to do so in situations in which assisting such a person would not put oneself at risk of harm, and in which police or others are not able to provide the needed assistance.

The moral and legal issues in this area are complex (Chapter 7). However, in my view in general it ought to be unlawful for a person, A, to refrain from assisting another person, B, under the following conditions: (a) B's life is at immediate risk, (b) A's intervention is necessary if B is to survive, and (c) A can assist with minimal cost to him- or herself. Indeed, there ought to be a variety of so-called Good Samaritan laws, and the reason for this is that human rights ought to be protected, and some Good Samaritan laws protect human rights.

So I hold that in general violations of human rights ought to be criminalized. If this were the case – and it already is to a considerable extent – then the police would have a central role in relation to the enforcement of human rights by virtue of having a role in relation to the enforcement of the criminal law.

One of the interesting implications of this conception is that there would be a shift in the line of demarcation between the so-called police service role and the law enforcement role (especially criminal law enforcement role) of police. Typically, the police service role is contrasted with the law enforcement role; the rescue operations of Water Police, or of police dealing with dangerous mentally deranged persons, are supposedly service roles, not law enforcement roles. In one sense, the contrast here is already overdrawn; the law with respect to the safe utilization of watercraft needs to be enforced, as does the law in relation to dangerous mentally deranged persons. Moreover, questions of policing *methods* should not be confused with questions of what actions ought to be criminalized and what ought not. In relation to some criminal offence, for example, juvenile gangs engaged in assaults, it might be more productive for police to engage in preventative strategies, such as restorative justice techniques, rather than simply arresting/charging and locking up offenders. More important, insofar as Good Samaritan laws with respect to so-called positive moral rights were enacted, then many police activities previously regarded as service roles would become in part law enforcement roles (indeed, roles of enforcing criminal laws). But it is important to stress here that the criminalization of violations of certain positive moral rights is entirely consistent with an overall reduction in acts regarded as criminal, such as decriminalization of laws in relation to cannabis and prostitution. After all, smoking cannabis and selling sex are not activities that in themselves necessarily violate anyone's moral rights.

Thus far we have sought to make a connection between moral rights and the law, on the one hand, and law enforcement and the institution of the police, on the other. This has enabled us to present, albeit in very general terms, the view that the collective end of policing is a collective good, namely, to enforce an aggregate of certain moral rights – justifiably enforceable moral rights of the members of the jurisdiction in question. However, there are other competing views. One such influential contrasting view holds that the law embodies social morality in general.[15] On this view, insofar as the role of the police was to enforce the law, then their role would be to enforce social morality.

It is tempting to view the role of the police as the enforcement of social morality understood as the structure of social norms in force in the community. (Here the notion of a social norm is that provided in Chapter 1, Section 2, namely, that of a regularity in behavior that is conformed to because it is believed to be the morally right thing to do.) This picture is an appealing one. However, it is inadequate in two respects.

First, the notions of a social norm, and of social morality, are relatively wide notions; considerably wider than the notion of a basic moral requirement that ought to be enshrined in the criminal law (or the legal system more generally). Note also that the notion of an action or omission required by a social norm is considerably wider than the notion of a duty correlative to a moral right. For the notion of a social norm – and therefore of social morality – embraces regularities in behavior (including omissions) that are the subject of some moral attitude. So they include behavior that is outside the purview of the criminal law, or indeed the law more generally. For example, social norms prescribe and proscribe sexual behavior that is not necessarily, or even generally, the subject of any legal requirement. Moreover, there is a great danger in widening the law to embrace all of social morality. Consider, in this connection, the threats to individual autonomy posed by puritanical polities such as that of Calvin's Geneva or, as mentioned above, agencies such as the Department for the Promotion of Virtue and the Prevention of Vice under the Taliban regime in Afghanistan (Rashid 2001, chap. 8).

Second, although behavioral conformity to a social norm is an objective social fact, social norms *qua* prescriptions are not necessarily objectively valid; everyone might be behaving in accordance with the social

---

[15] I take it that Lord Devlin's account is a version of this view (Devlin 1965).

norm, but from this it does not follow that they *ought to be* conforming to it. That is, the notion of a social norm – and of social morality – is an essentially subjective notion: it refers to the values and principles that are *believed in* by the members of some presumably morally sentient community; but beliefs, including moral beliefs, are not necessarily *true* beliefs. So social morality stands in contrast with objective notions, such as the notion of human rights. Or at least there is a contrast here for those of us who believe that the notion of a human right is an objective notion. It might be thought, nevertheless, that the subjective character of social morality is no obstacle to its being deployed – via the notion of the criminal law in particular – to define the proper role of the institution of the police. After all, the criminal law is itself subjective in the above sense. The criminal law is a de facto set of laws; it is not necessarily the set of laws that *ought to* exist by the lights of some objective moral standard.[16] And it might be thought that the proper role of the police is to enforce the law in general, and the criminal law in particular, as it is, not as it morally ought to be.

Once again, this is an issue to be addressed in more detail later in this chapter. Here I simply record my view that a normative account of the role of the police must be cast in terms of objective notions, not subjective ones. The de facto role of the police in apartheid South Africa was the enforcement of the laws of apartheid, and of the Serbian police, for example, the so-called Red Berets of the Serbian Interior Ministry of Belgrade, the ethnic cleansing of Muslims in Bosnia, but these are not the morally legitimate roles of police forces (see Silber and Little 1997, 224).

The upshot of the discussion thus far is that the view of police simply as enforcers of social morality is untenable. We cannot make a connection between the notion of social morality and the criminal law (especially), on the one hand, and the criminal law and the enforcement of the criminal law by the police, on the other, and thereby erect a normative theory of the role of policing as the enforcement of social morality. Rather, we ought to prefer the related, but competing, view that the fundamental role of the police is to protect legally enshrined (justifiably enforceable) moral rights, and for two reasons. First, the notion of justifiably enforceable moral rights is a suitably narrow one to qualify as the fundamental end of policing, unlike the notion of social morality. Second, the notion of justifiably enforceable moral rights is an objective notion, again

---

[16] The criminal law is not simply a set of laws. For some theoretical accounts of the criminal law, see Duff (1998) and Dworkin (1998).

unlike the notion of social morality. Putting matters simply, justifiably enforceable moral rights are an *objective* set of *fundamental* (actual or potential) social norms that are capable of being enshrined in enforceable law. As such, justifiably enforceable moral rights are an appropriate notion to provide the moral basis for policing, or at least the central and most important moral basis for policing.

So much for the discussion of human rights and social norms, and their relationship to the institution of the police. In the next section I consider in detail the relation between moral rights and the institution of the police.

### 3. MORAL RIGHTS AND THE INSTITUTION OF THE POLICE

According to the teleological account social institutions are to be defined in terms of their collective ends, specifically, collective ends that are also collective goods. However, in relation to policing, as with other relatively modern institutions – the media is another example (Chapter 10) – there is an opacity as to what precisely its fundamental collective ends are.[17]

Indeed, it is sometimes argued that there can be no overarching philosophical theory or explanatory framework that spells out the fundamental nature and point of policing, and that this is because the activities that police engage in are so diverse.

Certainly the police are involved in a wide variety of activities, including control of politically motivated riots, traffic control, dealing with cases of assault, investigating murders, intervening in domestic and neighborhood quarrels, apprehending thieves, saving people's lives, making drug busts, shooting armed robbers, dealing with cases of fraud, and so on. Moreover, they have a number of different roles. They have a deterrence role as highly visible authority figures with the right to deploy coercive force. They also have a law enforcement role in relation to crimes already committed. This latter role involves not only the investigation of crimes in the service of truth, but also the duty to arrest offenders and bring them before the courts so that they can be tried and – if found guilty – punished. And police also have an important preventative role in relation to crime and disorder. How, it is asked, could we possibly identify any defining features, given this diverse array of activities and roles?

---

[17] An earlier version of the material in this section and the one following it appeared in Miller (1998b) and another in Miller and Blackler (2005).

One way to respond to this challenge is to first distinguish between the activities or roles in themselves and the collective end that they serve, and then try to identify the collective good served by these activities (Chapter 2, Section 2). So riot control is different from traffic control, and both are different from drug busts, but all these activities have a common end, or at least a delimited set of ends. Moreover, this common end or set of ends is a collective good, or at least a delimited set of such goods. The collective goods to be aimed at by police will include upholding the law, maintaining social order, and preserving human life.[18]

Indeed, policing seems to involve an apparent multiplicity of ends. However, some ends, such as the enforcement of law and the maintenance of order, might be regarded as more central to policing than others, such as financial or administrative ends realized by, say, collecting fees on behalf of government departments, issuing speeding tickets, and serving summonses.

But even if we consider only so-called fundamental ends, there is still an apparent multiplicity. For example, there is the end of upholding the law, but there is also the end of bringing about order or conditions of social calm, and there is the end of saving lives. Indeed, Lord Scarman relegates law enforcement to a secondary status by contrast with the peace-keeping role (Scarman 1981). Moreover, the end of enforcing the law can be inconsistent with bringing about order or conditions of social calm, a point that Skolnick famously argues (Skolnick 1966).

Can these diverse and possibly conflicting ends be reconciled? As discussed above, we suggest that they can, and by recourse to the notion of justifiably enforceable moral rights. The first point here is that the criminal law in particular is, or ought to be, fundamentally about ensuring the protection of certain moral rights, for example, the right to life.

The second point is that social order, conditions of social calm, and so on, which are at times contrasted with law enforcement, are in fact, we suggest, typically necessary conditions for moral rights to be respected. A riot or barroom brawl or violent domestic quarrel is a matter for police concern precisely because it involves the violation of moral rights, including the rights to protection of person and property. Consider, in this connection, interregnum periods of disorder between the ending of military hostilities and the establishment of civil order, such as the

---

[18] Different theorists have seen one of these goals as definitive. See, for example, Skolnick and Fyfe (1993).

looting, revenge killings, and so on, that took place on a large scale at the close of the most recent war in Iraq.

I have suggested that the collective good to be secured by the institution of the police is the protection of justifiably enforceable moral rights, or at least a specific aggregate of such moral rights, namely, those of the members of the jurisdiction in question. Moreover, by virtue of being a collective good such protection is something to which the members of the community have a joint right. But that is not all that needs to be said; we need also to speak of the *means* by which this end is to be achieved (Miller 1998b, 88).

Egon Bittner has propounded a very different theory of policing to the one we have suggested. However, his account is insightful. Bittner focuses attention on the means deployed by police to secure their ends. He has in effect defined policing in terms of the use or threat of coercive force. He offers the following definition of policing: "a mechanism for the distribution of non-negotiable coercive force employed in accordance with the dictates of an intuitive grasp of situational exigencies" (Bittner 1980, 5).

Bittner's account of policing is inadequate because it fails to say anything about the ends of policing. Moreover, coercion is not the only means deployed by the police. Other typical means include negotiation, rational argument, and especially appeal to human and social values and sentiment. Moreover, whole taxonomies of police roles have been constructed on the basis of different mixes of methods, such as negotiation and proximate ends of policing, such as maintaining peace. Consider Kleinig's taxonomy in terms of peace keepers, crime fighters, "social enforcers," and "emergency operators" (see, e.g., Kleinig 1996, 22–4). Here I need to stress that I am not advocating one or other of the possible configurations of these mixes. Hitherto I have spoken of the collective ends of policing, and especially the fundamental purpose of ensuring the protection of justifiably enforceable moral rights. Now we are speaking of the means by which to achieve that purpose, and of different roles (comprised of means and proximate ends) by means of which that ultimate purpose might be realized. Clearly there are different ways to achieve a given end; and there are different means, including different roles, by which to realize the fundamental and ultimate end of policing as we have described it. Whether to emphasize the crime-fighter or the peace-keeper role, for example, ought to be settled in large part on the basis of which is the most efficient and effective means to ensure the protection of (justifiably enforceable) moral rights. To this extent, my individualist, teleological theory of policing is – at least in principle – neutral on questions of police methodology, and in relation to disputes between advocates of law enforcement roles and service roles for police.

To return to Bittner: in drawing attention to coercion, he has certainly identified a distinctive feature of policing, one that separates police officers from, say, criminal justice lawyers and politicians.

Further, in stressing the importance of coercion, Bittner draws our attention to a fundamental feature of policing, namely, its inescapable use of what in normal circumstances would be regarded as morally unacceptable activity. The use of coercive force, including in the last analysis deadly force, is morally problematic; indeed, it is ordinarily an infringement of human rights, specifically the right to physical security and the right to life. Accordingly, in normal circumstances the use of coercive force, and especially deadly force, is morally unacceptable. So it would be morally wrong, for example, for some private citizen to forcibly take a woman to his house for questioning or because he felt like female company.

Use of coercive force, especially deadly force, requires special moral justification precisely because it is in itself at the very least harmful, and possibly an infringement of human rights; it is therefore in itself morally wrong, or at least, so to speak, a prima facie moral wrong. Similarly, locking someone up deprives them of their liberty and is therefore a prima facie moral wrong. It therefore requires special moral justification. Similarly with deception. Deception, including telling lies, is under normal circumstances morally wrong. Once again, use of deception requires special moral justification because it is a prima facie moral wrong. Intrusive surveillance is another prima facie moral wrong – it is an infringement of privacy. Therefore, intrusive surveillance requires special moral justification. And the same can be said of various other methods used in policing.

The point here needs to be made very clear lest it be misunderstood. Police use of coercion, depriving persons of their liberty, deception, and so on are morally problematic methods; they are activities that considered in themselves and under normal circumstances are morally wrong. Therefore, they stand in need of special justification. In relation to policing there is a special justification. These harmful and normally immoral methods are on occasion necessary to realize the fundamental end of policing, namely, the protection of (justifiably enforceable) moral rights. An armed bank robber might have to be threatened with the use of force if he is to give himself up, a drug dealer might have to be deceived if a drug ring is to be smashed, a blind eye might have to be turned to the minor illegal activity of an informant if the flow of important information he provides in relation to serious crimes is to continue, a pedophile might have to be surveilled if evidence for his conviction is to be secured. Such harmful and normally immoral activities are thus morally justified in policing, and morally justified in terms of the ends that they serve.

The upshot of our discussion thus far is that policing consists of a diverse range of activities and roles, the fundamental end of which is a collective good, namely, the securing of the (justifiably enforceable) moral rights of the members of the jurisdiction in question; but it is nevertheless an institution the members of which inescapably deploy methods that are harmful, methods that are normally considered to be morally wrong. Other institutions that serve moral ends, and necessarily involve harmful methods, or prima facie wrongdoing, are the military – soldiers must kill in the cause of national self-defense – and political institutions. Australia's political leaders may need to deceive, for example, the political leaders of nations hostile to Australia, or their own domestic political enemies.

I have suggested that policing is one of those institutions the members of which need at times to deploy harmful methods, methods that in normal circumstances are morally wrong. In response to this, we need first to ask ourselves why it is that morally problematic methods such as coercion and deception are inescapable in policing. Why could not such methods be wholly abandoned in favor of the morally unproblematic methods already heavily relied on, such as rational discourse, appeal to moral sentiment, reliance on upright citizens for information, and so on?

Doubtless in many instances morally problematic methods could be replaced. And certainly overuse of these methods is a sign of bad police work, and perhaps of the partial breakdown of police-community trust so necessary to police work. However, the point is that the morally problematic methods could not be replaced in *all* or even *most* instances. For one thing, the violations of those moral rights that the police exist to protect are sometimes violations perpetrated by persons who are unmoved by rationality, appeal to moral sentiment, and so on. Indeed, such persons, far from being moved by well-intentioned police overtures, may seek to coerce or corrupt police officers for the purpose of preventing them from doing their moral and lawful duty; hence the truth of the claim that the use of coercive force in particular remains the bottom line in policing, no matter how infrequently coercion is in fact used. For another thing, the relevant members of the community may for one reason or another be unwilling or unable to provide the necessary information or evidence, and police may need to rely on persons of bad character or methods such as intrusive surveillance.

So the use of harmful methods cannot be completely avoided. It remains important to realize that these methods are in fact morally problematic; to realize that coercion, depriving someone of their liberty, deception, invasion of privacy, and so on, are in fact in themselves harmful. Indeed, these methods constitute prima facie wrongdoing, and some of them constitute – under normal circumstances – human rights violations. In the next section I consider some of the elements of this means/end problematic in policing.

### 4. MORAL RIGHTS IN POLICING: MEANS AND ENDS

In drawing attention to the use of harmful methods by police, I am far from denying the moral acceptability of these methods. The key point is that the use of any particular harmful method may be morally justified in the circumstances.[19] When police officers act in accordance with the legally enshrined and morally justified principles governing the use of harmful methods, they achieve three things at one and the same time: they do what is morally right, their actions are lawful, and – given these laws are the result of properly conducted democratic processes – they act in accordance with the will of the community.

Nevertheless, the use of harmful methods in the service of moral ends – specifically the protection of (justifiably enforceable) moral rights – gives rise to a number of problems in policing. Here I will mention only four.

First, the working out of these moral principles and the framing of accompanying legislation is highly problematic in virtue of the need to strike a balance between the moral rights of victims and the moral rights of suspects.

Obviously suspects – people who are only suspected of having committed a crime, but who have not been tried and found guilty – have moral rights. Suspects have a right to life, a right not to be physically assaulted, and a right not to be subjected to undue psychological harassment or

---

[19] I am here speaking of morally acceptable harmful methods. Torture, for example, is a morally harmful method that arguably ought never to be used by police.

intimidation. More generally, suspects have a right to procedural justice, including the right to a presumption of innocence and a fair trial.[20]

On the other hand, the police and the criminal justice system do not principally exist to protect the rights of suspects. They exist to protect the rights of victims and to ensure that offenders are brought to trial for appropriate disposition.[21] Accordingly, if the police believe on the basis of adequate evidence that a particular person is guilty of a serious crime, then the police are obliged to do their utmost to arrest and charge the suspect, and to provide sufficient evidence to enable his or her successful prosecution.

However, there is inevitably a certain tension between these two moral requirements of the police – the requirement to respect the moral rights of suspects (including the duty to make available evidence that may assist a suspect) and the requirement to apprehend, and provide evidence to ensure the conviction of, offenders. The procurement of such evidence may inevitably involve the kinds of justified, but harmful, actions I have been speaking of.

This tension has to be somehow resolved by framing laws that strike a moral balance between, on the one hand, ensuring that the rights of suspects are protected and, on the other, providing the police with sufficient powers to enable them to successfully gather evidence and apprehend offenders (especially rights violators).

This tension, and any resolution of it, is further complicated by the social, institutional, and technological contexts in which they operate. A set of laws might be thought to have struck an appropriate ethical balance between the moral rights of suspects and the provision of necessary powers to police, until one considers the criminal justice institutional context. For example, if putting young offenders into the system merely has the effect of breeding criminals, then this needs to be a factor taken into consideration in framing laws, including laws governing the nature and extent of police powers. Similarly, technological developments, such as surveillance technology and high-level encryption products, can justify either restrictions on police powers or extensions to police powers.

A second problem in this area has already been mentioned. It arises when the three desiderata mentioned above come apart: that is, a problem

---

[20] Here I am assuming that rights to procedural justice are institutional *moral* rights.

[21] This is putting things simply, even simplistically, but it makes no difference to the main point I am seeking to make here. Consider, in this connection, the restorative justice movement; it sees itself as an alternative to punishment-oriented conceptions of the criminal justice system.

arises when what the law prescribes is not morally sustainable, or at least is not morally acceptable to the community or significant sections of the community. Dramatic examples of the gap between law and the morality of significant sections of the community include the discriminatory race laws in South Africa under apartheid, the laws against homosexuality in Britain in the first part of the twentieth century, and the current laws in relation to prostitution and cannabis in parts of Australia. Other kinds of examples include obvious loopholes and deficiencies in the law. For example, legislation in relation to telephone surveillance in Australia might be thought to reflect appropriate moral principles, yet other forms of surveillance using new technology are not yet subject to laws reflecting these principles.

In all these kinds of situations, police are placed in an invidious position, one calling for discretionary ethical judgment. It is a lose/lose situation. In the first kind of example, although they are under a moral obligation to enforce the law, they may be unsure that the laws they are enforcing are in fact morally justifiable. Certainly they are aware that the laws in question are regarded as immoral by significant sections of the community. Recourse to justifiably enforceable moral rights, including human rights, is helpful in this context. For insofar as such rights provide an objective moral standard, and insofar as this objective moral standard comes to be widely accepted, then the uncertainty arising from subjective moral standards will cease to be a problem.

In the second kind of example, the law may allow police to engage in activities they believe to be immoral, and that the community believes to be immoral, and yet engaging in these activities may enable them to secure convictions they would otherwise be unable to secure. Clearly the resolution of this problem lies in bringing the law into line with objective moral principles.

A third problem in this area remains even after the provision of laws that strike the appropriate moral balance mentioned above, and even when laws are not in need of revision. This problem seems to arise out of inherent features of police work.

There is a necessity for police to be given a measure of professional autonomy to enable them to exercise discretion. Thus, individual police officers have a significant measure of legal authority. (On general issues of autonomy and accountability in policing, see Moore and Wettenhall 1994.) A police officer is legally empowered to "intervene – including stopping, searching, detaining and apprehending without a warrant any person whom he, with reasonable cause, suspects of having committed any such offence or crime" – at all levels of society (*NSW Crimes Act* 1990, no. 40, section 352, subsection 2(a)).

Moreover, the law has to be interpreted and applied in concrete circumstances. There is a need for the exercise of discretion by police in interpretation and application of the law. Further, upholding and enforcing the law is only one of the ends of policing; others include maintaining of social calm and the preservation of life. When these various ends come into conflict, there is a need for the exercise of police discretion, and in particular the need for the exercise of discretionary *moral* judgment.

The unavoidability of the exercise of discretionary moral judgment in policing means that it will never be sufficient for police simply to learn, and act in accordance with, the legally enshrined moral principles governing the use of harmful methods. On the other hand, my normative teleological account of policing in terms of the collective good of the protection of (justifiably enforceable) aggregate moral rights provides the theoretical means to satisfactorily resolve some of these dilemmas requiring discretionary moral judgment.

A fourth, and final, problem concerns the proper scope of the institution of the police. It is evident that transnational crime is on the increase. Accordingly, national law enforcement agencies are increasingly involved in transnational (and therefore transjurisdictional) law enforcement collaboration. Further, there has been a growth in private policing, including in the area of criminal investigations of fraud and white-collar crime. It might be thought that these developments threaten an institutional conception of policing. Given these developments, does it still make sense to talk of the *institution* of the police? I suggest that it does still make sense. Very briefly, although the notion of an institution is tied to the realization of certain collective ends, it is not necessarily the notion of a compartmentalized entity unrelated to other like institutions. We can still think of a specific organization as an institution, notwithstanding the fact that it has strong and important collaborative connections with like institutions, and notwithstanding the fact that other somewhat dissimilar organizations perform similar roles. Of course, this says nothing about the desirability of these developments. On the teleological account of institutions that we are offering, whether or not transnational collaboration and/or private-sector policing is to be welcomed or spurned depends on its contribution to the collective good that justifies the institution of the police, namely, the protection of legally enshrined, justifiably enforceable, (aggregated) moral rights – a good to which members of the community have a joint moral right.

## 5. THE INSTITUTIONALIZATION OF TORTURE

In the aftermath of the September 11, 2001, attacks by Al-Qaeda operatives on the World Trade Center in New York and the Pentagon in Washington, D.C., in particular, there has been an increase in the powers of police and other security agencies to search, engage in intrusive surveillance, and detain, and even in relation to shoot-to-kill provisions. Perhaps the greatest area of controversy that has arisen is in relation to torture. Just when it looked as though the so-called third degree was a thing of the past, at least in Western police agencies, the U.S. administration began to argue for (in effect) so-called torture lite powers for security agencies in the context of the alleged "war on terror." This ought to be a matter of profound concern. Certainly it is entirely inconsistent with the normative theoretical account of policing elaborated above, an account that places the protection of the moral rights of citizens as the raison d'être or collective end of the institution of the police.[22]

This is not to say that there might not be one-off emergency situations in which torture of terrorists known to be in the process of setting off bombs is, all things considered, the morally best action to perform (Miller 2006b). However, it may seem to follow that institutional arrangements should be in place to facilitate torture in such situations. However, it is perfectly consistent to oppose any legalization or institutionalization of torture; and this is precisely what I want to do in the remainder of this chapter.

Jeremy Waldron and David Luban have drawn attention to the moral inconsistency and inherent danger in liberal democratic states legalizing and institutionalizing torture, a practice that strikes at the very heart of the fundamental liberal value of individual autonomy (Luban 2005; Waldron 2005). They have also detailed the tendency for a torture culture to develop in organizations in which torture is legalized or tolerated, a culture in which the excesses of torturing the innocent and the like take place, as in the U.S. military detention centers in Abu Ghraib in Iraq and Guantanamo Bay in Cuba, and in the Israeli secret service (General Security Service). Nevertheless, it is useful to sketch a general argument against the legalization and institutionalization of torture. The argument is consistent with, indeed at some points it is more or less the same as, the arguments of Luban and Waldron. However, the argument has some novel elements, not the least of which is the claim that

[22] Material in this section is derived from Miller (2006b).

the view that torture is morally justified in some extreme emergencies is compatible with the view that torture ought not to be legalized or otherwise institutionalized.

Most of the theorists who oppose the legalization and institutionalization of torture also (at least implicitly) reject the possibility, let alone actuality, of one-off emergencies in which torture is morally justified. The argument has been put that there are, or could well be, such one-off extreme emergencies in which torture is morally justified. So the first task here is to demonstrate that these two claims are not inconsistent. Specifically, it needs to be shown that it does not follow from the fact that torture is in some extreme emergencies morally justified that torture ought to be legalized, or otherwise institutionalized. So the claim is that it is just a mistake to assume that what morality requires or permits in a given situation must be identical with what the law requires or permits in that situation. This calls for some explanation.

The law in particular, and social institutions more generally, are blunt instruments. They are designed to deal with recurring situations confronted by numerous institutional actors over relatively long periods of time. Laws abstract away from differences between situations across space and time, and differences between institutional actors across space and time. The law, therefore, consists of a set of generalizations to which the particular situation must be made to fit. Hence, if you exceed the speed limit you are liable for a fine, even though you were only 10 kph above the speed limit, you have a superior car, you are a superior driver, there was no other traffic on the road, the road conditions were perfect, and therefore the chances of your having an accident were actually less than would be the case for most other people most of the time driving at or under the speed limit.[23]

By contrast with the law, morality is a sharp instrument. Morality can be, and typically ought to be, made to apply to a given situation in all its particularity. (This is, of course, not to say that there are not recurring moral situations in respect of which the same moral judgment should be made, nor is it to say that morality does not need to help itself to generalizations.) Accordingly, what might be, all things considered, the morally best action for an agent to perform in some one-off, that is, nonrecurring, situation might not be an action that should be made lawful. Consider the real-life example of the five sailors on a raft in the

---

[23] Schauer (2003) argues this thesis in relation to laws and uses the speed limit as an example. Arguably, Schauer goes too far in his account of laws and is insisting that the law is blunter than it needs to be. However, that does not affect what is being said here.

middle of the ocean and without food. Four of them decide to eat the fifth – the cabin boy – to survive.[24] This is a case of both murder and cannibalism. Was it morally justifiable to kill and eat the boy, given the alternative was the death of all five sailors? Perhaps not, considering that the cabin boy was entirely innocent. However, arguably it was morally excusable, and, indeed, the sailors, although convicted of murder and cannibalism, had their sentence commuted in recognition of this. But there was no suggestion that the laws against murder and cannibalism admit of an exception in such an extreme case; the sailors were convicted and sentenced for murder and cannibalism. Again, consider an exceptionless law against desertion from the battlefield in time of war. Perhaps a soldier is morally justifiable in deserting his fellow soldiers, given that he learns of the more morally pressing need for him to care for his wife who has contracted some life-threatening disease back home. However, the law against desertion will not, and should not, be changed to allow desertion in such cases.

So the law and morality not only can and do come apart; indeed, sometimes they *ought* to come apart. This is the first point. The second point pertains to the nature of the subinstitution of torture within the larger military, police, and correctional institutions.

Social institutions, including legal institutions and military, police, and correctional organizations, have both a massive collective inertia and a massive collective momentum by virtue of the participation in them of many agents over a long time who (a) pursue the same collective ends; (b) occupy the same roles and, therefore, perform the same tasks and follow the same conventions, social norms, rules, and procedures; and (c) share the same culture. Accordingly, social institutions and their component organizations are like very large ocean liners that cannot slow down, speed up, or change direction very easily. It follows that very careful thought needs to be given to the establishment of any additional structure of roles and associated practices that is to be woven into the fabric of the institution. For such an additional (embodied) role structure, once it becomes, so to speak, an integrated working part of the larger institution, is likely to be extremely difficult to remove; it is now a beneficiary of the inertia of the institution. Moreover such an additional, but now integrated, role structure participates in, and influences the direction of, the institution; it is now a contributing element to the momentum of the institution.

[24] Andrew Alexandra reminded me of this example.

So what can be said of the likely institutional fit between military, police, and correctional institutions, on the one hand, and the sub-institution of torture, on the other? The role structure of this sub-institution consists of torturers, torturer trainers, medical personnel who assist torturers, and the like.

It would be a massive understatement to say that historically the sub-institution of torture – whether in a lawful or unlawful form – has been no stranger to military, police, and correctional institutions. Moreover, the practice of torture is endemic in many, probably most, military, police, and correctional institutions in the world today, including democracies such as India and Israel. It is only in recent times and with great diffi-culty that torture in Australian prisons and police services, for example, has been largely eliminated, or at least very significantly reduced. The Australian, British, American, and like cases are important not only because they illustrate that torture can be endemic to liberal democratic institutions, but also because they demonstrate that liberal democratic institutions are able – given the political will, suitable reeducation and training, stringent accountability mechanisms, and so on – to success-fully combat a culture of torture.

Further, there is now empirical evidence that in institutional environ-ments in which torture is routinely practiced it has a massive impact on other practices and on moral attitudes. For example, in police organiza-tions in which torture is routinely used the quality of investigations tends to be low. Careful marshalling of evidence is replaced by beating up sus-pects. Again, police in organizations in which offenders are routinely tortured do not, unsurprisingly, tend to develop respect for the moral rights of offenders, suspects, or even witnesses. This is entirely consistent with the excesses detailed by Luban and Waldron in the U.S. military detention centers in Iraq and elsewhere, for example, the Abu Ghraib scandal, and in the case of the interrogations of suspected terrorists by the Israeli secret service. Indeed, these excesses are to be expected.

And there is this further point. The prevalence of torture in numer-ous military, police, and correctional institutions throughout the world has taken place notwithstanding that for the most part it has been both unlawful and opposed by the citizenry.

It is to be concluded from all this that for the most part military, police, and correctional institutions are, *qua* institutions, receptive to the practice of torture – even when it is unlawful – and that these insti-tutions *qua* institutions would relatively easily incorporate the legalized sub-institution of torture; accordingly, it is very easy to legalize torture and thereby grow and develop a torture culture in military, police, and correctional institutions.

An additional conclusion to be drawn is that should the legalized sub-institution of torture be integrated into any of these institutions, it would be very difficult to remove and would, even in liberal democracies, have a major impact on the direction, culture, and practices of these institutions. Again, this is what the historical and comparative empirical evidence tells, notwithstanding the initial and even continuing aversion of many, perhaps most, of the individuals in these institutions to torture as such. Consider the Israeli case. Limited forms of torture were legal in Israel before 1999, but illegal post-1999. However, evidently torture has by no means been eradicated since 1999. According to the Public Committee Against Torture, reporting on the period between September 2001 and April 2003:

> The affidavits and testimonies taken by attorneys and fieldworkers ... support the conclusions ... violence, painful tying, humiliations and many other forms of ill-treatment, including detention under inhuman conditions, are a matter of course. ... The bodies which are supposed to keep the GSS [General Security Service] under scrutiny and ensure that interrogations are conducted lawfully act, instead, as rubberstamps for decisions by the GSS. ... The State Prosecutor's Office transfers the interrogees' complaints to a GSS agent for investigation and it is little wonder that it has not found in even a single case that GSS agents tortured a Palestinian "unnecessarily." (Public Committee against Torture in Israel 2003)

Torture is a terrorist tactic. Indeed, arguably it is the terrorist tactic par excellence. Detonating bombs that kill the innocent has come to be regarded as the quintessential terrorist tactic. But this is presumably because terrorism has implausibly come to be identified only with non-state terrorism. At any rate, the point to be made here is that torture is a terrorist tactic, and for a liberal democracy to legalize and institutionalize it, that is, to weave the practice of torture into the very fabric of liberal democratic institutions, would be both an inherent contradiction – torture being an extreme assault on individual autonomy – and, given what we know about the practice of torture in military, police, and correctional institutions, highly damaging to those liberal democratic institutions. It would be equivalent to a liberal democracy legalizing and institutionalizing slavery on the grounds, say, of economic necessity. Legalized and institutionalized slavery is inconsistent with liberal democracy, as is legalized and institutionalized torture. So if legalized and institutionalized slavery and/or legalized and institutionalized torture are necessary because morally required, then liberal democracy is not possible in anything other than an attenuated form. But, of course, neither legalized/institutionalized slavery nor legalized/institutionalized torture is morally required, quite the contrary. At best, torture is morally justified in some one-off emergencies – just as murder and cannibalism might be morally excusable in a one-off emergency on the high seas, or desertion from the field of battle might be morally justifiable given a one-off emergency back home – but absolutely nothing follows as far as the legalization/institutionalization of torture is concerned.

The fact is that the recent history of police, military, and other organizations in liberal democracies has demonstrated that torture cultures and sub-institutions of torture can be more or less eliminated, albeit with considerable difficulty. The elimination of torture cultures and sub-institutions can be achieved only if torture is unlawful, the community and the political and organizational leadership are strongly opposed to it, police officers and other relevant institutional actors are appropriately educated and trained, and stringent accountability mechanisms – for instance, video recording of interviews, closed-circuit TV cameras in cells, external oversight bodies – are put in place. It is surely obvious that to reintroduce and indeed protect the practice of torture, by legalizing and institutionalizing it, would be to catapult the security agencies of liberal democracies back into the dark ages from whence they came.

The discussion has focused on the legalization and institutionalization of torture, where the practice of torture is understood in general terms; it ought to be now obvious why torture should not be legalized. However, some commentators, notably Alan Dershowitz, have argued that legalized torture could be justified if the torture in question was restricted to extreme emergency situations and subjected to appropriate accountability mechanisms. Specifically, he has argued for torture warrants of the kind introduced for a time in Israel.

The notion of torture warrants is supposedly analogous to surveillance and telephone interception warrants issued to police by a magistrate or other judicial officer. The idea is that privacy is a fundamental right, but it can be infringed under certain conditions, such as reasonable suspicion that the person whose privacy right is to be infringed is engaged in serious criminal activity, there is no alternative way to acquire the necessary information to convict him or her, and so on. In this kind of setup the magistrate, not the police, makes the decision as to whether or not these conditions obtain. Consequently the infringements of privacy rights are restricted and subject to stringent accountability mechanisms.

However, morally speaking, torture warrants are entirely different from telephone interception or surveillance warrants. First, torture is a far greater evil than the infringement of privacy. For one thing, having one's phone tapped or movements filmed is inherently much less distressing, harmful, and morally repugnant than the physical suffering and loss of autonomy involved in being strapped to a chair and, say, having someone drill into an unanesthetized tooth. On the spectrum of evils, torture is closer to murder and killing than it is to the infringement of privacy. For another thing, torture is a far more dangerous practice than infringing privacy. For the degree of the infringement of privacy can be minimized; for example, the information gained can relatively easily be kept strictly confidential by the police; moreover, there is no inherent reason for the police to illicitly widen a given infringement of privacy by breaching confidentiality. But in practice torture cannot be restricted likewise. The methods of torture and the process of torture exist on a continuum, and there is often an inherent reason to "push the envelope" and inflict ever more severe forms of physical suffering on victims; so-called torture lite becomes full-blooded, no-holds-barred torture. One of the consequences of this continuum of torture is the ever-present possibility that the victims of torture will not simply be tortured, but rather be murdered; and in point of fact countless people have died in the course of being tortured.

Second, as has already been argued, there is an inherent institutional receptivity of military, police, and correctional institutions to the practice of torture, a receptivity that is such that torture cultures will grow and flourish, notwithstanding Dershowitz's proposal that only tightly controlled and highly restricted forms of torture are to be legally admissible. This institutional receptivity has the consequence that inevitably large numbers of innocent people will be tortured – as happened, and continues to happen, in Israel. Indeed, even under tightly controlled and highly restricted forms of torture some innocent persons will inevitably be tortured – just as the privacy of innocent people is infringed under the existing telephone and surveillance warrant systems. Arguably, the infringement of the privacy of some – in fact, many – innocent persons is a price that we ought to be willing to pay for the sake of preventing serious crimes. However, it would be preposterous to argue that (inadvertently?) torturing numerous innocent people is a reasonable price to pay in return for the information provided by those of the tortured who are in fact guilty.

## 6. CONCLUSION

In this chapter I have applied my individualist, teleological model of social institutions to police organizations. I have argued that police ought to have as their fundamental collective end the protection of justifiably enforceable, aggregated moral rights (namely, those of all the members of some jurisdiction) and, furthermore, that their efforts in this regard ought to be constrained by the law. The realization of this collective end is a collective good to which the members of the jurisdiction in question have a joint moral right.

Insofar as the law is a constraint – at least in democratic states – then my view accommodates "consent" as a criterion of legitimacy for the police role. However, legality, and therefore consent, is only one consideration. Police work ought to be guided by moral considerations – namely, moral rights – and not simply by legal considerations. This enables me to avoid the problems besetting theories of policing cast purely in terms of law enforcement, or protection of the state, or even peace keeping. Such theories are faced with the obvious problem posed by authoritarian states, or sometimes even democratic states, that enact laws that violate human rights in particular.

I have also argued that the practice of torture is inherently antithetical to police organizations as social institutions; indeed, it is corrosive and corruptive of police institutions because it undermines the fundamental moral purpose of police work, namely, that of protecting human rights. The Bush administration in particular pursued a policy of advocating and (at least) condoning torture – albeit so-called torture lite – and in doing has profoundly compromised the moral values underpinning police institutions and liberal democracy more generally.

# 10

# The Business Corporation

## 1. BUSINESS ORGANIZATIONS OPERATING IN COMPETITIVE MARKETS

In this chapter I apply my individualist, teleological theory of social institutions to business corporations operating in competitive markets and, specifically, to media corporations and financial service providers. In doing so, I identify a process of corrosion, if not corruption, that is taking place in relation to the media as an institution. I also identify processes of corrosion and corruption in relation to financial service providers. Indeed, in the case of the latter, arguably, there is a more fundamental problem, namely, the absence of an agreed on institutional purpose (collective good) in terms of which corrosion and corruption can be determined.

Business organizations operating in competitive markets are producers and on-sellers of goods and services, some of which are needed by consumers, many of which are only desired. Thus agri-businesses produce food for the market, and food is a basic human need. On the other hand, ice creams, celebrity-focused magazines, and the like do not meet basic human needs, but only consumer desires.

Market-based organizations and public institutions are usually distinguished from one another, albeit the distinction is in some cases difficult to make. Sometimes public institutions are distinguished in terms of the type of goods that they provide, namely, goods that have the economic properties of nonrivalness and nonexcludability. Although the definition, and even existence, of these properties is contested, there is a certain intuitive sense to them. If a good is nonrival, then my enjoyment of it does not prevent or diminish the possibility of your enjoyment of it; for instance, a street sign is nonrival because my using it to find my way has no effect on your likewise using it. A good is nonexcludable if it is such that if anyone is enjoying the good, then no one can be prevented from enjoying it, for example, national defense. In the light of my general account of social institutions as existing to provide collective goods and the complexities of the relationship between public goods in the economic sense and collective goods in my sense, I will eschew this way of making the distinction.

Another way to make the distinction is in terms of the type of funding source; whereas business organizations rely for their funding on selling goods in a competitive market, public institutions are publicly funded by governments through taxes raised from the community at large. I will make use of this way of making the distinction and refer to the latter as public institutions.

Public institutions provide a range of public goods that are not typically provided by businesses. Such public institutions include the government itself and its administration; the criminal justice system, including the police, the law courts, and correctional institutions; and state educational institutions, for instance, many universities and schools. On the other hand, there are a range of social institutions, including schools, universities, and security agencies, that are sometimes commercial businesses and sometimes publicly funded institutions. So a question arises as to whether or not a given social institution should be exclusively a public institution or not. Should police services, for example, remain public institutions? In the light of the proliferation of private policing in areas such as ensuring the security of property and persons, and investigations (including of corporate fraud), this is by no means a purely theoretical question. Likewise in many jurisdictions in the United States, the United Kingdom, and Australia there are private prisons. On my favored individualist, teleological model of social institutions this question should be answered on a case-by-case basis in the light of the normatively required collective ends of the social institution or institutions at issue. However, the answer to this question will also partly depend on one's favored normative theoretical account of private-sector social institutions and, in particular, one's account of the modern business corporation.

As we saw in Chapter 1, Section 3, organizations per se have no intrinsic normative character. The same point was made about joint procedural mechanisms, such as exchange systems; they are neither good nor evil *qua* exchange systems (Chapter 1, Section 4).

On the other hand, most exchange systems do in fact have a normative dimension. As argued in Chapter 2, competitive markets and, therefore, business organizations competing in competitive markets have a normative dimension by virtue of the fact that they involve competition that has consequences, direct and indirect, for the distribution of economic benefits and burdens. To this extent moral principles of fair competition, property rights, promises, and so on are implicated in competitive markets. Moreover, business organizations in the actual world are not simply layered structures of joint action; typically, business organizations are hierarchical in structure and involve contractual relations between employers and employees. To this extent moral principles pertaining to individual autonomy in the context of the exercise of authority and power are implicated, as are moral principles in relation to the making and breaking of contracts.

On the other hand, competitive markets and business organizations *qua* institutions are different in an important respect from other social institutions (Chapter 2, Section 1). Let us try to get clear on what the difference is.

We need to invoke a threefold distinction in relation to institutional ends. First, the constitutive joint activity of an organization, or set of organizations, has a defining collective end, an end that is in part definitive of that activity. Let us refer to such ends as constitutive collective ends. Thus a car manufacturer has as a constitutive collective end the production and distribution of cars, a bakery the production and provision of bread, a university the acquisition, transmission, and dissemination of knowledge, and so on.

Second, an organization or set of organizations that is a social institution has a collective end that is also a collective good, that is, something that is jointly produced, desirable, and to which members of the community have a joint right (Chapter 2, Section 2). Thus the collective good of universities is the acquisition, transmission, and dissemination of knowledge, of bakeries the provision of bread, and of car manufacturers the enabling of transport. Notice that in some cases the constitutive collective end of an organization is identical with (or, at least, identical in part with) the collective good that it produces, such as in the case of universities; in other cases the relation is simply that of means to end, such as in the case of car manufacturers. In the former kind of case, the constitutive collective end is an intrinsic good, namely, a collective good; accordingly, to pursue the constitutive collective end is (at least in part) to pursue the collective good, and so the constitutive collective end is an end-in-itself. In the latter kind of case this is not necessarily so; rather, the realization of the constitutive collective end is simply a means to a collective good – a means that might be ineffective, and a means to an end that might be able to be realized by some other means, for example, as transport might be achieved by trains rather than by cars.

In short, we need to make a conceptual distinction between the constitutive collective end, on the one hand, and the collective end that is the collective good, on the other; we also need to note that in the case of some social institutions they are one and the same thing, and in others they are not.

Third, in the case of market-based organizations only, we need to note the existence of a third kind of collective end, namely, profit maximization (or at least, the making of a profit in the financial sense). The existence of profit maximization adds a complication in the case of market-based organizations that is not present in the case of other social institutions. In the case of market-based organizations, but not necessarily other social institutions, there are *three* collective ends, namely, the constitutive collective end, such as the production of cars, the collective good, such as transport, and profit maximization. Moreover, although this third collective end is not a collective good it is undoubtedly desired, namely, by owners; indeed, it is in the collective self-interest of owners to maximize profit. So profit maximization is a collective end to which the constitutive collective end is a means; for example, cars are produced and sold for profit.

Accordingly, there are now two potentially competing collective ends, namely, collective goods and profit maximization. However, as is well known, a solution of sorts has been offered to this problem, namely, the so-called invisible hand. The claim is that the single-minded and self-interested pursuit of profit will, as a matter of contingent fact, maximize collective benefits (on some construal of collective benefits, for instance, utilitarianism). Relativized to my account of social institutions, the claim is that the pursuit of the collective end of profit maximization as an end will, as a matter of contingent fact, realize the collective good definitive of the social institution in question.

Unfortunately, as will become evident in the discussion below, the empirical claim on which the efficacy of the invisible hand is predicated is contestable and, in some cases, evidently false. In particular, the claim is false in the case of some social institutions that have a constitutive collective end that is identical, at least in part, with their defining collective good, such as the media as an institution. For in these cases there is a tendency for the collective good to be discounted, or even regarded simply as a means to profit maximization – rather than the other way around. Perhaps this is to some extent inevitable, given the constitutive collective end; for instance, the acquisition and dissemination of news is a means to profit maximization, and yet the constitutive collective end is itself the collective good.

At any rate the normative principle that my account of social institutions compels me to advance is that profit maximization is, or ought to be, regarded simply as a *means* to the realization of collective goods; so profit maximization is only a proximate end, whereas the realization of collective goods is an ultimate end.

More generally, as argued in Chapter 2, business organizations operating in competitive markets per se ought to be viewed instrumentally, for example, as the means to realize collective goods. Note that in many cases these collective goods are indirectly produced; in particular the aggregated right to work for pay is a collective good that is indirectly produced by market-based businesses (as, indeed, it is by public-sector institutions).

The fact that business institutions have the self-interested pursuit of profit maximization as an end is both an opportunity and a potential source of problems. On the one hand, it enables business institutions to be used instrumentally in relation to a wide range of ends – not only desired ends but also desirable ends, such as private schools and universities, private hospitals, and private security firms. Here we will need to distinguish between the proximate end of the business and its ultimate end. Thus the proximate end of a private hospital might be the profit it earns for its owners. However, the ultimate end would be the provision of health services to the needy.

On the other hand, being mere institutional instruments, market-based organizations per se can easily be used to serve harmful purposes, for instance, corporations that produce and distribute tobacco or armaments.

Moreover, as noted above, those social institutions that produce a collective good that is identical (at least in part) with their constitutive collective end can suffer a process of corrosion or corruption once they are "privatized," or otherwise transformed into predominantly market-based enterprises. Some organizations within the print and electronic media sector are cases in point.

## 2. THE PRINT AND ELECTRONIC MEDIA AS SOCIAL INSTITUTIONS

Because the mainstream media, including tabloid TV, is pervasive – 75 percent of the discretionary (nonwork, nonsleep) time of Americans is spent watching TV (Gore 2007, 6) – it profoundly influences, directly or indirectly, the institutions of public communication and, thereby, social attitudes and public policy.

Most print and electronic media organizations in Western countries are commercial businesses, that is, business institutions.[1] However, these organizations also have a particular role as an institution of public communication. Specifically, they have an institutional role as the free press in the service of the public's right to know – the role of the Fourth Estate alongside the executive, legislature, and judiciary within a liberal democracy.

As a commercial business, indeed, a business corporation or structure of business corporations, the media produces saleable commodities (including advertisements), employs workers and managers, and has investors and owners. It is simply another business, or set of businesses, within the market economy. As such its end is economic: it exists to make profits, provide jobs, and satisfy consumer demand. As a public-sector industry funded by government, for example, the British Broadcasting Corporation, the Australian Broadcasting Corporation, and the like, it also has economic ends; it employs workers and managers and is to an extent market oriented; for example, "consumption" levels are of importance.

However, the point to be stressed here is that the print and electronic media have an important institutional purpose as the Fourth Estate, and do so whether they happen to be public institutions or corporations operating in a competitive market.

In distinguishing between the media as a business and as an institution of public communication – between its economic and its ethico-sociopolitical institutional purpose – it is not being maintained that the functions do not overlap and are not linked. Indeed, it is a commonplace of political, social, and normative theory that economic functions intermesh with normative social and political functions. This goes as much for the media as for many other major social institutions. However, the crucial issue here is the order of priority of these functions or ends. In the case of the print and electronic media – at least in its role as a public communicator of news and comment – its existence as a business corporation is, or ought to be, subservient to, indeed, an instrument in the hands of, its institutional function as the Fourth Estate. As argued above,

---

[1] An earlier version of the material in this section on the media appeared in Miller (1995c).

business organizations in competitive markets are not ends in themselves but ought to be viewed purely instrumentally; this is certainly so in the case of the print and electronic media business in respect to their collective end of public communication of news and comment.

Here it is important to reaffirm the distinction between the de facto ends of the media and the ends that it ought to have. Perhaps the principal end of the mainstream media in the United States is in fact to provide entertainment and make profits for corporations rather than function as the Fourth Estate.

There are a number of considerations in support of this empirical claim. First, much of mainstream media news and comment is "soundbites," dumbed-down reports, sport, celebrity "news," infotainment, advertorials, and the like; the content lacks descriptive breadth or analytical depth, and it typically appeals to the lowest common denominator. In short, much of the news content of the mainstream media is a form of entertainment, including "selling" a consumerist-oriented way of life.

Second, there is a high degree of concentration of ownership in the mainstream media. The mainstream U.S. media, including news and comment, is in large part owned by large corporate conglomerates for which news is simply one commercial product; for example, the parent company of the mainstream news provider NBC is General Electric (Cohen 2005, 18).

Third, mainstream media enterprises are often simply components of large corporate conglomerates, and most have close institutional relationships with corporations outside the media. According to Elliot Cohen, citing a recent U.S. university-based research study (Cohen and Fraser 2007, 14), "only 118 people compose the membership on the boards of directors of the ten big media giants. These 118 individuals in turn sit on the corporate boards of 288 national and international corporations."

Finally, there is evidently an unhealthy institutional relationship between these conglomerates and government (the U.S. government in particular). Consider the U.S. government's "influence" on independent reporting of the Iraq war by the mainstream media. In 2003 leading international CNN war correspondent Christine Amanpour reported that CNN in its reporting of the Iraq War had allowed itself to be intimidated by the Bush administration and was engaging in self-censorship (Cohen and Fraser 2007, 93).

From the perspective of a free press in the service of the public's right to know (the Fourth Estate), each of these four considerations is very troubling. Taken in combination they call into question the independence of these media enterprises and their journalists, and the truth, objectivity, and balance of the news reports that they disseminate. Consider the case of General Electric; it is both the parent company of NBC and a major supplier to the U.S. military. Given this, are NBC news reports on the war in Iraq, for example, to be entirely trusted?

One specific political consequence of the current state of these corporate media institutions relates to U.S. elections. As Al Gore (Gore 2007, 78) says:

> Since voters still have the real power to elect their leaders, those who wish to exchange wealth for power must do so, in part, by paying for elaborate public relations campaigns to try to shape the opinions of the millions who spend so much time watching television. At times it seems as if a genuine democratic conversation is taking place, but it flows mainly in one direction – from those who have raised enough money to buy the television advertising to those who watch the ads and have little effective means for communicating in the opposite direction.

As far as a normative theory is concerned – and from the perspective of my individualist, teleological account of social institutions in particular – we need to ask what the collective end or ends of the media ought to be; that is, what collective goods do they produce?

A further normative issue concerns moral rights as side constraints. As is the case with any organization or institution, the fulfillment by the media of its actual and/or legitimate purposes is constrained by the moral rights of individuals. In the case of the media – an institution of public communication – these rights include especially the right to privacy, to a fair trial, and not to be defamed. Arguably, in relation to at least some of these rights the media in the United States and elsewhere has been pushing the boundaries to the point that the rights in question are now routinely violated. Consider the privacy rights of, for example, members of the British Royal Family; the level of media scrutiny is evidently quite often a breach of the right to privacy.

Let us now put forward the following normative theoretical standpoint. In relation to news and comment in the context of a contemporary liberal democratic state, the media as an institution – whether it be publicly or privately owned – has the collective end of public communication in the public interest.

Here the reference to public communication is to some extent self-explanatory, albeit there are multifarious "publics" in a globalizing world. So the boundaries of the public do not necessarily mirror those of the nation-state in which the media institution might be based. Indeed, there are numerous international media institutions based in numerous countries and communicating to international audiences.

Thus it can reasonably be claimed that the news/comment institution of the media is principally a vehicle for public communication, just so long as it is understood that the public in question is in need of specification in the case of any particular media institution. Nor is this general claim undermined by the emergence of new communications technologies, some of which may well facilitate private interactive communication and do so to some extent at the expense of public and "one-way" communication.

The notion of public interest is much more problematic than that of public communication. Suffice it to say here that attempts to explain away the notion of the public interest in terms of sectional or class interests have been unsuccessful. So has the attempted reduction of the notion of the public interest to sets of individual preferences or desires. What is in fact in the public interest is not necessarily what the public wants to hear or "consume," still less what will generate profits for the media industry. Relativized to the concerns of the news media, the public interest can usefully be glossed as information that the members of the relevant public (whether it be local, national, international, or in some other way segmented) has a moral right to know. Moreover, by the lights of my individualist, teleological account of social institutions, the fulfillment of this right to know is a collective good; it consists of each member of the public in question having his or her right to know fulfilled. So this collective good is the fulfillment of an aggregated epistemic right.

A final point concerns the relationship between the defining collective good of the media as an institution and its commercial viability. I have already argued that the end of profit maximization ought to serve the collective good produced by the media. A further point is that if the elements of the media in the private sector are to survive, they will need to be commercially viable, and this will entail that what is communicated is to an extent what the public is prepared to consume. But the point to be stressed here is that if a particular media organization is not discharging its obligations as an institution, there is no great cause for concern if it does not survive.

## 3. COLLECTIVE ENDS OF THE MEDIA AS A SOCIAL INSTITUTION

Public communication in the public interest involves at least the following subsidiary collective ends and associated roles.

First, the media provide a public forum enabling communication by government and other institutions, and by interest groups and individual citizens, to the public at large, and enabling that communication to stand as a public record; this is the media as public forum.

Second, the media, or at least members of the media such as journalists, have the task of unearthing and disseminating information of importance to the public; this is the media as investigator. Crucially, this includes information about governmental policies and actions that enables citizens to hold the government and its members to account. A similar point holds in relation to the accountability of other institutions, including business corporations, to the citizenry.

Third, the media, or at least members of the media, themselves function as public communicators. In this role members of the media communicate both information and comment; this is the media as autonomous public communicator.

Moreover, the realization of these collective ends in respect of public communication is the chief justification for the existence of the (news and comment) media.

## Media as Public Forum

The media as a public forum enables individual members of the public and representatives of groups and organizations (including the government) to communicate to the public at large. In this aspect of its overall role, the freedom of the press derives from the basic human right of freedom of communication. More specifically, members of a community have a jointly held moral right to communicate to the rest of the community, that is, to engage in public communication; in the case of larger communities this right can be exercised by way of chosen representatives or spokespeople. In this respect public communication is akin to political participation (Chapter 2, Section 3); indeed, the joint right to public communication is in part an aspect of the joint right to political participation. In the context of the existence of the media as an institution, the members of the relevant public have a joint *institutional* moral right of access to the institutional channels of public communication in question, either directly or via their representatives or spokespeople.

The setting of some of these instances of public communication is a dispute, and it is in the public interest that the public be informed about this dispute, for example, the dispute in the United Kingdom in relation to membership in the European Community. These disputes can be about the truth of particular claims, such as concerning the alleged relation between Saddam Hussein and Al-Qaeda, or about the workability or justice of particular policies, for instance, affirmative action policies in relation to Australian Aboriginal education. Here the role of the media is simply to provide a forum for the various disputing parties, and thereby enable them to communicate to the public at large.

Other cases in this category are ones involving the communication of noncontested information. For example, the government may wish to make known the details of its budget. Here the media provides a mechanism for communication by members of the public (individuals or groups or organizations, including the government) to the public at large.

## Media as Investigator

The second category of communications involves the members of the media as investigators (investigative journalists). There are cases in which journalists investigate matters of public interest and unearth information that is of legitimate interest to the public, even if not of great importance; that is, journalists produce a collective epistemic good.

Here the freedom of members of the press to investigate and disseminate their findings to the public at large (i.e., to provide the collective epistemic good) ultimately derives from the public's aggregated right to know. Accordingly, in this aspect the freedom of the press is not a basic human right as is the human right of freedom of communication (Lichtenberg 1987), nor (in this aspect) does it derive from that human right.

Although the freedom of the press is not a basic human right, nevertheless, the role of the journalist is different from most other institutional roles in respect of the very high degree of freedom that ought to attach to it, if journalists are successfully to undertake their institutional role. Thus, unlike, say, doctors, the right to function as a journalist is not something that should be restricted to certified practitioners, or even to uncertified institutional actors, that is, to members of media organizations. Moreover, journalists functioning within media organization need to be protected from interference from owners, governments, and so on; they need, that is, to have a high degree of professional autonomy (Chapter 6, Section 1) if they are to discharge their responsibilities to the public in respect of the latter's right to know.

For its part the right to know of members of the public is prior to the establishment of the institution of the media; in this sense it is akin to the human rights to the basic necessities of life; indeed, this prior right is the raison d'être for the establishment of the institution of the media.

Accordingly, once a media institution is established, then journalists who are members of this media institution have institutional moral duties to investigate and disseminate information that it is in the public's interest to know, that is, to produce the epistemic collective good. Moreover the members of the relevant public now have an *institutional* joint moral right to have that information disseminated to them.

In respect of the members of the public's joint right to know, consider the role of the journalists Woodward and Bernstein in relation to Watergate, or the sections of the press in South Africa, including notably *The Weekly Mail,* that for many years brought to light various covert operations of the South African government and its security agencies. More recently, consider the revelations by the *New York Times* in 2005 of the Bush administration's illegal warrant-less wiretapping of U.S. citizens (Cohen and Fraser 2007, 22).

While this category of cases necessarily involves investigation, it also involves public communication; the journalist investigates to communicate his or her discovery to the public. A journalist is not simply a private detective unearthing information for a fee.

In the cases in which the media provides a forum for individuals and groups to exercise their right to public communication, or finds out and communicates what the public has a right to know, the media is not an autonomous public communicator. Rather, in these former cases the media exists to ensure that the rights to communicate and to know of members of the public (respectively) are realized.

## Media as Autonomous Communicator

The category of cases in which members of the media act as autonomous public communicators comprises such things as editorial comment and comment and analysis provided by members of the print and electronic media itself, as opposed to comment and analysis in the media provided by academics, community leaders, and others. Political and economic commentaries are prominent in this category.

In this category the media has an active role as an independent communicator. The media is not simply a mouthpiece or the provider of a forum for other communicators, nor is it simply discharging its obligation to provide information that the members of the public have a joint right to possess. Rather, in these cases the media is a genuinely autonomous communicator.

The housing of journalists, editors, and commentators in large media corporations and corporate conglomerates has evidently compromised the role of the media as an independent communicator. Consider in this connection Bill O'Reilly, the host of Fox News's *The O'Reilly Factor*. O'Reilly's comments place a right-wing "spin" on events and do not even attempt to respect the canons of objective argument; indeed, even his factual claims are suspect (Cohen and Fraser 2007, 83).

As already noted, the general justification for the existence of the media as a public forum is that members of the public – or at least their representatives or spokespersons – have a moral right to address the public at large. In this connection the recent arrival of the Internet is important. It enables a very large number of people to have access to very large audiences. On the other hand, it is not immune to interference and censorship: for example, with the complicity of the search engine giant Google, the authoritarian Chinese government employs tens of thousands of people to police Chinese citizens using the Internet by intercepting their communications, shutting down web sites, and so on (Cohen and Fraser 2007, 219). Moreover, recent policy decisions in the United States threaten to undermine Internet freedom by refusing to maintain its status as a "common carrier" akin to telecommunication systems such as telephone networks; common carriers are open to all, and control of communications rests entirely with users (Cohen and Fraser 2007, 218).

As already noted, the general justification for the existence of the media as an investigator/disseminator is members of the public's joint right to know in relation to certain matters of public interest and importance (their knowledge in this regard being a collective good). Here it is important to stress the importance of investigative journalism and some of the recent threats to it, including lack of resources and the targeting of journalists in conflict settings.

The general justification for the existence of the media as an autonomous public communicator is more problematic. Suffice it to say here that there are a range of pragmatic reasons why professional journalists and media commentators might be desirable. In the last analysis these reasons come down to the quality of the comment and analysis provided. Note that such reasons do not include the existence of a moral right to exist as an autonomous public communicator.

## 4. FINANCIAL SERVICES SECTOR

It is agreed on all sides that the global financial crisis taking place at the time of writing is the worst since the Great Depression. The main aspects of the problem are frozen credit markets, the subprime mortgage crisis, and an impending global recession. The crisis has involved major corporate investment and mortgage banking collapses and bailouts in the United States (Lehman, Freddie Mac, and Fannie Mae), United Kingdom (Northern Rock), and Europe (Fortis, Hypo), and it is having a devastating effect on homeowners who cannot pay their mortgages (foreclosures), retirees whose pension funds have plummeted in value, employees whose jobs are at risk in the recession, and taxpayers whose money is being injected into the banking system in vast quantities to rescue it (e.g., $700 billion by the U.S. government).

Unethical, including imprudent, practices have been identified as being among the principal causes of the crisis. These practices include (1) reckless and predatory lending by banks; (2) developing highly leveraged investment banks; (3) the selling of toxic financial products, notably nontransparent packaged bundles of mortgages (including subprime mortgages) assessed by ratings agencies as high quality because the investment banks that packaged them had good risk assessment processes, securitized and sold by banks to pension funds; (4) allowing the growth of unsustainable debt on the part of governments and, indeed, whole economies: for instance, the U.S. overseas debt accumulated in 2006 alone was $850 billion; and (5) the negligence and/or complicity of legislators and regulators in relation to all of the above.

However, the current financial problems share important features with recent, as well as not so recent, corporate collapses and scandals. Recall the corporate scandals of the 1980s in the United States and elsewhere: the stock market crash, a junk bond collapse, the bankruptcy of numerous highly leveraged clients, the prevalence of the unlawful practice of insider trading, and the fining and imprisonment of the likes of Michael Milken and Ivan Boesky. Milken paid fines in excess of US$600 million, Boesky over US$100 million.

And what of the collapse of Enron, WorldCom, One Tel, and HIH circa 2001? These had a devastating effect on shareholders, employees, and others. Moreover, they involved a range of unethical practices such as conflicts of interests, auditing failures, and corrupt (if not unlawful) practices, for example, Enron's "Special Purpose Entities," calculated to mislead shareholders in relation to actual performance.

Accordingly, the question arises: Are the corporate collapses and corruption scandals of the 1980s, 1990s, early 2000s, and now in 2008 in the United States, United Kingdom, Europe, Australia, and elsewhere part of a recurring cycle? Are there systemic deficiencies in the corporate sector itself, including in the global banking and financial services area?

Self-evidently, these corporate collapses were extraordinarily damaging economically, but apparently they might also be ongoing; perhaps the question is not whether there will be a recurrence, but rather when it will take place. If so, then these corporate collapses and corruption scandals might not be aberrations but rather symptoms of underlying systemic deficiencies in corporate law and regulation, and perhaps of structural deficiencies in the corporate sector itself, notably in the financial services area.

In this book I have argued that the basic normative question that needs to be asked of a business corporation, or financial market, is the same as for any other social institution, namely, What collective good(s) does it exist to provide? I have further argued that, normatively speaking, social institutions, including business corporations and markets, exist for ultimate – and not merely proximate – purposes or ends, namely, to provide collective goods, such as foodstuffs that meet aggregate needs, the coordination of buyers and sellers of such goods. Here Adam Smith's invisible hand mechanism is salient. The outcome of the workings of the invisible hand is the ultimate purpose of this institutional mechanism, the pursuit of financial gain, the proximate end.

I now suggest that in the case of the financial services sector in particular, the prior fundamental ethical question as to the ultimate institutional ends of this sector remains unanswered. Yet without an answer to this question an integrity system for the financial services sector – and a regulatory system insofar as it is concerned with institutional (ethical) integrity, as it surely must be – is quite literally without one of its basic purposes: it does not know what ethical ends it is seeking to embed in its target institution, that is, in the financial services sector.

As already noted, markets and business organizations, normatively speaking, have both *proximate* ends and *ultimate* ends. The proximate end of market actors might be to maximize their financial self-interest or the firm's profits or shareholder value – the means to these ends being the production of goods for consumption or the provision of services. However, such proximate goals are not the ultimate ends of markets or of the social institution of the modern corporation. *Qua* social institution, markets and corporations ought to (and in fact do, albeit imperfectly) serve larger purposes than this, such as to contribute to the material well-being of human societies.

To claim that the ultimate purpose of the institution of the modern corporation – a product, if ever there was one, of institutional design – is, for example, simply and only to maximize profits or shareholder value is, on this ends-based, that is, *teleological,* account of social institutions, to confuse proximate with ultimate purposes.

Thus the proximate end of corporate financial service providers in capital markets might be to maximize shareholder value, but the ultimate collective end is something beyond this, for example, to allocate savings efficiently or to make capital available at reduced costs to productive firms. This ultimate collective end of financial service providers is unlikely to be an intrinsic good; it is more likely to be a good derived from some further intrinsic good, for example, the collective goods, such as aggregate needed foodstuffs, provided by the so-called real economy.

Market fundamentalism tends to overrate the rights and contribution of owners and senior managers and downplay the contribution of middle- and lower-echelon workers. However, all participants in the joint production of a collective good have a derived *joint* right to fair and reasonable remuneration, for instance, shareholders, managers, and workers (officers and employees) in a factory that produces cars for profit have joint right. Moreover, all participants also have a set of derived jointly held obligations, such as a worker's moral duty to do a reasonable day's work, or a manager's (director's) fiduciary duties to shareholders not to recklessly put at risk their money, or shareholders' responsibility not to invest their money in corporations that are generating profits not by virtue of a superior economic performance but by bribing public officials to gain lucrative contracts.

Naturally, what counts as fair and reasonable remuneration is not logically equivalent to, or necessarily overridden by, the terms of any *legal* (including contractual) rights and duties; after all, the latter may constitute excessive executive remuneration.

## 5. INSTITUTIONAL INTEGRITY IN THE FINANCIAL SERVICES SECTOR

Any given integrity system for an institution must be tailored to the needs of that particular institution (Chapter 6, Sections 2 and 3).[2] Arguably,

[2] An earlier version of the material in this section appeared in Miller (2007b).

market actors, including financial service providers, present a number of relatively distinct problems when it comes to devising integrity systems to ensure ethical practice and the pursuit of ethical ends; or, at any rate, this assumption is a source of the following speculations concerning the integrity system or systems for these groups.

In the first place, and as noted above, market actors do not have an ethical purpose as their proximate end; rather, they have some commercial end, such as profit maximization. The ultimate end is one provided for by the invisible hand. Market actors pursue (individual and collective) self-interest, and – by virtue of the workings of the invisible hand – the material well-being of the society is provided for. In this respect market actors are unlike, say, doctors or hospitals. The latter can reasonably be required to have the promotion of life and health at the forefront of their concerns, that is, as their proximate as well as ultimate (professional and institutional) ends.

Economic self-interest, especially when linked to social status and power, is a powerful driver, and establishing markets in previously non-market economies, as well as deregulating previously heavily regulated market economies, has unleashed a great deal of hitherto dormant human energy. Moreover, the modern corporation as an institution, and the development of global financial markets, has enabled the mobilization of vast capital sums in the service of this human energy. (They have, of course, in turn relied heavily on scientific and technological developments.) One has only to visit Shanghai today and remember what it was like 20 years ago to appreciate the power of market forces (especially government-assisted market forces).

However, from an ethical point of view, the *institutionally structured* self-interested orientation of market actors – including corporations – may well give rise to an immediate problem. How is this institutionally structured impetus and habit of pursuing economic self-interest to be contained within reasonable limits and channeled in appropriate directions? Presumably, this is in part to be achieved by means of some mix of self-regulation and external regulation. However, it is also predicated on the guiding ethico-conceptual frameworks (as opposed to prevailing ideologies) and related self-understandings of these market actors. At any rate, this brings us to a second set of problems.

It is one of the principal tasks of those who design and oversee the market system, including governments and – under the direction of governments – regulators, to ensure that the ultimate purposes of markets (and, therefore, market actors) are in fact achieved, that is, to contain

and channel the pursuit of economic self-interest. Perhaps there is a lack
of clarity in the collective minds of governments and regulators in relation to their role in this regard. Politicians these days sometimes talk as
if the market were an intrinsic good, that is, good in itself and independently of its outcomes in terms of human material well-being – market
fundamentalism. But on the view elaborated above, markets need to be
conceived in purely instrumentalist terms; they are simply a means to an
(ultimate) end (even if this is not the end to be pursued by the market
actors themselves).

   Moreover, if one looks, for example, at the objectives of many
regulators, one typically finds only limited aims, such as to reduce crime
and protect consumers, and procedural concerns, such as to promote
competition and efficiency. There is little or no reference to what I have
been referring to as the ultimate ends of markets, that is, the outcome
the invisible hand is supposed to bring about. Rather, the image of regulation is one in which regulators are umpires whose sole job is to impartially enforce the rules of the game. But in games, the pleasure of playing
aside, there is only one end, namely, winning, and this is an end pursued
by the players not the umpires. But here the analogy between markets
and games breaks down; markets, unlike games, have an end beyond
"winning"; they have ultimate, as opposed to proximate, ends. In the
case of markets, "winning," for instance, making a profit, is only a proximate end and, as such, a means to a further and larger purpose, namely,
the material well-being of the society (both national and, in the case of
international financial markets, global).

   Further, there is the problem mentioned above of the ambiguous role
of national governments and regulators when it comes to global markets,
including global financial markets. National governments and their
regulators are to some extent partisan, and (understandably) seek to
look after the economic interests of their own industries and businesses,
including their financial service providers. Moreover, in the absence of
a uniform set of global regulations and a single global regulator with
real authority, regulators operating at a national level can be played off
against one another by multinational corporations.

   In the case of the global financial sector, regulation and integrity assurance are ultimately in the hands of national governments.
However, national governments – and their regulatory authorities – are
not simply umpires; they are also players in the financial – and, more
generally, corporate – "game." For example, the U.K. government –
and its financial regulator (the Financial Services Authority) – cannot

be expected to regulate entirely impartially in the interests of ethical ends and principles, given the substantial interest the U.K. government has in ensuring that the U.K. corporate and financial sector retains and increases the benefits accruing to it from global financial markets.

A third set of problems confronting the establishment of an integrity system or systems for some market actors, perhaps especially corporations and financial service providers, pertains to the so-called gate-keepers. For example, auditors conduct audits to determine financial propriety and performance, and enable disclosure thereof to regulators and shareholders. Again, credit rating agencies award AAA ratings to provide investors with independent guidance. However, in many cases auditing firms and credit rating agencies have had conflicts of interests; auditors conduct consultancies for the firms that they audit, and credit rating agencies are paid by the very banks whose toxic financial products they gave AAA ratings to.

Perhaps there is a fourth problem pertaining to various specific unethical practices, such as insider trading and conflicts of interest, one that derives in part from the decoupling of ultimate ethical purposes from the self-understanding of market actors, and from the regulation of market actors by governments and their regulatory agencies.

Perhaps fair competition is the ethical issue here? But competition in the corporate sector is inevitably unfair; appeals to fairness may (reasonably enough) carry little moral weight. Rather, the substantive moral objection to insider trading is presumably that in the long run if enough people practice it, then it undercuts the ultimate, not simply the proximate, ends of the corporate sector. Without compliance with a set of rules or laws that promote competition, the market will not deliver the outcomes promised by the invisible hand. However, this ultimate purpose of markets is not in the forefront of the minds of market actors, preoccupied as they are, and need to be, with the proximate ends of generating profit or maximizing shareholder value. This is perhaps especially the case in the financial services sector. For this sector is arguably at a double remove from the ultimate purposes of the market as a whole; in accordance with the invisible hand it seeks to provide finance to firms that in turn – and again in accordance with the invisible hand – generate the products actually required for the material well-being of the wider society. But if this ultimate purpose is lost sight of – in the self-understanding of market actors and in the policy making of and regulation by governments and regulators – then perhaps insider trading is bound to be viewed by market actors as much less serious an ethical (as opposed to legal) offence than in reality it is.

A fifth set of issues arise from various perverse incentives that can exist in local and global markets, including financial markets. Competition, including competitive markets, can and does provide discipline to market actors. However, this is not necessarily or always the case. Consider the so-called tragedy of the commons in which everyone pursuing their self-interest destroys the environment. Again consider bribery. It might be the case that for most corporations in some sector bribing officials is necessary to be competitive, given that even a small number of other corporations will engage in this practice. Compliance with a legally enforced ethical principle might be in a market actor's self-interest, but only if the enforcement mechanisms are such that everyone (or most) comply. Similarly, there might be competitive pressure to invest in unethical corporations, given the highly lucrative returns, and given that one's competitors are doing so. Again, when liability does not appropriately track ethical responsibility this can lead to perverse incentives. An incentive structure, for example, in which market actors are allowed, indeed, encouraged, to take great financial risks with other people's money to achieve enormous financial benefits for themselves (and not simply for the investors and shareholders), yet can do so without commensurate legal and financial liability attaching to themselves in the event of things going wrong, is surely tailor-made for corruption. Accordingly, there is a need for institutional redesign of a kind that either decreases the potential financial benefits to such market actors, or increases their liability, or introduces some mixture of both.

More generally, the collective responsibilities of industries to realize their institutional purposes, including the collective responsibilities of financial service providers in capital markets, typically consist of highly dispersed individual responsibilities that attach to individual persons within firms, individual firms within the industry, institutions without the industry, and so on. The collective responsibility, for example, to lower the cost of capital is not one that can be discharged by any one, or even a small group, of market actors within a given capital market. Given the diffuse character of such collective responsibilities – and its attendant incentive structure – many industries, financial service providers included, will not discharge these collective responsibilities, and, as a consequence, these industries will not adequately realize their institutional purposes. Hence the need (and resultant responsibility) on the part of governments in particular to intervene to adjust these incentive structures and, if necessary, to design in appropriate institutions or subelements thereof.

Perverse incentive structures can be addressed by recourse to interventions that reconfigure the incentive structures (Rose-Ackerman 1999). Such interventions can take the form of solving jurisdictional problems in global settings, and increasing enforcement options and/or the intensity of enforcement. Thus Joseph Stiglitz (Stiglitz 2006) suggests that "Any country in which the corporation (or the substantial owners of the corporation) has assets should provide a venue in which suits can be brought or in which enforcement actions to ensure payment of liabilities can be undertaken. The corporation may incorporate where it wants, but this should not make it any less accountable for its actions in other jurisdictions" (Stiglitz 2006, 206–28). Stiglitz has other suggestions in this regard. In addition, he suggests global widening of the possibility of class action in relation to corporate price fixing. While obviously of great importance, these jurisdictional and enforcement methods are not always sufficient. Other options are themselves market based, such as to reduce supply of a product or service by factoring in real costs (and requiring that they be paid), reduce demand for a product by high sales tax, or limiting availability. Some of these options involve ambitious innovations to the market system itself, including the global financial system. For example, Stiglitz has proposed a radical extension of the concept of Special Drawing Rights to create a new global reserve currency that would help stabilize financial markets and make reserves available for wealth creation projects in impoverished countries, increasing literacy, reducing poverty-related diseases, addressing global warming, and other "ultimate" market ends (Stiglitz 2006, chap. 9). Still other options are based on the importance of reputation to the self-interest of market actors; for example, ethics reputational indices might be established to seek to draw attention to their unethical practices or orientations. Here, as elsewhere, it might be useful to deploy a strategy of mobilizing the link between self-interest and good reputation.

A sixth and final cluster of problems derives in part from the foregoing ones and pertains to education, ethos, and ideology. If the prevailing ethos or culture of an organization, and perhaps even ideology of central elements of a sector, downplays ethical considerations in favor of self-interest, then it should hardly surprise when self-interest overrides compliance with ethical principles, even ones enshrined in the law. This is no doubt especially the case in a context of high temptation and opportunity, on the one hand, and low risk of detection

and conviction, on the other, for instance, insider trading in some corporate settings. The point here is not that the majority of individuals
themselves engage in corrupt or unethical practices, but rather that
in certain cultural or ideological contexts they may well refrain from
reporting or otherwise preventing a minority from doing so. Many
key elements of integrity systems, such as ethics codes, codes of practice, education programs, and the like, do not exist for the most part
directly to prevent or deter the few people who are wrongdoers from
doing wrong, but rather to ensure that the many are intolerant of the
wrongdoing of the few. In this context it is perhaps worth pointing out
that most fraudsters are detected and convicted as a consequence of
the disclosures of their colleagues.

## 6. CONCLUSION

In this chapter I have argued that as a consequence of their lack of
any intrinsic normative character, markets and business organizations
should be viewed in purely *instrumental* terms; and the job of normative
theory becomes that of providing such organizations with a contextu-
ally appropriate purpose, such as, in some cases at least, the provision of
needed material goods for the society at large.

I have utilized my individualist, teleological theory of social institutions to outline a normative account of the media, including identifying the moral purposes that are internal to it. I have also detailed
a process of corrosion or corruption that is taking place and that is
in large part a function of the market-based framework in which the
media as an institution now operates. I suggest that the contemporary
media is in danger of becoming predominantly a set of consumer-
focused business enterprises, rather than an adequately functioning
Fourth Estate.

Finally, I have focused on a second set of contemporary business
corporations, namely, financial service providers. These are global
institutions of enormous influence. However, they suffer from a fundamental defect, particularly from the perspective of my teleological normative theory of social institutions; as they stand they do not
have a coherent and guiding institutional purpose. To claim that the
ultimate purpose of the institution of the modern corporation – a
product, if ever there was one, of institutional design – is, for example, simply and only to maximize profits or shareholder value is, on
this ends-based, that is, *teleological*, account of social institutions, to

confuse proximate with ultimate purposes. Thus the proximate end of corporate financial service providers in capital markets might be to maximize shareholder value, but the ultimate purpose is something beyond this, for example, to make capital available at reduced cost to productive firms. Here there is a need for theoretical articulation and practical implementation.

# 11

# Institutions and Information and
# Communication Technology

Technical developments in information and communication technology in conjunction with the twin processes of globalization and the deregulation of markets have in recent times led to the establishment of what might be regarded as a relatively new form of social institution, namely, one that is both trans-societal and technology-centered. The Internet is perhaps the most obvious candidate. I doubt that such socio-technical systems ought to be regarded as social institutions per se. Rather, I view them as akin to rail and other transport systems, that is, complex technical systems that serve human collective ends, but that are not in themselves constituted by human action (as is necessarily the case with social institutions). On the other hand, such technical systems are clearly in part constitutive of some social institutions, such as a university's intranet, and in the case of information and communication technology, this appears to be increasingly so (Friedman 2007).

In this chapter I undertake two main tasks.[1] First, I apply my collective end theory (Miller 2001b, chaps. 2 and 5) of joint action and my individualist, teleological account of social institutions, and their associated technical notions of joint procedures, joint mechanisms, and collective ends, to the institutional processes of the acquisition of certain forms of social knowledge.[2] The focus here is on analyzing the communication, storage, and retrieval of knowledge by means of information and communications technology (ICT) in terms of the teleological model and, more specifically, the collective end theory. Second, I apply my theory of

---

[1]  An earlier version of the material in this section appeared in Miller (2008a).
[2]  So my task here is in within the general area demarcated by, for example, Alvin Goldman (1999).

collective responsibility to the communication, storage, and retrieval of morally significant knowledge by means of ICT.

Accordingly, we need to distinguish between the genus, joint action, and an important species of joint action, namely, what I will call joint *epistemic* action. In the case of the latter, but not necessarily the former, participating agents have epistemic goals, that is, the acquisition of knowledge.

We also need to distinguish between actions, whether individual, joint, or epistemic actions (including joint epistemic actions), that do not make use of technology and those that do. For example, A and B might travel to work together by walking. Alternatively, A and B might travel to work together by taking a train. Again, A might communicate to B the proposition that A is not going to work today, and do so by uttering the English sentence "I am not going to work today." Alternatively, A might send an e-mail to B to this effect. The latter, but not the former, speech act involves the use of technology, as was the case with traveling together by train.

So there are two major hurdles for the attempt to apply my teleological theory of social institutions and my collective end theory of joint action to joint epistemic action that makes use of technology – and specifically of ICT. The first hurdle is to see how the communication, storage, and retrieval of knowledge could reasonably be conceived of as joint action at all. The second hurdle is to see how the communication, storage, and retrieval of knowledge by means of ICT in particular could reasonably be conceived of as joint action.

Likewise, there are two major hurdles for my attempt to apply my account of collective moral responsibility to joint epistemic action that makes use of ICT. The first hurdle is to see how agents could be collectively responsible for the communication, storage, and retrieval of morally significant knowledge. The second hurdle is to see how agents could be collectively responsible for the communication, storage, and retrieval of morally significant knowledge by means of ICT in particular.

## 1. JOINT ACTION AND ICT

As we know, joint actions are actions involving a number of agents performing interdependent actions to realize a collective end (Miller 2001b, chap. 2). (See Chapter 1.)

Recent developments in ICT have greatly extended the range of joint actions. For example, new forms of joint work have arisen, such as

Computer Supported Collaborative Work (CSCW or Groupware) (see, e.g., Bentley et al. 1997). Workers located in different parts of the world can over lengthy time periods function as a team working on a joint project with common goals. The workers can make use of a common electronic database, their communications with one another via e-mail and/or video-teleconferencing can be open to all, and the contributing actions of each can be a matter of common knowledge, for example, via a Basic Support for Cooperative Work (BSCW) Shared Workspace system. Moreover, there can be ongoing team discussion and a coordinated team response to problems as they arise via such systems.

Again, as we saw in Chapter 1, basic joint actions can also be distinguished from joint procedures. An agent has a joint procedure to X, if he X's in a recurring situation, and does so on condition that other agents X. Moreover, joint procedures are followed to achieve collective goals, for example, to avoid car collisions. Joint procedures are, in fact, conventions (Miller 2001b, chap. 3).

As noted in Chapter 1, it is important to distinguish conventions from social norms. Social norms are regularities in action involving interdependence of action among members of a group, but regularities in action that are governed by a moral purpose or principle (Miller 2001b, chap. 3). For example, avoiding telling lies is a social norm.

Again, we can also distinguish between joint procedures (in the above sense) and joint mechanisms.[3] Examples of joint mechanisms are the device of tossing a coin to resolve a dispute and voting to elect a candidate to office.

In some cases, that these joint mechanisms are used might be a matter of having a procedure in my earlier sense. Thus, if we decided that (within some specified range of disputes) we would always have recourse to tossing the coin, then we would have adopted a procedure in my earlier sense. Accordingly, such joint mechanisms are joint *procedural* mechanisms.

Joint actions are interdependent actions directed toward a common goal or end, that is, a collective end (Miller 2001b, chap. 2).

An interesting feature of the above-mentioned CSCW systems is their capacity to structure preexisting relatively unstructured practices, such as group decision making, in the service of the collective ends of efficiency and effectiveness. For example, Group Decision Support Systems can provide for simultaneous information sources for the participants in the

---

[3] Joint procedures and joint mechanisms are not mutually exclusive.

decision-making process, ensure equal time for the input of participants, establish key stages and time frames for the decision-making process, and so on.

## 2. COMMUNICATION, INFORMATION, AND JOINT ACTION

Let me now consider a particular category of joint actions, namely, joint actions involved in the communication, storage, and retrieval of information. My concern is principally with various kinds of intentional linguistic communicative acts, and with various kinds of intentional cognitive or epistemic actions, namely, ones that purport to convey information. Here, by information I simply mean true propositional content, including what is only implicitly propositional content, for example, when I write my address on a form. Such information includes the contents of statements such as the "The world is flat" or "Thomas Friedman says the world is flat" or larger chunks of information such as a witness's formal statement to the police or the information held in an HR database on the employment history of all the current employees of some organization.

The communication of information is a fundamental human activity, and it includes, but is not restricted to, speech acts in ordinary face-to-face interaction. Specifically, the practice of communication of information has been transposed to communication and information systems, such as the Internet.

Communication of information in its simplest form involves a speaker (the communicator) and a hearer (the recipient of information) and meaningful content (what is communicated). (My use of the term *meaning* is intended to indicate that I do not have in mind unintentional communication or communication that is not transparent to the hearer.)

Roughly, the speaker intentionally produces an utterance to get the hearer to recognize that the speaker has as an end to get the hearer to believe some proposition p; this is the speaker's singular action. The hearer intentionally attends to the speaker's utterance in order to come to know the proposition the speaker has as an end that the hearer come to believe; this is the hearer's singular action. Moreover, there is a collective end: the hearer coming to know something, namely, that the proposition (whatever it is) that the speaker has as an end that the hearer come to know is a true proposition.

Note that the content of the collective end is not the proposition p per se; albeit the speaker has as an individual end that the hearer come to believe p (at least in many cases; see below). Note further that the realization of the collective end is something above and beyond the realization of either one of the singular intentions of the speaker and the hearer; its realization is not identical with the speaker producing an utterance and thereby getting the hearer to recognize that the speaker has as an end that the hearer believe p, nor with the hearer's attending to the speaker's utterance and thereby coming to know the proposition the speaker has as an end that the hearer come to believe. Finally, there is speaker and hearer common knowledge in relation to the performance of these singular actions and the existence of this collective end. So evidently acts of communicating information are joint actions. But let us get clearer on acts of communicating information.

I offer the following Gricean-style (Grice 1989b) analysis of the act of communication of information. Utterer U in producing utterance x communicates information to audience A, if and only if (1) U utters x having as an end that A come to know that the proposition expressed by x is true and A attends to x having as an end that A come to know that the proposition expressed by x is true; (2) U intends A to recognize U's end in (1) (in part on the basis of x); (3) A comes to know that the proposition expressed by x is true on the basis of (a) A's fulfilling U's intention (2) and (b) A's belief that speaker U has as an end to avoid producing a false belief in A.

Note that condition (3)(b) is the truth-aiming and trust element of communication of information. Note also that there will need to be a further condition attached to (3)(b), namely, that it is common knowledge between A and U that U intentionally provided a good reason for A believing that U intends to avoid producing a false belief in A. Condition (3)(b), in the context of this further common knowledge condition, provides for the "making out that what one says is true" element of the communication of information. Note finally that the analysis is consistent with the hearer coming to believe that some proposition is true without actually knowing what the content of the proposition is that he believes to be true. Indeed, even the utterer might not know what this content is.

So far so good for many, if not most, acts of the communication of information. But what of those communications in which the speaker intends the hearer to believe what is false or in which the hearer does not accept what the speaker says? In these cases, that the hearer receives information from the speaker is *not* the collective end of the speaker and hearer. So we need to make an adjustment in relation to our conception of the communication of information as joint action. That the hearer receive information from the speaker is, *normatively* speaking, the collective end of acts of communicating information. In short, the point of acts of communicating information is for the speaker to transmit information to the hearer. This is consistent with this collective end not being realized, or even not being pursued, on some occasions.

It might be argued that one cannot freely choose to believe a proposition and that, therefore, the hearer coming to believe some true proposition that the speaker has as an end that the hearer come to believe is not an action. Accordingly, communicating information is not a joint action, because one of the alleged individual actions, that is, the hearer's coming to believe some proposition, is not really an action. Doubtless, many comings to believe are not under the control of the believer, for instance, perceptual beliefs. However, many acts of judgment in relation to the truth of certain matters are akin to judgments in relation to what actions to perform. The hearer, I suggest, is typically engaged in an act of judgment in relation to what a speaker communicates for the simple reason that the hearer is engaged in a process of defeasible inference making, first, to the speaker's ends, intentions, and beliefs and, second, from those ends, intentions, and beliefs to the truth of the proposition communicated. In particular, the hearer knows that in principle the speaker might be engaged in deception, or might simply have made an error.

Deception is itself often an act of will; one can simply *decide* to tell a lie, for example. Accordingly, an audience needs to *trust* a speaker. Trust in this sense is not simply reliance; it is not simply a matter of the audience reasonably believing on the basis of, say, inductive evidence that the speaker will not tell a lie. For the speaker can make a decision to tell a lie on this occasion here and now, notwithstanding his history of telling the truth; and the audience knows this. So, at least in the typical case, the speaker over time in effect *decides* to trust the speaker; so there is a volitional element in the hearer's coming to believe. For this reason, if for no other, a hearer's coming to believe in the context of an act of communication of information of the kind in question is an action.

Moreover many, if not most, communications involve a process of reflective reasoning on what the speaker has asserted; this reasoning is in part a process of testing the truth and/or validity of the propositions being advanced by the speaker (and believed by the speaker to be true). Indeed, the speaker often expects the audience to engage in such reflection and testing.

The upshot of all this is that the speaker's coming to believe what the speaker asserts is a process mediated by an act of inferential judgment with an element of volition; for this reason the comings to believe in question are appropriately described as *the result* of a joint action, the main component actions of which are (a) the speaker's complex intention to get the hearer to believe some proposition and (b) the speaker's judgment that the proposition being advanced is true (a judgment based in part on the inference that the speaker intends the hearer to believe the proposition and would not intend to get the hearer to believe a false proposition).

It is consistent with this conception of communications as joint actions that communications, nevertheless, are joint actions in an importantly different – indeed, weaker – sense from joint actions that do not have as their collective end the transmission of cognitive states.

Moreover, linguistic communication – and linguistic assertion in particular – is joint action in some further senses. For one thing assertion normally involves conventions, that is, joint procedures. Thus, there is a convention to utter the word "Sydney" when one wants to refer to Sydney, and to utter "is a city" when one wants to ascribe the property of being a city.

Further, assertion is a joint action normally involving joint mechanisms and, specifically, joint institutional mechanisms. As we saw above, joint mechanisms have the characteristic of delivering different actions or results on different occasions of application. Typically, this involves a resultant action.[4]

Language in general, and assertion in particular, appears to consist in part of joint mechanisms involving resultant actions.[5] Assume that there are the following joint procedures in a community: utter "Sydney" when you have as an end reference to Sydney; utter "'Paris" when you have as an end reference to Paris; utter "is a city" when you have as an end ascription of the property of being a city; utter "is frequented by tourists" when you have as an end ascription of the property of being frequented by tourists. Then there might be the resultant joint action to utter "Paris is a city" when you have as an end ascription to Paris of the property of being a city; and there might be the second and different, resultant joint action to utter "Sydney is frequented by tourists" when you have as an end ascription to Sydney of the property of being frequented by tourists. It is easy to see how, by the inclusion of a conjunctive operation indicated by

---

[4]  Grice (1989, 129) first introduced this notion.
[5]  Grice (1989, 129–31) developed his notion of a resultant procedure (as opposed to a resultant action) for precisely this purpose.

"and," additional linguistic combinations might yield multiple additional resultant actions, for example, the communication effected by uttering "Paris is a city and Paris is frequented by tourists."

Although it is self-evident that, say, the English language is governed by a structure of conventions and social norms, it is perhaps less clear what purposes or ends it serves *qua* institution. Obviously, at the microlevel individual speakers and hearers have collective ends, such as the speaker, S, and the hearer, H, at spatiotemporal point, P, both have as a collective end that H understand what it is that S is intending to communicate.

However, there are a number of collective ends that all or most or many speaker-hearers of English have, and that constitute *institutional* ends. For example, each speaker-hearer has as an end that each be able – at least in principle – to communicate with each of the other speaker-hearers; for example, A wants to be able to communicate with B and C, but A also wants B to be able to communicate with C (and similarly for B and C). Moreover, each speaker-hearer has as an end that each be able – at least in principle – to understand what has been communicated in the past, including by at least some speaker-hearers who are no longer present; for example, present "audiences" want to be able to understand the information directories, autobiographies, and the Bible produced by past "speakers." Further, each speaker-hearer has as an end that the communications of each be able – at least in principle – to be understood in the future, including by some not yet existing speaker-hearers, and by some not yet existing speaker-hearers in circumstances in which they themselves are no longer in existence; for example, past "speakers" want the information directories, autobiographies, and the Bible that they produced to be understood by future "audiences."

Armed with this individualist, teleological account of communication as a species of joint action, I turn now to information and communication technology systems. I will consider three broad areas: communication of information, storage of information, and retrieval of information.

### 3. COMMUNICATION, STORAGE, AND RETRIEVAL OF INFORMATION BY MEANS OF ICT

As argued above, a communicative act is a species of joint action, and the practice of linguistic communication among a group of speaker-hearers an institutional practice (if not a social institution per se). Thus far we have considered only communication in face-to-face contexts. However, communication in written form is also joint action; it is simply that the relevant speaker-intentions are embodied in written, as opposed to spoken, form. Here we should also note that one and the same communication can be directed to multiple hearers. Moreover, the multiple hearers can constitute a single audience by virtue (at least in part) of their common knowledge that each is an intended audience of the assertion. Further, each of these multiple hearers, whether they collectively constitute a single "audience" or not, can "hear" the communication at different times and/or at different spatial locations. Indeed, written language enables precisely this latter phenomenon; a speaker can assert something to an audience that is in another part of the planet, such as by means of an air-mail letter, or, indeed, in another historical time period, such as an assertoric sentence written in a history book authored a hundred years ago. Finally, "a speaker" can consist of more than one individual human being. Consider a selection committee that makes a recommendation that Brown be appointed to the position in question. Each of the members of the committee is taken to be endorsing the proposition that Brown ought to be appointed. This endorsement is expressed in a written statement, let us assume, that is signed by each of the members of the committee. Note here that such an assertion made by a collective body is to be understood as involving a joint institutional mechanism in my above-described sense of that term. The input consists of each member of the committee putting forward his or her views in relation to the applicants, including the reasons for those views. The output consists of the endorsement of Brown by all of the members of the committee. The mechanism is that of deliberation and argument having as a collective end that one person is endorsed by everyone. Accordingly, there is no need to invoke mysterious collective agents that perform speech actions and have mental states, such as intentions, that are not simply the speech acts and mental states of individual human beings.

Once linguistic communications can be embodied in written form they can be stored in books and the like. Once stored they can be retrieved by those with access to the book storehouse in question. For example, assertions can be written down in book format and the resulting book stored with other such books in that well-known social institution known as a library.

Such communicative acts and structured sets of assertions and other speech acts, that is, books and other written documents, that are accessible in this way constitute repositories of social knowledge; individual members of a social group can come to know the propositions expressed in these written sentences, and can come to know that others know these propositions, that is, there is common knowledge of the propositions in question.[6]

Most important for our purposes here, such storage and retrieval of information in libraries and the like is an institutional arrangement serving collective ends, for example, the ends of the acquisition of common knowledge and of multiple "hearer" acquisition of knowledge. Moreover, the procedures by means of which such knowledge is stored and retrieved typically involve joint procedures (conventions) and joint procedural mechanisms. An example of this is classificatory systems used in libraries. The system itself consists in part of a set of conventions that ascribe numbers to designated subject areas and in part of an ascription to each book of a number, the latter number being based on matching the content of the book with one of the subject areas. However, both librarians and borrowers jointly use the system. The library staff store books in accordance with the system, and borrowers retrieve books in accordance with the system. So the input of the joint mechanism is the storage of a book in accordance with the classificatory system. The output is the retrieval of that book by means of the same system. Note that, in the case of paper-based books, there is a physical location (a shelf space) associated with each number and each book; each book is stored in and retrieved from that shelf space.

ICT systems, such as the Internet, enable assertions to be performed more rapidly and to far greater numbers of "hearers." In so doing, an important difference has arisen between such technology-enabled communication and ordinary face-to-face communication. In the latter case, the speaker and the hearer are simply performing so-called basic actions, that is, actions that they can perform at will and without the use of a mediating instrument or mediating technology. Like raising one's arm, speaking is in this sense a basic action, albeit in the context of an audience a basic joint action. On the other hand, driving in a screw by means of a screwdriver, or sending an assertion by e-mail, is not a basic action in this sense (Goldman 1999, chap. 6).

As we shall see below, the fact of this technological intermediary, ICT, raises issues of moral responsibility in relation to the design, implementation, maintenance, and use of this technology-enabled communication, issues that do not, or might not, arise for face-to-face acts of assertion. Consider, for example, the possibility of communicating instantaneously to a large number of people or of filtering out certain addresses and

[6] On the concept of common knowledge see, e.g., Heal (1978).

communications. At each of these stages there is joint action, such as that of the team of designers. Moreover, there are new conventions and norms, or new versions of old ones, governing these joint actions at each of these stages, for example, the norm not to continue to send advertisements to an e-mail recipient who has indicated a lack of interest.[7]

ICT also enables the storage and retrieval of databases of information and the integration of such databases to constitute ever larger databases. Such electronic databases enable the generation of new information not envisaged by those who initially stored the information in the database, for example, by combining elements of old information. Such generation of new information on the part of a "retriever" can be an instance of a joint procedural mechanism.

Consider a large database of police officers in a police organization. The database consists of employment history, crime matters reported and investigated, complaints made against police, and so on. A large number of people, including police and administrative staff, have stored, and continue to store, information in this database. This is joint action. Moreover, when another police officer accesses the database for some specific item of information, this is also joint action; it is, in effect, an assertor informing an audience, except that the assertor does not know who the audience is, or even if there is to be an audience.

Now consider a police officer engaged in an anti-corruption profiling task. He first constructs a profile of a corrupt police officer, for example, an officer who has at least five years police experience, has had a large number of complaints, works in a sensitive area such as narcotics, and so on. At this stage the officer uses an ICT search engine to search the database for officers that fit this profile. Eventually, one police officer is identified as fitting the profile, say, Officer O'Malley. This profiling process is the operation of a joint procedural mechanism. First, it relies on the differentiated, but interlocking, actions of a number of agents, including those who initially stored the old information from which the new information is derived, and the anti-corruption officer who inserted the profile into the search engine. Moreover, as is the case with all joint *procedural* mechanisms, this profiling process is repeatable and repeated; for example, different profiles can be and are searched for. Second, the new information, namely, that O'Malley fits the profile, is the resultant action; it is derived by means of the profiling mechanism from the inputs of the profile in conjunction with the stored data. However, that O'Malley

---

[7] On moral problems of computerized work environments, including what he calls "epistemic enslavement," see van den Hoven (1998).

fits a certain profile is not in itself part of the profiling mechanism per se. Third, there is the profiling mechanism itself.

The resultant action of the use of the profiling mechanism is akin to the resultant action of the use of a voting system and to the resultant action involved in ascribing a property to the subject referred to in a subject-predicate sentence. As with the voting and the ascription of a property cases, at one level of description identifying O'Malley was an intentional action, that is, it was intended that the person(s) who fits this profile be identified. (As it was intended that the person with the most votes win the election; and it was intended that Paris be ascribed the property of being a city.) At another level of description it was not intended, that is, it was not intended or known that O'Malley would fit the profile. (As it was not intended by all the voters that Jones win the election; and it was not intended by the *audience* that he or she comes to believe that the speaker believes that Sydney is a city, given that the speaker has [a] referred to Sydney and [b] ascribed the property of being a city.)

A further example of a joint procedural mechanism in ICT is a so-called expert system (Cass 1996). Consider the following kind of expert system for approving loans in a bank. The bank determines the criteria, and weightings thereof, for offering a loan and the amount of the loan to be offered; the bank does so for a range of different categories of customer. These weighted criteria and associated rules are "designed-in" to the software of some expert system. The role of the loan officer is to interview each customer individually to extract relevant financial and other information from them. Having extracted this information, the loan officer simply inserts it as input into the expert system. The expert system processes the information in terms of the weighted criteria and associated rules designed into it, and provides as output that the customer does or does not meet the requirements for a loan of a certain amount. (Naturally, the decision whether or not to approve the loan is an additional step; it is a decision based on the information that the customer meets, or does not meet, the requirements for being offered a loan.) The loan officer then tells the customer his loan request has either been approved or not approved, based on the information provided by the expert system. I am assuming that the overall context of this scenario is customers and banks seeking to realize a collective end, namely, the provision of bank loans to appropriate customers.[8] This is a series of joint actions involving

---

[8]  I will ignore the inherent elements of conflict; for example, some customers who want loans are unable to afford them, banks often want to lend at higher rates of interest than customers want to pay.

information input from customers and the application of criteria to that information by the bank. However, it is also the application of a joint procedural mechanism, because there is differentiated, but interlocking, input (information from the customer, application of criteria on the part of the bank) and a derived resultant action (customer does or does not meet the requirements for a loan) that can, and does, differ from one application of the mechanism to the next. In our example the joint procedural mechanism has been embodied in the expert system.

### 4. COLLECTIVE RESPONSIBILITY FOR THE COMMUNICATION, STORAGE, AND RETRIEVAL OF INFORMATION

Let me now apply my account of collective responsibility to the communication, storage, and retrieval of knowledge.[9]

Before doing so we need to recall the discussion of collective moral responsibility in Chapter 4. Specifically, we distinguished four senses of individual responsibility and four counterpart senses of collective responsibility, namely, natural, institutional (including responsibility based on occupying a position of institutional authority over other persons), and moral responsibility.

In Chapter 4 we also made the following important claim in relation to collective moral responsibility in particular: If agents are collectively responsible for the realization of an outcome, in the first or second or third senses of collective responsibility, and if the outcome is morally significant, then – other things being equal – the agents are collectively morally responsible for that outcome, and can reasonably attract moral praise or blame, and (possibly) punishment or reward for bringing about the outcome.

As is by now evident, I reject the proposition that nonhuman agents, such as institutions or computers, have mental states and can, properly speaking, be ascribed responsibility in any noncausal sense of that term. Specifically, I reject the notion that institutions per se, or computers, can legitimately be ascribed moral responsibility, either individual or collective moral responsibility.[10] Accordingly, in what follows I am going to locate moral responsibility for morally significant communication, storage, and retrieval of information with individual human beings.

---

[9] The material in this and the following sections is derived from Miller (2001b, chap. 8).
[10] For an outline of this kind of view, see Ladd (1988).

Moral responsibility for epistemic states is importantly different from moral responsibility for actions as such. Nevertheless, it is legitimate to ascribe moral responsibility for the production of morally significant epistemic states. In particular, it is legitimate to ascribe collective moral responsibility for morally significant epistemic states that are, at least in part, the collective ends of joint actions, for example, of assertions and other communicative acts.

Many epistemic states are, or ought to be, dependent on some rational process such as deductive inference. In this sense the epistemic state is "compelled" by the evidence for it; there is little or no element of volition. Accordingly there is a contrast with so-called practical decision making. The latter is decision making that terminates in an action; the former is inference making that terminates in an epistemic state.

However, this contrast can be exaggerated. For one thing, the compulsion in question is not necessarily, or even typically, such as to guarantee the epistemic outcome; nor is it necessarily, or even typically, a malfunction of the process if it does not guarantee some epistemic outcome. For another thing there are, or can be, volitional elements in inference making that terminates in epistemic states; we saw this above in relation to an audience's decision to trust in a speaker's sincerity.

At any rate, my general point here is that theoretical reasoning is sufficiently similar to practical reasoning for it to be possible, at least in principle, to ascribe responsibility to a theoretical reasoner for the epistemic outcomes of their theoretical reasoning. One can be held responsible for the judgments one makes in relation to the truth or falsity of certain propositions, given the need for conscientious inference making, unearthing of facts and so on. Therefore, one can be held morally responsible for such judgments, if they have moral significance.[11]

Clearly many such judgments have moral significance in virtue, at least in part, of the truth or falsity of the propositions being communicated and/or the sincerity of the communicator. Lying and making defamatory claims, for example, are regarded by many as basic forms of moral wrongdoing. Moreover, in those cases where the lie or the defamation is perpetrated by a number of individuals acting together, for example, a defamatory newspaper article, then the moral responsibility will be joint or collective moral responsibility.

---

[11] I accept the arguments of James A. Montmarquet (1993, chap. 1) to the conclusion that one can be *directly* responsible for some of one's beliefs, that is, that one's responsibility for some of one's beliefs is not dependent on one's responsibility for some action that led to those beliefs. In short, doxastic responsibility does not reduce to responsibility

And there can be moral responsibility for negligence with respect to the truth (so to speak). Consider a scientist who comes to believe that the universe is expanding, but does so on the basis of invalid, indeed, very sloppy, calculations. Such a scientist would be culpable in a further sense if he communicated this falsity to others or stored the data in a form accessible to others. Moreover, a second scientist who retrieved the data and came to believe it might also be culpable if, for example, he failed to determine whether or not the data had been independently verified by other scientists.

Now, suppose that it is not an individual scientist who engages in such invalid and sloppy work, but a team of scientists. This is an instance of collective moral responsibility for scientific error. Again, there would be culpability in a further sense if the team communicated the falsity to others, or stored the data in a form accessible to others. Moreover, other scientists who retrieved the data and came to believe it might also be culpable if, for example, they failed to determine whether or not the data had been independently verified by other teams of scientists.

A further category of morally significant data is information in respect of which there is, so to speak, a duty of ignorance. This category may well consist of true propositions. However, the point is that certain persons ought not to have epistemic access to these propositions. Examples of this are propositions governed by privacy or confidentiality rights and duties. Again, if these violations are jointly perpetrated by a number of individuals, then the moral responsibility will be collective responsibility.

So a person can reasonably be held morally responsible for coming to believe, communicating, storing, or retrieving false propositions where the basis for this ascription of moral responsibility is simply the moral significance that attaches to false propositions; other things being equal, falsity ought to be avoided. In addition, a person can reasonably be held morally responsible for coming to believe, communicating, storing, accessing, or retrieving true propositions in respect of which he or she has a duty of ignorance. Moreover, such moral responsibility can be individual or collective responsibility. What of beliefs that are morally significant only because they are necessary conditions for morally unacceptable actions or outcomes?

---

for actions. However, if I (and Montmarquet) turn out to be wrong in this regard, the basic arguments in this chapter could be recast in terms of a notion of doxastic responsibility as a form of responsibility for actions.

Moral responsibility for adverse outcomes is sometimes simply a matter of malicious intent; it is in no way dependent on any false beliefs. Suppose that A fires a gun intending to kill B and believing that by firing the gun he will kill B. Suppose further that A does in fact kill B, and that it is a case of murder. A's wrongful action is dependent on his malicious intention. It is also dependent on his true belief; however, there is no dependence on any false beliefs. Here it is by virtue of A's malicious intention that his action is morally wrong and he is morally culpable.

Now assume that A does not intend to kill B, but A nevertheless kills B because A fires the gun falsely believing that it is a toy gun. Here A is culpable by virtue of failing to ensure that he knew that the gun was a toy gun. That is, it is *in part* by virtue of A's epistemic mistake that he is morally culpable. A did not know that it was a real gun, but he should have known this.

Let us consider a similar case, but this time involving a third party who provides information to A. Suppose C asserts to A that the gun is a toy gun and that, therefore, if A "shoots" B with the gun, A will not harm, let alone kill, B. Agent A has reason to believe that C is telling the truth; indeed, let us assume that C believes (falsely) that the gun is a toy gun. C is at fault for falsely asserting that the gun is a toy gun. However, A is also at fault for shooting B dead, albeit in the belief that it was a toy gun. For A should have independently verified C's assertion that the gun was a toy gun; A should not simply have taken C's word for it. Indeed, the degree of fault A has for killing B is not diminished by the fact that C informed A that it was a toy gun.

Now consider a scenario similar to the above one, except that C is a doctor who gives A some liquid to inject into B. B is unconscious as a consequence of having been bitten by a snake, and C asserts sincerely, but falsely, to A that the liquid is an antidote. Assume that the liquid is in fact a poison and that B dies as a consequence of A's injection of poison. Assume further that the snake venom is not deadly; it would have only incapacitated B for a period. C is culpable by virtue of his epistemic error; he is a doctor and should have known that the liquid was poison. What of A? He relies on his belief that C's assertions in relation to medicine are true; and that belief has a warrant, namely, the fact that C is a doctor. Presumably, A is not morally culpable, notwithstanding his epistemic error.

However, consider the case where C is not a doctor but is, nevertheless, someone with a reasonable knowledge of medicines, including antidotes; he is a kind of amateurish "doctor." Here we would be inclined, I take it, to hold that both A and C were jointly morally responsible for B's death. For whereas A was entitled to ascribe to C's assertion a degree of epistemic weight, he was not entitled to ascribe to it the kind of weight that would enable him (A) to avoid making his own judgment as to whether or not to inject the liquid into B.

The upshot of the discussion thus far is that in relation to harmful outcomes arising from avoidable epistemic error on the part of more than one agent, there are at least three possibilities. First, the agent who *directly* – that is, not via another agent – caused the harm is individually and fully culpable, the culpability in question being negligence. Second, the agent who *directly* caused the harm is not culpable. Third, the agent who *directly* caused the harm and the agent who *indirectly* caused it (by misinforming the agent who directly caused it) are jointly culpable. The question remains as to whether each is fully culpable, or whether their responsibility is distributed and in each case diminished. Here I assume that there can be both sorts of case.

Thus far we have been discussing situations involving harmful outcomes arising from avoidable epistemic error. But we need also to consider *some* cases involving harmful outcomes that have arisen from true beliefs. Assume that an academic paper describing a process for producing a deadly virus exists under lock and key in a medical library; the contents of the paper have not been disseminated, because there are concerns about bioterrorism. Assume further that the scientist who wrote the paper decides to communicate its contents to a known terrorist in exchange for a large amount of money. The scientist is morally culpable for communicating information, that is, true propositions. This is because of the likely harmful consequences of this information being known to terrorists in particular. Here we have the bringing about of a morally significant epistemic state for which an agent is morally culpable; but the epistemic state in question is a *true* belief.

So there is a range of cases of morally significant epistemic states for which agents can justifiably be held morally responsible, and these include epistemic states for which agents can justifiably be held collectively morally responsible.

This being so, it is highly likely that in some cases the individual and collective responsibility in question will not only be for the communication of false beliefs, but also for the storage and retrieval of false data. Given that speakers can be, individually or collectively, morally responsible for communicating falsehoods that cause harm, it is easy to see how they could be morally responsible for storing falsehoods that cause harm.

For example, a librarian who knows that an alleged medical textbook contains false medical claims that if acted on would cause death might, nevertheless, choose to procure the book for her library and, thereby, ensure that it will (a) be read and (in all probability) (b) be acted on with lethal consequences. What of responsibility for the retrieval of information?

Let us recall the example of an academic paper describing a process for producing a deadly virus that exists under lock and key in a medical library; the contents of the paper have not been disseminated because there are concerns about bioterrorism. Now suppose that in exchange for a large amount of money the librarian (not the scientist who wrote the paper) forwards a copy of the paper to a known terrorist.

I have been speaking of moral culpability for morally significant communication, storage, or retrieval of information; however, the moral significance has consisted of the harmfulness attendant on the communication, storage, or retrieval of the information in question. Naturally, moral responsibility could pertain to morally *desirable* communication, storage, and retrieval of information.

### 5. COLLECTIVE RESPONSIBILITY FOR THE COMMUNICATION, STORAGE, AND RETRIEVAL OF INFORMATION BY MEANS OF ICT

Thus far I have provided an account of collective responsibility for the communication, storage, and retrieval of information. Finally, I turn to the special case of collective moral responsibility for the communication, storage, and retrieval of information by means of ICT.

We have already seen that assertions are a species of joint action, and in the case of morally significant assertions, speakers and audiences can reasonably be held collectively morally responsible for the comings to believe consequent on those assertions. Insofar as ICT involves the communication, storage, and retrieval of morally significant assertions, users of ICT who are speakers and audiences can likewise reasonably be held collectively morally responsible for the comings to believe consequent on those computer-mediated assertions.

Expert systems provide a somewhat different example. We saw above that many expert systems are joint procedural mechanisms. In cases in which the resultant action of a joint mechanism is morally significant, then those who participated in the joint mechanism can reasonably be held collectively morally responsible, albeit some might have diminished responsibility, and others full responsibility. Thus voters can be held responsible for the fact that the person with the most votes was elected. Likewise, the customers and the bank personnel – including those who determine the criteria for loan approvals – can be held collectively morally responsible for a loan being approved to, say, a person who later fails to make his or her payments. And the police who enter data into a police database, the police who develop and match profiles against stored data, and the senior police who orchestrated this profiling policy can be held collectively morally responsible for the coming to believe on the part of some of the above that, say, O'Malley fits the profile in question. Naturally, the degree of individual responsibility varies from officer to officer, depending on the precise nature and extent of their contribution to this outcome.[12]

An additional point in relation to moral responsibility and expert systems is that the designers of any such system can, at least in principle, be held jointly morally responsible for, say, faults in the system or, indeed, for the existence of the system itself. Consider a team that designs a computerized delivery system for nuclear weapons.

In conclusion, I make two general points in relation to moral responsibility and ICT expert systems in particular. First, there is an important distinction to be made between the application of mechanical procedures, whether by humans or computers, on the one hand, and the *interpretation* of moral principles, laws, and the like, on the other hand. This point is in essence a corollary of the familiar point that computers and other machines do not mean or interpret anything; they lack the semantic dimension. So much John Searle (1984) has famously demonstrated by means of his Chinese rooms scenario. Moreover, computers do not assert anything or come to believe anything. Specifically, assertions and propositional epistemic states are truth-aiming and, as such, presuppose meaning or semantics. To assert that the cat is on the mat, the speaker has to refer to the cat and ascribe the property of being on the mat. However, asserting that the cat is on the mat is an additional act to that of meaning something in the sense of expressing some propositional content by, say, uttering a sentence.

---

[12] There are a host of other issues of moral responsibility raised by expert systems, including in relation to the responsibility to determine who ought to have access to what sources of information. The provision to library users of computer-based information directly accessible only to librarians is a case in point, e.g., sources of information potentially harmful to third parties. For a discussion of these issues, see Ferguson and Weckert (1993).

At any rate laws, but not mechanical procedures, stand in need of interpretation and, therefore, require on occasion the exercise of interpretative judgment. The law makes use of deliberately open-ended notions that call for the exercise of discretion by judicial officers, police, and so on, for example, the notion of reasonable suspicion. And some laws are deliberately framed so as to be left open to interpretation – so-called fuzzy laws. The rationale for such laws is that they reduce the chances of loopholes being found, loopholes of the kind generated by more precise, sharp-edged laws. Moreover, laws often stand in need of interpretation in relation to situations not encountered previously or not envisaged by the lawmakers. Consider a well-known South African case in which a policeman arrested a man for speaking abusively to him over the phone, claiming the offence had been committed in his presence. The court ruled that the place at which the offence was committed was in the house of the defendant and that therefore the crime had not been committed in the presence of the policeman. So the ruling went against the police officer. But it was not obvious that it would. At any rate the interpretation of laws is not always a straightforward matter, yet it is a matter that will be adjudicated. Accordingly, judicial officers, police, and, indeed, citizens necessarily make interpretative judgments that can turn out to be correct or not correct. There is no such room for interpretative judgment in the case of mechanical procedures. Either the procedure applies or it does not, and, if it is not clear whether or not it is to be applied, the consequence is either recourse to a default position, for example, it does not apply, or to a malfunction. The implications of this discussion are (a) many laws are not able to be fully rendered into a form suitable for mechanical application and (b) expert systems embodying laws might need additional ongoing interpretative human expertise. Accordingly, such expert systems ought to be designed so that they can be overridden by a human legal expert.[13]

Second, conformity to conventions, laws, and mechanical procedures, on the one hand, is importantly different from conformity to moral principles and ends. It is just a mistake to assume that what morality requires or permits in a given situation must be identical with what the law requires or permits in that situation, much less with what a mechanical procedure determines.

As was argued in Chapter 9, the law in particular and social institutions more generally are blunt instruments. They are designed to deal

---

[13] For more detail on this kind of issue, see Kuflik (1999).

with recurring situations confronted by numerous institutional actors over relatively long periods of time. The law, therefore, consists of a set of generalizations to which the particular situation must be made to fit. This general point is even more obvious when it comes to mechanical procedures.

By contrast with the law and with mechanical procedures, morality is a sharp instrument. Morality can be, and typically ought to be, made to apply to a given situation in all its particularity. Accordingly, what might be, all things considered, the morally best action for an agent to perform in some one-off, that is, nonrecurring, situation might not be an action that should be made lawful, much less one designed in to some computer or other machine. The implication here is that by virtue of its inherent particularity moral decision making cannot be fully captured by legal systems and their attendant processes of interpretation, much less by expert systems and their processes of mechanical application of procedures. Moral decision making has an irreducibly discretionary element. Accordingly, expert systems embodying moral principles ought to be designed so as to be able to be overridden by a morally sensitive human being, if not by a human moral expert (Kuflik 1999).

## 6. CONCLUSION

In this chapter I have applied the collective end theory of joint action and the individualist, teleological model of social institutions, and their associated technical notions of joint procedures, joint mechanisms, and collective ends, to the institutional processes of the acquisition, storage, retrieval, and dissemination of certain forms of social knowledge, and especially those relying on information and communication technology. In addition, I have applied my theory of collective responsibility to the communication, storage, and retrieval of morally significant knowledge by means of ICT.

# 12

# Government

## 1. GOVERNMENT AS A META-INSTITUTION

As we have seen, according to my individualist, teleological theory of social institutions, the ultimate justification for the existence of fundamental human institutions such as government, the education system, the economic system, and the criminal justice system, is their provision of some collective good or goods to the community[1] (see also Miller 2001b, chap. 6).

Moreover, these collective goods are, normatively speaking, the collective ends of institutions, and as such they conceptually condition the social norms that govern, or ought to govern, the constitutive roles and activities of members of institutions, and therefore the deontic properties (institutional rights and duties) that attach to these roles. Thus, a police officer has certain deontic powers of search, seizure, and arrest, but these powers are justified in terms of the moral good – legally enshrined human rights, say – that it is, or ought to be, the role of the police officer to maintain.

It is also worth reiterating that there is no easy rights versus goods distinction. Human rights certainly function as a side constraint on the behavior of institutional actors. But equally, the securing of human rights can be a good that is aimed at by institutional actors.

Further, a defining property of an institution is its substantive functionality (or *telos*), and so a putative institutional entity with deontic properties, but stripped of its substantive functionality, typically ceases to be an institutional entity, at least of the relevant kind; would-be surgeons who cannot perform surgery are not surgeons. Equally, would-be police

---

[1]  The material from the opening two sections is derived from Miller 2001b, chap. 4.

officers who are incapable of conducting an investigation, or who cannot make arrests or exercise any form of authority over citizens, are not really police officers. Here, by "substantive functionality," I have in mind the specific defining ends of the institution or profession. In the case of institutions, including professions, the defining ends will be collective ends; they will not in general be ends that an individual could realize by his or her own action alone. In short, the theory of institutions, and of any given institution, is my *teleological* theory.

Moreover, as noted earlier, institutions in general, and any given institution in particular, require both a *descriptive* teleological theory, and a *normative* teleological theory.

Thus far I have spoken in terms of the theory of institutional action where institutions have been taken to be different and separate "entities." However, there is also a need for a theoretical account of the *interrelationships* between different institutions. There is some evidence that in recent decades in the Western liberal democracies, public-sector institutions have been unacceptably weakened as a consequence of policies coming under the banner of so-called economic rationalism (Chapters 8, 9, and 10). Such policies include the privatization of law enforcement agencies and prisons, and the outsourcing by government of administrative functions and computing services. More specifically, after 9/11 the doctrine of institutional separation has to an extent been undermined, notably in the United States, as a consequence of a shift in power in favor of the executive at the expense of the legislature (Dean 2007). The so-called war on terrorism has provided a pretext for this executive overreach. I will return to this issue in the final section of this chapter.

As far as the *nature* of the relationship between institutions is concerned, on our teleological account this is to be determined primarily on the basis of the extent to which the differential defining collective ends of institutions are complementary rather than competitive, and/or the extent to which they mesh in the service of higher-order collective ends. In this connection, consider the complementary ends of the institutional components of the criminal justice system, namely, the police (a collective end to gather evidence and arrest suspects), the courts (a collective end to try and sentence offenders), and the prisons (a collective end to punish, deter, and rehabilitate offenders). Again, consider the complementary (collective) ends of the legislature, the executive, and the judiciary in the liberal democratic state.

However, I also need to reiterate the point that I made in the Introduction to this book – a point that I believe has been evidenced in many of the normative accounts of particular social institutions in Part B – namely, that social institutions are not necessarily to be understood as the constitutive elements of a holistic, for example, organicist, conception of a society. For one thing, many social institutions are trans-societal or trans-national, for example, the international financial system. For another thing, the normative reach of many social institutions, such as universities and many media organizations, goes beyond the society or nation in which they are located.

In times of institutional crisis, or at least institutional difficulty, problem-solving strategies and policies for reform need to be framed in relation to the fundamental ends or goals of the institution or set of complementary institutions, which is to say they need to be contrived and implemented on the basis of whether or not they will contribute to transforming the institution or institutional structure in ways that will enable it to provide, or better provide, the collective good(s) that justify its existence.

As far as the institution of government is concerned, I note three important respects in which it is to be distinguished from many other institutions.

Firstly, government is a meta-institution. We have seen that many social institutions are organizations or systems of organizations. For example, capitalism is a particular kind of economic institution, and in modern times capitalism consists in large part in specific organizational forms – including multinational corporations – organized into a system. I have also noted that some institutions are *meta-institutions:* they are institutions (organizations) the principal activities of which consist of organizing other institutions. One such important meta-institution is government. The tasks of a contemporary government consist in large part of organizing, including designing and redesigning, other institutions (both individually and collectively). Importantly, governments have as a collective end to see to it that other institutions realize their specific collective ends, for example, that universities pursue the collective end of knowledge acquisition and dissemination. More generally, governments have as a collective end to see to it that other institutions function in the interests of the community as a whole. Thus governments regulate and coordinate economic systems (see Chapter 10), educational institutions (see Chapter 8), and police organizations (see Chapter 9) and do so, or ought to do so, in the public interest.

Here I note that since many social institutions are not society or nation specific, the role of governments in terms of regulation and coordination of another institution is not necessarily bilateral (so to speak) or even one-many. It may be that many governments need to be involved in the regulation and coordination of a single social institution, such as the global capital market system.

Naturally, in claiming that governments are meta-institutions I do not want to deny that governments ultimately govern individual citizens; for certainly they do. However, in large part contemporary governments govern individual citizens *indirectly* via some other institution, for instance, the tax office or the police. Indeed, the edifice of laws enacted by successive governments in respect of the actions of individual citizens is itself an institutional arrangement that intercedes between government and citizen.

A second important property of governments is their vulnerability to collective acceptance. Consider Peter Sellars in the movie *Being There*. Sellars plays the role of a gardener who for various reasons begins to be treated by the staff of the president, and ultimately by everyone, as if he were the president of the United States. Eventually, he might even have run for office and be elected. Unfortunately, he has no understanding of the political system, or of relevant policies, and has no leadership qualities whatsoever. Nevertheless, it seems to be the case that the gardener is, or has become, the president by virtue of collective acceptance.

Institutional authorities are vulnerable to a degree that other institutions, such as language, are not. As Searle points out, the communist government of the Soviet Union turned out to have clay feet (Searle 1995, 91). Once people chose not to obey its directives, it was finished; it simply ceased to function or exist as a government. However, it is difficult to see how many other institutions such as, for example, the English language could go out of existence in such spectacular fashion; for it depends on millions of often disconnected communicative interactions between millions of different people.

There is a reason for the vulnerability of institutional authorities, especially political authorities. In the special case of institutional authorities deontic properties are *ontologically dependent* on collective acceptance: no collective acceptance, no deontic properties. The point here is not simply that, say, rulers cannot *exercise* their right to rule if their right to rule is not collectively accepted. Rather, a ruler does not even possess a *right* to rule unless she is able to exercise authority over her subjects. This seems to be a general feature of the deontic properties of those in authority (whatever kind of authority they might possess), and of political authorities in particular.

I note that this point concerning the vulnerability of political institutions by virtue of their ontological dependence on collective acceptance needs to be distinguished from consent-based theories of government, for example, the representative theory of liberal democratic government. The latter (of which more below) is a specific normative theory of one species of government; the former is a property of all governments, consent-based or otherwise.

A third important property of government is its use of coercive force and, specifically, the normative claim that government is entitled to a monopoly on the use of coercive force on pain of a return to the state of nature. Here we do not have to accept Hobbesian contractarianism or other unpalatable forms of authoritarianism. What is uncontroversial is that contemporary liberal democratic governments govern largely by way of *enforceable legislation* and could not do otherwise. (What is also uncontroversial is that there are moral limits on governmental power, and the moral legitimacy of governments – and therefore their right to legislate and to use coercive force to enforce the law – depends in part on their respecting those limits. I return to this latter point below.)

In the discussion of police institutions (Chapter 9) I argued that the principal collective end of police organizations was the protection of justifiably enforceable, legally enshrined, moral rights. The requirement that the justifiably enforceable moral rights be legally enshrined ties the institution of the police to the institution of government and, in particular, to the legislature. The police exist in part to enforce the laws the government introduces and, specifically, those laws that embody justifiably enforceable moral rights.

However, there are many laws that do not appear to embody justifiably enforceable moral rights. Many of these laws prescribe actions (or omissions), the performance (or nonperformance) of which provides a social benefit. Consider the laws of taxation. The benefits provided by taxation include the provision of roads and other services to which arguably citizens do not have a basic moral right, and certainly not a justifiably enforceable moral right (see Chapter 9 for a discussion of the notion of basic moral rights in play here). On the other hand, taxes also enable the provision of benefits to which citizens do have justifiably enforceable moral rights, for instance, medicine for life-threatening diseases, basic welfare, and so on.

I argued in Chapter 9 that certain legally enshrined moral rights are justifiably enforced by police, as are laws that indirectly contribute to the securing of these rights. The moral rights in question are justifiably enforceable moral rights. But, to reiterate, there are many laws that are not of this sort. Many of these latter laws are fair and reasonable, and the conformity to them enables collective goods to be provided. But what is the justification for their enforcement by police? I will shortly argue that the fact that they provide collective benefits, and/or that they are fair and reasonable, does not of itself provide an adequate justification for their enforcement. Perhaps consent to the enforcement of just and reasonable laws that enable the provision of collective benefits provides an adequate moral justification for such enforcement. Here there is an issue with respect to the degree and type of enforcement that might be in this way justified; deadly force may not be justified, even if it is consented to in relation to fair and reasonable laws that enable collective benefits to be provided. Moreover, as is well known, there is a problem in relation to consent. Evidently there is not in fact explicit consent to most laws, and the recourse to tacit consent seems not to offer a sufficiently strong and determinate notion of consent.

At any rate, I want to make two preliminary points here in relation to what is nothing more than a version of the traditional problem of the justification for the use of coercive force by the state to enforce its laws.[2] First, self-evidently there is no obvious problem in relation to the enforcement of laws that embody *justifiably enforceable* moral rights, including human rights. Moreover, there may well be other laws that can justifiably be enforced (up to a point) on the grounds that not only are they fair, reasonable, and productive of social benefits, but in addition citizens have consented to their enforcement (up to that point).

Second, I want to suggest that, notwithstanding our first point, there are fair, reasonable, and socially beneficial laws with respect to which enforcement is not morally justified. Further, there may not be an adequate justification for enforcement of some of these laws, even if enforcement were to be consented to. The reason for this is that the nature and degree of enforcement required to ensure compliance with these laws – say, use of deadly force – is not morally justified.[3] Certainly recourse to deadly force – as opposed to nondeadly coercive force – is not justified

---

[2]  See Dworkin (1998, 190). There are questions here in relation to the *exclusive* right of the state to enforce moral rights. Arguably, the state has only an exclusive right to punish, but not an exclusive right to enforce in the narrow sense of protection against rights violations.

[3]  This is consistent with there being a moral obligation to obey these laws; we are speaking here of the justification for the *enforcement* of such laws. For an account of the moral justification for obeying the law, see Miller (2001b, 141–51). See also Luban (1988, chap. 3).

in the case of many unlawful actions; specifically, unlawful actions not regarded as serious crimes. Indeed, this point is recognized in those jurisdictions that have made it unlawful for police to shoot at many categories of "fleeing felons" (see Miller and Blackler 2005, chap. 3). It is more often than not now unlawful, because immoral, to shoot at, say, a fleeing pickpocket.

Before turning to a detailed discussion of the problem of political obligation, the problem of the moral justification for obedience to the law, I need to discuss the moral limits placed on government by virtue of human rights, on a certain conception of human rights. As I have just mentioned, it is morally unacceptable for police to shoot at a fleeing pickpocket. The reason for this is that pickpockets – like everyone else – have a basic moral right to life, and that right to life is not forfeited or even suspended merely by virtue of committing a crime of petty theft. (Indeed, as will become clear shortly, I do not hold to a forfeiture account of human rights.)

Moreover, I want to press an additional point here. In my view the right to life is inalienable, as is the right to freedom. Accordingly, neither a pickpocket nor anyone else can extinguish, by consent or otherwise, their right to life or their right to freedom. Naturally, the right to life and the right to freedom can be overridden under certain circumstances; indeed, I hold the view that these rights can even be suspended under certain circumstances. However, these rights cannot be alienated. Thus no one is able to forfeit their right to freedom by selling themselves into slavery.

Let me now briefly discuss my claim that human rights, in particular, can be suspended before returning directly to the issue of the moral limits placed on government by human rights. We saw in Chapter 9 that any right not to be killed, right to freedom, or other basic moral right that an individual might have is dependent on, or in some way linked to, that individual's discharging his or her obligation not to violate the rights of others. The further suggestion that I want to make here is that the linkage in question has to be relativized to the offender and his or her victim. This relativization reflects the different structure of moral relations that holds between a third party, the offender, and the victim, on the one hand, and that holds between the offender and victim, on the other hand.

In a case of self-defense, the defender is not obligated to respond to the life-threatening attack in a way that a third person is obligated to respond. One's legitimate interest in one's own life, and the responsibility for it, is different from another person's legitimate interest in, or responsibility for, one's life. Similarly, in a murder scenario, the victim is not under an obligation to punish the offender in the way in which a third party, including the state, might be obligated to punish. And so a victim, but not necessarily a third party, can forgive an offender.

Given these considerations, I suggest the following fault-based internalist (suspendable) rights-based theory (FIST) (Miller 1993). You have a right not to have your basic moral rights infringed by me, and I have a concomitant obligation not to infringe your rights. However, you suspend your rights if you satisfy the following conditions: (1) you infringe my right(s) or threaten to infringe my right(s); (2) you intentionally infringe my right(s) (or form the intention to do so), and you are responsible for doing so (or at least for forming the intention to do so); and (3) you do not have a strong and decisive moral justification for infringing my right(s) (or intending to do so), and you do not, with respect to a strong and decisive moral justification for infringing my right(s), believe that you have it, and believe this with good reason.

According to this view, each person, X, has a set of suspendable moral rights, including the right not to be killed and the right to various freedoms. Thus, X has a right not to be killed by Y, a right not to be killed by Z, etc. X also has a set of suspendable obligations not to kill – X has an obligation not to kill Y, an obligation not to kill Z, etc. Here X's right not to be killed generates an obligation on the part of Y, Z, etc., not to kill X; X's right to be free generates an obligation on the part of others not to infringe his freedoms, and so on.

These rights are such that when one member of the set of rights is suspended, the other rights (with their concomitant obligations) remain in force. Thus if A's right not to be killed by B is suspended, then B no longer has an obligation not to kill A. However, A still has a right not to be killed by C, and thus C's obligation not to kill A remains in force.

It must also be noted that the basic moral rights in question, including the right not to be killed, cannot only be suspended but can also be overridden. So, although A might still have a right not to be killed by C, it might be the case that it is morally permissible for C to kill A. This would be the case were A's right not to be killed by C overridden (but not suspended).

According to FIST, the fact that a victim stands in a different way to an offender than a third party does makes a crucial difference to the kind of moral justification available to the third party for intervening to harm the offender. This is so, whether it involves preventing a rights violation or punishing a rights violator. The third party, including the state, has a choice – if he can decisively intervene either to prevent the rights infringement or to punish the offender – between two sets of rights infringement, one with a moral justification and the other without a moral justification. From the point of view of the third party, both the victim and the offender have a right not to have their rights infringed, and consequently the third party has a strong obligation not to harm the offender (or the victim). However, the third party has a choice between harming an offender and allowing an innocent person's rights to be infringed (the victim) and go unpunished. In such a case the third party ought to choose to protect the rights of the would-be victim or to redress the wrong done by punishing the offender. Here the third party's obligation not to infringe the rights of the offender is not suspended; rather, it is overridden. The duty of the third party to protect the rights of the would-be victim or to redress the wrongs done to that person, coupled with the fact that the offender is at fault, is generally sufficient to override the offender's rights.

At this point I explicitly invoke, on the one hand, the Lockean idea of persons in a so-called state of nature transferring to the state *some* of their rights in exchange for enhanced protection of their basic rights more generally. For example, persons in a state of nature hand over their prior right to punish rights violators; and victims, in particular, transfer to the state their prior right to punish those whose rights have been suspended by virtue of them having violated the rights of the aforesaid victims. They do so in order that their basic rights to life and freedom are better protected than in the state of nature. Crucially, they do not transfer, or otherwise alienate, their basic rights to the state. They retain the right to life and to various freedoms, and these rights are suspended only in the circumstance that the rights bearer in question violates some other person's rights.

It follows from this broadly Lockean conception of human rights that there are moral limits on government, and they are of two general kinds. First, there are those limits that exist by virtue of the *contingent fact* that citizens have not authorized (legitimately consented to) the government to act outside those limits. Hence a democratic government cannot, or ought not to, embark on a protracted war without the consent of the citizenry. (This is consistent with a government acting in self-defense in the context of an unexpected armed attack and, then, seeking and gaining retrospective authorization to do so.) If it does so, it is going beyond what it has been authorized to do. Second, there are those (theoretically more restricted) limits that exist by virtue of the inalienability of some basic moral rights, such as the right to life and the right to freedom; these limits exist because governments *could not be authorized* by their citizens to exceed them. Thus there is no circumstance in which a liberal democratic government could legitimately be authorized to enslave its citizenry; for instance, if a majority or even all of the citizens consented to enslavement, this would not provide a legitimate authorization.

## 2. SOCIAL NORMS AND LAWS

In Chapter 1 I outlined an account of social norms according to which social norms are regularities in behavior to which agents conform because they believe that they have a duty to conform or that they otherwise morally ought to conform (Miller 1997a, 2001b, chap. 4). Given this account of social norms it is easy to see why citizens feel they ought to obey many of the laws of the land, and in particular criminal laws. For the criminal law is an explicit formulation (backed by penal sanction) of the most basic of a society's social norms. Citizens believe that they ought not to flout the laws against murder, theft, rape, assault, and so on, because these citizens have internalized a system of social norms that proscribes such behavior. Putting matters simply, for the most part any given citizen does not commit murder in part because he or she believes it is wrong for him or her to murder, and in part because others believe it is wrong for him or her to murder.

Unfortunately, there are some citizens who have not internalized the system of social norms, or who have not sufficiently internalized that system. Accordingly, there is a need to buttress the system of social norms by the construction of a criminal justice system. The latter system involves the detection of serious moral wrongdoing, and the trial and punishment of offenders.

This account of compliance with laws explains why citizens feel an obligation to obey the criminal law, but it does not provide a justification for an objective obligation to obey the criminal law. Nor does it explain the felt obligation – let alone any objective obligation – to obey laws which are not criminal laws.

Let me deal with the former problem first. Any objective obligation to obey the criminal law will be based on the objective moral merits of the specific criminal laws in question. For example, there is an objective moral obligation to obey the law against murder because the social norm proscribing murder is not only a subjectively felt obligation, it is also an objective moral obligation deriving from the human right to life. The criminal law, the social norm, and the objective moral principle coincide. Moreover, many, if not all, such laws are justifiably enforceable by virtue of the seriousness of the moral breach that flouting such laws entails. So it is a short step, as we saw in Chapter 9, to infer that such laws are justifiably enforceable by the police in particular.

How do matters stand when a given criminal law does not coincide with a relevant objective moral principle? In the case where the criminal law in question infringes some central moral principle or right then there is no moral obligation to obey the law. For example, in South Africa under apartheid it was a criminal offence under the Immorality and Mixed Marriages Act for persons belonging to different race groups to have sexual relations with one another or to get married.

However, in other cases there might still be an obligation to obey criminal laws that do not infringe important objective moral principles, or that infringe only relatively minor objective moral principles. For example, in some states of Australia it is a minor criminal offence to possess marijuana. Arguably, such criminal laws – although they ought to be repealed because they unnecessarily restrict certain freedoms – do not violate any important rights. So perhaps such criminal laws, while unjustifiable, ought to be obeyed. I suggest that if such laws ought to be obeyed, they ought to be obeyed in virtue of a general obligation to obey the law generated by other considerations. What other considerations? Considerations that generate the objective obligation to obey laws that do not embody moral (or immoral) principles, that is, much of the non-criminal law. In other words, we have come to our second problem. In the remainder of this section I will offer a detailed treatment of this problem and the various attempts to deal with it.

It has proved difficult to provide the required rational underpinning for this felt moral obligation to obey the law. For example, theories in terms of consent to obey the law seem unable even to get to first base; most citizens have simply never consented to obey the law. More recently, Hart (1973) and Rawls (1964) have developed the so-called argument from fair play. Roughly the idea is that (many) laws should be construed as mutually beneficial cooperative schemes. But if so, it is unfair to disobey the law when one has accepted its benefits; as a beneficiary one is under a moral obligation to obey the law even if it is not in one's interest to do so.

However, the argument from fair play has come under attack, including from Robert Nozick (1974, 90) and John Simmons (1979, 101), and these attacks have in turn provoked a reworking of the argument by David Luban. In this section I criticize Luban, but do so with an eye to improving the argument from fair play. My discussion makes use of the teleological account of social institutions and, especially, the Collective End Theory developed in Chapter 1.

Luban in his influential book *Lawyers and Justice* (1988, 35–49) argues that the justification for a moral obligation of citizens to obey at least some laws – laws that are not evil, unfair, or hopelessly stupid (Luban 1988, 35) – lies in the fact that each of these laws constitutes an important, or at least, reasonable, cooperative scheme (Luban 1988, 41) for the members of the citizenry, and that to break such a law is unfair to those who obey it. It should be noted that even if Luban's argument demonstrates that there is an obligation to one's (law-abiding) fellow citizens to obey these laws, he has not shown that these law-abiding citizens have a right to enforce compliance with these obligations.

Luban mentions (Luban 1988, 38, 41) four conditions in his discussion of the moral obligation to obey a law: (1) the law is generally beneficial – the so-called generality requirement (Luban 1988, 43) to the effect that the law benefits citizens and does so in a fair and nondiscriminatory way, (2) most citizens comply with the law, (3) citizens accept the benefits of the law, (4) the law is an important, or at least reasonable, cooperative scheme.

Luban (1988, 38–39) claims that conditions 1, 2, and 4 are jointly sufficient to establish an obligation to obey a law.

Luban also argues against Simmons's claim (Simmons 1979, 125) that condition 3 is necessary. That is, Luban rejects the claim that there is an obligation to obey a law only if the person thus obligated had an opportunity to decline the benefit arising from that law, and chose to accept the benefit.

Simmons thinks (3) is necessary because being an active participant – as opposed to merely conforming to the law – is necessary, and (3) is a necessary condition for being an active participant.[4]

It is not clear whether Luban accepts Simmons's view that (3) is a necessary condition for being an active participant (hereafter, participant) in a law. What is clear is that Luban, in claiming that (1), (2), and (4) are jointly sufficient to generate an obligation to obey a law,

---

[4] Luban (1988, 38) and Simmons (1979, 122–5). According to Simmons, to be an active or real participant one must have at least tacitly consented or played some sort of active role in the cooperative scheme. Simmons (1979, 123).

commits himself to rejecting the proposition that being a participant is a necessary condition for having the obligation to obey a law (Luban 1988, 38).

Luban's initial point is that the benefits of most laws are in fact thrust on the citizen; citizens are in general not in a position to reject the benefits laws confer.

But the fact, if it is a fact, that the benefits of laws are thrust on citizens, does not in itself show that participating in laws is not necessary for being under the obligation to obey the law. In the first place, it might not be the case that a necessary condition for participation in a law is that there has been an opportunity to refuse the benefits.

In the second place, it might be that (a) participation is a necessary condition for having the obligation to obey the law, (b) there is no participation because the benefits of laws are in fact thrust on citizens, and therefore, (c) there is no obligation to obey the law.

Luban does not think he needs to *assume* that there is in fact an obligation to obey the law (Luban 1988, 39). He takes himself to have an argument against the claim that being in a position to decline benefits is a necessary condition for being obligated to a law. Indeed, he takes himself to have a further argument for the stronger claim that conditions 1, 2, and 4 jointly constitute a sufficient condition for having the obligation to obey the law. Let me now turn to Luban's arguments.

Luban argues that there are cases in which it is unfair to free-ride even though there is no opportunity of declining benefits (Luban 1988, 39). In such cases one is under an obligation not to free-ride. Luban's argument, if valid, would show that being in a position to decline benefits is not a necessary condition for having the appropriate obligation.

Luban puts forward a number of cases to try to demonstrate this point. One such case is that of failing to help clean up glass on one's street, and then making full use of the fact that the street has been cleaned up by others. (The street will be cleaned up by others whatever one does.)

This case is different, he suggests, from failing to assist others to plant and to tend flowers on the median strip of the street. (The case is similar to the street cleaning example in that the others will plant the flowers whatever one does, and one is not in a position to decline this benefit.)

Luban suggests that the difference is that in the first example it is essential that the street be cleaned. That is, Luban at this point introduces condition 4. More precisely, Luban suggests that the more important or reasonable a cooperative scheme is, the less it matters if the benefit received is actively accepted. Acceptance does not matter in the glass example, but does in the gardening example. In the glass example, but not the gardening example, free-riding is unfair and disrespectful to one's fellows (Luban 1988, 42).

Luban's examples demonstrate that being in a position to decline benefits is not a necessary condition for having the obligation to contribute to a cooperative scheme. However, I will argue that being in a position to decline benefits is not a necessary condition for being a participant in a cooperative scheme. Therefore being a participant may well be a necessary condition for being obligated to contribute to a cooperative scheme. Further, I reject Luban's view that the conjunction of conditions 1, 2, and 4 provides a sufficient condition for having the obligation to obey the law.

Before proceeding any further, it may be helpful to get clear about individuals' rights and obligations in the standard cooperative scheme. In such a scheme there are two levels of "activity": the level of contribution and the level of acceptance of benefits. Individuals perform a contributory individual action to realize a collective end (Chapter 1). In cooperative schemes the collective end consists of some good or benefit. In the case of laws, typically (although not invariably) the collective end can be realized without the participation or contribution of everyone, and the collective end realized is a collective good. (A collective good is one such that if it exists it is able to be enjoyed by everyone. Clean air is an example.) Accordingly, in the case of laws there is the possibility of free-riding.

In cooperative schemes, obligations and rights arise as follows. If an individual contributes to the scheme, then the individual has a right to the benefit. If an individual does not contribute, then he has no right to the benefit, unless by the consent of those who contributed to the provision of that benefit, for example, if they offer the benefit as a gift.

This gives rise to at least three possibilities. In two of these the agents fail to contribute.

First, there is the agent who both contributes and accepts the benefits. This agent is a standard participant and he is under an obligation to contribute.

Second, there is the bona fide nonparticipating agent who refuses to contribute and refuses the benefit. Such an agent is not under an obligation to contribute.

Third, there is the free-riding agent who always takes the benefits, and yet fails to contribute unless it is necessary in order for the scheme to succeed. He is under an obligation to contribute having taken the benefits.[5]

A problem arises in cases in which it is not possible (or not possible without considerable difficulty or hardship) for an agent to refuse the benefit provided by some cooperative scheme. Can agents be obligated to contribute to the scheme if they cannot refuse the benefits? Such problematic cases include Luban's flower example and his glass example.

In cases where agents are not in a position to decline a benefit, what makes any given person a bona fide nonparticipant – without rights to benefits or obligations to contribute – rather than a free-riding participant who wants to exercise a right to a benefit, but does not want to discharge his obligation to contribute? (Simmons 1979, 122).

What makes an agent a free-riding participant, as opposed to a nonparticipant, in such cases, is what makes an agent a free-riding participant in any case, namely, the fact that the agent would contribute if it were necessary to provide the benefit. The free-riding participant, unlike the nonparticipant, would contribute if he had to, for participants – whether free-riders or not – are committed to realizing the purpose or end of the cooperative scheme.[6] So Luban's flower example involves a nonparticipant and his glass example, a free-riding participant. And this is the reason, *contra* Luban, why the agent in the glass example, but not the flower example, is under an obligation to contribute to the cooperative scheme. The agent in the glass example, being a participant, is under an obligation to contribute.

It might be argued that in cases in which the benefit is imposed, there is no way of determining whether an agent is a free-riding participant or a bona fide nonparticipant.

I reject this argument. There is all sorts of evidence to distinguish free-riders from nonparticipants. There can be evidence for the agent's willingness to contribute if his contribution is necessary to realize the collective end of the scheme. For example, in the Luban glass case, if the free-rider has a expensive car with thin tires, needs to drive to work, and swept up glass the time before when most people were out of town, then we have evidence that he is a participant seeking to free-ride. (I will

---

[5] Such an agent needs to be distinguished from the exploiting nonparticipant, the agent who takes benefits whenever he can but never contributes even if it is necessary for the scheme to succeed. Such an agent is a parasite rather than a free-rider.

[6] Cooperative schemes are best understood as a species of joint actions; joint actions involve a collective end that can be achieved only by the actions of the individuals, each agent contributing only if the others do. See Miller (1992a, 1992b, and Chapter 1).

say more about the evidence for free-riding in relation to laws, below.)
Another kind of evidence would be the agent's attitude to the contributions of other agents. For example, in the Luban gardening example, if
the agent said nothing to the neighbors when he noticed that the flowers
were not being tended, and, indeed, were beginning to die off, then we
could assume that he was a nonparticipant in the cooperative scheme.
He is not prepared to do anything to rescue the scheme.

I conclude that although Luban has shown that being in a position to
decline a benefit is not a necessary condition for having the obligation to
obey the law, he has not shown that being a participant is not a necessary
condition for having the obligation to obey the law.

Let me now turn to Luban's view that taken together conditions 1, 2,
and 4 constitute a sufficient condition for generating an obligation to
obey the law. (Naturally, if 1, 2, and 4 are – jointly – sufficient, then being
a participant is not necessary.)

Condition 2 is that most citizens in fact comply with a law. If most people do not comply with a law, then the law is failing to realize its collective
end and it becomes difficult to see how under these circumstances an
individual could be under an obligation to obey it. So condition 2 looks
as though it must be a necessary condition for generating an obligation
to obey a law. What of conditions 1 and 4?

Luban terms condition 1 the generality requirement. This condition
amounts to Luban's above-mentioned requirement that a law be fair and
neither stupid nor evil. For presumably a cooperative scheme that is not
stupid, evil, or unfair is so in virtue of the following facts. First, it provides a benefit which outweighs the cost of contributing to it, and there is
no known and clearly preferable alternative way of securing the benefit.
Second, it benefits *everyone* and does not require anyone to contribute
a greater share than anyone else in relation to the benefit that person
receives.

Condition 2, taken in conjunction with condition 1, is not sufficient to
generate an obligation to contribute to a cooperative scheme. For, in the
first place, the benefit in question may be quite trivial, and contributing
to the provision of trivial benefits is not a matter of moral obligation.

In the second place, a given agent may well have some alternative
course of action that will provide him with some other benefit which may
be of greater importance to him than the benefit to be derived from participating in the cooperative scheme. It is not that the benefit provided
by the cooperative scheme is trivial. It is just that some other individually
attainable benefit is more important to that agent.

Are conditions 1 and 2, taken in conjunction with condition 4, sufficient to generate an obligation to obey the law? Condition 4 rules out trivial benefits. However, there is nothing in these three conditions to rule out the possibility of an agent who does not want to contribute to a cooperative scheme because he wishes to pursue some other individually attainable benefit which is of greater importance to him.

Suppose, for example, that the roads in some neighborhood become snowed over. The members of the community regularly go out and clear the snow off the roads. But suppose there is a somewhat reclusive composer who is actually prepared to forgo driving during the relatively short winter rather than see to it that the roads are passable. The composer's life would be made fairly difficult by impassable roads. For example, he would not get any fan mail, and would have to stockpile food. However, he would rather this than have to regularly perform the somewhat arduous and time-consuming task of shoveling snow.[7]

Sometimes an agent or agents have an obligation to conform to a scheme that burdens that agent or agents, but that significantly benefits another agent or agents. But such an obligation has little to do with the fairness of a cooperative scheme. Rather, it concerns the importance or moral value of the collective end realized by the cooperative scheme. Such obligations arise, especially, in cases of need – as opposed to desire for a benefit – and the greater the need, the greater the disadvantage one ought to be prepared to suffer to help fulfill that need. The need in question may belong to a majority or a minority of the participants in the scheme. In the latter case the collective end of the scheme does not consist of a collective good or benefit.

Suppose that in the snow clearing example it was known to the composer that some other members of the community needed access to a hospital in the city. There would now be an obligation on the members of the community, including the composer, to ensure that the roads were kept clear. But this has little to do with the fairness of contributing to a scheme from which one benefits. The composer is obliged to help the infirm, irrespective of the fact that to do so does not benefit him.

The upshot of this discussion is that there are (at least) two sorts of basis for an obligation to contribute to a cooperative scheme. There is the obligation, if any, deriving from the moral value or importance attaching to the collective end realized by the cooperative scheme. Fairness is

---

[7] This is not an example of the individual having an excuse for not contributing, as would be the case if he were ill or had to mind the children. See Luban (1988, 45).

the other basis of the obligation to contribute. The obligation of fairness derives from the fact that having become a participant in a cooperative scheme, and therefore a beneficiary of it, one is under an obligation to do one's part to realize that benefit.

In the case of some cooperative schemes, there is no moral obligation to become a participant. However, in some of these, if one is a participant, fairness demands that one contribute. In other cases it is morally incumbent on agents to secure some collective end, irrespective of whether the cooperative scheme that secures this end is a fair one. In still other cases considerations of both fairness and the moral value of the collective end of a cooperative scheme generate obligations to contribute.

I have argued that Luban fails to demonstrate that (a) being an active participant is not a necessary condition for being under an obligation to obey a law and (b) conditions 1, 2, and 4 are sufficient for generating the obligation to obey the law.

I have also argued that one source of Luban's problems is a failure adequately to accommodate the distinction between the fairness of a cooperative scheme and the value of the collective end that the scheme might realize. I want now to argue that a further source of Luban's problems is that his account is focused too narrowly on the individual law or cooperative scheme.

If the moral obligation to obey laws is to be properly understood whole structures of laws – whole structures of cooperative schemes – need to be considered. For if this is done it becomes clear that in many instances the apparently bona fide nonparticipant is actually a participant in the overall structure of cooperative schemes, but is nevertheless unfairly trying to opt out of certain individual constituent schemes. He is in reality a free-rider. He wants to opt out of those individual constituent schemes that benefit others but not him, although he expects others to participate in individual constituent schemes that benefit him but not them. In such cases the free-rider is involved in an inconsistency, and hence unfairness, across individual cooperative schemes. The law is a good example of such a system of cooperative schemes. Many laws benefit only some individuals. However, the issue is whether the whole system of laws on balance benefits everyone and to a reasonable extent. If so, then, failing to contribute in the case of a particular law may well be inconsistent and unfair to law-abiding citizens. Here breaking the law is simply a special case of unfair free-riding in a cooperative arrangement of the sort envisaged by Luban. As such, breaking the law will constitute a failure to discharge a moral obligation.

And there is this further point. It may be that the collective end realized by the whole structure of laws, say, the collective end of good order, may be so important that everyone is under an obligation to obey the law, even though the structure of laws is unfair. This is not to say that the importance of realizing the collective end of the system of laws might in some cases not be outweighed by the unfairness of that system.

How do we determine in relation to a given instance of law breaking whether it is a case of free-riding or of nonparticipation? In respect of law breaking we need to distinguish on the one hand, between individual law breaking and law breaking by collectives, and on the other between breakage of an individual law and rejection of the system of laws or of large fragments of a system. I have already suggested that in relation to fairness what is important is the whole system of laws. It is whether or not an individual or group participates in the *whole* system of laws that is important.

I suggest that in relation to systems of laws or large fragments of systems, there can be clear evidence that some group is essentially a nonparticipant being forced to participate. That group consisting of black South Africans provides one clear example of this. This does not show that with respect to *all* groups desirous of nonparticipation there could be evidence. Presumably there are instances where there could not be evidence. But in any society where a group has a strong desire not to participate, and where there is some space to vent opposition to the system of laws (or some large fragment of the system) there is likely to be such evidence. What of the individual in relation to the system of laws?

Let us set aside those laws which embody social norms and express moral prohibitions, such as laws against murder. I suggest that it is almost never the case that the set of the remaining laws of some legal system – or large fragments of the set of the remaining laws – are such that *one person only* (or even a handful of people) would rather not be a participant in those laws. Rather it is almost always the case that it is some *group* of individuals that would prefer not to participate. Typically such a group will consist of those individuals who are being burdened in various ways by the system of laws. But in that case in most situations where there is some space for groups to express their desire not to participate in the system of laws, the individual will be able to manifest his or her desire not to participate in that system of laws; he or she will be able to do so in consort with other individuals who have a similar desire.

In this section I have argued the following: (1) *contra* Luban, the notion of an active participant in a mutually beneficial cooperative scheme can be used to generate the obligation to obey the law, provided there is evidence that the participants would have complied with the law and accepted its benefits if this was necessary for the realization of the collective end of the cooperative scheme; (2) Luban fails to demonstrate that one is under an obligation to obey a law if the law is a generally beneficial and important cooperative scheme that most people comply with (but are not active participants in); (3) we need to distinguish between a moral obligation generated by the fairness of a law and one generated by the moral value of the collective end secured by a law, and accept that both kinds of moral obligation can be used to justify obedience to the law.

Finally, I return to the question of the enforcement of laws. In Chapter 9 we saw that some laws, for example, many criminal laws such as the law proscribing wrongful killing, directly embody moral obligations of great strength, indeed, justifiably enforceable moral obligations. It now turns out that some individual laws realize collective ends of great moral importance; given the importance of these collective ends, the enforcement of such laws is likely to be morally justifiable. Finally, it turns out that some systems of laws, or fragments of systems of laws, might realize collective ends of such importance that the enforcement of these constituent laws is justifiable, notwithstanding the fact that the enforcement of any one of these laws considered on its own is not morally justifiable. That said, it remains the case that there are significant limits on the extent of coercion that is justified to enforce any one of these laws on a single occasion. Perhaps it is legitimate to arrest someone who refuses to pay legitimately incurred speeding fines; but it could not be legitimate to use deadly force against such a person.

## 3. TERRORISM, STATES OF EMERGENCY, AND GOVERNMENTAL ABUSE OF POWER

The September 11, 2001, attacks on the World Trade Center in New York and the Pentagon in Washington, D.C., catapulted terrorism to the top of the U.S. political agenda and produced immediate and profound global consequences, not only politically and militarily, but also economically.[8] There have been a number of subsequent specific terrorist bombings of civilians, including in Bali in 2002, Madrid in 2004, London in 2005, New Delhi in 2005, and Mumbai in 2006. In addition, there have been ongoing terrorist attacks in a number of theaters of internecine

[8] Much of the material in this section is taken from (Miller 2008b).

war, including in Iraq, Kashmir, Sri Lanka, and the Israeli-Palestinian conflict in the Middle East. In some of these contexts there appears to be an escalation in the number of terrorist attacks, such as in Iraq. In other contexts there appears to be a ratcheting up of a given terrorist group's lethal capability; for example, in 2006 the Lebanon-based terrorist organization Hezbollah for the first time launched a series of rocket attacks on Israeli cities from Lebanon (to which the Israelis responded with bombing raids on Beirut and other Lebanese cities). These specific and ongoing attacks have ensured that terrorism remains in the international media headlines and at the world's political center stage.

The counter-terrorist response to Al-Qaeda on the part of the United States and its allies has taken place at a number of levels. There has been increased resourcing and restructuring of security forces, for example, the new Department of Homeland Security in the United States. There has been a ramping up of security measures and an increase in police powers. Airport security has been tightened, for example, there has been an increase in data collection and in monitoring and surveillance (some of it apparently unlawfully undertaken by the National Security Agency after being authorized by President Bush in breach of the Foreign Intelligence Surveillance Act, which prohibits warrantless domestic wiretappings),[9] and police have been given wider powers to detain without trial suspects or even nonsuspects who might have information. In addition, foreign nationals suspected of being terrorists have been incarcerated indefinitely, such as at Guantanamo Bay in Cuba. At a strategic military level, the United States has invaded Iraq and sent armed forces into Afghanistan to combat Al-Qaeda and its supporters in the Taliban.

The overall effects of these measures are difficult to determine (with some notable exceptions). Arguably, it now seems clear that the United States has exacerbated, rather than reduced, the problem of global Islamic terrorism by invading and occupying Iraq. Iraq has become a potent symbol of the U.S.-Islam confrontation as expressed by bin Laden and a breeding ground for terrorists.

Second, liberal democratic values and the rule of law have been significantly compromised by these measures. For example, the absolute ban on torture has been questioned by the Bush administration, and, indeed, torture has been practiced by the U.S. military in Abu Ghraib prison in Iraq. Moreover, in invading Iraq, President Bush clearly misled

---

[9] First reported in the *New York Times* in December 2005.

Congress and, as a consequence, was legally liable to impeachment even though this was unlikely for political reasons. In the United Kingdom there is provision for indefinite detention of suspects without bringing them to trial, if they do not have British citizenship and expelling them would present a real risk of their being tortured.[10] In Australia, new antiterrorist legislation (ASIO Bill No. 2) permits ASIO (Australian Security Intelligence Organisation) to detain and question persons who are not even suspects, if it is believed these innocents could provide relevant information.[11]

In short, recent acts of terrorism by Al-Qaeda and others have led to an abuse of governmental power on the part of the United States and some other liberal democratic states. President Bush sought to mask this abuse of executive authority by characterizing the threat of terrorism as a threat of cataclysmic proportions; apparently the threat of terrorism is so grave and so different as not to be able to be accommodated within a traditional liberal democratic institutional framework. In particular, he and his supporters, for example, his legal advisor John Woo, have sought to disparage the adequacy of the terrorism-as-crime framework in favor of a terrorism-as-war framework.

By contrast, I take it that the so-called terrorism-as-crime framework – as opposed to the terrorism-as-war framework – is the preferred and, therefore, default, framework when a liberal democratic state is suffering lethal attacks from a terrorist organization. More precisely, the terrorism-as-war framework should be applied only under the following general conditions:[12] (1) the terrorism-as-crime framework cannot adequately contain serious and ongoing terrorist attacks; (2) the application of the terrorism-as-war framework is likely to be able adequately to contain the terrorist attacks; (3) the application of the terrorism-as-war framework is proportionate to the terrorist threat; (4) the terrorism-as-war framework is applied only to an extent, for example, with respect to a specific theater of war but not necessarily to all areas that have suffered, or might suffer, a terrorist attack, and over a period of time, that is necessary; (5) all things considered, the application of the terrorism-as-war framework will have good consequences in terms of security, and

[10] Sections 21 to 32 of the Anti-Terrorism, Crime and Security Emergency Bill 2001 now allow detention without trial where the option of deportation is not available. Article 3 of the European Convention on Human Rights, to which the United Kingdom is a signatory, forbids torture and inhuman treatment. See Haubrich (2003, 15).
[11] See Lynch and Williams (2006, 33–4).
[12] These conditions mirror many of the conditions in the *ius ad bellum* of Just War Theory.

better overall consequences, for example, in terms of lives lost, freedoms curtailed, economic impact, institutional damage, than the available alternatives.

Accordingly, it is only when the liberal democratic state cannot adequately contain the terrorist activity of a specific terrorist organization that the terrorist-as-war model might need to be applied, for instance, in a theater of war involving ongoing, large-scale terrorist attacks and military counter-strikes by government security forces. The Israeli-Hezbollah conflict is arguably a case in point. Moreover, even if the terrorist-as-war model is to be applied in a given theater of war it would not follow that it should be applied outside that theater of war. Thus, even if it is desirable and necessary to apply the terrorism-as-war model to the armed conflict between Al-Qaeda combatants and U.S. forces in Afghanistan seeking to destroy Al-Qaeda military bases and personnel, it would not follow that it was desirable or necessary to apply it to Al-Qaeda operatives functioning in the U.S. homeland.

I further take it that, notwithstanding President George Bush's pronouncements, the United States is not literally at war with terrorism per se. For terrorism per se is not an organization, nor is a terrorist ideological movement necessarily an organization. Moreover, there are some terrorists and terrorist groups, for example, Timothy McVeigh (the Oklahoma City bomber), that are not the sort of entities that are able to conduct a war. Moreover, there are many terrorist groups – whatever their military capacity might be – that are simply not engaged in a war with the United States. It is obviously false that the United States is at war with all the dozens of disparate terrorist groups all over the world, Islamic and otherwise, and at war also with numerous nation-states that engage in terrorism, such as North Korea. Nor is the threat to the United States posed by Al-Qaeda in particular of the same order of magnitudes as (say) that posed by the Soviet Union in its heyday; the latter could have annihilated the United States at any time (albeit, thereby, assured its own destruction).

Let me, then, directly address the question: How should a well-ordered, liberal-democratic state respond to such a large-scale, one-off, terrorist attack by a nonstate actor during peacetime?

Such attacks should be treated, first, as disasters, and, as such, they call for the imposition of a legally circumscribed, geographically limited state of emergency during the period of the disaster and its immediate aftermath, but not beyond, and certainly not for a prolonged period. Second, if the terrorist actions in question are perpetrated outside a theater of war then they should be treated as crimes, that is, the most appropriate framework to apply is the terrorism-as-crime framework – as opposed to the terrorism-as-war framework.

My reason for preferring the imposition of a state of emergency and the application of the terrorism-as-crime framework to one-off, large-scale terrorist attacks is as follows. Such a terrorist attack is clearly a crime; the further questions are, first, whether it is also an act of war and, second, whether the terrorist attack has been undertaken in what was, or what now is, a theater of war. Here I am not disputing that the 9/11 attack by Al-Qaeda on the World Trade Center is assimilable to an act of war, given the nature, goals, and military capability of Al-Qaeda as an organization. Nor am I disputing the legitimacy of the U.S. military operations against Al-Qaeda in Afghanistan; Afghanistan is a theater of war, and U.S. forces are justifiably engaged in a military campaign to capture and kill Al-Qaeda terrorist-combatants. Whether or not a one-off, large-scale terrorist attack should be treated as an act of war depends in part on the nature, goals, and lethal capability of the person or persons that mounted the attack. However, I am disputing that by virtue of the 9/11 attack, New York became a theater of war. So my specific point here is that a single terrorist attack by a nonstate actor – even a large-scale attack – does not of itself constitute a war and, therefore, should not necessarily be regarded as having been undertaken in what was, or now is, a theater of war. Even if Timothy McVeigh's bombing in Oklahoma City had killed 3,000 people, it would not have meant that the U.S. was at war or that Oklahoma City had become a theater of war. Accordingly, such one-off, large-scale terrorist attacks do not in themselves warrant the application of the terrorism-as-war framework; the terrorism-as-crime framework will suffice.

In this respect such decisions are not different in principle from other one-off decisions made in relation to acute moral dilemmas arising from peacetime disasters. Some such decisions (made under a state of emergency) pertain to criminal actions, such as a government's decision to order police to shoot looters in the context of a flood disaster. Other decisions do not pertain to any criminal actions, such as a government's decision to order police to cordon off an area of a city to prevent the further spread of a pandemic, that is, to enforce a large-scale quarantine, with the consequence that those who are not infected but who live within the area cordoned off will very likely become infected and die.

The general points to be extracted here are fivefold. First, states of emergency should not be assimilated to theaters of war; although some areas declared to be under a state of emergency, for example, some regions under martial law, are theaters of war, many are not. Specifically, some contexts involving a one-off, large-scale terrorist attack, such as the Al-Qaeda attack on the World Trade Center, warrant the declaration of a state of emergency but are, nevertheless, not theaters of war.

Second, disastrous occurrences in liberal-democratic states in peacetime, including large-scale, one-off terrorist attacks, do not justify an increase in the *standing* powers (as opposed to the *emergency* powers granted for the limited period of the disastrous occurrence) of governments to order the use of, or security personnel to use, deadly force against offenders, terrorists or otherwise; and even disasters do not justify, for example, the granting to governments and/or security personnel of a legal power to deliberately kill innocent citizens.

Third, any imposition of a state of emergency must be comprehensively legally circumscribed in respect of (a) the geographical area in which it is in force and the time period, (b) the conditions under which it can be imposed (and the conditions under which it must be terminated), and (c) the precise powers granted to government and security agencies during the state of emergency. Moreover, the imposition of states of emergency, and the granting and use of emergency powers, must be subject to judicial oversight.

Fourth, notwithstanding the granting of emergency powers, the default framework to be applied domestically by well-ordered, liberal-democratic states to large-scale, one-off terrorist attacks is the terrorism-as-crime – not the terrorism-as-war – framework. For the terrorist attack and the security response to it do not constitute an internal war within the liberal-democratic state. (This is consistent with the application of the terrorism-as-war framework in the case of externally based terrorist groups to which the terrorism-as-crime framework has not been successfully applied by relevant external states.)

## 4. CONCLUSION

In this chapter I have applied my individualist, teleological theory to the institution of government and concluded that government is a meta-institution that has as a principal task the organization and maintenance of other social institutions for the public good. I have argued that there are significant moral limits on government by virtue of the moral rights of citizens, including inalienable moral rights.

In relation to the obligation to obey the law, I have suggested that many laws embody objective moral principles, and, therefore, there is a moral obligation to obey these laws. Moreover, in some case the moral obligations in question are justifiably enforceable.

Further, I have argued that *pace* Luban laws can be assimilated to cooperative schemes and, thereby, rendered explicable in terms of the Collective End Theory. In the case of some such schemes, there is no moral obligation to become a participant. However, in some of these, if one is a participant, fairness demands that one contribute. In other cases it is morally incumbent on agents to secure some collective end, irrespective of whether the cooperative scheme that secures this end is a fair one. In still other cases considerations of both fairness and the moral value of the collective end of a cooperative scheme generate obligations to contribute.

Finally, I have discussed a contemporary version of a historically familiar form of governmental corruption, namely, abuse of governmental power; in this instance the abuse of executive power by U.S. president George Bush in the context of recent terrorist attacks.

# Bibliography

Alderson, John. 1998. *Principled Policing*. Winchester, Mass.: Waterside Press.

Alexandra, Andrew, Tom Campbell, Dean Cocking, Seumas Miller, and Kevin White. 2006. *Professionalisation, Ethics and Integrity*. Sydney: Professional Standards Council.

Alexandra, Andrew, and Seumas Miller. 1996. "Needs, Moral Self-consciousness and Professional Roles." *Professional Ethics* 5, nos. 1–2: 43–61.

Althusser, Louis. 1971. *Lenin and Philosophy and Other Essays*. Trans. Ben Brewster. London: New Left Books.

Anderson, Elizabeth. 1999. "What Is the Point of Equality?" *Ethics* 109, no. 2: 287–337.

Anscombe, G. E. M. 1981. "On the Source of the Authority of the State." In Anscombe, ed. *The Collected Philosophical Papers of G. E. M. Anscombe*, vol. 3: *Ethics, Religion and Politics*. Oxford: Basil Blackwell.

*Australian, The*. 2002. "HIH Regulator Deceived." January 24.

Barlow, David Edward, and Steven Gerard Brandl. 1996. *Classics in Policing*. Cincinnati: Anderson Publishing.

Barnes, Barry. 1995. *The Elements of Social Theory*. Princeton: Princeton University Press.

Barry, Christian, and Sanjay Reddy. 2008. *International Trade and Labor Standards*. New York: Columbia University Press.

Bellow, Adam. 2003. *In Praise of Nepotism: A Natural History*. New York: Doubleday.

Benn, Stanley I. 1988. *A Theory of Freedom*. Cambridge: Cambridge University Press.

Benson, Paul. 1991. "Autonomy and Oppressive Socialisation." *Social Theory and Practice* 17, no. 3: 385–408.

Bentley, R., W. Appelt, U. Busbach, E. Hinrichs, D. Kerr, K. Sikkel, J. Trevor, and G. Woetzel. 1997. "Basic Support for Cooperative Work on the World Wide Web." *International Journal of Human-Computer Studies* 46, no. 6: 827–46.

Bhaskar, Roy. 1979. *The Possibility of Naturalism*. Brighton: Harvester.

Bittner, Egon. 1980. *The Functions of Police in Modern Society*. Cambridge, Mass.: Gunn and Hain.

Blackler, John, and Seumas Miller. 2000. *Police Ethics: Case Studies for Police Managers.* Canberra: Charles Sturt University.

Blake, Michael. 2001. "Distributive Justice, State Coercion and Autonomy." *Philosophy & Public Affairs* **30**, no. 3: 257–96.

Bloor, David. 1997. *Wittgenstein, Rules and Institutions.* London: Routledge.

Bradley, F. H. 1927. "My Station and Its Duties." In Bradley, *Ethical Studies.* Oxford: Oxford University Press.

Bratman, Michael. 1987. *Intentions, Plans and Practical Reason.* Cambridge, Mass.: Harvard University Press.

———. 1992. "Shared Cooperative Activity." *Philosophical Review* **101**, no. 2: 327–41.

———. 1993. "Shared Intention." *Ethics* **104**: 97–113.

Broad, C. D. 1928. *The Mind and Its Place in Nature.* London: Kegan Paul.

Campbell, Tom, and Seumas Miller, eds. 2004. *Human Rights and Organizations.* Dordrecht: Kluwer.

Carr-Saunders, A. M., and P. A. Wilson. 1933. *The Professions.* Oxford: Oxford University Press.

Cass, K. 1996. "Expert Systems as General-Use Advisory Tools: An Examination of Moral Responsibility." *Business and Professional Ethics Journal* **15**, no. 4: 61–85.

Christman, John. 1991. "Autonomy and Personal History." *Canadian Journal of Philosophy* **21**, no. 1: 1–24.

Clarke, Frank, Graeme Dean, and Kyle Oliver. 2003. *Corporate Collapse: Accounting, Regulatory and Ethical Failure.* Rev. ed. Cambridge: Cambridge University Press.

Coffee, John. 2007. "Law and the Market: The Role of Enforcement." Paper delivered at the conference "Private Equity, Corporate Governance and the Dynamics of Capital Market Regulation," Australian National University, Canberra.

Cohen, Elliot, ed. 2005. *News Incorporated: Corporate Media Ownership and Its Threat to Democracy.* New York: Prometheus Books.

Cohen, Elliot, and B. W. Fraser. 2007. *The Last Days of Democracy: How Big Media and Power-Hungry Government Are Turning America into a Dictatorship.* New York: Prometheus Books.

Cohen, G. A. 1978. *Karl Marx's Theory of History: A Defence.* Oxford: Clarendon Press.

Cohen, Howard, and Michael Feldberg. 1991. *Power and Restraint: The Moral Dimension of Policework.* New York: Praeger.

Cohen, Philip R., and Hector J. Levesque. 1991. "Teamwork." *Nous* **25**, no. 4: 487–512.

Collingridge, M., and Seumas Miller. 1997. "Filial Responsibility and the Care of the Aged." *Journal of Applied Philosophy* **14,** no. 2: 119–28.

Copp, David. 1976. "*Individuals, Collectives and Moral Agency.*" Ph.D. dissertation, Cornell University.

———. 2007. "The Collective Moral Autonomy Thesis." *Journal of Social Philosophy* **38,** no. 3: 369–388.

Cravens, Karen, Elizabeth Goad Oliver, and Sridhar Ramamoorti. 2003. "The Reputation Index: Measuring and Managing Corporate Reputation." *European Management Journal* **21**, no. 2: 201–12.

Cullity, Garrett. 2006. *Moral Demands of Affluence*. Oxford. Oxford University Press.

Davidson, Donald. 1973. "Freedom to Act." In Ted Honderich, ed. *Essays on Freedom of Action*. London: Routledge and Kegan Paul.

Davis, Michael. 1998. *Thinking like an Engineer*. Oxford: Oxford University Press.

Dean, John W. 2007. *Broken Government: How Republican Rule Destroyed the Legislative, Executive and Judicial Branches*. New York: Viking.

De George, Richard T. 1997. *Academic Freedom and Tenure: Ethical Issues*. New York: Rowman and Littlefield.

Devlin, Patrick. 1965. *The Enforcement of Morals*. Oxford: Oxford University Press.

Dubnick, Melvin. 2007. "The Fundamental Error of Accountability Processes." In Justin O'Brien, ed. *Private Equity, Corporate Governance and the Dynamics of Capital Market Regulation*. London: Imperial College of London Press.

Duff, R. Antony, ed. 1998. *Philosophy and the Criminal Law: Principle and Critique*. Cambridge: Cambridge University Press.

Dummett, Michael. 1973. *Frege: The Philosophy of Language*. London: Duckworth.

Durkheim, Émile. 1957. *Professional Ethics and Civil Morals*. Routledge: London. 1964. *Rules of Sociological Method*. New York: Free Press.

Dworkin, Gerald. 1988. *The Theory and Practice of Autonomy*. Cambridge: Cambridge University Press.

Dworkin, Ronald. 1979. "Academic Freedom." *Philosophical Papers* 8, no. 1: 1–10. 1998. *Law's Empire*. Oxford: Hart Publishing.

*Economist, The*. "White Man's Shame," September 25, 89.

Eitan, N., C. Hoerl, T. McCormack, and J. Roessler. 2005. *Joint Attention: Communication and Other Minds*. Oxford: Oxford University Press.

Elster, Jon. 1989. *Nuts and Bolts for the Social Sciences*. Cambridge: Cambridge University Press.

Etzioni, A. 1975. *A Comparative Analysis of Complex Organizations*. 2nd ed. Washington, D.C.: George Washington University.

Ferguson, S., and J. Weckert. 1993. "Ethics, Reference Librarians and Expert Systems." *Australian Library Journal* 42, no. 3: 3–13.

Freadman, Richard, and Seumas Miller. 1992. *Re-thinking Theory: A Critique of Contemporary Literary Theory and an Alternative Account*. Cambridge: Cambridge University Press.

French, Peter A. 1984. *Collective and Corporate Responsibility*. New York: Columbia University Press.

Friedman, Thomas. 2007. *The World Is Flat: A Brief History of the Twenty-First Century*. New York: Picador.

Fusaro, Peter C., and Ross M. Miller. 2002. *What Went Wrong at Enron: Everyone's Guide to the Largest Bankruptcy in U.S. History*. New York: Wiley.

Gert, Bernard. 2004. *Common Morality: Deciding What to Do*. Oxford: Oxford University Press.

Giddens, Anthony. 1976. *New Rules of Sociological Method*. London: Hutchinson. 1984. *The Constitution of Society: Outline of the Theory of Structuration*. Cambridge: Polity Press.

Gilbert, Margaret. 1989. *On Social Facts*. London: Routledge.

1992. *Social Facts*. Princeton: Princeton University Press.

Goldman, A. 1999. *Knowledge in a Social World*. London: Oxford University Press.

Goldstein, Herman. 1990. *Problem Oriented Policing*. New York: McGraw-Hill.

Gore, Al. 2007. *The Assault on Reason*. New York: Penguin.

Graham, Keith. 2002. *Practical Reasoning in a Social World*. Cambridge: Cambridge University Press.

Grice, Paul. 1989. "Utterer's Meaning, Sentence-meaning and Word-meaning." In Grice, *Studies in the Way of Words*. Cambridge, Mass.: Harvard University Press.

Griffin, James. 1996. *Value Judgement: Improving Our Ethical Beliefs*. Oxford: Oxford University Press.

2008. *On Human Rights*. Oxford: Oxford University Press.

Hardin, Russell. 1988. *Morality within the Limits of Reason*. Chicago: University of Chicago Press.

Harre, Rom. 1979. *Social Being*. Oxford: Blackwell.

Harre, Rom, and E. H. Madden. 1975. *Causal Powers: A Theory of Natural Necessity*. Oxford: Basil Blackwell.

Hart, H. L. A. 1973. "Bentham on Legal Rights." In A. Simpson, ed. *Oxford Essays in Jurisprudence*, vol. 2. Oxford: Oxford University Press.

1978. "Are There Any Natural Rights?" In A. M. Quinton, ed., *Political Philosophy*. Oxford: Oxford University Press.

Haubrick, D. 2003. "September 11, Anti-Terror Laws and Civil Liberties: Britain, France and Germany Compared." *Government and Opposition* **38**, no. 1: 10–23.

Heal, J. 1978. "Common Knowledge," *Philosophical Quarterly* **28**: 116–31.

Heffernan, William C. 1985. "The Police and Their Rules of Office: An Ethical Analysis." In William C. Heffernan and Timothy Stroup, eds. *Police Ethics: Hard Choices for Law Enforcement*. New York: John Jay College Press.

Heidenheimer, Arnold J., and Michael Johnston, eds. 2002. *Political Corruption: Concepts and Contexts*. 3rd ed. London: Transaction Publishers.

Hempel, C. G. 1965. "Theoreticians' Dilemma." *Aspects of Scientific Explanation*. New York: Free Press.

Hill, Richard S. 1986. *Policing the Colonial Frontier: The Theory and Practice of Coercive Social and Racial Control in New Zealand, 1767–1867*. Wellington, New Zealand: Government Printer.

Hindess, Barry. 2001. "Good Government and Corruption." In Peter Larmour and Nick Wolanin, eds. *Corruption and Anti-Corruption*. Canberra: Asia Pacific Press.

Hirschman, Albert O. 1970. *Exit, Voice and Loyalty*. Cambridge, Mass.: Harvard University Press.

Hodson, Nick. 2007. "Why Auditors Can't Find Fraud." In Justin O'Brien, ed. *Private Equity, Corporate Governance and the Dynamics of Capital Market Regulation*. London: Imperial College of London Press.

Hoff Sommers, Christina. 1986. "Filial Morality." *Journal of Philosophy* **88,** no. 3: 439–56.

Hollis, Martin. 2002. *The Philosophy of Social Science: An Introduction*. Rev. ed. Cambridge: Cambridge University Press.

Hopkins, Jonathan. 2002. "States, Markets and Corruption: A Review of Some Recent Literature." *Review of International Political Economy* 9, no. 3: 574–90.

Human Rights and Equal Opportunity Commission. 1997. *Bringing Them Home: Report of the National Inquiry into the Separation of Aboriginal and Torres Strait Islander Children from Their Families*. Sydney: Commonwealth of Australia.

Jackall, Robert. 1988. *Moral Mazes: The World of Corporate Managers*. New York: Oxford University Press.

Jaspers, Karl. 1960. *The Idea of the University*. London: Peter Owen.

Kant, Immanuel. 1785. *Groundwork of the Metaphysics of Morals*. Various editions.

1943. *Critique of Pure Reason*. Trans. J. Meiklejohn. New York: Wiley.

1979. *The Conflict of the Faculties*. Trans. Mary J. Gregor. New York: Abaris.

Kekes, John. 1989. *Moral Tradition and Individuality*. Princeton: Princeton University Press.

Kilney, Geoff. 2008. "Doha Collapse." *Australian Financial Review*, July 31.

Kleinig, John. 1996. *The Ethics of Policing*. Cambridge: Cambridge University Press.

Klitgaard, Robert, Ronald Maclean-Abaroa, and H. Lindsey Parris. 2000. *Corrupt Cities: A Practical Guide to Cure and Prevention*. Oakland, Calif.: ICS Press.

Kuflik, A. 1999. "Computers in Control: Rational Transfer of Authority or Irresponsible Abdication of Autonomy?" *Ethics and Information Technology* 1, no. 1: 173–84.

Ladd, J. 1988. "Computers and Moral Responsibility: A Framework for an Ethical Analysis." In C. Gould, ed. *The Information Web: Ethical and Social Implications of Computer Networking*. Boulder: Westview Press.

Lane, Melissa. 2004. "Autonomy as a Central Human Right and its Implications for the Moral Responsibilities of Corporation." In T. Campbell and S. Miller, eds. *Human Rights and the Moral Responsibilities of Corporate and Public Sector Organisations*. Dordrecht: Kluwer.

Lewis, David. 1969. *Convention: A Philosophical Study*. Cambridge, Mass.: Harvard University Press.

Lichtenberg, Judith. 1987. "Foundations and Limits of Freedom of the Press." *Philosophy and Public Affairs* 16, no. 4: 329–55.

Luban, David. 1988. *Lawyers and Justice: An Ethical Study*. Princeton: Princeton University Press.

2005. "Liberalism and the Unpleasant Question of Torture." *Virginia Law Review* 91, no. 6: 1425–61.

Lynch, A., and G. Williams. 2006. *What Price Security? Taking Stock of Australia's Anti-Terror Laws*. Sydney: UNSW Press.

Mackenzie, Catriona. 2001. "On Bodily Autonomy." In S. K. Toombs, ed. *Philosophy and Medicine: Handbook of Phenomenology and Medicine*. Dordrecht: Kluwer.

Manicas, Peter. 2006. *A Realist Philosophy of Social Science: Explanation and Understanding*. Cambridge: Cambridge University Press.

May, Larry. 1987. *The Morality of Groups*. Notre Dame, Ind.: University of Notre Dame Press.

1996. *The Socially Responsible Self.* Chicago: University of Chicago Press.

May, T., ed. 1991. *Collective Responsibility.* Lanham, Md.: Rowman and Littlefield.

Mayntz, Renate. 2004. "Mechanisms in the Analysis of Social Macro-Phenomena." *Philosophy of the Social Sciences* 34, no. 2: 237–59.

Mill, John Stuart. 1869. *On Liberty.* Various editions.

Miller, Seumas. 1982. "Lewis on Conventions." *Philosophical Papers* 11, no. 2: 1–8.

1984. "Performatives." *Philosophical Studies* 45, no.2: 247–60.

1985. "Speaker-Meaning and Assertion." *South African Journal of Philosophy* 2, no. 4: 48–54.

1986a. "Truthtelling and the Actual Language Relation." *Philosophical Studies* 49, no. 2: 281–94.

1986b. "Conventions, Interdependence of Action and Collective Ends." *Nous* 20, no. 2: 117–40.

1987. "Conventions, Expectations and Rationality." *Southern Journal of Philosophy* 4, no. 2: 48–55.

1992a. "Joint Action." *Philosophical Papers* 21, no. 3: 275–99.

1992b. "On Conventions." *Australasian Journal of Philosophy* 70, no. 4: 435–44.

1993. "Killing in Self-defence." *Public Affairs Quarterly* 7, no. 4: 325–40.

1995a. "Intentions, Ends and Joint Action." *Philosophical Papers* 24, no. 1: 51–67.

1995b. "Socio-political Action, Ethics and Literature." *Philosophy and Social Criticism* 21, no. 3: 93–111.

1995c. "Freedom of the Press." *Politikon* 22, no. 1: 24–36.

1997a. "Social Norms." In G. Holmstrom-Hintikka and R. Tuomela, eds. *Contemporary Action Theory, Volume 2: Social Action.* Dordrecht: Kluwer–Synthese Library Series.

1997b. "Individualism, Collective Responsibility and Corporate Crime." *Business and Professional Ethics Journal* 16, no. 4: 19–46.

1998a. "Collective Responsibility, Armed Intervention and the Rwandan Genocide." *International Journal of Applied Philosophy* 12, no. 2: 223–39.

1998b. "Corruption and Anti-Corruption in the Profession of Policing." *Professional Ethics* 6, nos. 3–4: 83–106.

2000a. "Speech Acts and Conventions." *Language Sciences* 22, no. 2: 155–66.

2000b. "Academic Autonomy." In C.A.J. Coady, ed. *Why Universities Matter.* Sydney: Allen and Unwin.

2000c. "Shootings by Police in Victoria: The Ethical Issues." In Tony Coady, Steve James, Seumas Miller, and Michael O'Keefe, eds. *Violence and Police Culture.* Melbourne: Melbourne University Press.

2001a. "Collective Responsibility." *Public Affairs Quarterly* 15, no. 1: 65–82.

2001b. *Social Action: A Teleological Account.* Cambridge: Cambridge University Press.

2003a. "Institutions, Collective Goods and Moral Rights." *ProtoSociology* 18–19: 184–207.

2003b. "Individual Autonomy and Sociality." In Frederick F. Schmitt, ed. *Socializing Metaphysics: The Nature of Social Reality.* Lanham, Md.: Rowman and Littlefield.

2004. "Group Rights Revisited." *Philosophical Papers.* November: 187–206.

2005. "Corruption." In *Stanford Encyclopedia of Philosophy*, ed. Edward N. Zalta. Winter edition. Available at: plato.stanford.edu/archives/fall2005/entries/corruption.

2006a. "Collective Moral Responsibility: An Individualist Account." In Peter A. French, ed. *Midwest Studies in Philosophy* xx: 176–93.

2006b. "Torture." In Edward N. Zalta, ed. *Stanford Encyclopedia of Philosophy*. Spring edition. Stanford, Calif.: Stanford University Press.

2007a. "Social Institutions." In Edward N. Zalta, ed. *Stanford Encyclopedia of Philosophy*. Winter edition. Stanford, Calif.: Stanford University Press.

2007b. "Institutions, Integrity Systems and Market Actors." In J. O'Brien, ed. *Private Equity, Corporate Governance and the Dynamics of Capital Market Regulation*. London: Imperial College of London Press.

2007c. "Joint Action: The Individual Strikes Back." In S.L. Tsohatzidis, ed. *Intentional Acts and Institutional Facts: Essays on John Searle's Social Ontology*. Dordrecht: Springer.

2007d. "Civilian Immunity, Forcing the Choice and Collective Responsibility." In Igor Primoratz, ed. *Civilian Immunity*. Oxford: Oxford University Press.

2007e. "Against the Collective Moral Autonomy Thesis." *Journal of Social Philosophy* 38, no. 3: 389–409.

2008a. "Collective Responsibility and Information and Communication Technology." In J. van den Hoven and J. Weckert, eds. *Moral Philosophy and Information Technology*. New York: Cambridge University Press.

2008b. *Terrorism and Counter-Terrorism: Ethics and Liberal Democracy*. Oxford: Blackwell Publishing.

2009a. "Applied Ethics: Problems and Perspectives." *Philosophia* 37, no. 2: 185–201.

2009b. "Justification in Ethics." In John-Stewart Gordon, ed. *Morality and Politics: Reading Boylan's A Just Society*. Lanham, Md.: Rowman and Littlefield.

Miller, Seumas, and John Blackler. 2005. *Ethical Issues in Policing*. Aldershot: Ashgate.

Miller, Seumas, and Pekka Makela. 2005. "The Collectivist Approach to Collective Moral Responsibility." *Metaphilosophy* 36, no. 5: 634–51.

Miller, Seumas, Peter Roberts, and Ed Spence. 2005. *Corruption and Anti-Corruption*. Upper Saddle River, N.J.: Prentice Hall.

Montmarquet, J.A. 1993. *Epistemic Virtue and Doxastic Responsibility*. Lanham, Md.: Rowman and Littlefield.

Moore, David, and Roger Wettenhall, eds. 1994. *Keeping the Peace: Police Accountability and Oversight*. Canberra: University of Canberra.

Newman, John Henry. 1854. *The Idea of a University*. Various editions.

Noonan, John T. 1984. *Bribes*. New York: Macmillan.

North, Douglass C. 1990. *Institutions, Institutional Change and Economic Performance*. Cambridge: Cambridge University Press.

Nozick, Robert. 1974. *Anarchy, State and Utopia*. Oxford: Blackwell.

Nye, Joseph. 1967. "Corruption and Political Development: A Cost-Benefit Analysis." *American Political Science Review* 61, no. 2: 417–27.

Parsons, Talcott. 1968. *The Structure of Social Action*. New York: Free Press.
  1982. *On Institutions and Social Evolution.* Chicago: University of Chicago Press.
Pearson, Zoe. 2001. "An International Human Rights Approach to Corruption." In Peter Larmour and Nick Wolanin, eds. *Corruption and Anti-Corruption*. Canberra: Asia Pacific Press.
Pelikan, Jaroslav. 1992. *The Idea of the University: A Reexamination*. New Haven, Conn.: Yale University Press.
Peterson, M. Jeanne. 1978. *The Medical Profession in Mid-Victorian England*. Berkeley: University of California Press.
Pettit, Philip. 1990. "Virtus Normativa: Rational Choice Perspectives." *Ethics* **100**, no. 4: 725–55.
  2001. *A Theory of Freedom*. Cambridge: Polity Press.
Pincoffs, Edmund L., ed. 1975. *The Concept of Academic Freedom*. Austin: University of Texas Press.
Pogge, Thomas. 2007. "Severe Poverty as a Human Rights Violation." In T. Pogge, ed. *Freedom from Poverty as a Human Right*. Oxford: Oxford University Press.
  2008. *World Poverty and Human Rights*. 2nd ed. London: Polity.
Polanyi, Michael. 1951. *The Logic of Liberty: Reflections and Rejoinders*. London: Routledge and Kegan Paul.
Pritchard, Michael S. 1998. "Bribery: The Concept." *Science and Engineering Ethics* **4**, no. 3: 281–86.
Public Committee against Torture in Israel. 2003. *Back to a Routine of Torture: Torture and Ill-Treatment of Palestinian Detainees during Arrest, Detention and Interrogation (September 2001 – April 2003)*. Jerusalem: Public Committee Against Torture in Israel.
Radcliffe-Brown, A. R. 1958. *Method in Social Anthropology: Selected Essays*. Ed. M. N. Srinivas. Chicago: University of Chicago Press.
Rashid, Ahmed. 2001. *Taliban: The Story of the Afghan Warlords*. London: Pan Books.
Rawls, John. 1964. "Legal Obligation and the Duty of Fair Play." In S. Hook, ed. *Law and Philosophy*. New York: New York University Press.
  1972. *A Theory of Justice*. Cambridge, Mass.: Harvard University Press.
  1999. *The Law of Peoples*. Cambridge, Mass.: Harvard University Press.
Rose-Ackerman, Susan. 1999. *Corruption and Government: Causes, Consequences and Reform*. Cambridge: Cambridge University Press.
Rossouw, G. J. 2000. "Defining and Understanding Fraud: A South African Case Study." *Business Ethics Quarterly* **10**, no. 4: 885–95.
Ryan, Alan. 1970. *The Philosophy of the Social Sciences*. London: Macmillan.
Said, Edward. 1994. *Representations of the Intellectual: The 1993 Reith Lectures*. London: Vintage.
Sartre, Jean-Paul. 1948. *Existentialism and Humanism*. London: Methuen.
Scarman, Lord. 1981. *The Scarman Report: The Brixton Disorders 10–12 April 1981*. Harmondsworth: Penguin.
Schauer, Frederick. 1981. *Free Speech: A Philosophical Inquiry*. Cambridge: Cambridge University Press.
  2003. *Profiles, Probabilities and Stereotypes*. Cambridge, Mass.: Belknap Press.

Schmidtz, David. 1994. "Choosing Ends." *Ethics* **104**: 226–51.
Schmitt, Frederick F. 2003. *Socializing Metaphysics: The Nature of Social Reality.* Lanham, Md.: Rowman and Littlefield.
Schotter, Andrew. 1981. *The Economic Theory of Institutions.* Cambridge: Cambridge University Press.
Scott, W. Richard. 2001. *Institutions and Organisations.* 2nd ed. London: Sage.
Searle, John. 1975. "Two Concepts of Academic Freedom." In Edmund L. Pincoffs, ed. *The Concept of Academic Freedom.* Austin: University of Texas Press.
    1983. *Intentionality: An Essay in the Philosophy of Mind.* Cambridge: Cambridge University Press.
    1984. *Minds, Brains and Science.* London: Pelican.
    1990. "Collective Intentions and Actions." In P. Cohen, J. Moran, and M. Pollack, eds. *Intentions in Communication.* Cambridge, Mass.: MIT Press.
    1995. *The Construction of Social Reality.* London: Penguin.
Selgelid, Michael. 2008. "A Full-Pull Program for the Provision of Pharmaceuticals: Practical Issues." *Public Health Ethics* **1**, no. 2: 134–45.
Sen, Amartya. 2002. *Rationality and Freedom.* Cambridge, Mass.: Harvard University Press.
Shue, Henry. 1996. *Basic Rights.* Princeton. Princeton University Press.
Silber, Laura, and Allan Little. 1997. *Yugoslavia: Death of a Nation.* London: Penguin.
Simmons, A. J. 1979. *Moral Principles and Political Obligation.* Princeton: Princeton University Press.
Singer, Peter. 1972. "Famine, Affluence and Poverty." *Philosophy and Public Affairs* **1**, no. 3: 229–43.
    1981. *The Expanding Circle: Ethics and Sociobiology.* New York: Farrar, Straus and Giroux.
    2007. Uehiro Lectures delivered at Oxford University.
Skolnick, Jerome H. 1966. *Justice without Trial.* New York: Macmillan.
Skolnick, Jerome H., and James J. Fyfe. 1993. *Above the Law: Police and the Excessive Use of Force.* New York: Free Press.
Soros, George. 2008. *The New Paradigm for Financial Markets: The Credit Crisis of 2008 and What It Means.* New York: Perseus Books.
Spencer, Herbert. 1971. *Structure, Function and Evolution.* Ed. S. Andreski. London: Michael Joseph.
Stewart, James B. 1992. *Den of Thieves.* New York: Simon and Schuster.
Stiglitz, Joseph. 2006. *Making Globalization Work: The Next Steps to Global Justice.* New York: Penguin.
Sykes, Trevor. 1984. *The Bold Riders: Behind Australia's Corporate Collapses.* Sydney: Allen & Unwin.
Thompson, Dennis. 1995. *Ethics in Congress: From Individual to Institutional Corruption.* Washington, D.C.: Brookings Institute.
Tuomela, Raimo. 1995. *The Importance of Us: A Philosophical Study of Basic Social Notions.* Stanford, Calif.: Stanford University Press.

2002. *The Philosophy of Social Practices: A Collective Acceptance View.* Cambridge: Cambridge University Press.

Tuomela, Raimo, and Karlo Miller. 1988. "We-Intentions." *Philosophical Studies* **53**, no. 3: 367–89.

Turner, Jonathan H. 1979. *United Nations Code of Conduct for Law Enforcement Officials.* New York: United Nations.

1997. *The Institutional Order: Economy, Kinship, Religion, Polity, Law, and Education in Evolutionary and Comparative Perspective.* New York: Longman.

van den Hoven, Jeroen. 1997. "Computer Ethics and Moral Methodology." *Metaphilosophy* **28**, no. 3: 1–12.

1998. "Moral Responsibility, Public Office and Information Technology." In I. Snellen and W. van de Donk, eds. *Public Administration in an Information Age.* Amsterdam: IOS Press.

Varess, F. 2002. "The Buck Will Stop at the Board? An Examination of Directors' (and Others') Duties in the Light of the HIH Collapse." *Commercial Law Quarterly* **3** (March–May): 12–31.

Waldron, Jeremy. 2005. "Torture and Positive Law: Jurisprudence for the White House." *Columbia Law Review* **105**, no. 6: 1681–1750.

Walzer, Michael. 1983. *Spheres of Justice.* New York: Basic Books.

Warwick, Donald P. 1981. "The Ethics of Administrative Discretion." In Joel L. Fleishman, Lance Liebman, and Mark H. Moore, eds. *Public Duties: The Moral Obligations of Public Officials.* Cambridge, Mass.: Harvard University Press.

Weber, Max. 1949. *The Methodology of the Social Sciences.* Glencoe, Ill.: Free Press.

2008. "Property Rights and the Resource Curse" *Philosophy and Public Affairs* **36**, no.1: 2–32.

Wiggins, David. 1987. "Claims of Need." In Wiggins, *Needs, Values, and Truth.* Oxford: Basil Blackwell.

1991. "Claims of Need." In Wiggins, *Needs, Values, Truth: Essays in the Philosophy of Value.* 2nd ed. Oxford: Blackwell.

Willis, Evan. 1989. *Medical Dominance: The Division of Labour in Australian Health Care.* Rev. ed. Sydney: Allen and Unwin.

World Bank. 1997. *Helping Countries Combat Corruption. The Role of the World Bank.* Washington, D.C.: World Bank.

Zimmerman, Michael J. 1985. "Sharing Responsibility." *American Philosophical Quarterly* **22**, no. 2: 115–22.

# Index

Afghanistan, 250, 258, 341, 343, 344
AIG (U.S. company), 2
Al-Qaeda, 269, 287, 341, 342, 343, 344, 345
Althusser, Louis, 93
Amanpour, Christiane (CNN), 283
American Medical Association, 182, 189
Amin, Idi, 159
Aristotle, 37, 174
Arthur Anderson (U.S. company), 187
attitudes
  affective attitudes, 44
  cognitive and conative attitudes, 19, 38, 44
  collective approval, 109, 110
  generic attitudes of approval, 109
  I-attitudes and we-attitudes, 38, 39
  interdependence of attitude/action, 109
  interpersonal attitudes and relations, 18, 19
  irreducibly collective attitudes and entities, 39
  moral approval and disapproval, 98, 102, 103, 104
  mutual consciousness, 18, 19, 38
  propositional attitudes, 31, 39
Australian Broadcasting Corporation (ABC), 282
Australian Security Intelligence Organisation (ASIO), 342

autonomy, 98, 105, 107, 239, 255,
  *See also* academic autonomy
  (universities); Collective Moral
  Autonomy Thesis (Copp,
  David); individual autonomy;
  institutional autonomy;
  professional autonomy
  (professions)
  "thick" and "thin" senses of
    autonomy, 255
  autonomy and independence, 93
  concept of autonomy, 241
  diminished/enhanced autonomy,
    101, 104, 116, 275
  diminished/enhanced autonomy
    and moral agency, 99
  four dimensions of autonomy
    autonomous agents self-
      reflective, 240, 241
    autonomy presupposes social
      forms, 241
    independence from external
      control, 239
    internal features of autonomy,
      240
  intellectual autonomy, 239
  right to autonomy, 66, 68, 69, 215

Barnes, Barry, 29
Basic Support for Cooperative Work
  (BSCW) Shared Workspace
  system, 302
Bernstein, Carl, 288

357

Pogge, Thomas, 209, 210, 211–12,
    213, 214–16, 220, 224,
    *See also* poverty (global)
Health Impact Fund (HIF), 221–23,
    224
positive obligations to assist/
    negative obligations not to
    harm, 210
Polanyi, Michael, 242
police, 7, 57, 58, 87, 325, 326
as enforcers of social morality,
    258–60
fundamental ends of policing, 261
law enforcement/peace-keeping/
    police service roles, 247, 251,
    257, 261, 276
legal constraints on police, 247
military and policing institutions,
    252, 253
moral rights of victims and
    suspects, 265–66
morally problematic methods, 264,
    265
normative teleological account of
    policing, 2, 7, 245, 246, 253,
    268, 276
paramilitary police forces, 252
police accountability, 267
police discretion, 267, 268
police use of torture. *See* torture
primary and secondary purposes of
    policing, 246
private policing, 268, 278, 322
proper scope of policing, 268
use of deception, 263, 264
variety of police activities, 260, 261,
    264
poverty (global), 2, 80, 159, 209, 212,
    214, 215, 218, 219, 220, 221,
    224
global disease burden. *See* Health
    Impact Fund (Pogge, Thomas)
international welfare institutions.
    *See* welfare institutions
moral obligation to assist poor, 202,
    203, 204, 205, 206, 207,
    208, 209

poverty-related diseases, 218, 222,
    224, 297
resource curse, 221
professions, 7, 92, 237
defining properties of professions
    expert knowledge, 181, 182, 187,
        226
institutionalization, 182
professional autonomy, 92, 182,
    183, 186–88, 267, 287
professions and market-based
    occupations (professional-
    client relationship), 180, 181
pursuit of collective goods, 179,
    180
emerging professions, 7, 183, 199,
    229
integrity systems. *See* integrity
    systems
non-professional occupational
    groups, 179, 182, 187
normative teleological account of
    professions, 179
professional accountability, 188,
    197
professional development
    programs, 195, 198
professional integrity as role
    specific, 190
professional liability, 187
professional negligence, 181, 191
professional reputation, 191, 198,
    *See also* integrity systems
"triangle of virtue," 197, 200
Reputation Index, 197, 297
professional-role occupants, 189
special rights and duties, 183
structure, function and culture of
    professions, 190
unethical professional practices,
    191

Radcliffe-Brown, A. F., 29
Rawls, John, 10, 21, 83
difference principle, 86, 88
fair play argument, 331,
    *See also* Hart, H. L. A.

For EU product safety concerns, contact us at Calle de José Abascal, 56–1°,
28003 Madrid, Spain or eugpsr@cambridge.org.

 www.ingramcontent.com/pod-product-compliance
Ingram Content Group UK Ltd.
Pitfield, Milton Keynes, MK11 3LW, UK
UKHW042211180425
457623UK00011B/151